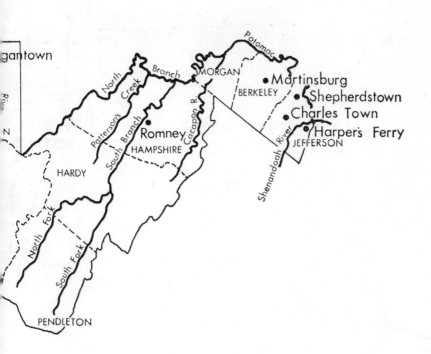

gantown

North Branch

Patterson's Creek

South Branch

Cacapon R.

MORGAN

BERKELEY

• Martinsburg

• Shepherdstown

• Charles Town

• Romney

HAMPSHIRE

JEFFERSON

Harpers Ferry

Shenandoah River

Potomac

HARDY

North Fork

South Fork

PENDLETON

WEST VIRGINIA
Rivers and Counties in 1830
• Cities and Towns

The Allegheny Frontier

The Allegheny Frontier

West Virginia Beginnings, 1730-1830

by Otis K. Rice

The University Press of Kentucky
Lexington: 1970

Standard Book Number 8131-1190-0
Library of Congress Catalog Card Number 75-94069

COPYRIGHT © 1970 BY THE UNIVERSITY PRESS OF KENTUCKY

A statewide cooperative scholarly publishing agency serving Berea College, Centre College of Kentucky, Eastern Kentucky University, Kentucky State College, Morehead State University, Murray State University, University of Kentucky, University of Louisville, and Western Kentucky University.

Editorial and Sales Offices: Lexington, Kentucky 40506

To my Father & Mother

CHARLES ORION RICE
1897-1936

&

MARY CATHERINE BELCHER RICE
1896-1962

Contents

Illustrations and Maps

Preface

The lingering effects of the frontier experience of the United States were nowhere more pronounced than in the Allegheny Highlands. Indeed, in most of these mountainous areas the pioneer period blended almost imperceptibly into a settled rurality which retained characteristics of the frontier throughout most of the nineteenth century. These isolated uplands suffered an arrested development and in the mid-twentieth century constituted a substantial portion of that area of the country labeled—sometimes scornfully, sometimes sympathetically—Appalachia.

The present study makes no attempt to deal comprehensively with the history of the entire Allegheny frontier; rather, its focus is upon that segment which lay within West Virginia. Situated in the very heart of the Alleghenies and the only state to lie wholly within Appalachia, West Virginia exemplified to a remarkable degree the influences and peculiarities of the Allegheny frontier. Moreover, her pioneering process consumed no less than a full century. Examination of the West Virginia portion, therefore, should illuminate the frontier experience of the entire Allegheny area.

By 1735, or less than a decade after West Virginia's first settlers established themselves along the Potomac lowlands, pioneers had begun to push toward the eastern slopes of the Alleghenies; but so rugged was most of the terrain of the state that another century elapsed before settlers penetrated isolated mountain areas. During that time, however, customs, manners, and folkways associated with the frontier took firm root. An ethnic complexion radically different from that of the Tidewater and Piedmont was established. Religious affiliations, in which Protestant evangelical churches claimed the vast majority of the population, were formed and assumed enduring significance. Virtually every problem to face education in the twentieth century appeared in microcosm in the early nineteenth. An absentee ownership of much of its land and resources was fastened upon the state's people, and the portents of waste and exploitation were clearly discernible. Voices of protest against economic exploitation and government apathy could be distinctly heard, but even then they were drowned in the seas of indifference. West Virginia's experiences were not unique, but were shared by western Pennsylvania, southwestern Virginia, and eastern Kentucky, as well as other parts of the Appalachians.

In this study I have attempted to keep the people themselves in the foreground. Their story is one of both heroism and defeat. The heroes are not Washingtons, Jeffersons, or Lincolns—the Allegheny section of West Virginia produced no such towering giants—but common folk who struggled to conquer a wilderness, establish a reign of law where none existed, implant and preserve moral and religious values, foster education, and call into practice the concepts of equality and freedom set forth in the Declaration of Independence. The joyous notes of their endeavors, however, were all too frequently accompanied by the dolorous tones of anti-intellectualism, resignation to circumstances, and inability to master adverse political, social, and economic forces. In their achievements and in their failures West Virginians were representative of most of the pioneers of the Alleghenies.

Two points regarding terminology require mention. I have used the name West Virginia throughout the study because no other description quite fits the area included. My attention to the extreme Eastern Panhandle, which lies in the Valley of Virginia, is justifiable, I believe, because it provides data for comparison and contrast with sections of the Alleghenies subject to Virginia authority. My use of the word "transmontane" refers, unless otherwise made clear, to the trans-Allegheny portions of West Virginia and not to the part of Virginia west of the Blue Ridge. I have applied the term "Allegheny" to the entire mountainous area of the state and "trans-Allegheny" to the portion lying west of the Allegheny Front.

Terminal points of the topical chapters vary. For example, the chapter dealing with political affairs ends with the Virginia Constitutional Convention of 1829–1830 and the culmination of some two decades of agitation by westerners for constitutional reform. Educational developments, on the other hand, have been carried to the mid-1840's, when efforts of two generations of pioneers to establish free schools were dealt a blow by legislation which was permissive only. Similarly, I have considered religious issues such as missions, temperance, and slavery, which were not resolved, in some cases, until the 1840's.

In the course of my research and writing I have incurred deep obligations. My greatest debt is to Thomas D. Clark, now Distinguished Professor of History at Indiana University. Dr. Clark suggested the need for the study while I was a student at the University of Kentucky, helped to determine its dimensions and focus, and gave encouragement and sound advice at every major point. Much of the original research was done with the aid of a dissertation year fellowship provided by the Southern Fellowships Fund. Further research was made possible by grants-in-aid from the American Association for State and Local History during the summers of 1961 and 1965. West Virginia Institute of Technology, through its Faculty Research Committee, generously provided funds for maps and illustrations. The illustrations were taken from the West Virginia Collection of the West Virginia University Library and from the original sketches of Joseph H. Diss Debar in the West Virginia Department of Archives and History Library.

The staffs of the libraries of the West Virginia Department of Archives and History, West Virginia University, University of Virginia, Virginia State Library, University of Kentucky, Duke University, and West Virginia Institute of Technology have been helpful in every way. Special words of appreciation are due Mrs. Hattie Ashworth, Mrs. Elizabeth Bowen, and Mrs. Mary Jenkins of the West Virginia Department of Archives and History, Mrs. Pauline Kissler of West Virginia University, and Mrs. Mary Gray of Duke University. The Reverend Lawrence Sherwood of Oakland, Maryland, generously made available his resources on West Virginia Methodism. Miss Ruth St. Clair of the Mathematics Department of West Virginia Institute of Technology read several chapters and offered valuable criticisms.

Finally, my student assistants, Harold D. Shaffer and Philip J. Welch, rendered yeoman service in the laborious tasks of typing and proofreading. Neither they nor others who have given assistance can be held responsible for remaining errors; to them I can lay complete claim.

Chapter One

A Land Wild and Tremendous

The Allegheny Highlands, consisting of an eastern escarpment known as the Allegheny Front and a westward-sloping and hilly expanse of the Appalachian Plateau, are one of the most distinctive physiographic regions of the United States. Embracing the western parts of Pennsylvania and Maryland, most of West Virginia, and southwestern Virginia, they are part of the Appalachian system, which extends from the St. Lawrence Valley to Georgia and Alabama. This great chain separates the Atlantic coastal plains from the interior of the North American continent and in colonial times stood as an almost inpenetrable barrier to westward expansion. For English settlers, the only two relatively unobstructed routes to the transmontane country were the Mohawk Valley and the paths which cut around the southern end of the Appalachians, but these approaches were held securely by the Iroquois and Cherokees, respectively. Most of the other reasonably accessible passages lay through the Alleghenies. Partly for this reason, the most significant thrusts of the frontier into the mountains and the Ohio Valley were made by Virginia, Pennsylvania, and Maryland.

The Alleghenies played a crucial role in determining patterns of exploration and settlement of the transmontane West, but they exerted more enduring effects in molding the features of pioneer life and in shaping the political, social, and economic thought of those who settled in their midst. In these upland regions an unusually stubborn and unyielding nature imposed an abnormally prolonged frontier environment upon settlers and firmly implanted customs, folkways, and attitudes commonly associated with the American pioneering experience. With more than 20,000 of its 24,000 square miles lying within the Allegheny Highlands, West Virginia was more completely a part of and bore more indelibly the stamp of this mountain frontier than any other state.

Any consideration of the influences of geography upon the Allegheny frontier, however, must take into account a larger environmental setting, extending from the Atlantic Ocean to the Great Lakes and the Mississippi Valley. Within much of this broader expanse, land forms lie in long folds, which generally follow a northeast-southwest direction. Prominent physiographic features are the Tidewater, the Appalachian Highlands, including the Piedmont, Blue Ridge, Valley and Ridge Province, and Appalachian Plateau, and the Central Lowland.[1]

Of major importance to the development of the Allegheny Highlands, and particularly to the West Virginia sections, were the Tidewater and the Piedmont. In Pennsylvania, Maryland, and Virginia they were the locus of political power from colonial times until well into the nineteenth century. Extensive cultivation of tobacco on the flat lowlands and gently rolling acres of eastern Virginia and Maryland gave rise to a plantation economy and aristocratic traditions, while the growth of business and mercantile interests in eastern Pennsylvania bred its own social and economic elite. Modes of life along the seaboard were largely alien to the Allegheny Highlands, and political and economic clashes between the coastal aristocracy and the mountain yeomen constitute a major theme in the history of the Allegheny frontier.

Between the Allegheny frontier and the Tidewater and the Piedmont lay the Blue Ridge, which extends like a vast wall across Virginia, Maryland, and Pennsylvania. Broken only by wind gaps and by passes carved by streams such as the Potomac, the New, and branches of the James, the Virginia Blue Ridge placed almost insurmountable physical difficulties in the path of westward-moving pioneers. It combined with the colony's land policy after 1730 to prevent any heavy exodus of population from eastern Virginia to lands west of the Blue Ridge.

[1] Nevin M. Fenneman, *Physiography of the Eastern United States* (New York, 1938), pp. 1-342, 449-536, but especially pp. 8-13, 35-38, 121-33, 139-45, 163-77, 195-203, 226-55, 279-319; Charles H. Ambler and Festus P. Summers, *West Virginia: The Mountain State*, 2d ed. (Englewood Cliffs, N. J., 1958), pp. 3-12; U. S., Works Projects Administration, Writers' Program, *West Virginia: A Guide to the Mountain State* (New York, 1941), pp. 8-20.

In Pennsylvania, on the other hand, the elevations of the Blue Ridge are lower than in Virginia. Settlers moving westward during the first half of the eighteenth century found it comparatively easy to thread their way through the mountains by following the Delaware, Susquehanna, and Juniata rivers and their tributaries. Indeed, most of the pioneers of the trans-Blue Ridge country were immigrants from Pennsylvania and New Jersey or recent arrivals from Europe. Barred by Pennsylvania authorities from taking up lands west of the Alleghenies, thousands turned southward upon reaching the Valley and Ridge Province. Some acquired lands in Maryland, but the vast majority continued into Virginia, crossing the Potomac at such points as Shepherdstown and picturesque Harper's Ferry, the latter described by Thomas Jefferson as "wild and tremendous" but also as "placid and delightful."[2]

Cradled between the Blue Ridge and the Allegheny Front, the Valley and Ridge Province is essentially a long depression known locally in Pennsylvania as the Great Valley and in Virginia as the Valley of Virginia or the Shenandoah Valley. From a width of about eighty miles between Williamsport and Harrisburg in Pennsylvania, the Valley tapers to a breadth of about sixty-five miles along Virginia's northern boundary and about fifty miles on her southern border. The soils of much of this Appalachian Valley, particularly in the Virginia portion, are enriched by a limestone base and well-drained by rivers and numerous subterranean streams, sinks, and caverns. Early settlers found them especially well adapted to the cultivation of grains, including wheat, corn, rye, oats, and barley, and to the raising of flax, beans, and root crops. Moreover, the Valley abounded in luxuriant natural grasses ideally suited to the grazing of livestock. Partly because of these advantages for agriculture and partly because of Virginia land policy, most of the available lands had been occupied by 1750, or within about a quarter of a century after the planting of the first settlements.

[2] Fenneman, *Physiography of the Eastern United States*, pp. 168-71; Ellen Churchill Semple and Clarence Fielden Jones, *American History and Its Geographic Conditions*, rev. ed. (Boston, 1933), p. 63, and map, pp. 64-65; Thomas Jefferson, *Notes on the State of Virginia*, ed. William Peden (Chapel Hill, N. C., 1955), p. 19; Thomas Perkins Abernethy, *Three Virginia Frontiers* (University, La., 1940), pp. 58-62.

Contributing to the population pressure in the Valley, and ultimately to its release, was the network of rivers along which the great human procession moved. Because they are older than the mountains, most rivers of the central and southern portions of the Appalachian Highlands do not follow the general northeast-southwest direction of the mountain ranges. Instead, they have cut transverse channels through the Blue Ridge and the Allegheny Mountains. Most of the rivers draining the northern part of the Valley, such as the Susquehanna, Potomac, and James, flow from west to east. Those of the southern portions, including the Watauga, Holston, French Broad, and New, flow from east to west.

By connecting the eastward-flowing streams of Pennsylvania, Maryland, and Virginia with the westward-bound waters at its southern end, the Valley became a major arterial route in the great westward movement. Once they had reached the southern part of the Valley, substantial numbers of pioneers followed the Watauga, Holston, Clinch, and French Broad rivers to fertile lands along the Tennessee or turned eastward by way of Staunton River Gap to the Carolina Piedmont. Others pressed through the Cumberland Gap to the Cumberland River valley or the lush Kentucky Bluegrass country. By contrast, the forbidding crests of the Allegheny Front, the ruggedness of the terrain immediately to its west, and the lack of relatively easy access routes into the interior discouraged migration of the Valley's surplus population into much of West Virginia.[3]

Two streams, the Potomac and the New, however, opened adjacent areas of West Virginia to emigrants from the Valley. The upper Potomac region, which embraces about one-sixth of the area of West Virginia, is in many respects a giant arm of the Valley of Virginia. Hundreds of pioneers who ascended the Potomac from the Virginia Piedmont or who followed Pennsylvania routes to the vicinity of Harper's Ferry or Shepherdstown continued up the river and settled along such West Virginia

[3] U. S., Department of Agriculture, *Soils and Men: Yearbook of Agriculture, 1938* (Washington, D. C., 1938), pp. 1033, 1037-38; Freeman H. Hart, *The Valley of Virginia in the American Revolution, 1763–1789* (Chapel Hill, N. C., 1942), pp. 7-11; Semple and Jones, *American History and Its Geographic Conditions,* pp. 63-67.

streams as the Opequon, Great Cacapon, Little Cacapon, North Branch, South Branch, and Patterson's Creek. Along these watercourses they found rich lands with limestone soils well suited to the production of wheat, corn, fruits, vegetables, and grasses. Uplands provided excellent pasturage for livestock. Farther south, the New River provided a route by which the frontier made its first precarious advance into Allegheny regions of southern West Virginia. Mountain valleys along the New and its tributaries, the Greenbrier and the Bluestone, absorbed a part of the burgeoning population of the southern part of the Valley.[4]

Beyond the Alleghenies, the Ohio River became a second great artery by which population was carried into the interior regions of the United States. The forks of the Ohio was the western terminus of three important routes which, during the late eighteenth and early nineteenth centuries, channeled settlers from the middle Atlantic states and Europe into the Ohio Valley. Two of the routes connected Philadelphia with the Ohio. The first passed by way of the West Branch of the Susquehanna to Kittanning on the Allegheny and then followed that river to its confluence with the Monongahela. The second followed either the Juniata River or Forbes' Road to the Loyalhanna and continued to the forks of the Ohio via the Allegheny. Serving those who set out from more southerly points, such as Baltimore and Alexandria, was a third route, which meandered with the Potomac to Fort Cumberland and extended to the Youghiogheny or to Redstone Old Fort on the Monongahela by way of Nemacolin's Path, or Braddock's Road.

Northwest of the Ohio lay an abundance of excellent farmland, easily accessible to the land-hungry pioneer. A heavy base of glacial drift produced soils capable of supporting a variety of crops and a high type of animal husbandry. Moreover, the absence of extensive forests enabled the settler to bring the land under cultivation without the arduous task of clearing it of heavy stands of timber. In providing an easy route to these fertile Central Lowlands and additional approaches to the rich

---

[4] U. S., D. A., *Soils and Men,* pp. 1022-23; Ambler and Summers, *West Virginia,* p. 7.

Kentucky country, the Ohio served as a major course of empire, carrying thousands of pioneers into both the Old Northwest and the Old Southwest.[5]

Part of the great wave of settlement which surged westward by way of the Ohio during the post-Revolutionary War years was deposited on West Virginia soil. The areas of the state most attractive to Ohio Valley pioneers were the lowlands along the river itself, the lower portions of Wheeling, Fish, Fishing, and Middle Island creeks, and lands along the Little Kanawha, Kanawha, Guyandotte, and Big Sandy rivers. The Ohio lowlands, reaching like long fingers deep into the Appalachian Plateau, embrace about 6,000 square miles of West Virginia, but level land, most of it in the form of flood plains, seldom exceeds two miles in width. Although these alluvial soils proved exceptionally fertile, the pioneer nevertheless found that attractive lands were relatively scarce. Of the 125,000 people who lived in trans-Allegheny regions of the country in 1790, only 20,000 resided in West Virginia. By contrast, the population of Kentucky rose from 12,000 in 1783 to approximately 70,000 in 1790.[6]

The two great avenues of migration—the Valley of Virginia and the Ohio River—lay along the borders of West Virginia, and neither fed its stream of settlers directly into the state. Instead, both exerted their main force upon areas beyond West Virginia. To be sure, the Allegheny Highlands caught a part of the overflow, but in general the sweep was in wide arcs around the mountainous areas, leaving much of West Virginia, like similar sections of Pennsylvania, Virginia, and Kentucky, a vast island only lightly touched by the tide of settlement.

This deflection of the frontier movement from any due-west course was nowhere more pronounced than in West Virginia. There the Alleghenies cut a great swath a hundred miles or more in width through the state and give it a mean elevation of 1,500 feet, the highest of any state east of the Mississippi River.

[5] Semple and Jones, *American History and Its Geographic Conditions*, pp. 74-75, 85. For a map showing these routes, see Nicholas B. Wainwright, *George Croghan: Wilderness Diplomat* (Chapel Hill, N. C., 1959), p. 11.

[6] U. S., W. P. A., *West Virginia*, pp. 10-11; Ambler and Summers, *West Virginia*, p. 103; Thomas D. Clark, *A History of Kentucky* (Lexington, Ky., 1954), p. 75.

Numerous peaks rise to 3,000 feet, and Spruce Knob towers 4,860 feet above sea level. Striking in majesty and grandeur, the mountains abound in awe-inspiring formations such as Seneca Rock, Blackwater Falls, Canaan Valley, and the New River gorge. The face of the hills changes with the seasons. In spring, the Alleghenies bud with new life; in summer, they become verdant and heavily luxuriant; in autumn, their multi-colored foliage blazes with indescribable splendor; and in winter, they stand stark but strong against wind and snow.

The pragmatic pioneer was less concerned with the primeval beauty of the hills than with their wildlife and resources. The slopes of the Alleghenies supported heavy stands of white oak, red oak, chestnut, dogwood, hickory, beech, ash, gum, linn, walnut, cherry, sugar maple, poplar, birch, and pawpaw. Mingled with these growths were stately evergreens, including white pine, cedar, spruce, and hemlock. Forest-clad hills and valleys were the haunts of the timber wolf and panther and of the deer, elk and black bear. They provided cover for the wild turkey, red fox, squirrel, raccoon, groundhog, opossum, and rabbit. Within a few years of their arrival, pioneer hunters had almost exterminated some of these animals. Bears and elk constituted valuable sources of food, and wolves and bears had to be eliminated as a menace before livestock could be raised successfully. Small herds of bison roamed the valleys of the Alleghenies, but they were never very numerous. The last buffalo noted in West Virginia was killed in 1825 at the mouth of the Tygart Valley River.

Scattered throughout the Alleghenies the settler found glades and savannahs, often "covered with luxurious grass." They had no trees, but they abounded in small shrubs which sheltered the grass from the drying heat of summer and the freezing cold of winter. The natural grasses provided excellent pasturage for livestock and helped to make such areas as the South Branch of the Potomac and the Greenbrier uplands important centers in the early American cattle industry.[7]

[7] U. S., W. P. A., *West Virginia*, pp. 9, 15, 17-18; Ambler and Summers, *West Virginia*, pp. 6-7; U. S., D. A., *Soils and Men*, p. 1022-23; Anne Royall, *Sketches of History, Life, and Manners, in the United States* (New Haven, Conn., 1826), pp. 29, 39-40, 76-77.

Although much of the land of the Alleghenies was too steep and the soil too thin and stony for easy cultivation, the pioneer quickly discovered that the mountainous terrain was by no means totally unfit for agriculture. In the central Alleghenies the growing season averaged about 180 days per year, the rainfall about 45 inches, well distributed over the year, and the mean temperature 52 or 53 degrees. The savannahs of the Greenbrier area, like numerous other parts of the highlands, produced good crops of wheat, rye, oats, flax, and "the best Irish potatoes," and picturesque mountain valleys, in many cases surprisingly fertile, provided excellent yields of corn, small grains, hay, and vegetables. Many sections of the Alleghenies, nevertheless, defied cultivation, and considerable quantities of land were often left in brushy pasture. Moreover, in some places the valleys became veritable canyons "shaded to fearful darkness with lofty spruce and laurel." Descriptive appellations, such as "the shades of death," were often bestowed—and not inappropriately—upon these forbidding scenes.[8]

The Allegheny Highlands themselves fostered and preserved conditions commonly associated with the frontier. From the forests the settler obtained bountiful supplies of wild game, nuts, berries, and fruits for food, animal skins for clothing and bedding, wood for warmth, cooking, and building cabins, roots and herbs for medicinal uses, and mast for the scrubby livestock which were left to fend for themselves. The pioneer readily adapted to this environment, in which natural abundance was prone to stifle industry and ambition, and a primitive hunting-grazing-farming economy persisted in mountainous regions long after neighboring areas had cast off the crudities of the frontier.

Contributing to the prolongation of primitive ways of life were difficulties in transportation and communication, themselves largely the result of rough terrain and rugged mountains. Settlements were often separated from one another by constraining mountain walls, which accentuated the isolation always common to the frontier. These barriers not only limited contacts between the Allegheny pioneers and outside areas, but they also

8 U. S., D. A., *Soils and Men,* pp. 1022-23, 1122,

fostered strong particularistic feelings even among the mountain folk.

Particularism was nowhere more marked than in the West Virginia Alleghenies. The Potomac River and its tributaries tied the Eastern Panhandle, or that part of the state east of the Allegheny Front, to the social, economic, and political life of the Valley of Virginia and to such eastern commercial centers as Washington and Baltimore. The Monongahela and its major tributaries, the Cheat, Tygart Valley, and West Fork, turned north-central portions of the state toward western Pennsylvania and ultimately toward either the Ohio Valley or the Pennsylvania seaboard. Other Ohio River tributaries, including several large creeks along the river's upper reaches and the Little Kanawha, Kanawha, Guyandotte, and Big Sandy rivers, drew their hinterlands into the economic orbit of the Ohio and Mississippi valleys. Equally close ties, both economic and political, bound the quick-to-mature Greenbrier and upper New River areas to the Valley of Virginia. Similarly, life along the Guyandotte and the Tug Fork of the Big Sandy bore a striking similarity to that of eastern Kentucky.

Of more than ordinary importance to the penetration of the mountain fastnesses was the network of Indian trails which traversed the Alleghenies. First made by wild animals in their endless search for grazing lands and salt licks, these trails were well-worn by centuries of use. The Indians followed the animal paths in their quest for game and in their trading and warring activities. Later the trails facilitated the advance of fur traders, explorers, and settlers into the mountains.

The major north-south route used by the Allegheny pioneers was the Warrior Path, which ran through almost the entire length of the Appalachian Valley. Although the path provided an avenue for intertribal commerce, the great stillness of the Valley was perhaps more often broken by the war whoop than by the laughter and revelry of trading expeditions. At Packhorse Ford, or Shepherdstown, where the trail crossed the Potomac, war parties often engaged in deadly combat. One branch of the Warrior Path, which connected the Valley of Virginia with Indian villages along the Scioto River and Lake

Erie by way of Cumberland Gap, became a significant thorough-
fare by which the frontiersmen pushed into the trans-Appalachian country. The southern segment of the Warrior Path
developed into the Great Philadelphia Wagon Road, which connected the Pennsylvania capital with frontiers as remote as the
Carolina Piedmont.

Of special significance, perhaps, to the West Virginia frontier
was the Seneca, or Shawnee, Trail, possibly a branch of the old
Catawba War Path. Following the South Branch of the Potomac
and the North Fork of that stream to Seneca Creek, it crossed
Cheat Mountain to Shaver's Fork of Cheat River before turning
west to Elkins, which appears to have been an important meeting
place for Indian trails. From there, one branch of the trail led
down the Greenbrier to Lewisburg and continued southward to
North Carolina by way of Bluefield. Other branches radiated out
from Elkins by way of Jim Shaver's Ridge, Laurel Hill, Belington,
Clover Run, and Parsons, to Oakland, Maryland, and via Beverly,
Huttonsville, Mingo Flats, and the Little Kanawha to the Ohio
River.

Other important Indian trails connected the central Alleghe-
nies with the Shawnee country in Ohio. The Little Warrior's
Trail, the northernmost of the paths and the chief route by which
Shawnee raiding parties entered the Monongahela Valley, passed
by way of New Martinsville, Fishing Creek, Indian Creek, and
White Day Creek, to the Cheat River area. A second route, the
Scioto–Monongahela Trail, connected the Lower Shawnee Town
with the Monongahela region by way of Neal's Station near
Parkersburg, West Union, Middle Island Creek, Ten-Mile Creek,
and Morgantown, before turning north into Pennsylvania. A
branch of the latter trail continued up the Little Kanawha from
Parkersburg to Bulltown and then crossed a divide between
Elk and Gauley rivers to the vicinity of Webster Springs. The
Little Kanawha Trail tied the east-west routes to the complex
Seneca system of north-south pathways in the eastern part of
the state.

The Shawnees and other western tribes made use of two other
routes in their hunting and warring expeditions. The first,
known as the Kanawha, or Buffalo, Trail, passed up the Kanawha

to Cedar Grove and then followed Kelly's, Bell, Twenty-Mile, and Rich creeks to Ansted, before winding its way along Meadow River and Muddy Creek to the Greenbrier Valley, where it, too, joined the Seneca Trail. Another branch of the trail entered the state near Huntington and followed the ancient Teays Valley to St. Albans, where it connected with the main route. Western Indians also reached the Greenbrier and Bluestone regions by following another branch of the Kanawha Trail which passed by way of Paint Creek, Beckley, and Flat Top Mountain. The other important path by which the Shawnees entered the southern Alleghenies lay along the Big Sandy, Tug Fork, and Clear Fork and extended into the Valley of Virginia.

One other major path, significant in east-west movements, was McCullough's, or the Traders, Trail, which became an important outlet for settlers of the Monongahela Valley, and gave them access, by way of Wardensville, Moorefield, and Mount Storm, to supply centers such as Winchester.

Strangely enough, the first white visitors found the Alleghenies almost devoid of Indians. Scores of mounds and earthworks, such as those of the upper Ohio Valley, and along the Kanawha River from Loup Creek to St. Albans in West Virginia, and in Westmoreland, Crawford, and Fayette counties in Pennsylvania, and thousands of artifacts found in widely scattered areas indicate that most of the Allegheny region was occupied by Indians during prehistoric times. The reasons for their leaving are not entirely clear, but they were probably closely related to the Iroquois conquests of the mid-seventeenth century. Of the tribes which remained in West Virginia at the time of the first white penetrations, the most important were a few Shawnees with villages on the lower Kanawha and at Old Town on the Ohio, Tuscaroras along the Potomac, and a small band of Delawares in the Northern Panhandle, which includes the tier of counties between Pennsylvania and Ohio. On the other hand, Indians regularly visited the mountainous areas to hunt and fish and to obtain supplies of salt from such centers as Malden on the Kanawha and Bulltown on the Little Kanawha. Moreover, the Alleghenies were covered with a welter of conflicting claims, chief of which in West Virginia were those of the Iroquois, Cherokees, and

Shawnees. Disputes over these lands led to serious intertribal strife, and much Indian blood was shed on West Virginia soil.[9]

Neither the Indian, concerned with hunting and salt-making, nor the early settler, seeking farms and grazing lands, fully appreciated the riches of the Alleghenies. Indeed, nature had carefully hidden some of her greatest treasures from their sight. Her vast stores of coal, oil, and gas remained almost untouched until the latter half of the nineteenth century. Salt deposits, in the form of brine and rock salt, were tapped only where they were near the earth's surface. On the other hand, the Allegheny pioneer attacked the forests, the soils, and the wildlife with a prodigality unknown to the Indians. In the process, he developed attitudes which enabled him and his descendants to view with but little concern the rapacious greed and wanton destruction which later laid waste so much of the natural wealth.

[9] General descriptions of major Indian trails in the state are in Ambler and Summers, *West Virginia*, pp. 15-25; U. S., W. P. A., *West Virginia*, pp. 97-99; James Morton Callahan, *Semi-Centennial History of West Virginia*, (n.p., 1913), pp. 9-13; Reuben Gold Thwaites and Louise Phelps Kellogg, eds., *The Revolution on the Upper Ohio, 1775–1777* (Madison, Wis., 1908), pp. 181-83.

Chapter Two

Westward to the Alleghenies

During the seventeenth century the energies of the middle Atlantic colonies and those of the upper South were absorbed in the development of their Tidewater and Piedmont areas, and not until well into the eighteenth century did they direct a major thrust westward toward the Alleghenies. In the extension of settlement beyond the Blue Ridge, Virginia assumed a conspicuous lead. Prior to the 1750's she directed the main force of her advance into her Valley and Ridge Province, particularly into the Valley of Virginia and along the upper Potomac. The only other settlements of consequence were made by Pennsylvanians in the valley of the Juniata and in the vicinity of Bedford, then known as Raystown.

Paving the way for the settler's advance, however, were the fur trader and the land speculator. The fifteen years following the Stuart Restoration in England were of signal importance for the extension of the Virginia fur trade, and before they were over Virginia explorers had penetrated the Blue Ridge at several points. The governor of the colony, Sir William Berkeley, was, in keeping with the spirit of the times, an ardent expanionist and himself deeply involved in the fur business. With his encouragement and through the active endeavors of prominent traders such as William Byrd and Abraham Wood, several expeditions, undertaken for the purpose of tapping new sources of furs, were dispatched westward. It was this trading activity which first pointed the movement of the Virginia frontier in the direction of West Virginia.

The first of the expeditions were undertaken by John Lederer, who in 1670 made three journeys into unknown areas along Virginia's frontiers. Lederer's first expedition carried him to the Blue Ridge northwest of present Charlottesville and the second to the Catawba River near the North Carolina–South Carolina border. On his third journey he proceeded from the falls to the headwaters of the Rappahannock River, scaled the steep slopes of the Blue Ridge, and from the vicinity of Front Royal gazed upon the Shenandoah Valley. Aside from his contributions to geographical knowledge—and questions as to Lederer's veracity have made some of the contributions highly suspect—the expedition was of little immediate importance.

Far more significant was an expedition which left Fort Henry on the Appomattox River in 1671. Dispatched by Abraham Wood, the builder and commandant at the fort, the party's two most prominent members were Thomas Batts, its leader, and Robert Fallam, who kept a journal of its progress. Proceeding westward by way of the Staunton and Roanoke rivers, the little band came upon a westward-flowing stream which they named Wood's River. They followed the stream, later known as New River, to Peters' Falls near the West Virginia–Virginia border. Markings on trees along their route clearly showed that other white men had been on New River previously, and, in fact, on their return journey they met William Byrd with a considerable number of men. Nevertheless, the verifiable discovery of New River by Batts and Fallam added important strength to England's claim to the Ohio Valley and to much of the Allegheny area.

Two years later, in 1673, Wood dispatched another expedition from Fort Henry. This party, under the direction of James Needham, sought the Cherokee villages on the headwaters of the Tennessee. Friendly relations were established with the Cherokees, and Gabriel Arthur, an illiterate but intelligent youth, was left with the Indians during the following winter. During his stay Arthur sometimes accompanied the Indians on their forays against enemy tribes. One such expedition, against the Shawnees, carried the Indians across West Virginia and into Ohio. Their route lay along a northward-flowing stream which emptied into the Kanawha at the site of a village of friendly Moneton Indians, probably at present St. Albans. From there, it followed the Kanawha to the Ohio country. In all likelihood, Arthur was the first white man to visit the Kanawha Valley.

The flurry of exploration which led to penetrations of the

Allegheny Highlands ended by 1675. By that time the Susque-hannocks and other tribes, whose lands adjoined the Virginia settlements, had become increasingly hostile, and war broke out between them and the colonists. The following year, Bacon's Rebellion, the most serious uprising in Virginia or any other colony prior to the American Revolution, prevented further exploration of the west. This lull in activity was followed by the death of Abraham Wood in 1680. During the ensuing decade, unsettled conditions in England, culminating in the Glorious Revolution of 1688, put an end to any sustained interest in westward expansion.[1]

Pennsylvanians were somewhat slower in venturing into the Alleghenies for fur-trading activities. In fact, the first white trader to enter western Pennsylvania was apparently a Dutch-man, Arnout Viele, sent out by the governor of New York in 1692 to lure the Shawnees into the English sphere of influence. The occupation of the Allegheny Valley by Delawares and Shawnees in 1724 provided the first great impetus to the fur trade in western Pennsylvania. In 1725 James Le Tort estab-lished a trading post at the forks of the Susquehanna, and within a few years he was joined by several other traders, who estab-lished profitable connections with the Shawnees on the Alle-gheny.

Meanwhile, with the arrival of Governor Alexander Spots-wood in 1710, Virginia again undertook serious attempts to extend her frontiers westward. By that time the wave of Virginia population was rolling toward the Blue Ridge, and both spec-ulators and settlers were seeking new farmlands. Moreover, the government of Virginia regarded buffer settlements beyond the

[1] For the journals of the Lederer, Batts and Fallam, and Needham and Arthur expeditions, as well as an excellent introduction to seventeenth-century explora-tions by Virginians, see Clarence Walworth Alvord and Lee Bidgood, *The First Explorations of the Trans-Allegheny Region by Virginians, 1650–1674* (Cleveland, Ohio, 1912), pp. 131-71, 181-226. See also Douglas L. Rights and William P. Cumming, *The Discoveries of John Lederer, with Unpublished Letters by and about Lederer to Governor John Winthrop, Jr.* (Charlottesville, Va., 1958), pp. 69-95; Lyman Carrier, "The Veracity of John Lederer," *William and Mary Quarter-ly*, 2d Series, XIX (October, 1939), 435-45; Fairfax Harrison, "Western Explora-tions in Virginia between Lederer and Spotswood," *Virginia Magazine of History and Biography*, XXX (October, 1922), 323-40.

Blue Ridge as essential to the protection of the valuable Piedmont plantations from the French and Indians. In 1716 Governor Spotswood, himself an expansionist and land speculator, led an expedition, consisting of fifty gentlemen, with Indian guides and Negro servants, up the Rappahannock, across the Blue Ridge by way of Swift Run Gap, and into the Shenandoah Valley. The vast panorama of superb farmlands which greeted Spotswood and his associates clearly presaged a movement of the Virginia frontier into the Valley of Virginia.[2]

Indeed, for several years before Spotswood made his famous expedition, land speculators and prospective settlers had evinced an interest in lands in the Shenandoah Valley. As early as May, 1703, Louis Michel, a resident of Bern, Switzerland, then on his second visit to America, wrote from Germantown, Pennsylvania, that he, along with "eight experienced Englishmen" and four Indians, was about to undertake an expedition to "the rather unknown western regions, of which the Indians here have wonders to tell, on account of their high mountains, warm waters, rich minerals, fruitful lands, large streams and abundance of game which is found there." Michel asserted that his journey was inspired in part by an "old curiosity, to seek out unknown things and to collect the wonders of nature" and partly by "the intention to take up land, if . . . feasible."

In the same year, Michel became associated with George Ritter, a druggist of Bern. Shortly afterward, Ritter petitioned the council of Bern for permission to transport himself and four or five hundred other persons of that canton to Pennsylvania or to "the borders of Virginia," if a grant of land could be procured from the English queen. He proposed to draw these immigrants from Reformed Protestants and from such economic groups as merchants, artisans, traders, manufacturers, and farmers. Ritter's plans, however, resulted in no immediate emigration from Switzerland.

Three years later, in 1706, while again visiting America, Michel undertook another journey to the west in search of lands and

<hr />

[2] Leonidas Dodson, *Alexander Spotswood, Governor of Colonial Virginia, 1710–1722* (Philadelphia, 1932), pp. 237–41.

minerals. On this expedition he was accompanied by seasoned woodsmen, including the Pennsylvania traders James Le Tort, Peter Bezalion, and Martin Chartier. In their quest, the party explored the region around Harper's Ferry, at the confluence of the Shenandoah and Potomac rivers, and Michel sketched a map of the area.

Upon his return to Switzerland in 1708, Michel, armed with accounts of good farmland and attractive mineral resources, excited the interest of another resident of Bern, Baron Christopher de Graffenried. Sensing an opportunity to promote the liberty and welfare of his countrymen and at the same time to recoup his declining fortune, Graffenried joined forces with the Ritter group. In another memorial to the English Crown, he and his associates, on July 13, 1709, specifically requested a grant of land on the Shenandoah. In pressing his petition, Ritter declared that the Swiss colonists would be willing to pay quitrents and would ask only one concession—that, because of their religious beliefs, they might have a minister from their own country.

Several factors combined to deprive the Shenandoah area of the thrifty, industrious, and God-fearing colonists whom Graffenried eventually transported to America. Unfortunately, the activities of Michel and his companions around the forks of the Potomac in 1706 and 1707 aroused the apprehensions of the Conestoga Indians. At a council held at Philadelphia on February 24, 1707, the Conestogas complained of the encroachments to the government of Pennsylvania, whereupon the colonial authorities warned Michel and others that unless they had special permission to engage in such expeditions, they should repair at once to Philadelphia or to their usual places of abode, or "answer to the Contrary at their Peril." Another difficulty lay in the uncertainty as to the ownership of the lands around the forks of the Potomac. Even though Pennsylvania might give her blessing to the proposed settlement, the locality selected lay within territory claimed by both the proprietors of Maryland and the English grantees of the Northern Neck of Virginia. Perhaps most important of all in the decision of the Swiss immigrants to turn to North Carolina was an offer of the proprietors of that colony to provide them with lands and to grant to Graffenried himself 10,000 acres and the title of landgrave.[3]

Although the Swiss interest led to no settlement in the lower Shenandoah Valley, there are suggestions that other settlers may have taken up lands in nearby areas prior to 1730. Information regarding these alleged occupations, however, is of a nebulous—but nonetheless tantalizing—character. The minutes of a council held by the Conestoga Indians and Governor William Keith of Pennsylvania at Conestoga on July 18, 1717, record a complaint by the Indians that about two months previously, while they were hunting beyond the "ffurthermost Branch of the Potomack," they had come upon "about Thirty Christians, armed Horsemen, & about as many Indians." The Conestogas wanted to know "what Christians were settled Back in the Woods behind Virginia & Carolina." Some writers have concluded from this information that a settlement existed at the time in the Harper's Ferry area. More explicit are the records of the Philadelphia Synod of the Presbyterian Church, which show that on September 19, 1719, "the people of Potomoke, in Virginia" requested "an able gospel minister to settle amongst them." These records also reveal that the following year Reverend Daniel McGill visited Potomoke, where he "remained for some months and put the people in church order." The site of Potomoke cannot be positively identified, but there is reason to believe that it was Shepherdstown.

An old West Virginia tradition that Morgan Morgan, a Welshman, made the first settlement in the state at Bunker Hill in Berkeley County in 1726 can no longer be accepted. It is now known that Morgan served as a coroner in Delaware from 1726

[3] William J. Hinke, trans. and ed., "Letters regarding the Second Journey of Michel to America, February 14, 1703, to January 16, 1704, and His Stay in America till 1708," *Virginia Magazine of History and Biography*, XXIV (June, 1916), 295-97, 301-302; Charles E. Kemper, ed., "Documents relating to Early Projected Swiss Colonies in the Valley of Virginia, 1706–1709," *ibid.*, XXIX (January, 1921), 6, 14, and map facing p. 1; *Minutes of the Provincial Council of Pennsylvania from the Organization to the Termination of the Proprietary Government [1683–1775]*, 10 vols. in *Colonial Records of Pennsylvania*, 16 vols. (Philadelphia, 1851–1853), II, 403-404. Hereafter cited as *Colonial Records of Pennsylvania*. See also Thomas Perkins Abernethy, *Three Virginia Frontiers* (University, La., 1940), p. 37; Charles H. Ambler and Festus P. Summers, *West Virginia: The Mountain State*, 2d ed. (Englewood Cliffs, N. J., 1958), p. 34.

through 1729 and that he did not purchase lands in West Virginia until November, 1730. This information suggests that Morgan did not arrive before 1730, and perhaps not before 1731. If, as is often asserted, German settlers took up residence at Shepherdstown in 1727, the claim that Morgan was the state's first permanent settler must be abandoned.[4]

Although a few settlements, beginning with Adam Müller's acquisition of a homesite at Elkton in the Shenandoah Valley in 1726, had been made, no substantial occupation of territory west of the Blue Ridge occurred before the early 1730's. The remoteness of the upper Potomac and lower Shenandoah from the inhabited parts of the Tidewater and Piedmont and their separation from the latter by the formidable Blue Ridge Mountains presented hazards of a magnitude not previously encountered in the pattern of frontier advance in Virginia. Ordinarily, the pioneer of the Tidewater and the Piedmont had carved his new homestead within communicating distance of friends and neighbors and had carried with him knowledge and resources which had enabled him to begin life successfully in an environment not unlike that to which he had been accustomed. The move west of the Blue Ridge, on the other hand, meant isolation, virtually no contact with former acquaintances, exposure to attack by Indians, and a degree of self-sufficiency which the lone pioneer family did not possess. Only the simultaneous migration of a number of families could provide the security against Indian incursions, the psychological reassurance needed in times of loneliness, illness, and death, and the probability of the maintenance of familiar and cherished institutions.

Virginia officials believed that, in spite of these difficulties and the rival claims of Maryland and Pennsylvania, there were numerous advantages to be derived from the occupation of the backcountry. An area of settlement west of the Blue Ridge would provide a buffer zone between the Piedmont and the Indians,

---

[4] *Colonial Records of Pennsylvania,* III, 19-20; Charles E. Kemper, "Some Valley Notes," *Virginia Magazine of History and Biography,* XXIX (October, 1921), 420-21; Ambler and Summers, *West Virginia,* p. 107n; Millard Kessler Bushong, *A History of Jefferson County, West Virginia* (Charles Town, W. Va., 1941), pp. 8-9; Albert Bernhardt Faust, *The German Element in the United States,* 2 vols. (Boston, 1909), I, 190.

help prevent the encroachment of the French upon the lands, and promote trade with the western tribes. As early as 1701 the General Assembly sought to encourage settlement of the backlands by making available tracts of from 10,000 to 30,000 acres to organized groups, or "societies," each of which should include not less than 20 armed fighting men, who would build a palisaded fort near the center of their settlement. Although each member of such societies might receive a 25-acre town lot, 200 acres of farm and grazing lands, and exemption from taxes for 20 years, the plan apparently excited little interest. As a result, most Virginia land grants continued to be made to individuals, but patents of a thousand acres became more and more common. These grants entailed a cash payment of ten shillings and an annual quitrent of two shillings per hundred acres by the grantee and the requirement that at least three acres out of each fifty be brought under cultivation.[5]

Modification of the land laws about 1730 brought the speculator into prominence in the extension of the Virginia frontier. Under the new plan, promoters received grants, most of which ranged from 10,000 to 100,000 acres, on the condition that they seat one family for each thousand acres. They were required to settle families who lived outside Virginia and to fulfill their contracts within two years. On the other hand, they were permitted to defer payment of all fees until the issuance of their patents. Prominent among the numerous speculators who obtained grants of land west of the Blue Ridge during the 1730's were Joist Hite and Robert McKay of Pennsylvania, William Beverley (the grandson of the first William Byrd), Benjamin Borden of New Jersey and his associates, and James Patton, a Scotch-Irish ship captain, who, after transporting many of his fellow countrymen to Beverley's lands, set out upon speculative ventures of his own. The land speculators and their descendants formed the backbone of the new aristocracy which developed in the Valley of Virginia.

The westernmost of these grants lay either entirely or partially within West Virginia. In 1730 the council of Virginia provided John and Isaac Van Meter, sons of the elder John Van Meter,

[5] Abernethy, *Three Virginia Frontiers*, pp. 46, 53-54.

whom tradition credits with a visit to the South Branch of the
Potomac as early as 1725, with 40,000 acres of land on the
usual terms. Of these lands, a 20,000-acre grant to the younger
John Van Meter lay in the fork between the Shenandoah and
the Potomac and extended to the Opequon and its southern
branch. On October 28 of the same year Alexander Ross and
Morgan Bryan of Pennsylvania obtained 100,000 acres, which
was to be located west and north of "the River Opeckon" and to
extend to the North Mountain and the Potomac or to be taken
from any other part of the Shenandoah Valley not already
granted. Charles Chiswell and his associates on May 5, 1735,
having been unsuccessful in finding sufficient land along the
Potomac and the Pennsylvania line to satisfy the 60,000 acres
previously granted them, asked for and received the acres yet
due them in the region "between the Rivers little Cacaper & great
Cacaper." One of the tracts in the 30,000-acre grant to Edward
Barradall and John Lewis lay between two ridges of the North
Mountains "upon a River running to the South South West of
another called Kackapa," a reference perhaps to Lost River in
Hardy County.[6]

Prohibited from recruiting settlers from eastern Virginia,
promoters attempting to settle lands between the Blue Ridge
and the Alleghenies drew heavily upon the population of New
Jersey and Pennsylvania and upon the vast numbers of Germans, Scotch-Irish, and Swiss then pouring into America from
Europe. The Germans constituted the vanguard of the new
immigrant wave and usually took up lands in the northern part
of the Valley of Virginia in the counties of Frederick, Shenandoah, and Rockingham. The Scotch-Irish, who followed close
behind them, settled in Berkeley County or moved farther south
to Augusta, Rockbridge, and Botetourt counties. Many of these
settlers, as well as those from eastern Virginia, had formerly been
indentured servants and had moved into the Valley as their
contracts expired. Although Virginia speculators ordinarily

[6] *Ibid.*, pp. 54-57; H. R. McIlwaine, Wilmer Hall, and Benjamin J. Hillman, eds.,
Executive Journals of the Council of Colonial Virginia, 6 vols. (Richmond, Va.,
1925-1966), IV, 223-24, 229, 232-33, 249-50, 253, 258, 270, 289, 319, 326, 336,
347, 350-51, 375-76, 395, 408-409; V, 82-83, 113, 134, 444. The visit of the
elder John Van Meter to the South Branch is in Samuel Kercheval, *A History of the
Valley of Virginia,* ed. Oren F. Morton, 4th ed. (Strasburg, Va., 1925), p. 55.

charged three pounds per hundred acres for their lands, or about six times the price at which lands could be purchased directly from the government, they rendered services, such as the extension of credit to purchasers and attention to legal details at distant courthouses, which settlers regarded as sufficient to offset the additional price. The attractiveness of these lands was further augmented by Virginia's willingness to allow religious dissenters in the backcountry to practice their own beliefs.[7]

The cosmopolitan character of the Valley of Virginia was reflected in the population of Jefferson and Berkeley counties, in West Virginia. Between 35 and 40 percent of the settlers who took up lands in Jefferson County and in the eastern part of Berkeley County were Virginians of English extraction, who moved west by way of Vestal's and Snickers' gaps. Jefferson County, the most accessible to these routes of migration from eastern Virginia, received the largest English population. Berkeley County, on the other hand, attracted a greater proportion of the Scotch-Irish. Both counties absorbed a substantial part of the German migration, with Martinsburg and Mecklenburg, later known as Shepherdstown, becoming centers of German settlement. In the two counties, as a whole, the Germans and Scotch-Irish were about equal in numbers, each nationality accounting for about 30 percent of the population. By the middle 1740's settlements in which the two nationalities figured prominently had expanded far beyond the bounds of the two counties and dotted the banks of Opequon, Back, and Tuscarora creeks and the two Cacapon rivers. By that time, too, Germans and Scotch-Irish made up substantial portions of the population of the South Branch and Patterson's Creek.[8]

[7] Abernethy, *Three Virginia Frontiers*, p. 55; Faust, *German Element in the United States*, pp. 187-200, 265-68; John W. Wayland, *The German Element of the Shenandoah Valley of Virginia* (Charlottesville, Va., 1907), pp. 20-56; Wayland F. Dunaway, *The Scotch-Irish of Colonial Pennsylvania* (Chapel Hill, N. C., 1944), pp. 103-107. A map showing the ethnic composition of the Valley at the time of the American Revolution is in Freeman H. Hart, *The Valley of Virginia in the American Revolution, 1763–1789* (Chapel Hill, N. C., 1942), pp. 5-7.

[8] Miles Sturdivant Malone, "The Distribution of Population on the Virginia Frontier in 1775" (Ph.D. dissertation, Princeton University, 1935), pp. 3, 87-88, 93, and maps, pp. i-ii; William H. Foote, *Sketches of Virginia, Historical and Biographical*, 2d ed., rev. (Philadelphia, 1856), pp. 15-16; Ambler and Summers, *West Virginia*, p. 35.

Drawing upon a vast reservoir of depressed but optimistic humanity, the Virginia speculators unquestionably provided much of the initial impetus for settlement of the Valley of Virginia and the upper Potomac. For example, Joist Hite, who acquired lands from the Van Meters, was granted a patent to his lands on June 12, 1734, on the basis that he had seated the required number of families on his tracts lying at the forks of the Potomac and the Shenandoah. By April 23, 1735, Alexander Ross and Morgan Bryan had transported seventy families to their lands, some of them undoubtedly in West Virginia.[9] Once the migration was in motion, however, the influence of the speculators appears to have diminished.

Virginia speculators immediately encountered rival claims of Lord Fairfax to the Northern Neck of Virginia. The rights of the English nobleman originated in a patent to lands "bounded by and within the heads" of the Potomac and Rappahannock rivers, made by Charles II of England in 1669 to a group of seven staunch supporters of the Stuarts in their difficulties with Parliament. By inheritance and sale, the proprietary passed through various hands until in 1719 Thomas, sixth Lord Fairfax, became sole owner. The agent of Lord Fairfax, the able Robert Carter of Corotoman, asserted the claims of the proprietor to lands as far west as the headsprings of the southern fork of the Rappahannock and the highest branch of the Potomac. Carter contested the right of Virginia to grant lands in the lower Shenandoah and upper Potomac valleys and thereby called into question all patents to lands in the Northern Neck.[10]

In 1733 Lord Fairfax petitioned the Crown to proclaim his rights and to restrain the government of Virginia from granting lands within the area which he claimed. As a result of his representations, the Crown ordered a survey of the Northern Neck in 1736, with the lines to be run by commissioners, part of whom were to be appointed by Fairfax and part by the government of Virginia. The commissioners, however, were

[9] McIlwaine, Hall, and Hillman, eds., *Executive Journals of the Council of Colonial Virginia*, IV, 223, 326, 347.

[10] One of the most convenient summaries of the history of the Fairfax proprietary is in Douglas Southall Freeman, *George Washington: A Biography*, 7 vols. (New York, 1948-1957), I, 447-527.

unable to agree upon a boundary. Virginia's representatives insisted that the Fairfax tract was bounded on the west by a line running from the forks of the Rappahannock to the mouth of the Shenandoah and that it included about 2,033,000 acres. Fairfax, on the other hand, was adamant in demanding the boundaries set forth by Carter, or an area of 5,282,000 acres. After a long delay, Fairfax appeared in person before the Privy Council and proposed that, in return for the validation of his grant, he would confirm all royal titles in the disputed area, waive all past due quitrents, and give the Crown the arrearages due under royal grants. On that basis, the Crown on April 6, 1745, confirmed the rights of Fairfax to a tract extending to the headsprings of the Rapidan and to the westernmost spring of the North Branch of the Potomac. At the latter point the famed Fairfax Stone was erected in 1746 to mark the uttermost limits of the Fairfax grant. Except for patents already issued by Virginia and recognized by the proprietor, this disposition of the conflict placed in the hands of Lord Fairfax the lower Shenandoah Valley, which included Jefferson and Berkeley counties and that portion of the Alleghenies embraced in Morgan, Hardy, Hampshire, and Mineral counties and parts of Grant and Tucker counties in West Virginia.[11]

Significantly, Fairfax introduced into his domain a feudal system of landholding. Some of his best lands he laid out in large manors. The South Branch, or Wappacomo, Manor, lying along the South Branch of the Potomac and principally in Hardy County, contained 55,000 acres. The Patterson's Creek Manor consisted of 9,000 acres. The manors were subdivided into tracts ranging from 9 to 625 acres, depending upon the needs of individual purchasers, with most families acquiring from 100 to 300 acres. Apparently, not more than 10 percent of the settlers on the Fairfax estate held their lands in fee simple.

[11] Nine documents relating to the Fairfax survey are in Miscellaneous MSS, Box CII, West Virginia Department of Archives and History Library. These documents have been reproduced in Elizabeth Cometti, ed., "Concerning the First Survey of the Northern Neck," *West Virginia History*, II (October, 1940), 52-64. See also [Thomas Lewis], *The Fairfax Line: Thomas Lewis's Journey of 1746*, ed. John W. Wayland (New Market, Va., 1925), pp. 37-41, and Harold Bruce Fortney, "Maryland–West Virginia, Western Boundary," *West Virginia History*, XIX (October, 1957), 16-19.

Others held their properties under a system of lease and release. Of them Fairfax required a down payment, or composition money, and an annual quitrent payable on St. Michaelmas Day, with fees varying according to the amount and value of the land held.[12]

Although many local historians and antiquarians have attacked the quitrents and have berated Fairfax for his restrictions upon the killing of elk, deer, buffalo, beaver, and other game, the truth is that the Englishman's terms were not such as to discourage settlement. By the summer of 1747 homesteads extended for sixty miles along the South Branch, with Germans, Scotch-Irish, and English making up most of the population. A rental list of Fairfax's lands reveals that many of the most prominent South Branch families began life there as tenants on the lord's estate. Among them were the Heath, Van Meter, Hornback, Hite, Harness, Armentrout, Inskeep, McNeal, Renick, Shobe, and Cunningham families. In addition to numerous Germans, who were "interspersed among the English," the Patterson's Creek Manor included Scotch-Irish and a scattering of Low German and Dutch settlers.[13]

Settlement of the Eastern Panhandle of West Virginia, like that of other mountainous areas, often had the character of a folk movement. Typical of such migrations was that of six families who took up lands in the Fort Seybert area of Pendleton County in 1747. The party included the families of Roger Dyer, his son William, his son-in-law Matthew Patton, John Patton, Jr., John Smith, and William Stephenson. Two of the six families were closely related to Dyer, and the others appear to have been friends and neighbors of Dyer during the time he lived in Pennsylvania and at Moorefield on the South Branch of the Potomac. These families purchased lands from Robert Green, who, with James Wood and William Russell, had acquired in 1746 and 1747 nineteen tracts totaling 15,748 acres on the South Branch

<hr />

[12] Hu Maxwell and H. L. Swisher, *History of Hampshire County, West Virginia* (Morgantown, W. Va., 1897), pp. 396-98.

[13] Undated Lord Fairfax Rental List, South Branch Manor, South Branch Valley MSS, West Virginia Department of Archives and History Library; William J. Hinke and Charles Kemper, eds., "Moravian Diaries of Travels through Virginia," *Virginia Magazine of History and Biography*, XII (January, 1904), 226, and XII (July, 1904), 56-57.

above the lands of Lord Fairfax. Following the arrival of the Dyer party, Green's lands filled rapidly with settlers. Between 1748 and 1751, Dyer began to sell lands from his "Upper Tract," and by 1753 twenty-one families, including the Dunkles, Conrads, Seyberts, Rulemans, Propsts, and Keisters, and mostly of German origin, had acquired holdings. Within ten years after the settlement of the Dyer group, the population along the headwaters of the South Branch of the Potomac numbered about forty families.[14]

By the time of the French and Indian War the population of the Valley of Virginia had reached a saturation point and that of the Eastern Panhandle of West Virginia, concentrated largely in the lower Shenandoah Valley and along the tributary streams of the upper Potomac, numbered 7,000 to 8,000. Hampshire County, which had been created in 1754 in response to the demands of the inhabitants of the South Branch and Patterson's Creek, reported 558 tithables and 12 Negroes in 1756. In determining population at that time, the number of tithables was ordinarily multiplied by four. On the basis of this formula, Hampshire County would have had about 2,200 people. Frederick County had 2,173 tithables and 340 Negroes, or a population of about 10,000, of whom about 5,000 lived in the extreme Eastern Panhandle of West Virginia.[15]

Although many of the settlers of the lower Shenandoah Valley and along the upper Potomac and its tributaries lived in all the crudeness commonly associated with a new frontier, they escaped many of the regressions in civilization which accompanied movement into other parts of the Alleghenies. The erosiveness of the frontier in the former areas was most apparent in its effects upon organized religion and formal education, but the strength of family units and the cohesiveness of national groups, particularly among the Germans, exerted social pressures

[14] Oren F. Morton, *A History of Pendleton County, West Virginia* (Franklin, W. Va., 1910), pp. 33-38. See also, for example, an indenture between Aldrich and Elizabeth Coonrad and John Fisher, September 2, 1806, McCoy Family Papers, West Virginia University Library.

[15] R. A. Brock, ed., *The Official Records of Robert Dinwiddie, Lieutenant Governor of the Colony of Virginia, 1751–1758*, 2 vol. (Richmond, Va., 1883-1884), II, 352-53.

which preserved moral and ethical standards to which the settlers had been accustomed. The requirement that speculators seat families rather than individuals as a condition for obtaining patents for their lands thus proved to have significant social implications, and it must not be overlooked in assessing the role of the land speculator in the peopling of the Valley of Virginia and the Potomac section of West Virginia.

Significantly, too, the upper Potomac settlements were spared during their first quarter of a century that almost constant danger from Indian attack which plagued settlers who occupied the trans-Allegheny regions between the outbreak of the French and Indian War and Anthony Wayne's victory at Fallen Timbers in 1794. In 1722, before any advance into the Potomac section began, Virginia signed the Treaty of Albany with the Six Nations and thereby gained the right to make settlements south of the Potomac and east of "the high ridge of mountains." The Indians were not wholly satisfied with the agreement, inasmuch as it deprived them of the use of the Warrior's Path, their chief line of communication with the Cherokees, provided for no payment for the lands ceded, and was interpreted by Virginia authorities as involving the cession of all Indian lands east of the Alleghenies. The displeasure of the Six Nations, however, was not sufficient to impede seriously the settlement of the Shenandoah and upper Potomac regions, and in 1744, through the efforts of Conrad Weiser, the Indians signed the Treaty of Lancaster, which affirmed cessions of lands as far west as the crests of the Alleghenies.[16]

Geographical conditions in the Shenandoah Valley and in the lowlands along the upper Potomac also accelerated the resurgence of time-honored social and economic institutions. Like the Blue-grass region of Kentucky and the Nashville Basin, these areas were blessed with rich limestone soils, which very early gave rise to an important grazing industry and the introduction on a limited scale of plantation-type agriculture. When Moravian missionaries passed through the South Branch settlements in 1747 and 1748, they found Germans who had already constructed

[16] For the Treaty of Lancaster, see Lois Mulkearn, ed., *George Mercer Papers relating to the Ohio Company of Virginia* (Pittsburgh, Pa., 1954), pp. 401-403.

barns large enough to accommodate gatherings for religious services. In 1762 the Virginia General Assembly recognized the stability of the upper Potomac frontier by incorporating the towns of Mecklenburg, later Shepherdstown, and Romney.[17] By the time of the American Revolution, the lower Shenandoah Valley abounded with well-developed estates, including Adam Stephen's "Bower," Horatio Gates' "Traveler's Rest," and Samuel Washington's "Harewood." Andrew Burnaby later declared that in spite of their "inexperience of the elegancies of life," the residents along the Shenandoah—and his observations would have been equally applicable to those on the upper branches of the Potomac—possessed "what many princes would give half their dominions for, health, content[ment], and tranquillity of mind."[18]

Finally, the movement of people into the Shenandoah and upper Potomac valleys was but a part of a much larger migration, which was in the mainstream of American history. Here were found attractions for agriculture and an ease of transportation equal to those of other areas of the country open to settlement at the time. Moreover, the chaotic land system, which later discouraged prospective immigrants from acquiring lands in the Allegheny sections of Virginia, was not in effect in the upper Potomac and lower Shenandoah valleys during the forty years in which most of their early settlers arrived.

Just prior to the French and Indian War, settlers also began to occupy the Greenbrier Valley. The Greenbrier population was largely an overflow from the great concentration of Scotch-Irish settlers who had pushed up the Shenandoah Valley and into Augusta, Botetourt, and Rockbridge counties. According to tradition, an unidentified lunatic from Frederick County, who was prone to wander off during the seizures with which he was afflicted, discovered the Greenbrier River in 1749. This tradition, however, is hardly tenable, since the Greenbrier region was by

[17] Hinke and Kemper, eds., "Moravian Diaries of Travels through Virginia" (July, 1904), pp. 56-57; Ambler and Summers, West Virginia, p. 50.
[18] Freeman H. Hart, The Valley of Virginia in the American Revolution, 1763–1789 (Chapel Hill, N. C., 1942), p. 24; Andrew Burnaby, Travels through the Middle Settlements in North-America, in the Years 1759 and 1760 with Observations upon the State of the Colonies (London, 1775), p. 33.

that time well known and was already being taken up by land speculators.

Older accounts almost universally name Jacob Marlin and Stephen Sewell as the first settlers in the Greenbrier area. Although they were alone in the wilderness, they reportedly disagreed on matters of religion and took up separate dwellings, but otherwise remained good friends. Eventually Marlin returned to the Valley settlements, but Sewell, if tradition be true, moved farther west, to the mountain which bears his name, and was killed by the Indians. It is worthy of note that Sewell was one of 18 persons who on November 2, 1752, were granted 30,000 acres of land "between the Green Briars to the South and the Youghyoughganie to the North, bearing the Name of Mannangelie upon a River called Goose River, beginning at a Run known by the Name of Muddy Run." His interest in land speculation and the notation of William Preston that he was killed not on Sewell Mountain but on Jackson's River, east of the Greenbrier area, suggests that Sewell may have been scouting for lands in the Greenbrier country and may not have been a bona fide settler.[19]

On the other hand, there is proof that the settlement of the Greenbrier Valley had begun by 1750. In returning from his famous exploring expedition for the Loyal Company, Dr. Thomas Walker journeyed eastward from Kentucky by a route which crossed West Virginia via New River, Greenbrier River, and Anthony's Creek and then led over the Alleghenies to Jackson's River by way of Ragged Creek. Walker noted in his journal that Anthony's Creek, a tributary of the Greenbrier, afforded "a great deal of Very good Land, and it is chiefly bought." In general, the lands along the branches of the Greenbrier were considered better than those along the river itself, and the highlands were "very good in many places." At the time of Walker's

[19] Alexander Scott Withers, *Chronicles of Border Warfare*, ed. Reuben Gold Thwaites, new ed. (Cincinnati, Ohio, 1903), pp. 56-57; McIlwaine, Hall, and Hillman, eds., *Executive Journals of the Council of Colonial Virginia*, V, 172-73, 409; John Stuart, "Memorandum, 1798 July 15th," in Ruth Woods Dayton, *Greenbrier Pioneers and Their Homes* (Charleston, W. Va., 1942), p. 367; Preston's Register of Persons Killed, Wounded, or Taken Prisoner . . . , Draper MSS, 1QQ83, State Historical Society of Wisconsin (Microfilm in West Virginia Department of Archives and History Library). Hereafter cited as "Preston's Register."

expedition, some settlers had already established "plantations" on the branches of the Greenbrier.[20]

The first settlements of the Greenbrier area were apparently promoted by the Greenbrier Company. Composed of John Robinson, Sr., Thomas Nelson, Jr., William Beverley, Robert Lewis, Beverley Robinson, Henry Weatherbourne, John Lewis, William Lewis, Charles Lewis, John Craig, and John Wilson, its membership represented both political influence and experience in settling western lands. By the end of 1754 Andrew Lewis had surveyed more than 50,000 acres in the Greenbrier Valley.[21]

The locations of the Greenbrier settlements confirm to some extent Thomas Walker's appraisal of the lands. Most of the settlers—numbering some fifty families—who had taken up lands by 1753 resided on Anthony's Creek, Howard's Creek, Spring Lick Creek, Muddy Creek, Knapp's Creek, in the locality known as the Sinks, and along the Greenbrier itself. Among these pioneers were the families of John Keeney, James Burnside, Thomas Campbell, Samuel Carroll, Archibald Clendenin, Andrew Lewis, George, Frederick, and John See, Matthias and Felty Yocum, Lemuel Howard, James Ewing, Patrick Davis, William Renick, and John and Robert Fulton.[22]

About the same time settlers began to press beyond the mountains encircling the western part of the Potomac drainage area. In 1753 Robert Files and David Tygart, for whom Files Creek and Tygart Valley River are named, settled near Beverly, either on or near the Seneca Trail. Here Files, his wife, and five of their children were killed by Indians in 1754. The Tygart family, warned by a surviving son of Files, managed to escape to the South Branch settlements.[23]

---

[20] Thomas Walker, *Journal of an Expedition in the Spring of the Year 1750*, ed. William Cabell Rives (Boston, 1888), pp. 66-67.

[21] McIlwaine, Hall, and Hillman, eds., *Executive Journals of the Council of Colonial Virginia*, V, 172-73; John Stuart, "Memoir of Indian Wars, and Other Occurrences," Virginia Historical and Philosophical Society *Collections*, I (Richmond, Va., 1833), 38.

[22] J. T. McAllister, "Incidents in the Pioneer, Colonial and Revolutionary History of the West Virginia Area," in Henry S. Green, *Biennial Report of the Department of Archives and History of the State of West Virginia, 1911–1912, 1913–1914* (Charleston, W. Va., 1914), p. 21. A settlement was also made in 1753 at Culbertson's, later Crump's, Bottom in Summers County by Andrew Culbertson. Draper MSS, 12CC272.

[23] "Preston's Register"; Withers, *Chronicles of Border Warfare*, pp. 74-75.

Unique in many respects among West Virginia settlements prior to the French and Indian War was that made by Israel, Grabriel, and Samuel Eckerlin at Dunkard Bottom on Cheat River. These brothers, emigrants from Schwarzenau in Germany, had joined the Brethren, or Dunkards, before leaving their homeland. Soon after their arrival at Germantown, Pennsylvania, they became associated with the Cloister at Ephrata. The gifted but strong-willed brothers soon disagreed with the management of Ephrata, and in 1754 Israel and Samuel Eckerlin, Alexander Mack, Jr., and Peter Miller moved to an isolated section of Virginia and established themselves on New River at a place which they called Mahanaim. Within a few years the Eckerlins returned to Ephrata. Again they became dissatisfied, and in 1750 they renounced the society altogether and rejoined the Brethren at Germantown. The following year they harkened once more to the call of the frontier, but this time they crossed the Alleghenies, settling first in Greene County, Pennsylvania, and later on the Cheat River lands, where they lived the ascetic life which so appealed to them.

With the outbreak of the French and Indian War, the Eckerlin brothers, who were ardent pacifists, fell under a cloud of suspicion. In 1756, while he was returning from Winchester with supplies, Samuel was stopped by wary settlers and detained at Fort Pleasant on the South Branch of the Potomac. After some delay, he was placed under an armed guard and permitted to return to Dunkard Bottom. The sight which Eckerlin and his escort beheld when they arrived at Dunkard Bottom proved that there had been no ground for suspecting the brothers of collaborating with the Indians, for they found the cabin in ashes and Gabriel and Israel missing, both evidently captured by the Indians.

Much speculation has centered around the ultimate plans of the Eckerlins in the Cheat River Valley. During their residence there, they acquired over 6,000 acres of land. They engaged in extensive hunting and agricultural activities and at one time required twenty-eight packhorses to transport their products to market. It has been suggested that they may have intended to form a monastic society there. Other writers believe that, in the light of their demonstrated capability for business and management, the Eckerlins hoped to profit from speculations in land.[24]

Most of the settlements in and west of the Alleghenies prior to the French and Indian War lay in West Virginia, but a few attempts were made to establish habitations in western Pennsylvania. The latter, including those of Christopher Gist near Mt. Braddock and William Stewart at Connellsville, however, were abandoned in 1754 when Washington was driven from Fort Necessity. At the outbreak of hostilities between England and France in the Ohio Valley, the only settlements deep in the Alleghenies were those in the Greenbrier Valley. Early in the war even these spearheads were wiped out, and the great dividing ridges of the Alleghenies became a visible line of demarcation between English settlements and the Indian country. Moreover, immigration into the upper Potomac Valley ceased altogether, and existing settlements as far east as Winchester were threatened with destruction. Fifteen years were to elapse before the international situation and Indian relations would permit any sustained movement beyond the crests of the Alleghenies.

[24] Foster Melvin Bittinger, *A History of the Church of the Brethren in the First District of West Virginia* (Elgin, Ill., 1945), pp. 21-28; Oren F. Morton, *A History of Preston County, West Virginia,* 2 vols. (Kingwood, W. Va., 1914), I, 47.

Chapter Three

Barbarous Circumstances

Unlike the peaceful and uninterrupted advance of immigrants into the Valley of Virginia and the upper Potomac region, the movement of settlers into trans-Allegheny areas was impeded by rivalries which led to one of the great international confrontations in American history. By 1748 competition between those ancient enemies, England and France, was approaching a climax, and the Ohio Valley, of which trans-Allegheny West Virginia was a part, had become a focal point of tension. Neither country regarded the Treaty of Aix-la-Chapelle, which had just ended nearly ten years of bloody European strife, as more than a truce in their long struggle, and in the six years following its signing both nations pressed claims to the Ohio Valley. Their claims rested in part upon discovery—England's by Batts and Fallam and France's by La Salle. But both nations had extensive fur trading operations in the Ohio Valley, and both had made settlements along tributary streams—France in the Illinois country, and England along the Monongahela and the Greenbrier.

Virginia, whose charter of 1609 gave her a boundary extending two hundred miles north and south of Old Point Comfort and east and west from sea to sea, had especially strong claims of her own to the Ohio Valley, but her leaders knew that she could not challenge France alone. When James Patton, the Valley speculator, sought a grant of 200,000 acres on the "branches of the Mississippi" in 1743 on the usual condition that he seat one family for each thousand acres, Governor William Gooch denied his request "lest it might occasion a Dispute betwixt them and the French, who claimed a Right to Land on those waters." Besides, said Gooch, there was no advantage in having a "hand full of Poor People" settled there. However, the governor promised to give Patton's application priority over any later requests and to approve it should war break out between England and France.[1]

Two events in 1744 induced Virginia to abandon her cautious policy concerning the transmontane country and actively to encourage expansion into the area. On March 15, following the signing of the treaty known as the Family Compact by France and Spain, the War of Jenkins' Ear between England and Spain and the War of the Austrian Succession, in which France and Prussia were aligned against Austria, merged, as expected, into a general European conflict. With England and France again in opposing camps, Virginia felt more secure in adopting an aggressive policy with respect to the Ohio Valley. Moreover, the conclusion of the Treaty of Lancaster with the Six Nations on July 2, which Virginia interpreted as involving the cession by the Indians of all lands west of the Alleghenies, made a vigorous policy a certainty.[2]

In implementing the decision to press her claims to the Ohio Valley, Virginia again attempted to make the speculator the intermediary between the settler and the wilderness. This technique had proved remarkably successful in the peopling of the Valley of Virginia. She again offered promoters 1,000 acres of land for each family seated and extended the time allowed for making the settlements to four years rather than the customary two. Between April 26, 1745, and May 7, 1754, the council of Virginia granted to speculators more than 2,500,000 acres, most of it lying west of the Alleghenies. Ten of the grants, embracing 450,000 acres, lay entirely in trans-Allegheny West Virginia. In addition, most of the 200,000-acre grant to the Ohio Company was to be located within a triangular area bounded by the crests of the Alleghenies and the Ohio and Kanawha rivers.[3]

The first of the grantees, the Greenbrier Company, whose membership represented both political influence and experience

[1] James Patton to John Blair, January, 1753, Draper MSS, 1QQ75.

[2] Lois Mulkearn, ed., *George Mercer Papers relating to the Ohio Company of Virginia* (Pittsburgh, Pa., 1954), p. 403.

[3] *Ibid.*, pp. 289-94; H. R. McIlwaine, Wilmer Hall, and Benjamin J. Hillman, eds., *Executive Journals of the Council of Colonial Virginia*, 6 vols. (Richmond, Va., 1925-1966), V, 172-73, 195, 206, 231, 258, 282-83, 295-97, 377, 409, 426-27, 436-37, 454-55, 470.

in settling western lands, was in many respects the most successful in making settlements in West Virginia.[4] By the end of
1754 Andrew Lewis had surveyed more than 50,000 acres in the
Greenbrier Valley for the company. The settlers whom Dr.
Thomas Walker noted along the Greenbrier in his famous exploring expedition of 1750 were placed there by the Greenbrier
Company.

Other speculative ventures were less successful. Walker's own
group, the Loyal Company, with a princely domain of 800,000
acres, made a few surveys in the upper and middle New River
area and apparently settled a few families in West Virginia.
Henry Downs and his associates lost a 50,000-acre grant in the
Greenbrier area for failure to settle any families. Another combination, headed by Samuel Klug, seeking lands between the
Greenbrier and Monongahela rivers, likewise did nothing to
fulfill its obligations, unless the journey of one of the partners,
Stephen Sewell, into the Greenbrier region in 1751 was connected
with its affairs. Speculators in other West Virginia lands eventually forfeited their rights because of inability to make settlements. In most cases the tracts which they chose lay along
the Ohio River, 200 miles or more from existing settlements.
Families taking up these lands would be dangerously exposed
to Indian attack and would inevitably constitute a first line of
defense. Such fears probably prevented the settling of 10,000-
acre tracts at the mouth of the Kanawha granted to Thomas
Lewis and Ambrose Powell in 1752, as well as 5 tracts awarded
Richard Corbin and 24 associates in 1753 and 1754, including
50,000 acres at the mouth of Fishing Creek, 100,000 at the mouth
of the Kanawha, 40,000 at the mouth of Buffalo Creek, 20,000
at the mouth of Lalots [Le Tort's] Creek, and 50,000 at the mouth
of the Little Kanawha.[5]

The remaining group, the Ohio Company, received its lands

[4] McIlwaine, Hall, and Hillman, eds., *Executive Journals of the Council of
Colonial Virginia*, V, 172-73; John Stuart, "Memoir of Indian Wars, and Other
Occurrences," Virginia Historical and Philosophical Society *Collections,* I (Rich-
mond, Va., 1833), 38.

[5] Draper MSS, 12CC272-73; "A List of Early Land Patents and Grants," *Vir-
ginia Magazine of History and Biography*, V (October, 1897), 175, 179; Mc-
Ilwaine, Hall, and Hillman, eds., *Executive Journals of the Council of Colonial
Virginia*, V, 377, 436-37, 470.

on terms somewhat different from those imposed upon its rivals. Organized by Thomas Lee and including Thomas Cresap, Augustine Washington, George Fairfax, Francis Thornton, and Nathaniel Chapman among its many members, it petitioned Governor Gooch in 1747 for 500,000 acres of land for purposes of settlement and carrying on a trade with the Indians. Although he had authority to do so, Gooch declined to make the grant and, instead, referred the request to the Board of Trade, which in turn laid it before the Privy Council. After prolonged study and the addition of other members including John Hanbury, the influential London merchant, to the original group, the Privy Council instructed Gooch to make the grant. By the terms of its charter, the company received 200,000 acres "betwixt Romanetto's and Buffalo's Creek, on the South Side of the River Alligane, otherwise the Ohio, and betwixt the two creeks and the Yellow Creek on the North Side of the River, or in such other Parts of the West of the Great Mountains as shall be adjudged most proper by the Petitioners for making settlements thereon." For its part, the company was required to settle one hundred families within seven years and to build and garrison a fort on its land for their protection. When it had complied with these provisions, it might obtain an additional 300,000 acres adjoining the original tract subject to similar conditions.[6]

From the beginning, the Ohio Company faced a formidable array of difficulties. Traders from Pennsylvania and New York viewed the grant with menacing hostility. Moreover, the Six Nations argued that they had not ceded their trans-Allegheny lands in the Treaty of Lancaster. At the same time Indians north of the Ohio, allied with the Six Nations and encouraged by the French, assumed an increasingly belligerent attitude. A partial improvement in the company's position vis-à-vis the unfriendly tribes resulted from the Treaty of Logstown, which James Patton, Joshua Fry, Lunsford Lomax, Conrad Weiser, and Andrew Montour, representing Virginia but reflecting the interest

[6] Kenneth P. Bailey, *The Ohio Company of Virginia and the Westward Movement, 1748–1792: A Chapter in the History of the Colonial Frontier* (Glendale, Calif., 1939), pp. 24-31; Alfred P. James, *The Ohio Company: Its Inner History* (Pittsburgh, Pa., 1959), pp. 1-27; McIlwaine, Hall, and Hillman, eds., *Executive Journals of the Council of Colonial Virginia*, V, 295-96.

of the Ohio Company, concluded with the Iroquois, Shawnee, Delaware, and Wyandot tribes in August, 1752. By the terms of the agreement, the Indians reluctantly and protestingly recognized Virginia's claims to lands south of the Ohio River, and the company promised to build a fort to protect the Indians from French retaliation.[7]

Other problems arose with speculators whose claims conflicted with those of the Ohio Company. John Mercer of the Ohio Company charged that the Corbin group had obtained all of their five tracts along the Ohio River by devious methods. According to Mercer, they had first learned of the lands from an Ohio Company map, which Governor Robert Dinwiddie, himself a member of the Ohio Company, laid before the council of Virginia, and had profited from the exertions and expenses of the Ohio Company in making claims of their own. Although the Ohio Company had in 1751 and 1752 sent Christopher Gist on two exploring expeditions which had given it valuable information on trans-Allegheny West Virginia, including perhaps areas claimed by Corbin and his partners, the allegations of Mercer cannot be entirely substantiated.[8]

The immediate and ultimate results of the Ohio Company's activities were of no more than modest significance in advancing the Allegheny frontier. The company succeeded in locating only eleven families on its lands. All settled in Pennsylvania at Redstone Old Fort on the Monongahela, and none took up lands in West Virginia. For purposes of conducting its Indian trade, however, it built a storehouse in 1749 on the West Virginia side of the Potomac opposite the mouth of Wills Creek. This storehouse became a local business center where residents along the upper Potomac exchanged livestock and grains for such articles as blankets, red strouding, and "half-thicks," a coarse cloth originally made in Lancashire, England. Originally a two-story double log building, it was replaced in 1752 by a larger

---

[7] Bailey, *Ohio Company of Virginia*, pp. 125-37; Mulkearn, ed., *George Mercer Papers relating to the Ohio Company*, pp. 52-66, passim; James, *Ohio Company*, pp. 64-65.

[8] Mulkearn, ed., *George Mercer Papers relating to the Ohio Company*, pp. 7-40, 69, 72, 143, 225, 241-42, 526-27n, 577-78n, and map opposite p. 72; Draper MSS, 1QQ76.

and more substantial structure, which became the westernmost outpost in Virginia's system of defenses during the French and Indian War.[9]

On the other hand, the activities of the Ohio Company and other speculators undoubtedly helped spark countermoves by the French. In 1749 the Marquis de la Galissoniere, governor of New France, dispatched Captain Celoron de Blainville on an expedition down the Ohio with instructions to bury lead plates which asserted the claim of France to the Ohio Valley. These plates were embedded at strategic points, including the confluence of the Kanawha and the Ohio. Taking advantage of Indian apprehensiveness with regard to British plans for settlement in the Ohio Valley, French authorities began by means of persuasion, presents, and intimidation to lure the Ohio tribes away from their connections with the Iroquois, and by 1753 they had brought them firmly under French control. By that time, too, they had, through seizures of English traders and pressures upon the Indians, virtually ended the English fur trade north of the Ohio. In order to prevent further English expansion into the upper Ohio Valley, France also began construction of a ring of forts, including Fort Presqu' Isle at Erie, Fort Le Boeuf at the mouth of French Creek, and Fort Venango at Franklin, Pennsylvania.[10] These French moves cut off all prospects of any immediate advance of English settlement into the Ohio Valley.

In the face of French aggressiveness, Virginia took upon herself the burdens of empire. In October, 1753, Robert Dinwiddie, her vigorous governor, sent young George Washington to Fort Le Boeuf with a message to its commander, the Chevalier de St. Pierre, charging the French with encroaching upon English territory. St. Pierre rejected the English claims and made it clear that France would not yield the Ohio Valley. Upon his

[9] Bailey, *Ohio Company of Virginia*, pp. 74-78, 156, 213-14, 221; U. S., Works Progress Administration, Writers' Program, *Historic Romney, 1762–1937* (n. p., 1937), p. 47.

[10] Virgil A. Lewis, *First Biennial Report of the Department of Archives and History of the State of West Virginia* (Charleston, W. Va., 1906), pp. 166-70; Bailey, *Ohio Company of Virginia*, pp. 93, 163-76; Nicholas B. Wainwright, *George Croghan: Wilderness Diplomat* (Chapel Hill, N. C., 1959), pp. 17, 26-27, 50-51; Lawrence Henry Gipson, *The British Empire before the American Revolution*, 12 vols. to date (New York, 1936-   ), IV, 273-74.

return to Williamsburg, Washington recommended to Dinwiddie that Virginia offset the French advantages by building a fort at the forks of the Ohio. Dinwiddie acted upon his advice, and in January, 1754, sent a work party of thirty-seven men under Captain William Trent to construct the fort. In April he dispatched Washington with another force of 150 men, mostly from Frederick and Augusta counties, to garrison the fort. En route Washington met the work party returning homeward, with news that a much larger French force had seized the partially completed fort, driven the English construction crew from the forks of the Ohio, and then set about building their own defense, later known as Fort Duquesne. Washington chose to continue on to his original destination rather than return home with the work party. Near present Uniontown, Pennsylvania, he encountered a small detachment of French troops commanded by Coulon de Jumonville, and a skirmish took place in which Jumonville was killed. Certain that the French would retaliate, Washington hastily threw up a small defense which he called Fort Necessity. On July 3, 1754, the French assaulted the little fort and forced Washington to surrender. By the terms of capitulation, Washington was permitted to withdraw with honors of war but was compelled to agree that he would refrain from any efforts to construct fortifications in the Ohio Valley for one year.[11]

Unconfirmed, but plausible, reports now began to circulate that the French planned to follow up their successes at the forks of the Ohio by establishing their defense perimeter along the crests of the Alleghenies rather than along the Ohio itself. For this purpose, it was rumored, they were sending 400 men to build forts on the Greenbrier, New, and Holston rivers, an action which would have jeopardized all of Virginia's claims in the trans-Allegheny region.[12]

[11] Douglas Southall Freeman, *George Washington: A Biography*, 7 vols. (New York, 1948-1957), I, 327-437; Gipson, *British Empire before the American Revolution*, VI, 20-43.

[12] Robert Dinwiddie to Earl of Albemarle, August 15, 1754, R. A. Brock, ed., *The Official Records of Robert Dinwiddie, Lieutenant-Governor of the Colony of Virginia, 1751–1758*, 2 vols. (Richmond, Va., 1883-1884), I, 282; Dinwiddie to Earl Granville, August 15, 1754, *ibid.*, p. 283; Dinwiddie to James Abercromby, August 15, 1754, *ibid.*, p. 286; Dinwiddie to James Hamilton, September 6, 1754, *ibid.*, p. 308.

Dinwiddie was now convinced that Virginia could not parry the French threat alone, and he appealed to England for help. In response to his plea, the British government ordered Sir Edward Braddock, with two regiments of British regulars, to Virginia. With 1,400 Redcoats and 450 Virginia militia, Braddock set out by way of Fort Cumberland and the Nemacolin Trail for the forks of the Ohio. Conducted without Indian allies, impeded by the lack of roads for transporting artillery and supply trains, and led by an officer inexperienced in modes of fighting common to the American frontier, the expedition's success depended upon a surprise stroke against the French post, believed to be relatively weak in manpower. On July 9, 1755, when it was within about ten miles of Fort Duquesne, the French and their Indian allies ambushed Braddock's army, cutting it to pieces and mortally wounding Braddock himself. The remnants of the army, which had seemed to Washington so grand on its outward march, returned home humiliated and broken.

The disastrous consequences of the Braddock campaign were nowhere more keenly felt than among the frontier settlements of West Virginia. Braddock's fiasco, together with English attacks upon Crown Point and Niagara, dispelled any illusions concerning the nature of the struggle in the Ohio Valley. In the summer of 1755 the French and their Indian allies, particularly the Shawnees, Delawares, and Mingoes, took the offensive and spread terror throughout the backcountry of Virginia, Maryland, and Pennsylvania. Settlements in present West Virginia bore the brunt of the attacks upon Virginia's frontiers. Hopes that they might absorb the shock of the onslaught, however, proved ill-founded, and large numbers of the hitherto unmolested settlers, with little protection against the savage fury, became panic-stricken and sought safety in flight.[13] Dinwiddie insisted that this exposure of the frontier could have been averted had Colonel Thomas Dunbar, Braddock's second-in-command, rallied the troops after the surprise attack and launched a counter attack

[13] Dinwiddie to Arthur Dobbs, July 23, 1755, *ibid.,* II, 111; Louis Knott Koontz, *Robert Dinwiddie: His Career in American Colonial Government and Westward Expansion* (Glendale, Calif., 1941), pp. 332-43.

or had he stationed his men at Fort Cumberland instead of setting up winter quarters at Philadelphia in the middle of the summer.[14]

Typical of the reign of terror which prevailed in the border areas were the blows which fell upon the Greenbrier settlements. In late August, 1755, Indians attacked a small fort in which fifty-nine people had gathered. Within four days they killed thirteen of the people who were "forted" and twelve others who remained outside the walls, captured two girls, burned eleven houses, and slaughtered or drove off about 500 cattle and horses. The remaining residents of the Greenbrier Valley fled across the mountains to safety. Captain Peter Hog proposed that a contingent from Fort Dinwiddie be sent to the Greenbrier area to harvest the crops, lest the Indians use them for winter forage, but his recommendation went unheeded, and the Greenbrier Valley remained depopulated until 1761. Dinwiddie, as usual, was highly critical of the behavior of the fleeing settlers. Deploring the loss of crops and cattle, he asserted that there were only a fourth as many Indians in the attack as there were people in the fort and that if the settlers had shown any resistance the enemy would "have run away like sheep."[15]

Conditions in the upper Potomac Valley were no better. On October 4, 1755, Adam Stephen reported that about 150 Indians were in the vicinity of Fort Cumberland. They had broken up into small parties and had effectively isolated some small settlements, including those on Patterson's Creek. According to Stephen, they had left nothing but "desolation and murder heightened with all barbarous circumstances, and unheard of instances of cruelty," with smoke from the burning plantations darkening the day and hiding neighboring mountains from view. Stephen predicted that unless relief were immediately provided the people, there would soon not be a settler west of Monocacy

[14] Dinwiddie to Thomas Robinson, August 7, 1755, Brock, ed., *Official Records of Robert Dinwiddie*, II, 139.

[15] Accounts of the attack are given in Dinwiddie to Andrew Lewis, September 15, 1755, *ibid.*, p. 198; Dinwiddie to James Overton, September 20, 1755, *ibid.*, pp. 210-11; Dinwiddie to John McNeill, September 27, 1755, *ibid.*, pp. 218-19; Peter Hog to George Washington, September 23, 1755, Stanislaus Murray Hamilton, ed., *Letters to Washington and Accompanying Papers*, 5 vols. (Boston, 1889-1902), I, 93-94; "Preston's Register"; Freeman, *George Washington*, II, 120-21.

and Winchester. Meanwhile, Frederick County militia sent to bolster the defenses along the South Branch were threatening to return home rather than face annihilation. Heavy responsibility for the defense of the South Branch area therefore fell upon the settlers themselves, but many of them refused to join with the militia until they had first moved their families to places of safety.[16]

Fearing that the scalping of about a hundred settlers on the upper Potomac and the flight of scores of others might result in a collapse of all defenses in the area, George Washington, who had been named commander of all Virginia troops, left Winchester on either October 21 or 22 for a personal examination of the situation. At Little Cacapon, where he found Andrew Lewis' command encamped, he saw one farm from which the family had departed, leaving household effects yet in place, corn and oats in the barn, and livestock wandering about in the fields. At a farm on Patterson's Creek, he found that the owner had been killed by the Indians, hastily buried by neighbors, and then dug up and partially eaten by wolves, while nearby lay the ruins of his burned house and devastated cornfields. Similar scenes Washington encountered again and again. Everywhere he found the settlers surly and embittered that the government had not given them adequate protection. Washington was so discouraged by what he saw that he contemplated resigning his command.[17]

Prospects for the coming winter looked bleak indeed for the upper Potomac settlements. No durable peace was possible until the French were driven from the forks of the Ohio, which was the key to their power in the Ohio Valley and to their control of the Indian tribes. Although the Virginia assembly, after Braddock's failure, voted 40,000 pounds for the defense of the

[16] Adam Stephen to Washington, October 4, 1755, Hamilton, ed., *Letters to Washington*, I, 103-104; George Washington to William Vance, October 10, 1755, John C. Fitzpatrick, ed., *The Writings of George Washington from the Original Manuscript Sources, 1745–1799*, 39 vols. (Washington, D. C., 1931-1944), I 194-95; Washington to Dinwiddie, October 11, 1755, *ibid.*, pp. 201-206.

[17] Freeman, *George Washington*, II, 128-32; Charles Lewis, "Journal of Col. Charles Lewis," *West Virginia Historical Magazine*, IV (April, 1904), 111; Washington to Dinwiddie, October 11, 1755, Fitzpatrick, ed., *Writings of George Washington*, I, 202.

frontiers, Dinwiddie had no intention of sending an expedition against the French position before the spring of 1756. Even then he preferred to use the thousand men which he was then raising as part of a larger intercolonial force. Meanwhile, with winter approaching, it was difficult to provide food, clothing, and supplies for the troops and even more difficult to weld men so averse to discipline and authority into an effective fighting force. The only break in a cloud of despair was the willingness of the Cherokees to provide 150 warriors for an expedition against their old enemies, the Shawnees, but Dinwiddie and his military commanders well knew that defensive activities alone were likely to provoke impatience and disgust among the Cherokee warriors.[18]

Opposed throughout the fall of 1755 to any offensive move against the French and Indians, Dinwiddie began by December to urge an expedition against the Shawnees at the earliest possible moment.[19] The continued outcries and petitions of the frontier inhabitants convinced him that steps must be taken to restore morale among both the militia and the frontier settlers. Moreover, failure to take offensive action would almost inevitably result in the defection of the Cherokees, who had already caused apprehension in Virginia by their failure to provide warriors for the Braddock campaign. With little to lose by providing men to accompany the Cherokees, the governor could hardly afford to reject their offer. When Thomas Ingles, a trusted frontiersmen, informed the governor that he had information from two women who had recently escaped their Shawnee captors that the Indians were then in their towns, Dinwiddie concluded that a limited offensive was essential.[20] He was not prepared for an attack

[18] Hayes Baker-Crothers, *Virginia and the French and Indian War* (Chicago, 1928), pp. 85-86. See also Dinwiddie to Arthur Dobbs, December 13, 1755, Brock, ed., *Official Records of Robert Dinwiddie*, II, 290; Dinwiddie to Washington, December 14, 1755, *ibid.*, p. 292; Dinwiddie to Richard Pearis, December 15, 1755, *ibid.*, p. 296.

[19] Dinwiddie to Peter Hog, December 15, 1755, Brock, ed., *Official Records of Robert Dinwiddie*, II, 294-95; Dinwiddie to William Preston and John Smith, December 15, 1755, *ibid.*, pp. 295-96; Dinwiddie to Richard Pearis, December 15, 1755, *ibid.*, pp. 296-97; Dinwiddie to Obadiah Woodson, December 15, 1755, *ibid.*, pp. 297-98; Dinwiddie to Robert Hunter Morris, January 2, 1756, *ibid.*, p. 310.

[20] Dinwiddie to Horatio Sharpe, January 2, 1756, *ibid.*, p. 308. Dinwiddie's information regarding the Shawnees is noted in Dinwiddie to George Washington,

upon Fort Duquesne, but he believed that a surprise strike by Cherokee warriors and Virginia militia upon the Shawnee towns might relieve the distressed Virginia frontiers.

The Sandy Creek Expedition, as the retaliatory movement against the Shawnee towns by way of the Big Sandy River was called, was under the command of Major Andrew Lewis, whom Washington, at the request of Dinwiddie, had dispatched from Winchester. At Fort Frederick, near Ingles Ferry on the New River, the appointed place of rendezvous, Lewis assembled about 340 men, including 200 to 320 rangers and from 80 to 130 Cherokees. They included militia companies of Captains Peter Hog, Samuel Overton, William Preston, John Smith, Obadiah Woodson, Archibald Alexander, and Robert Breckinridge and volunteer companies under James Dunlap and John Montgomery. Two Cherokee warriors, Round O and Yellow Bird, were also given commissions.[21]

From the time it left Fort Frederick on February 18, the expedition encountered a disheartening array of difficulties and disappointments. Heavy rains slowed its advance as it moved via the North Fork of the Holston, Burke's Garden, and the upper Clinch to the headwaters of the Big Sandy, which it reached on February 28. Thereafter the terrain became increas-

---

January 22, 1756, Hamilton, ed., *Letters to Washington*, I, 170. The women captives who supplied the governor with this information were undoubtedly Mary Ingles, who had been taken prisoner at the time of the attack on Draper's Meadows in the summer of 1755, and an unidentified Dutch woman. Both escaped their Indian captors and made their way to the New River settlements. See David E. Johnston, *A History of the Middle New River Settlements and Contiguous Territory* (Huntington, W. Va., 1906), p. 22, and John P. Hale, *Trans-Allegheny Pioneers: Historical Sketches of the First White Settlers West of the Alleghenies*, 2d ed. (Charleston, W. Va., 1931), pp. 23-83.

[21] Dinwiddie to Washington, December 14, 1755, Brock, ed., *Official Records of Robert Dinwiddie*, II, 292; Washington to Dinwiddie, January 13, 1756, *ibid.*, p. 315; Dinwiddie to Earl of Halifax, February 24, 1756, *ibid.*, p. 348; Dinwiddie to Commodore Keppel, February 24, 1756, *ibid.*, p. 357; Dinwiddie to James Abercromby, February 24, 1756, *ibid.*, p. 358; Dinwiddie to Horatio Sharpe, March 8, 1756, *ibid.*, p. 366; Dinwiddie to Henry Fox, March 20, 1756, *ibid.*, p. 373; Washington to Lewis, December 27, 1755, Fitzpatrick, ed., *Writings of Washington*, I, 258; William Preston Journal (hereafter cited as "Preston Journal"), Draper MSS, 1QQ97; Lyman C. Draper, "The Expedition Against the Shawanoe Indians in 1756," *Virginia Historical Register*, V (April, 1852), 63. For a detailed account of the ill-fated undertaking, see Otis K. Rice, "The Sandy Creek Expedition of 1756," *West Virginia History*, XIII (October, 1951), 5-19.

ingly rugged. On February 29 the men crossed the rain-swollen Big Sandy sixty-six times in fifteen miles and had to abandon several packhorses. By March 3 food supplies began to run low and rations for each man had to be reduced to one-half pound of flour per day and such meat as could be killed. Three days later the troops were complaining loudly of the hardships and lack of food and threatening to return home. Thomas Morton one dissatisfied member of the expedition, declared that by this time they "were now in a pitiable condition, our men looking on [one] another with Tears in their Eyes, and lamenting that they had ever Enter'd in to a Soldier's life." In the camps, he said, there "was little else but cursing, swearing, confustion [sic] and complaining," all made worse by the selfishness of the officers.[22]

But worse was yet to come. The packhorses now began to give out. The Cherokees, whose morale yet remained high, proposed the building of bark canoes for carrying the ammunition and the small remaining store of provisions downstream, and Lewis ordered that all axes be put to that use. By March 7 prospects for any success by the expedition had vanished, and many of the ill-disciplined, but nonetheless realistic, men announced their intentions of returning home. William Preston noted that by then "hunger appeared in all our Faces & most of us were got Weak & Feeble & had we not got Releif [sic] I Doubt not but several of the men would have died of hunger, their Cries and Complaints were Pitiful & Shocking & more so as the Officers could not give them any help, for they were in equal want with the men."[23]

Lewis tried in vain to persuade the men to press on to their objective. They declared that "if they Proceeded any Further they must Inevitably Perish with hunger which they Looked upon to be more Inglorious than to Return & be yet Serviceable to their Country when properly Provided for." With desertions already beginning, Lewis and his officers held a council of war at Sandy Creek on March 15 and decided to give up the

---

[22] "Preston Journal," 1QQ102-11; "Morton's Diary," *Virginia Historical Register and Literary Note-Book,* IV (July, 1851), 144.
[23] "Preston Journal," 1QQ110-13; "Morton's Diary," pp. 145, 147.

expedition. By early April disorganized groups from Lewis' forces began straggling back into the settlements.[24]

The failure of the Sandy Creek Expedition, the only offensive action undertaken by Virginia during the French and Indian War, opened the West Virginia frontier to new attacks by the French and Indians. Disappointed Virginians, with Dinwiddie the most vehement, unleashed a flood of accusations against its leaders. Charges were placed against Lewis himself, but he was cleared of any neglect or misconduct.[25] Indeed, the rugged terrain, inclement weather, swollen streams, and failure to find sufficient game to sustain the men en route were conditions over which no person had control. Nor could Lewis bear heavy responsibility for the poor discipline, since he had been given no time to whip his army into a high state of readiness. On the other hand, if blame must be placed upon any person, a substantial part of it must fall upon Dinwiddie, whose impatience and urge to haste resulted in the dispatch of an expedition which lacked the preparation and the supplies needed for a successful undertaking.

Elsewhere in West Virginia, the war followed its usual pattern for the Allegheny frontier—an incessant series of forays by French and Indians against isolated settlements and small, inadequately manned forts. Typical of such attacks was that made upon Captain John Mercer and his men on April 18, 1756. Stopping at Fort Edwards while en route to Fort Enoch, Mercer and some forty or fifty men went out to search for horses. While yet within sight of the stockade, they were attacked by Indians, who killed Mercer, his ensign, and fifteen of the men. The incident well illustrates the precarious state of frontier defenses. The fall of Fort Edwards, only twenty miles from Winchester, would expose the entire Shenandoah Valley to Indian attack. Alarmed at that possibility, Washington ordered the delivery

[24] "Preston Journal," 1QQ117-18, 121; John Pendleton Kennedy and H. R. McIlwaine, eds., *Journals of the House of Burgesses of Virginia [1619–1776]*, 13 vols. (Richmond, Va., 1905-1915), *1756–1758*, p. 369.

[25] Dinwiddie to George Washington, April 8, 1756, Brock, ed., *Official Records of Robert Dinwiddie*, II, 382; Dinwiddie's Instructions to Lewis, *ibid.*, p. 321; Kennedy and McIlwaine, eds., *Journals of the House of Burgesses, 1756–1758*, pp. 369, 380.

of additional ammunition to the fort before nightfall of April 19, directed the militia of Frederick and adjoining counties to march to its relief, and dispatched Captain Henry Harrison to take command of the beleaguered post.[26]

Indeed, defenses on the upper Potomac appeared to be crumbling. Men who were ordered from Winchester to the South Branch surreptitiously disappeared, and whole companies fell apart before the time of departure for the frontier. Numerous settlers, despairing of any help, were reported ready to capitulate to the French rather than face extermination. Alarming rumors that about four hundred Indians were in the Patterson's Creek area threw many of the remaining settlers into a panic. Fearing that these reports might intimidate Captain John Ashby into surrendering his fort at the mouth of that stream, Washington ordered him to resist to the utmost in case he were attacked. Should it become evident that the fort would be overwhelmed, Ashby should blow it up and retreat to Fort Cumberland.[27]

By the spring of 1756 Virginia was faced with the necessity of either providing adequate defenses for the upper Potomac settlements or preparing for their disintegration. She chose the first alternative. In March, 1756, the General Assembly directed "that a chain of forts shall be erected, to begin at Henry Enochs on the Great-Cape-Capon, in the county of Hampshire, and to extend to the South-Fork of the Mayo-River, in the county of Halifax, to consist of such a number, and at such distance from each other, as shall be thought necessary and directed by the governor, or commander in chief of this colony." Dinwiddie

[26] Freeman, *George Washington,* II, 180-81; Charles Carter to Washington, April 22, 1756, Hamilton, ed., *Letters to Washington,* I, 227; Dinwiddie to Washington, April 23, 1756, *ibid.,* pp. 227-28; Washington to Harrison, April 19, 1756, Fitzpatrick, ed., *Writings of George Washington,* I, 319-20; Washington to Lord Fairfax, April 19, 1756, *ibid.,* pp. 320-21; Washington to William Stark, April 20, 1756, *ibid.,* pp. 321-22; Washington to Edward Hubbard, April 20, 1756, *ibid.,* p. 322; Washington to Lord Fairfax, April 21, 1756, *ibid.,* p. 323; Washington to Commanding Officers of Prince William and Fairfax, April 21, 1756, *ibid.,* pp. 323-24.

[27] Memorandum respecting the Militia, April and May, 1756, Fitzpatrick, ed., *Writings of George Washington,* I, 351-52; Washington to Henry Harrison, April 21, 1756, *ibid.,* p. 324; Washington to Dinwiddie, April 22, 1756, *ibid.,* p. 326; Washington to Dinwiddie, April 24, 1756, *ibid.,* p. 330; John Ashby to Washington, April 15, 1756, Hamilton, ed., *Letters to Washington,* I, 220-21.

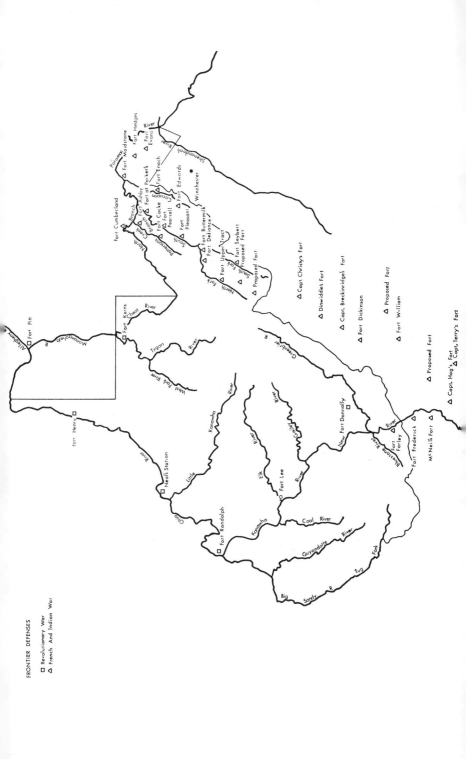

FRONTIER DEFENSES

☐ Revolutionary War
△ French And Indian War

entrusted Washington with the decision as to the locations of these forts and charged him with responsibility for their construction.

As planned by Washington, the forts provided a line of defense which ran from the Potomac in the north, southward along Patterson's Creek and thence across the dividing ridges to the upper South Branch, and then along that stream to its headwaters in Pendleton County, West Virginia. From there it crossed what is now the West Virginia–Virginia line and continued along the western edge of the Valley of Virginia to the upper reaches of the James and the Roanoke, before turning eastward to the Mayo River.[28] Significantly, the proposed defense system represented an abandonment of any efforts to cover the Greenbrier area. On the other hand, it envisioned protection for the upper Potomac settlements as far west as Patterson's Creek.

The apportionment of defense allocations underscored the importance of the settlements on Patterson's Creek and the South Branch. Declaring that "an invasion is most to be dreaded on this Quarter," Washington directed that 9 of the 22 forts and 1,045 of the 2,000 men required for their garrisons be placed on the West Virginia frontier. Moreover, while Washington was willing to delegate responsibility for the exact locations and construction of the southern units in this defense system to Captain Peter Hog, he himself undertook a general supervision of the West Virginia defenses. He believed that the latter were more important to the defense of the upper Potomac than Fort Cumberland, which was so situated that it could not provide adequate protection without an excessive number of men. Of the nine forts projected for the West Virginia tributaries of the Potomac, that of Cocke's, or Fort Cox as it was sometimes called, was of greatest importance. Its complement of 500 men was one-fourth

[28] William Waller Hening, comp., *The Statutes-at-Large: Being a Collection of All the Laws of Virginia from the First Session of the Legislature in the Year 1619*, 13 vols. (Richmond, Va., 1809-1823), VII, 17-18; Dinwiddie to Washington, May 8, 1756, Brock, ed., *Official Records of Robert Dinwiddie*, II, 406; Dinwiddie to Washington, June, 1756, *ibid.*, p. 434. For a map showing locations of these forts, see Charles H. Ambler, *George Washington and the West* (Chapel Hill, N. C., 1936), p. 119.

the total assigned to the entire system. Other West Virginia forts in the chain were Fort Ashby on Patterson's Creek, Parker's Fort, Fort Pleasant, Fort Upper Tract, and the fort at Trout Rock, all on the South Branch, Fort Enoch on the Cacapon, and Fort Maidstone on the Potomac at the mouth of the Cacapon.[29]

The strengthening of fortifications on Patterson's Creek and the South Branch brought only a temporary abatement in the danger faced by the upper Potomac settlers. For a time Washington was optimistic and declared on July 10, 1756, that the posts had already had "the desired effect—The inhabitants of that fertile district, keep possession of their Farms; and seem resolved to pursue their Business under cover of them."[30] By late summer, however, Indian depredations increased in number and severity, including several isolated attacks near Fort George on the South Branch. These encounters produced their share of pioneer heroes, including Samuel Bingaman, who killed six of his eight Indian assailants before he himself lost his life. But mixed with acts of heroism were instances of selfishness, if not outright cowardice. At The Trough on the South Branch, men from Fort Buttermilk became engaged in a struggle with the Indians which lasted for several hours, during the course of which "their guns got right hot." When men gathered in Van Meter's Fort, which was within sight of the battle, refused to send help, the little band of fighters swam across the river and sought refuge at the fort. The commander of the post, however, refused to open the gates and the fleeing party was forced to take refuge at Lynch's Fort, two miles farther on. On September 17 the Indians carried their attacks to Fort Neally on the Opequon, where they massacred the garrison and captured a number of people living in the vicinity.[31]

By this time Washington viewed the situation on the upper Potomac with increasing gravity. On September 8 he wrote Din-

---

[29] Louis Knott Koontz, *The Virginia Frontier, 1754–1763* (Baltimore, Md., 1925), pp. 104-105, 157-59; Washington Remarks on the Council of War, November 5, 1756, Fitzpatrick, ed., *Writings of George Washington,* I, 487-91.

[30] Koontz, *Virginia Frontier,* p. 158.

[31] Statement of George Yocum, Draper MSS, 12CC147; Samuel Kercheval, *A History of the Valley of Virginia,* ed. Oren F. Morton, 4th ed. (Strasburg, Va., 1925), pp. 73, 75-77, 88.

widdie from Winchester that for some time the only substantial body of settlers remaining were those on the South Branch and that it had been difficult to prevail upon them to stay. If they once gave way, he declared, there would not be a soul between Winchester and Fort Duquesne except the few soldiers in the little forts on Patterson's Creek.[32] Yet the remaining South Branch settlers held their ground despite attacks made upon them during the winter and in the spring of 1757. Still seeking to preserve this shaky line of defense, a council of war held at Fort Cumberland in April, 1757, recommended that additional troops be posted on the South Branch "in order to preserve that valuable Settlement—to induce the people to plant a sufficiency of Corn; and to prevent by that means, the vale of Winchester from becoming the Frontier."[33]

With the spring of 1758 the Indians became bolder than ever. On April 27 they attacked and burned Fort Upper Tract, killing Captain James Dunlap and twenty-two men. The next day they moved to Fort Seybert and killed or captured thirty persons who had sought refuge there, after promising, according to one version of the incident, to spare the lives of those who would surrender. Later that same year they struck farther east and burned Fort Warden.[34]

In spite of these sanguinary events the year 1758 opened more auspiciously than any since the beginning of the war. Efforts of Sir William Johnson, whom the British had placed in charge of relations with the Northern Indians, George Croghan, his deputy, and Teedyuskung, the self-styled king of the Delawares, and others had succeeded in August, 1757, in restoring peace between the English and the Delawares and Shawnees. In the fall of 1757 the imaginative and audacious William Pitt was called upon to save the reeling British Empire. The war which had begun in 1754 in the Ohio Valley had by then merged into a full-scale European conflict with worldwide implications. In a "diplomatic revolution," Great Britian and Prussia were pitted

---

32 Washington to Dinwiddie, September 8, 1756, Fitzpatrick, ed., *Writings of George Washington*, I, 466.

33 Quoted in Koontz, *Virginia Frontier*, p. 163.

34 *Ibid.*, pp. 144-45; Kercheval, *History of the Valley*, pp. 87, 91-92.

against France, Austria, and Spain. Pitt was convinced that Prussia was capable of handling the military situation in Europe and that England should concentrate her energies upon winning the war on the overseas fronts. In America, where the conflict had until 1758 been marked by a series of disasters for England, there was a special need for an invigorated war effort. Pitt took the first step toward turning defeat into victory by advancing young and brilliant officers from the ranks to high positions. Among them were James Wolfe, John Forbes, and Jeffrey Amherst, whose military genius enabled England to drive France from the North American continent.

The campaigns launched in 1758 brought notable achievements for British arms, the one conspicious exception being the failure of General James Abercromby to capture Fort Ticonderoga, a gateway to Quebec, and his loss of 2,000 of his 15,000 troops in the vain endeavor. Within three weeks of Abercromby's defeat, however, another English force of 12,000 men under Amherst and Wolfe captured Louisbourg, the eastern approach to Quebec. Another army under Colonel John Bradstreet moved westward up the Mohawk Valley, constructed Fort Stanwix, and then descended upon Fort Frontenac, which surrendered after a day's bombardment. The capture of Louisbourg and Fort Frontenac nullified the effects of the French retention of Ticonderoga and opened the way to the interior of Canada.

Conditions on the West Virginia frontier, however, were more immediately affected by an expedition against Fort Duquesne in the fall of 1758. Under the command of General John Forbes, an army of 6,000 men moved across Pennsylvania, cutting its road as it progressed. Confronted with overwhelming English power, the French commandant at Fort Duquesne ordered the fortification blown up, and the French withdrew from the forks of the Ohio. With English occupation of that strategic point and their erection of Fort Pitt, the remaining tribes of the Ohio Valley turned against their former allies. Within a few months only Fort La Baye, Detroit, Mackinac, and the Illinois villages remained in French hands. The capture of the forks of the Ohio also relieved the pressures on the West Virginia frontier. Settlers of the Potomac region began to return to their homes, and a few, prematurely as it turned out, even began to cross the Alleghenies.

In the summer of 1759 the great struggle reached its climax with Wolfe's capture of Quebec. The loss of that bastion of French power by Montcalm left no doubt as to the final outcome of the conflict in North America. A year later, Montreal, the last major stronghold remaining in French hands, surrendered. The war dragged on for two more years in Europe, but with the French capitulation at Montreal, the fate of her North American empire was sealed.

The Treaty of Paris of 1763 settled the question which for Allegheny pioneers had been uppermost at the outset of the war. The Ohio Valley was open to the American settlers. Transmontane West Virginia, like the entire Allegheny region, had been won from the French; its future belonged to the English and to the determined settlers. Powerful Indian tribes, however, yet claimed the region, and its occupation by the impatient pioneers was for the moment no more than a dream.

Chapter Four

Across the Alleghenies

Impatient settlers and land-hungry speculators who expected the British occupation of the forks of the Ohio in 1758 and the spectacular successes over the French on other fronts the following year immediately to open the trans-Allegheny regions were to suffer keen disappointment. In fact, at the very outset of the French and Indian War the British government, stunned by the defection of all the western tribes to the French, had set up machinery for imperial supervision of Indian affairs and had in effect served notice that in the future it would not countenance an unregulated expansion westward. Moreover, the increasing restiveness of traditionally friendly tribes, including the Six Nations, convinced many colonial officials that the collapse of French power must not be accompanied by new encroachments upon Indian lands. In 1758 the Treaty of Easton, concluded by Sir William Johnson on behalf of the proprietors of Pennsylvania with the Six Nations, stipulated that the part of Pennsylvania west of the Alleghenies should remain an Indian hunting ground and be closed to white settlement. Colonel Henry Bouquet, the commandant at Fort Pitt, not only upheld the line but, in 1761, in a broad interpretation of imperial approval of the Treaty of Easton, extended its provisions to include the trans-Allegheny areas of Maryland and Virginia.[1]

Bouquet's proclamation was made in the face of immense pressure from Virginia land speculators. In 1759 the Ohio Company, acting first through Thomas Cresap and later through George Mercer, sought to enlist Bouquet's support for its claims and his aid in procuring German and Swiss settlers by offering him 25,000 acres of land. When Bouquet refused, the company carried its case to London, where it brought its full influence to bear upon British officials. Speculators also endeavored to use Governor Robert Dinwiddie's promise of February, 1754, to set aside 200,000 acres of land for volunteers in Virginia's military forces as a means of forcing Bouquet's hand. Seeking to obtain lands around the forks of the Ohio, several ranking military officers of Virginia, including George Mercer and George Washington, made it clear that they were prepared to "leave no stone unturned" in their efforts to acquire the forbidden lands. At their behest, Lieutenant Governor Francis Fauquier, who professed to be uncertain as to whether the coveted lands lay within Virginia or Pennsylvania, interceded with the home government, but the Board of Trade refused to make the grant.[2]

Fauquier was not easily discouraged. On September 1, 1760, he again approached the Board of Trade, this time on behalf of the Greenbrier and Loyal companies. Their lands on Greenbrier and New rivers, Fauquier pointed out, had been "tolerably seated for some time," but the settlers had been driven out during the French and Indian War. Without doubt, these two organizations had stronger cases than the Ohio Company, for settlers on their lands held titles legally obtained before the war. The Board of Trade therefore vacillated on the ground that it lacked sufficient information to render "any explicit Opinion," and contented itself by enjoining Fauquier to refrain from any action which might "in any degree, have a tendency" to arouse the Indians.[3]

This pronouncement of the Board of Trade probably explains the return of settlers to the Greenbrier region in 1761. In that year Archibald Clendenin settled about two miles west of Lewisburg and Frederick See and Felty Yocum located on Muddy Creek. By the summer of 1763 more than fifty persons were

[1] Jack M. Sosin, *Whitehall and the Wilderness: The Middle West in British Colonial Policy, 1760–1775* (Lincoln, Nebr., 1961), pp. 42-43; Kenneth P. Bailey, *The Ohio Company of Virginia and the Westward Movement, 1748–1792: A Chapter in the History of the Colonial Frontier* (Glendale, Calif., 1939), pp. 222-24; Nicholas B. Wainwright, *George Croghan: Wilderness Diplomat* (Chapel Hill, N. C., 1959), pp. 17, 26-27, 50-51; Albert T. Volwiler, *George Croghan and the Westward Movement, 1741–1782* (Cleveland, Ohio, 1926), pp. 137-39; Clarence Walworth Alvord, *The Mississippi Valley in British Politics: A Study of the Trade, Land Speculation, and Experiments in Imperialism Culminating in the American Revolution*, 2 vols. (Cleveland, Ohio), I, 121-22.

[2] Sosin, *Whitehall and the Wilderness*, pp. 43-45; Bailey, *Ohio Company of Virginia*, pp. 223-27; Kenneth P. Bailey, *Thomas Cresap: Maryland Frontiersman* (Boston, 1944), pp. 111-14.

[3] Quoted material is from Sosin, *Whitehall and the Wilderness*, pp. 45-46.

again residing in the Greenbrier Valley. Considering the in-
decision of the Board of Trade, the initiative for the return of
settlers to the Greenbrier region could have come either from
the pioneers themselves or from the Greenbrier Company, which
may have sought to use settlement as a means of keeping its
claims alive.

The settlement of Thomas Decker and others at the mouth of
Decker's Creek at Morgantown in 1758, on the other hand, was
almost certainly a spontaneous movement by impatient frontiersmen. The Decker settlement was premature in that it was
made prior to clarification of the demarcation line established
by the Treaty of Easton. In the spring of 1759 it was wiped
out by Delaware and Mingo Indians.[4]

The apprehension of the western tribes, of which the attack
upon the Decker settlement was but one manifestation, mounted
to a crescendo of discontent during the winter of 1762–1763.
Following the occupation of the forks of the Ohio by Forbes,
British fur traders and land speculators, the latter often in the
guise of traders, swarmed into the Indian country, where they
exploited the tribes with more than their usual zeal. Although
some Indian leaders placed credence and even hope in rumors
of a resurrection of French power, most realized that they were
now at the mercy of the British. Nor were the attitudes of
British military authorities reassuring. Lord Jeffrey Amherst,
the commander in North America, advocated a policy of ex-
terminating the Indians by infecting them with smallpox, while
Bouquet favored the use of trained dogs to hunt and destroy
them. Amherst's announcement in 1762 that the customary
gifts would not be distributed to the tribes during the coming
winter seemed to the Indians an ominous portent and brought
unrest to a head.[5]

---

[4] John Stuart, "Memorandum, 1798 July 15th," in Ruth Woods Dayton, *Greenbrier Pioneers and Their Homes* (Charleston, W. Va., 1942), pp. 367-68; James
Morton Callahan, *Semi-Centennial History of West Virginia* (n. p., 1913), p. 20.

[5] Although the suggestions of Amherst and Bouquet were not made until the
summer of 1763, they were indicative of an unwillingness of important officials to
buy Indian friendship at a time when Britian faced financial difficulties. Howard
H. Peckman, *Pontiac and the Indian Uprising* (Princeton, N. J., 1947), pp. 226-27;
Randolph C. Downes, *Council Fires on the Upper Ohio: A Narrative of Indian
Affairs in the Upper Ohio Valley until 1795* (Pittsburgh, Pa., 1940), pp. 105-22;
Volwiler, *George Croghan and the Westward Movement*, pp. 159-64.

Seeking to stay the power and terminate the threats of the British, the western tribes, spurred on by Pontiac, an Ottawa chieftain, began to lay plans for concerted attacks upon British strongholds during the coming spring. On May 7, 1763, Pontiac struck a heavy blow at Detroit, and later that month Shawnees and Delawares laid siege to Fort Pitt. One by one, other British posts were attacked, and by the end of July only Detroit, Fort Pitt, and Fort Niagara were yet in British hands.

Two relief expeditions, ordered out by Amherst, saved the British military position in the west. The first, under the command of Captain James Dalyell, carried supplies which enabled Detroit to withstand the Indian onslaught. The other, led by Bouquet, defeated the Indians at Bushy Run and raised the siege of Fort Pitt. These reverses discouraged the Indians and weakened their confederacy. In the summer of 1764 most of the tribes met with Sir William Johnson at Fort Niagara and made their peace with the British. Those which held out, including the Shawnees and Delawares, were subdued later that summer by expeditions under Bouquet and Colonel John Bradstreet. A year later, George Croghan, the deputy of Sir William Johnson, met Pontiac near Fort Ouiatanon and arranged a peace with the recalcitrant leader.[6]

The fury unleashed by Pontiac fell heavily upon West Virginia's frontier settlements. In the summer of 1763 a band of about sixty Shawnees under Cornstalk invaded the Greenbrier region. Posing as friends, small parties visited the Muddy Creek settlements, including the homes of Frederick See and Felty Yocum, and killed or captured everyone present. The Indians next proceeded to the Big Levels, or present Lewisburg, and the house of Archibald Clendenin. There they found about fifty persons gathered to feast on three elk which Clendenin had just killed. As at Muddy Creek, they were accorded a warm welcome. At a prearranged signal, the Indians again threw off the mask of friendship and, with one exception, killed or captured every person there. The only survivor, Conrad Yocum,

---

[6] Standard accounts of Pontiac's War are Peckham, *Pontiac and the Indian Uprising*, and Francis Parkman, *History of the Conspiracy of Pontiac* (Boston, 1851). Peckham challenges Parkman's contention that Pontiac was an all-powerful chieftain and that the uprising was a well-organized rebellion.

who suspected treachery, left the house on the pretext of hobbling his horse and fled across the mountains to the Jackson River settlements. For a second time within eight years a terrible visitation from the Indians had annihilated the Greenbrier settlements.[7]

A rather typical incident in the annals of frontier tragedy was the fate which befell the family of Archibald Clendenin. Reputed already to have been so "scarified" by past encounters with the Indians that "he looked like an old raccoon dog," Clendenin was among those killed. His wife and infant child were among the captured. As the Indians and their captives were passing over Keeney's Knob, Mrs. Clendenin handed her young child to another woman prisoner. She quickly stepped into a thicket, sped back to the Big Levels, where she covered the body of her scalped husband, and then fled to the safety of the Jackson River settlements. Soon after her escape, her child began to cry. The outraged Indians, declaring that they would "bring the cow to her calf," seized the infant by the heels and dashed its head against a tree until it was dead.[8]

Indian depredations also took a heavy toll in the Eastern Panhandle. Particularly hard hit was the Cacapon River area, where about twenty-three persons were killed or captured in June, 1764. Among the prisoners was the wife of Owen Thomas, who had been killed the previous summer. While crossing the South Branch, Mrs. Thomas eluded her captors by jumping into the stream and floating with the current until she reached Williams' Fort, two miles below Hanging Rock. Her daughter saved herself by running nine miles to Stephen's Fort on Cedar Creek.[9]

Only the timely action of Governor Fauquier in calling out a thousand militia from Hampshire and adjoining counties prevented even greater disaster among West Virginia's Allegheny

[7] Stuart, "Memorandum, 1798 July 15th," p. 368; Alexander Scott Withers, *Chronicles of Border Warfare*, ed. Reuben Gold Thwaites, new ed. (Cincinnati, Ohio, 1903), pp. 93-95.

[8] Statement of James Wade, Draper MSS, 12CC11-12; John Stuart, "Memoir of Indian Wars, and Other Occurrences," Virginia Historical and Philosophical Society *Collections*, I (Richmond, Va., 1833), 39-40; Stuart, "Memorandum, 1798 July 15th," p. 368; Withers, *Chronicles of Border Warfare*, pp. 94-95; Peckham, *Pontiac and the Indian Uprising*, pp. 217-18.

[9] Samuel Kercheval, *A History of the Valley of Virginia*, ed. Oren F. Morton, 4th ed. (Strasburg, Va., 1925), pp. 98-101.

settlements. Under the command of Colonel Adam Stephen and Major Andrew Lewis, the forces were divided into small companies of about thirty men each. They manned the little forts, guarded the mountain passes through which the Indians gained access to the settlements, and pursued the attackers when they made forays against the settlers.[10] Not until Bouquet defeated the Indians at Bushy Run and Johnson concluded peace with most of the warring tribes the following year, however, did the West Virginia frontier again experience tranquillity.

On October 7, 1763, with the power of the Indian confederacy far from broken, the British government issued a sweeping proclamation forbidding settlement west of the Alleghenies. This policy angered both speculators and prospective settlers. David Robinson, a Virginia speculator, summed up their frustration in his sarcastic remark that land won by the blood and treasure of the people was now to be "given as a Compliment to our good Friends and faithfull Allies, the Shawnee Indians."[11] In western Pennsylvania squatters took up lands illegally, and troops from Fort Pitt had to be sent out to disperse them, burn their cabins, and destroy their crops. But whether because of respect for British authority or for Indian tomahawks, scalping knives, and firebrands, the Proclamation of 1763 proved remarkably effective in keeping settlers out of trans-Allegheny West Virginia. During the nearly six years that its original provisions were in effect, probably not more than a dozen persons took up residence west of the Allegheny Front.[12]

In the view of settlers and speculators, the one redeeming

[10] Francis Fauquier to William Preston, July 24, 1763, Draper MSS, 2QQ42; William Ingles to William Preston, September 13, 1763, *ibid.*, 2QQ43; Andrew Lewis to [William Preston], April 4, 1764, *ibid.*, 2QQ46-48; John Brown to William Preston, June 8, 1764, *ibid.*, 2QQ49; John Brown to [William Preston], undated, *ibid.*, 2QQ50-51; Louis Knott Koontz, *The Virginia Frontier, 1754–1763* (Baltimore, Md., 1925), p. 96.

[11] David Robinson to William Thompson, February 18, 1764, Draper MSS, 2QQ44-45. A good account of the evolution of the Proclamation of 1763 is in Sosin, *Whitehall and the Wilderness*, pp. 51-65.

[12] Typical of the situation in trans-Allegheny West Virginia was that of the Greenbrier region, where settlements were not attempted until 1769. Stuart, "Memorandum, 1798 July 15th," p. 368. Violations of the Proclamation of 1763 elsewhere, however, were apparently numerous, and speculators continued to mark out land on the Monongahela, Greenbrier, and New rivers. Sosin, *Whitehall and the Wilderness*, pp. 107-108.

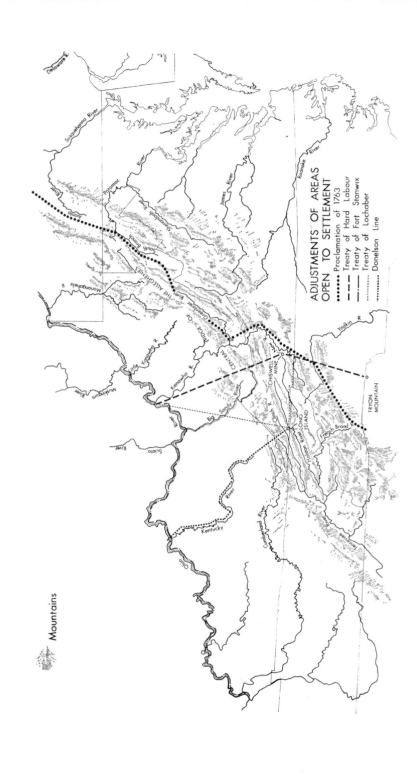

ADJUSTMENTS OF AREAS
OPEN TO SETTLEMENT

• • • • Proclamation of 1763
— — Treaty of Hard Labour
— Treaty of Fort Stanwix
· · · · Treaty of Lochaber
· · · · · Donelson Line

Mountains

feature of the Proclamation of 1763 was a provision whereby the demarcation line might legally be moved westward. Taking advantage of this opening, powerful Pennsylvania speculative groups, for whom Benjamin Franklin was a major spokesman, began to exert heavy pressure upon British authorities for a westward extension of the boundary. As a result of their representations, Lord Shelburne, who, as Secretary of State for the Southern Department, had charge of American colonial affairs, on January 5, 1768, authorized the drawing of a new line. On March 12, following a reorganization of the British cabinet, Lord Hillsborough, in the new post of Secretary of State for the American Department, directed Sir William Johnson and John Stuart, the Indian superintendents for the northern and southern districts, respectively, to begin negotiations with the Indians for a new line.

Hillsborough's instructions to Johnson and Stuart were explicit as to the location of the new boundary. They specified a line running from the Susquehanna to the Ohio River, thence along that stream to its confluence with the Kanawha, and from there in a straight course to Chiswell's mine on New River. This line purposely cleared the 200,000-acre military grant which Dinwiddie had promised Virginians in 1754 and which since that time had been demanded by the House of Burgesses.[13] This boundary would also allow those who held title to lands in the Greenbrier region legally to repossess their property.

Prior to final negotiations with the Cherokees over the southern portion of the boundary, John Stuart suggested to Hillsborough that the line be altered to run from Chiswell's mine to the mouth of the Kentucky River rather than to the confluence of the Ohio and the Kanawha. Stuart's proposal would have satisfied the most extreme aspirations of the Greenbrier and Loyal companies and would have freed all of southern West Virginia as well as much of eastern Kentucky of Cherokee claims. Hillsborough, however, refused to sanction any changes in the line originally recommended. As a consequence, the Treaty of Hard Labor,

---

[13] Thomas Perkins Abernethy, *Western Lands and the American Revolution* (New York, 1937), pp. 14-38; Sosin, *Whitehall and the Wilderness*, pp. 136-70, and map facing p. 70.

which Stuart signed with the Cherokees on October 17, 1768, established a boundary which was in scrupulous accord with Hillsborough's initial instructions.[14] The treaty extinguished Cherokee claims to all of trans-Allegheny West Virginia except the extreme southwestern section of the state.

The speculators found a more dependable friend in Sir William Johnson, who was charged with the redefinition of the northern part of the boundary. Before Johnson received instructions from Hillsborough to negotiate a new line, Samuel Wharton, William Trent, and George Croghan had called upon him at New London and secured the superintendent's support for their efforts to obtain a grant of land from the northern tribes. Wharton and Trent were the major spokesmen for the "Suffering Traders," who had allegedly lost 85,912 pounds in trading goods during Indian hostilities in 1763 and who now sought compensation in the form of land. Croghan also hoped to obtain recognition of and clear title to 200,000 acres in the vicinity of Fort Pitt and along the Youghiogheny granted to him in 1747 by the Six Nations.

Encouraged by their success in gaining the approval of the Indian superintendent, Wharton and Trent visited the northern tribes during the summer of 1768 and received assurances that the Indians would be willing to cede a tract of land to the "Suffering Traders" in their impending negotiations with Sir William Johnson. Wharton and Trent also discussed their proposals with Andrew Lewis and Thomas Walker, Virginia's commissioners in the Mohawk country, and apparently convinced themselves that, although the coveted lands lay within her bounds, Virginia would acquiesce in their cession to the "Suffering Traders."

The optimism of Wharton and Trent was not ill-founded. Although incontrovertible evidence is lacking, it appears reasonably certain that they reached an understanding with Lewis and Walker whereby the latter agreed to raise no objections to a large grant to the "Suffering Traders," provided the Indian boundary could be pushed westward from the mouth of the

[14] Sosin, *Whitehall and the Wilderness*, pp. 170-72; Abernethy, *Western Lands and the American Revolution*, pp. 60-64.

Kanawha, as directed by Hillsborough, to the mouth of the Tennessee. The fact that the Greenbrier and Loyal companies had by this time begun to encounter difficulties in their efforts to induce John Stuart to extend the southern boundary to the mouth of the Kentucky, together with Lewis' personal interests in the 200,000-acre military tract promised by Dinwiddie in 1754, adds plausibility to contentions that some *quid pro quo* arrangement existed between the "Suffering Traders" and the Virginia commissioners.

It is not surprising, therefore, that the Treaty of Fort Stanwix, which Johnson concluded with the Six Nations on November 5, 1768, involved gross violations of the instructions which the superintendent had received from Hillsborough. Without any authorization from the secretary, the treaty recognized the cession of a large tract to the "Suffering Traders" by the Six Nations. Known as Indiana, the grant embraced the area between the Little Kanawha River, Laurel Hill, the southern boundary of Pennsylvania, and the Ohio River, and included all of trans-Allegheny West Virginia north of the Little Kanawha with the exception of the Northern Panhandle.

Johnson also permitted, in direct disobedience of instructions from Hillsborough, a boundary which ran to the mouth of the Tennessee rather than to the junction of the Ohio and the Kanawha. The superintendent justified his action on the ground that the Six Nations had insisted that their claims extended to the Tennessee and that to have refused their proffered cession would have antagonized them and jeopardized the conclusion of any agreement.

Despite assurances by Johnson that the additional cession by the Six Nations did not infringe upon Cherokee claims to the land between the Kanawha and the Tennessee, Hillsborough and the Board of Trade roundly condemned Johnson's deviation from instructions. In May, 1769, Hillsborough informed Johnson that the ministry would withhold approval of the Indiana grant until the recipients had applied to the Crown for their tract and had offered a satisfactory explanation of the land transfer. The secretary ordered Johnson to refuse the lands west of the Kanawha, if he could do so without offending the Indians. In any case, he declared, the Crown had no intention of permitting settlement beyond the Kanawha.

Pressures from speculators and concern for Cherokee friendship led to a revision of the line approved at Hard Labor. The new governor of Virginia, Lord Botetourt, asked Lewis and Walker to discuss the question of an alteration with John Stuart. The result of their conversations was the Treaty of Lochaber of October 18, 1770, by which the line was moved westward. The new line ran from the North Carolina–Virginia border to a point near Long Island on the Holston River and thence in a straight course to the mouth of the Kanawha. This adjustment partially met the demands of the Virginia speculators and at the same time removed Cherokee fears that their Kentucky hunting grounds might be occupied.[15] The new cession, together with that of the Treaty of Fort Stanwix, extinguished the claims of the Six Nations and the Cherokees to trans-Allegheny West Virginia and left only the claims of tribes northwest of the Ohio as a threat to their occupation by white settlers.

The significance of the agreements reached at Hard Labor and Fort Stanwix to the Allegheny frontier of West Virginia is indicated by the great rush of settlers into the areas west of the mountains in the spring and summer of 1769. Thousands of settlers descended upon the area around the forks of the Ohio, and others threaded their way through the Valley of Virginia to lands along the Holston, Watauga, and Nolichucky. From that time until 1777, when the menace from British and Indians again halted their advance, they streamed across the Alleghenies in ever-increasing numbers. During these years they reoccupied the Greenbrier region, spread over nearly all the lowlands of the Monongahela Valley, advanced southward from Fort Pitt down the Ohio as far as the Little Kanawha, thrust important spearheads of settlement into the Kanawha Valley, and occupied many choice sites in the intervening mountains and valleys.

The movement into the Greenbrier country was the third

[15] Sosin, *Whitehall and the Wilderness,* pp. 172-80; Wainwright, *George Croghan,* pp. 253-58; George E. Lewis, *The Indiana Company, 1763–1798: A Study in Eighteenth Century Frontier Land Speculation and Business Venture* (Glendale, Calif., 1941), pp. 58-65.

attempt to plant permanent settlements there. In the vanguard of the new wave of settlers were Colonel John Stuart, Robert McClanahan, Thomas Renick, and William Hamilton, who located near Frankford in 1769. During the ensuing six years about three hundred families moved into the Greenbrier Valley, most of them taking up lands on Sinking Creek, Wolf Creek, Muddy Creek, in the Sinks of Greenbrier, at the Little Levels, or Hillsboro, and at the Big Levels, or Lewisburg. The Greenbrier population was drawn largely from the Scotch-Irish of the southern part of the Valley of Virginia. Prominent among the Greenbrier pioneers were the Boggs, Burnside, Clendenin, Donnally, Handley, Johnson, Keeney, Kelly, Kincaid, Lewis, Mathews, McClung, Nichols, Skaggs, Swope, and Woods families.[16]

Simultaneously with the reoccupation of the Greenbrier region, settlers began to press into the Monongahela Valley. A large part of these immigrants were from New Jersey, Pennsylvania, Maryland, and eastern Virginia and reached the lower or middle Monongahela by way of Forbes' or Braddock's roads. From there they moved upstream to the upper waters of the Monongahela. Another large contingent, emigrants from the upper Potomac, particularly the South Branch, cut through the passes in the Alleghenies to the Cheat and Tygart Valley rivers and then fanned out into most of the valleys of the upper Monongahela.[17]

Migration into the Monongahela Valley began on a modest scale. Daniel Burchfield settled on Flaggy Run in 1765 and John Morgan at Dunkard Bottom on Cheat River in 1766. Since these lands lay in the Indian country at that time, it seems very likely that Burchfield and Morgan were, like John Simpson, who established himself near Clarksburg in 1764, primarily hunters

[16] Stuart, "Memorandum, 1798 July 15th," p. 368; J. T. McAllister, "Incidents in the Pioneer, Colonial and Revolutionary History of the West Virginia Area," in Henry S. Green, *Biennial Report of the Department of Archives and History of the State of West Virginia, 1911–1912, 1913–1914* (Charleston, W. Va., 1914), pp. 21-24.

[17] James Morton Callahan, *History of the Making of Morgantown, West Virginia: A Type Study in Trans-Appalachian Local History* (Morgantown, W. Va., 1926), pp. 28-34; Hu Maxwell, *The History of Randolph County, West Virginia, from Its Earliest Settlement to the Present* (Morgantown, W. Va., 1898), pp. 177-79.

and trappers. With the opening of the trans-Allegheny area by the treaties of Hard Labor and Fort Stanwix, David Frazer, John Judy, Charles Martin, William Morgan, Samuel Owens, James Parsons, and perhaps others, took up lands along the Monongahela itself and on the Cheat River and Sandy Creek in 1769.[18]

After 1769 settlement on the Monongahela advanced rapidly. Tomahawk rights grew from four in 1768 to over 1,200 in 1776. Some of the greatest concentrations of population were along the Monongahela and small tributaries such as Decker's Creek, Booth's Creek, Indian Creek, Cobun's Creek, and Scott's Mill Run; the West Fork and such feeder streams as Dunkard Creek, Simpson's Creek, and Ten-Mile Creek; the Tygart Valley and its major tributary, the Buckhannon; and the Cheat River. Prominent family names among the settlers along the Monongahela, the Cheat, and the West Fork were Cobun, Collins, Davisson, Dorsey, Haymond, Ice, Judy, Martin, Miller, Nutter, Parsons, Pierpont, Scott, Shinn, Stewart, and Wade. In this wave of settlers were Zackwell Morgan, Michael Kerns, and John Evans, who located at Morgantown in 1772.[19]

Settlement in the Tygart Valley received its first impetus from John and Samuel Pringle, two brothers who had trapped and hunted there since their desertion from the garrison at Fort Pitt in 1761. Shortly after 1768, and probably in 1769, they led a party of settlers, which included Benjamin Cutright and Henry Rule, from the South Branch to the Buckhannon River Valley. About the same time John Hacker and others acquired lands on Hacker's Creek. Excellent hunting, an abundance of wild fruit, and fertile lands made the Tygart Valley especially attractive, and a large part of its best lands were taken by 1772. Accretions

[18] Monongalia County Land Grants, I (1782-1785), 56, 65, 122-23, 160, 175, 191, 195, 219. Transcripts in Office of the Auditor of the State of West Virginia (Originals in Virginia State Library). All references to manuscript land grants hereafter cited are to these transcripts. For John Simpson, see Withers, *Chronicles of Border Warfare,* p. 118, and Henry Haymond, *History of Harrison County, West Virginia* (Morgantown, W. Va., 1910), pp. 17-19.

[19] Charles H. Ambler and Festus P. Summers, *West Virginia: The Mountain State,* 2d ed. (Englewood Cliffs, N. J., 1958), p. 55; Monongalia County Land Grants, I (1782-1785), passim, and II (1785-1786), passim; Callahan, *History of the Making of Morgantown,* pp. 30-34; Callahan, *Semi-Centennial History of West Virginia,* p. 25.

to the Hacker's Creek and Buckhannon communities were so great in 1773 that grain crops were insufficient to provide bread for the burgeoning population, and the rich valley suffered distresses known in its history as "the starving year." Members of the Connelly, Hadden, Nelson, Riffle, Stalnaker, Warwick, Westfall, and Whiteman families were conspicuous among these early settlers. According to tradition, the Westfalls found and buried the bones of members of the Files family who had been killed by Indians in 1754.[20]

Settlement of the upper Ohio Valley section of West Virginia appears to have been slightly behind that of the Monongahela Valley. Although tradition credits Ebenezer, Silas, and Jonathan Zane and others with visiting and laying out lands in the Wheeling area in 1769 or even earlier, there is good reason to believe that these pioneers made no settlements at that time. George Washington, who in his own search for lands passed Wheeling Creek on October 24, 1770, made no mention of a settlement there.[21] Moreover, lands acquired by Ebenezer Zane, David Shepherd, John Wetzel, and Samuel McCulloch, reputedly the first settlers, were granted them, according to their own assertions, on the basis of settlements made in 1772 and later.[22] Indeed, few improvements seem to have been made in the upper Ohio Valley prior to 1772, but in that year and continuing until 1777 scores of pioneers acquired lands. By the end of 1777 they had taken

[20] David Crouch Interview, Draper MSS, 12CC225-26; Withers, *Chronicles of Border Warfare*, pp. 118-22, 125-27; Haymond, *History of Harrison County*, pp. 16-53.

[21] John C. Fitzpatrick, ed., *The Diaries of George Washington, 1748–1799*, 4 vols. (Boston, 1925), I, 403; Roy Bird Cook, *Washington's Western Lands* (Strasburg, Va., 1930), p. 19.

[22] Their settlements were: John McCulloch, Short Creek, 1773; David Shepherd, [Glen's?] Run, 1772; Samuel McCulloch, Short Creek and Wheeling, 1772; Andrew Zane, between Wheeling Creek and the Ohio River, 1772; John Wetzel, Wheeling Creek, 1773; Ebenezer Zane, Wheeling Creek, 1774; and Jonathan Zane, Ohio River and Wheeling Creek, 1776. Ohio County Survey Book, 1779–1786, pp. 19, 32, 36, 40, 122, 253 (Microfilm in West Virginia University Library). The Wetzels later declared that the family arrived at Wheeling Creek in 1770. See Wood County Legislative Petitions, December 8, 1803, Virginia State Library. All legislative petitions from West Virginia counties hereafter cited are in the Virginia State Library. John Mills, who "Deadened a few trees, made a little brush heap, & cut J. M. upon a tree" in order to establish a claim to 425 acres, which he allegedly sold to Ebenezer Zane, declared that his father built the first log cabin at Wheeling. For Mills' claim, see Draper MSS, 12CC236.

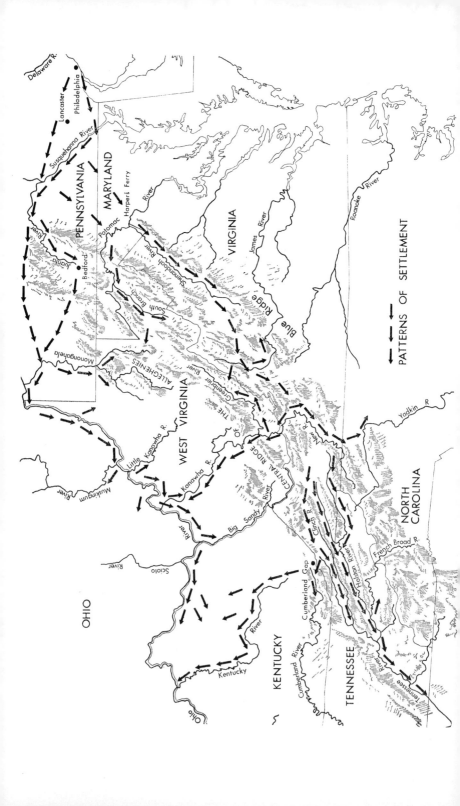

PATTERNS OF SETTLEMENT

Delaware R.
Philadelphia
Lancaster
Susquehanna River
PENNSYLVANIA
MARYLAND
Juniata
Bedford
Potomac River
Harper's Ferry
Shenandoah River
South Branch
ALLEGHENIES
Monongahela River
THE
WEST VIRGINIA
Little Kanawha R.
Muskingum River
OHIO
Scioto River
Kanawha R.
Big Sandy River
CENTRAL RIDGE
OF
Greenbrier River
VIRGINIA
James River
Blue Ridge
Roanoke River
Yadkin R.
NORTH CAROLINA
French Broad R.
Clinch R.
Cumberland Gap
Holston River
Kentucky River
KENTUCKY
Cumberland River
TENNESSEE
Tennessee River
Ohio

most of the good sites along the Ohio River and along such tributary streams as Buffalo, Short, Wheeling, Grave, Middle Island, Fish, and Fishing creeks.[23]

The advance of settlement along the upper Ohio south of the Northern Panhandle and in portions of the Monongahela Valley was perhaps impeded by the inclusion of the area within the Indiana grant. Knowledge of the Indiana Company's claim was widespread, and few settlers cared to risk the possibility of losing their improvements. James Chew, who had settled above the mouth of the Cheat River in April, 1772, also took up lands on the west side of the Monongahela, but, assuming that they belonged to the Indiana Company, had not by 1777 applied to any land office to register his claim.[24]

Farther south, the rich Kanawha Valley had begun to attract settlers. In 1773 several prospective immigrants, including James Campbell, Peter Shoemaker, James Pauley, and Walter Kelly, were there selecting lands. The first to attempt a settlement was Kelly, reputedly a refugee from the Carolina backcountry and a man of "bold and intrepid disposition." In 1773 he moved his family and a brother, "a young man of equally suspicious character," to Cedar Grove, twenty miles below the falls of the Kanawha and eighty miles from the Greenbrier habitations.

Kelly's settlement was of short duration. In the spring of 1774 Colonel John Stuart, who was in charge of the militia of the Greenbrier region, sent a messenger to warn Kelly of the increasing hostility of western Indians and of the danger of attack. Kelly sent his family and livestock back to the Greenbrier settlements, but he himself stayed behind. Remaining with him were John Field of Culpeper County, who was then surveying lands in the Kanawha Valley, a Scottish servant boy of Field, and a Negro girl belonging to Kelly. The Indians attacked

[23] Only eight improvements prior to 1772 are noted in Ohio County Survey Book, 1779–1786. Lands along these streams were surveyed for thirty-five persons in 1772; eighty-two, in 1773; seventy-five, in 1774; fifty-eight, in 1775; and thirty-two, in 1776. Ohio County Survey Books, 1779–1786 and 1786–1797.

[24] James Chew to George Morgan, May 18, 1777, W. P. Palmer and others, eds., *Calendar of Virginia State Papers and Other Manuscripts*, 11 vols. (Richmond, Va., 1875-1893), I, 287. See also depositions of William Powell, Simon Girty, and William Crawford, March 10, 1777, *ibid.*, pp. 279-82, and undated statements of Innes and Duval, *ibid.*, p. 297.

shortly after the departure of Kelly's family. Kelly and the Scottish boy were killed and the Negro girl was captured. Field escaped by temporarily hiding in a cornfield and then running, clad only in a hunting shirt, over the rugged Alleghenies to the Greenbrier settlements.[25]

The fate of Walter Kelly did not deter other settlers from pushing into the Kanawha Valley. In 1774 William Morris, Sr., occupied the Kelly homestead. His numerous relatives, including John, Leonard, Benjamin, and Carroll Morris, as well as Thomas Asbury, Joseph Carroll, Thomas Hughes, Sr., John Jones, and others took up lands at other points along the Kanawha. Many of these settlers had been residents of Culpeper County and presumably acquaintances of John Field. The rapidity with which the Kanawha Valley was occupied is indicated by the fact that when troops were withdrawn from Fort Randolph at the mouth of the Kanawha in 1778 at least sixty-nine persons—by no means all of the Kanawha Valley residents—abandoned their homes.[26]

For a time it appeared that all these Allegheny settlements of West Virginia would be included within Vandalia, a proposed fourteenth colony. The Vandalia scheme had its origins in the determined efforts of the Pennsylvania traders to retain the Indiana grant which they had received by the Treaty of Fort Stanwix. Fearing that the objections of Lord Hillsborough might lead to a refusal of the Board of Trade to confirm the award, the group sent Samuel Wharton to London in 1769 for the purpose of pressing its claim. Wharton proved unusually adept at cultivating the friendship and winning the support of powerful political figures in England, including Thomas Walpole, the influential London merchant. His skillful political maneuver-

[25] Lyman Chalkley, *Chronicles of the Scotch-Irish Settlements in Virginia, Extracted from the Original Court Records of Augusta County, 1745–1800*, 3 vols. (Rosslyn, Va., 1912), II, 68-69; Stuart, "Memoir of Indian Wars, and Other Occurrences," pp. 42-43; Withers, *Chronicles of Border Warfare*, pp. 159-61. Stuart is not to be confused with the Indian Superintendent for the Southern District.

[26] Roy Bird Cook, *The Annals of Fort Lee* (Charleston, W. Va., 1935), p. 4; Chalkley, *Chronicles of the Scotch-Irish Settlement*, II, 68-69; Affadavit of John Jones, May 12, 1835, Miscellaneous MSS, Box CII, West Virginia Department of Archives and History Library; Palmer and others, eds., *Calendar of Virginia State Papers*, II, 468-69.

ing produced a nearly solid phalanx of opposition to Hills-borough within the British cabinet and vastly enhanced the chances of confirmation of the Indiana grant.

Wharton's prospects grew even brighter in the summer of 1769 with the organization of the Grand Ohio Company, also known as the Walpole Company, which included some of the most important administrative and Parliamentary officials in Great Britain. This syndicate proposed to purchase 2,400,000 acres of land from the area ceded by the Six Nations in 1768 and to offer the Crown 10,460 pounds, or the exact amount which the government had paid the Indians for the entire cession. By merging its interests with those of the Walpole associates, the Indiana group would gain powerful political support and at the same time be spared the necessity of making a separate petition to the Crown.

When the proposal reached the Secretary of State for the American Department, Hillsborough made the startling suggestion that the Walpole Company enlarge its request to 20,000,000 acres, or enough land to set up a separate colony. The most plausible explanation of Hillsborough's action is that he expected the increase in area to push the price upward to about 100,000 pounds and thereby wreck the scheme. When a meeting of Wharton and Walpole with the Treasury Commissioners on January 14, 1770, resulted in an understanding that the price would remain at 10,460 pounds, it seemed that Hillsborough's attempts to foil the project had been in vain.

But there yet remained Virginia's claims to the lands and the interests of her speculative groups to be considered. Upon learning of the Walpole plan, Edward Montague, the agent of the House of Burgesses in London, promptly entered a caveat against the company's petition. On July 18, after months of delay, the Commissioners of Trade again took up the Walpole petition, but because of charges of illegal grants by the council of Virginia, and, perhaps out of regard for the rights of other vested interests, it again postponed action on the Walpole grant, at least until Virginia could answer the charges of improper disposal of her lands.

On the other hand, the overwhelming political power represented by the Walpole group either dissolved or minimized much of the opposition to the company's plans. George Mercer, dazzled by the prospect that he might become governor of the new colony, negotiated the absorption of the Ohio Company of Virginia by the Walpole Company in return for two of the seventy-two shares into which the latter's interests were divided. Although the Ohio Company repudiated the action of its agent, the Walpole Company apparently never became aware of its objections and conducted its own affairs on the assumption that the merger was in effect. The Walpole Company also quieted the fears of those who were to share in the 200,000-acre tract which Dinwiddie had promised the Virginia regiment in 1754 by agreeing that the required amount of land should be made available in one tract from the territory sought by the Walpole Company.

Even Virginia authorities raised less objection than anticipated. William Nelson, who, as president of the council, was acting governor following the death of Lord Botetourt, noted that all large grants made by Virginia, with the exception of those to the Loyal Company and to Colonel James Patton, had lapsed because of failure of grantees to meet the conditions upon which they had obtained their lands. Nelson accepted the promise of the Walpole Company that all prior rights to lands lying within the new colony would be respected and refused to set himself against the petition of the company. Nor did Thomas Walker, the powerful spokesmen for the Loyal Company, place obstacles in the path of the Walpole associates. Much of the land sought by the Loyal Company lay outside the area desired by the Walpole Company. Moreover, the agreements reached by the Loyal Company and the "Suffering Traders," whose interests were reflected in the Walpole plans, were apparently sufficiently satisfactory to overcome any differences that might have arisen over the Walpole request.

Despite the success in resolving conflicting claims, the Walpole Company was unable to obtain immediate action on its petition. But on July 1, 1772, after nearly two years of delay, the Committee for Plantation Affairs acted favorably upon its request. Lord Hillsborough steadfastly opposed the grant, but his position in the cabinet became so untenable that he resigned. On August 14, 1772, the day he left office, the Privy Council approved the petition of the Walpole Company.

The new colony, to be named Vandalia "in Compliment to the Queen," who took great pride in her alleged descent from the Vandals, was of magnificent proportions. Its boundary, as defined on May 6, 1773, followed the Kentucky River from its mouth to its source, ran from there to the intersection of the Holston River and the Virginia–North Carolina border, and along that border eastward to New River. The line then ran along New River to the mouth of the Greenbrier, thence along that stream and its northeast branch, across the Alleghenies until it met the line of Lord Fairfax, and along the Fairfax line to the headsprings of the North Branch of the Potomac, where it intersected the Maryland boundary. It then followed the Maryland line northward to the southern boundary of Pennsylvania, ran thence to the southwestern corner of Pennsylvania, and then along the Monongahela and the Ohio back to the mouth of the Kentucky.[27] All of West Virginia west of the crests of the Alleghenies was included within the boundaries of the proposed colony.

The new boundaries included significant additions of territory, so that the lands originally sought by the Walpole Company were not coterminous with the colony of Vandalia. The first important territory added was that lying west of a line running from the mouth of the Scioto River to the Cumberland Gap, and the other accretion consisted of the lands between the Virginia–North Carolina border and the Cumberland Mountains. The first of these additions was made possible by the running of the Donelson line in 1771, which shifted the Indian boundary even farther west than that specified by the Treaty of Lochaber and which included the territory sought by the Loyal Company in 1768. The extension of the line westward and the conviction of Thomas Walker and other Virginia promoters that the location of their lands within the Vandalia colony would in no way

---

[27] Lewis, *Indiana Company*, pp. 65-122; Sosin, *Whitehall and the Wilderness*, pp. 181-208; Alvord, *Mississippi Valley in British Politics*, II, 94-166 passim; Abernethy, *Western Lands and the American Revolution*, pp. 46-51, 74-76.

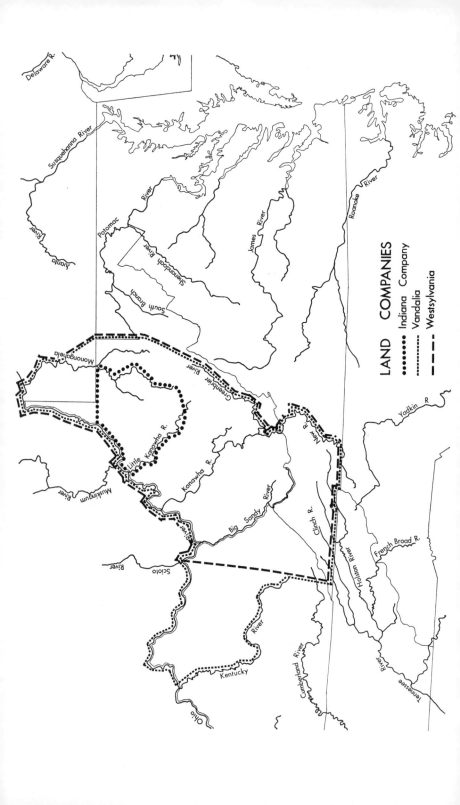

LAND COMPANIES

········· Indiana Company
·········· Vandalia
━ ━ ━ ━ Westsylvania

jeopardize their interests helps to account for the lack of opposition by Virginia speculators to the enlargement of the colony.[28]

But Vandalia was never to become the fourteenth colony. On July 14, 1773, the Crown Law Officers submitted a report questioning the possibility of collecting quitrents under the terms of joint tenancy proposed by the Walpole associates and the Commissioners of Trade and decrying the vagueness of the boundaries outlined. A more serious obstacle stemmed from the Boston Tea Party of 1773 and the Intolerable Acts, which provoked an air of crisis in the relations between Britain and her American colonies and ultimately wrecked any possibility of the creation of an additional colony.[29]

Meanwhile, Virginia speculators found a warm friend in the new governor, Lord Dunmore, who arrived in Williamsburg on December 12, 1771. Dunmore quickly succumbed to the speculative fever himself, and his four years as Virginia's chief executive were marked by an unusual burst of expansionist activity, the result of which was to hasten, if not actually to provoke, the conflict known as Dunmore's War.

As prospects for the establishment of Vandalia waned, Virginia speculators intensified their activities in the trans-Allegheny regions. On October 30, 1773, Thomas Bullitt, almost certainly with Dunmore's blessing, announced in Virginia and Pennsylvania newspapers that he planned to make military surveys in Kentucky in accordance with the Proclamation of 1763. The following spring he assembled a party which included James Douglas, Hancock Taylor, James Harrod, and Isaac Hite at the mouth of the Kanawha. Bullitt's group was joined by another party under James McAfee near the mouth of the Kentucky River. Preliminary to making surveys, Bullitt visited the Shawnees at Chillicothe and succeeded in making agreements with the Indians whereby the latter permitted the surveying and settling of Kentucky lands in return for assurances that they would be paid for their claims, which had been ignored in the Treaty of Fort Stanwix, and that they would continue to enjoy

28 Abernethy, *Western Lands and the American Revolution,* p. 77.
29 Sosin, *Whitehall and the Wilderness,* p. 208.

hunting rights in the territory south of the Ohio River. Disregarding the Donelson line, Bullitt surveyed tracts as far west as Louisville, some of which were granted by Dunmore to John Connolly and to close relatives and associates of George Croghan.[30]

The activities of the Bullitt and McAfee parties were but one manifestation of the cooperation between Dunmore and the land speculators, which increased in proportion to the declining fortunes of the Vandalia promoters. Dunmore now began to grant lands not only on the basis of Dinwiddie's commitment of 1754 but also under the terms of the Proclamation of 1763. Among the significant military grants made in West Virginia were 21,941 acres between Coal and Pocatalico rivers to John Fry and others; 51,302 acres at the mouth of the Kanawha to George Muse, Adam Stephen, Andrew Lewis, Peter Hog, and others; 28,400 acres at the mouth of the Little Kanawha to Robert Stobo, Jacob Van Braam, and others; and 28,627 acres along the Ohio and Big Sandy rivers to John Savage and 59 associates.[31]

Among those who profited substantially from the governor's policies was George Washington. With the instincts of a shrewd speculator, Washington acquired the rights of numerous veterans of the French and Indian War, and in the fall of 1770 he personally spent several weeks selecting choice sites along the Ohio and Kanawha rivers. He reaped immediate benefits from the decision of the governor and council to redeem Dinwiddie's pledge of 1754 and to make further grants under the Proclamation of 1763. Washington's lands along the Kanawha included 10,990 acres a few miles above Point Pleasant, 7,726 acres at the mouth of Pocatalico River, 2,000 at the mouth of Coal River, 2,950 on Tyler Creek, and 418 at Burning Spring, about 10 miles east of Charleston. On the Ohio he held 1,293 acres at Round

[30] Alexander Spotswood Dandridge to William Preston, May 15, 1774, Draper MSS, 3QQ26; Reuben Gold Thwaites and Louise Phelps Kellogg, eds., *Documentary History of Dunmore's War, 1774* (Madison, Wis., 1905), pp. 22-24, 125n; Downes, *Council Fires on the Upper Ohio*, pp. 156-57; Abernethy, *Western Lands and the American Revolution*, pp. 102-103; Randolph C. Downes, "Dunmore's War: An Interpretation," *Mississippi Valley Historical Review*, XXI (December, 1934), 311-19.

[31] Descriptions of these grants are in Edgar B. Sims, *Making a State* (Charleston, W. Va., 1956), p. 141.

Bottom, in Marshall County, 2,314 at Washington Bottom, below the mouth of the Little Kanawha, 2,448 near Ravenswood, and 4,394 at Millwood in Jackson County.[32]

Almost immediately Washington laid plans for settling his lands near the mouth of the Kanawha. His fears that the Vandalia project might undermine his rights were evidently allayed, and in advertising his property, he called attention to its location only a few miles from Point Pleasant, the proposed capital of Vandalia. Washington sought to attract immigrants from England, Scotland, Ireland, and German states by promising payment of passage money to America, suspension of all quitrents for a period of years, and religious freedom. In March, 1774, he sent more than twenty "hirelings and servants" from Mount Vernon to prepare his lands for settlers, but at Redstone, on the Monongahela, the party learned of imminent danger from the Indians and decided against proceeding farther.

Undiscouraged, Washington revived his plans in the spring of 1775. A new work force, under the direction of James Cleveland, succeeded in making improvements valued at more than 1,100 pounds on Washington's property. It erected three dwellings of four and five rooms each, ten cabins, and a barn, cleared twenty-eight acres of land, and planted potatoes, corn, and turnips, as well as nearly two thousand peach trees. Once again, increasing hostility of the Indians, together with the outbreak of the Revolutionary War and the subsequent abandonment of Fort Blair, which gave cover to the settlement, forced Washington to postpone further work on the enterprise.[33]

In creating opportunities for the speculators, Dunmore and the council of Virginia displayed little sympathy for the rights and aspirations of the yeoman farmer. Complaints arose almost immediately that soldiers were infringing upon the claims of others, and on December 16, 1773, Dunmore and the council

[32] Cook, *Washington's Western Lands*, pp. 43, 55-56, 61, 62, 64, 75, 81, 85, 97; Charles H. Ambler, *George Washington and the West* (Chapel Hill, N. C., 1936), pp. 135-51.
[33] Washington to Robert McMickan, May 10, 1774, John C. Fitzpatrick, ed., *The Writings of George Washington from the Original Manuscript Sources, 1745–1799*, 39 vols. (Washington, D. C., 1931-1944), III, 212; Cook, *Washington's Western Lands*, pp. 41-42, 47-52; Ambler, *George Washington and the West*, pp. 152-58.

directed that military surveys should not encroach upon existing settlements or upon prior surveys legally made. But at the same time, they served notice upon prospective settlers that they must expect to buy lands from either veterans with land warrants or from the Greenbrier and Loyal companies. The political power of the Loyal Company, and particularly of Thomas Walker, its guiding spirit, had been demonstrated on May 5, 1772, when in response to the company's complaints that residents of other colonies were illegally moving onto its lands, the governor and the council ordered the sheriff and other law enforcement officials to evict the settlers. Armed with this renewed recognition of its rights, the Loyal Company continued to make surveys, adding to the 156,164 acres which had been laid off by 1756 another 45,340 acres by the time of the Revolution. A large number of these surveys lay in the southeastern section of West Virginia.[34] The claims of the Greenbrier and Loyal companies, given new substance by the action of the governor and the council, remained to plague settlers of West Virginia for the next forty years.

Another of Dunmore's moves which was to prove of great significance for the West Virginia frontier was his forceful assertion of Virginia's claims to lands around the forks of the Ohio. For years the area had been in dispute between Virginia and Pennsylvania, but the great influx of settlers into the region following the Treaty of Fort Stanwix forced the matter to a head. The trouble arose from a vagueness in the Pennsylvania charter, which stipulated that the western boundary of the colony should be five degrees west of the Delaware. If this meant that the western boundary must conform to the meanderings of the Delaware River, Virginia by virtue of her charter of 1609 had a valid claim to the area. If the western boundary were to be a line run due north from a point five degrees west of the mouth of the Delaware, Pennsylvania's claim was stronger.

In sparring for advantage, Pennsylvanians took the first step and opened a land office west of the Alleghenies in 1769. Two years later the assembly of Pennsylvania created Bedford County, but designated as its seat a town, also called Bedford, east of

---

[34] See, for example, Archibald Henderson, *Dr. Thomas Walker and the Loyal Company of Virginia,* Reprint from *Proceedings* of the American Antiquarian Society (Worcester, Mass., 1931), p. 35.

the Alleghenies. In 1772 Pennsylvania remedied this defect by establishing Westmoreland County, which included all her territory west of the mountains. Numerous Virginians, led by Michael Cresap, formed an association to resist Pennsylvania authority, and about six hundred of them petitioned the Virginia assembly to provide them with a government.[35]

In the summer of 1773 Lord Dunmore visited Fort Pitt, ostensibly for a firsthand observation of the situation but also for the purpose of determining whether he should make land grants in the region. Dunmore convinced himself that Virginia should establish her authority over the area in dispute and that he had the right to grant lands there. Following the governor's return to Williamsburg, the council, on October 11, 1773, created the District of West Augusta, which embraced not only the disputed area around the forks of the Ohio but all of West Virginia west of the crests of the Alleghenies. The outbreak of the Revolutionary War and the advent of more pressing matters eclipsed the controversy over the boundary, and the dispute was not finally adjusted until 1784.[36]

Of more immediate importance for the West Virginia frontier was the alliance which Dunmore formed with George Croghan and John Connolly during his visit to Fort Pitt. Croghan's claim to 200,000 acres of land near the forks of the Ohio and on the Youghiogheny on the basis of a grant made to him by the Six Nations in 1747 was confirmed by the Treaty of Fort Stanwix in 1768, but Pennsylvania authorities steadfastly refused to recognize it. Croghan, hoping to secure his title through other means, had then become active in both the Indiana and Vandalia schemes. Faced in 1773 with the determined opposition of Pennsylvania on the one hand and the imminent collapse of the Vandalia enterprise on the other, Croghan was now ready to recognize Virginia authority over the disputed area around the forks of the Ohio provided he could obtain prior guarantees of his own claims. With Dunmore's affinity for land speculators and the propensity of both men to seek practical accommodation

---

[35] Abernethy, *Western Lands and the American Revolution*, pp. 91-97; Ambler and Summers, *West Virginia*, pp. 56-59.

[36] Abernethy, *Western Lands and the American Revolution*, pp. 136-38; Jack M. Sosin, *The Revolutionary Frontier, 1763–1783* (New York, 1967), pp. 56-60.

of differences in business matters, Dunmore and Croghan readily reached an understanding. Dunmore recognized the validity of Croghan's grant from the Six Nations, and, at Croghan's suggestion, named John Connolly, Croghan's nephew, his agent in charge of both civil and military affairs on the upper Ohio.[37]

Dunmore was well aware of Croghan's unsurpassed and almost mystical influence over the Indians, and he undoubtedly believed that almost no price was too high for the good will and services of such a man. But in elevating Connolly, whose virtues included little of wisdom, patience, or restraint, to a position of trust and authority, Dunmore could hardly have done more, if such had been his intent, to deepen the fear and insecurity of the frontiersmen or to inflame Indian animosity.

Unfortunately, the hostility of the western tribes was already at the kindling point. In April, 1773, George Yeader and Adam Strader, onetime hunting companions of Simon Kenton, were killed by Indians at the mouth of Elk River. By the spring of 1774 the danger all along the frontier, from western Pennsylvania to the Clinch and Holston valleys, had become acute. Part of the Indian indignation was directed at surveyors in the western country, whom they correctly regarded as harbingers of settlement. At the mouth of the Little Guyandotte a band of Shawnees attacked a surveying party under John Floyd, seized several of his men, held them prisoner for three days, and subjected them to several indignities before releasing them. A few weeks later the advance members of a surveying party which included George Rogers Clark and Michael Cresap were fired upon at the mouth of the Kanawha. The angry men chose Cresap as their leader and tried to prevail upon him to direct a movement against the Shawnee towns. It was only with difficulty that Cresap was able to persuade them to return to Wheeling until they could learn what action Virginia proposed to take with regard to the Indian outbreaks.[38]

The danger of unauthorized expeditions against the Indians

[37] Wainwright, *George Croghan*, pp. 286-88; Abernethy, *Western Lands and the American Revolution*, pp. 92-94.

[38] Downes, *Council Fires on the Upper Ohio*, pp. 157-58; Thwaites and Kellogg, eds., *Dunmore's War*, pp. xiii-xiv; Roy Bird Cook, *The Annals of Fort Lee* (Charleston, W. Va., 1935), p. 4.

vastly increased with an incendiary circular issued by John Connolly on April 21. Connolly declared that a virtual state of war already existed and called upon the settlers to arm themselves in anticipation of attack. Cresap, who upon his return to Wheeling was informed of Connolly's circular, overcame his reluctance to take the offensive and during the next few weeks led parties in several small encounters with the Indians in what was commonly known on the frontier as "Cresap's War." Typical of the actions was a skirmish near Grave Creek on April 27, in which a Shawnee and a white man were killed and a quantity of booty was taken from boats which the Indians abandoned.[39]

Without question, the most serious of the hostile actions was that which involved the killing of the family of Logan, a Mingo chieftain, at the mouth of Yellow Creek on April 30. The facts of the episode are difficult to establish, but the killing of two Mingoes on the north side of the Ohio the previous day undoubtedly started the train of events. In a dark mood because of the killings, four Indians, including the brother of Logan, crossed the Ohio to the residence of Joshua Baker. Soon afterward, a band of whites led by Daniel Greathouse arrived at the Baker house. Greathouse and his men plied the Indians with whiskey but allegedly grew angry when the Indians became boisterous and one of them swaggered about in a greatcoat belonging to one of the whites. Were these the only circumstances surrounding the event, they would suggest little more than a drunken brawl of historic proportions; but there is also evidence of premeditation in that Greathouse and his men engaged the Indians in a contest of markmanship and then killed them while their guns were unloaded. In all, eight Indians, including a brother and a sister of Logan, were killed. It was this loss which turned an old friend into an implacable enemy of the whites and resulted in Logan's personally taking thirteen scalps in retaliation.[40]

[39] John A. Caruso, *The Appalachian Frontier: America's First Surge Westward* (Indianapolis, Ind., 1959), pp. 124-27; Downes, *Council Fires on the Upper Ohio*, pp. 158-62.
[40] Thwaites and Kellogg, eds., *Dunmore's War*, pp. 9-19; Downes, "Dunmore's War: An Interpretation," pp. 322-24; Reminiscences of Judge Henry Jolly, Draper MSS, 6NN22-24; Deposition of Michael Cresap, Jr., *ibid.*, 2SS, Book 5, pp. 33-35;

By this time hopes for peace on the frontier were fast evaporating. John Connolly, hoping to curry favor with Dunmore and to perpetuate himself in power, was believed by traders in the Indian country deliberately to be seeking war. When Cornstalk, the Shawnee chieftain, had the white traders in his town safely escorted to Fort Pitt, Connolly attempted to seize the Indians who had accompanied them. George Croghan arranged an escape for the Indians, but Connolly's men overtook the fleeing Shawnees and killed one of them. Croghan was by now convinced that war was inevitable and bent all his efforts toward limiting the conflict. Partly as a result of his influence with such chiefs as Kiasutha of the Senecas and Grey Eyes and The Pipe of the Delawares, most of the tribes north of the Ohio remained quiet during the summer of 1774, and the depredations on the West Virginia frontier were largely the work of Logan and his friends and of the Shawnees.[41]

The summer of 1774 brought unusual tenseness to the Allegheny settlements of West Virginia. In late June Indians killed one man and wounded two others in an encounter in the Greenbrier region and laid siege to a house in which inhabitants had gathered. Alarms were spread throughout the area, particularly in the Walker's Creek and Bluestone settlements. Bands of Indians continued to roam around the Greenbrier region, forcing settlers to huddle together in the little fort and keeping scouts busy trying to learn the whereabouts and intentions of the Indians. On July 31 the Indians attacked the settlement at Muddy Creek, killing a brother and a sister of Walter Kelly, the unfortunate pioneer who had lost his own life some three weeks previously at his cabin at Cedar Grove.[42]

Dunmore sought to allay the fears of the frontier inhabitants by erecting a defense line along the Ohio. In early June Major William Crawford, acting upon instructions from John Connolly, began work on Fort Fincastle at Wheeling. On July 12 Dunmore

---

Recollections of Bazaleel Wells, *ibid.*, 2S, Book 2, pp. 5-6; Recollections of George Edgington, *ibid.*, 2S, Book 3, p. 34; Recollections of Michael Myers, *ibid.*, 4S132-34.

[41] Wainwright, *George Croghan*, pp. 288-93.

[42] William Christian to Joseph Cloyd, June 29, 1774, Draper MSS, 3QQ49; James Robertson to William Preston, August 1, 1774, *ibid.*, 3QQ69; Stuart, "Memoir of Indian Wars, and Other Occurrences," pp. 42-43.

himself instructed Colonel Andrew Lewis to proceed with militia raised in Augusta County to the mouth of the Kanawha and to build another fort there. Dunmore expressed the hope that communications could be kept open along the new defense perimeter from the mouth of the Kanawha to Fort Fincastle and thence to Fort Dunmore, as Fort Pitt had been renamed. Moreover, he even suggested that Lewis might attack the Shawnees in their towns and inflict whatever damage he could upon them.

The governor's plans called for other offensive movements. At Fort Fincastle Colonel Angus McDonald assembled about 400 men drawn from the Monongahela and Youghiogheny valleys for an expedition against the Shawnees. McDonald's army began its march on July 26 and proceeded without mishap until, within about six miles of its destination, it was suddenly ambushed by about thirty Indians. Stunned by the encounter, but suffering no disorganization, the army moved on to the Indian villages. But it found the towns deserted, engaged no Indian warriors in combat, and had to content itself with the destruction of the dwellings and the supplies of corn which had been left. As was usual in such cases, the lack of success of the McDonald expedition was followed by an increase, rather than a diminution, of Indian forays.[43]

Meanwhile, Dunmore had decided upon a far larger undertaking. On July 24 he informed Lewis that because of the "unhappy situation of the Divided People settled over the Alegany Mountain's," he himself was proceeding to Fort Dunmore to "put Matters under the best Regulation to Support that Country for a Barrier [and] give the Enemies a Blow that will Breake the Confederacy & render their plans abortive." The governor proposed to gather as large a force of militia as possible from Frederick, Berkeley, and Hampshire counties and to move them overland to Fort Dunmore and thence down the Ohio. He ordered Lewis to enlist men from Augusta, Botetourt, and Fincastle counties and to join him either at the mouth of the Kanawha or elsewhere along the Ohio. From the point of

[43] Dunmore to Andrew Lewis, July 12, 1774, Draper MSS, 46J7; Thwaites and Kellogg, eds., *Dunmore's War*, pp. 86-87, 151-56.

juncture the combined forces would strike into the Indian country.[44]

At Lewisburg, or Camp Union, his appointed place of rendezvous, Lewis gathered about 1,100 men. He resisted a last-minute effort of Dunmore to change his line of march to the mouth of the Little Kanawha and on September 6 ordered his advance units to move toward the mouth of the Kanawha. Lewis entrusted these units numbering about 600 men with 500 packhorses, 54,000 pounds of flour, and 108 cattle, to his popular younger brother, Charles. On September 12 Lewis and Colonel William Fleming, with 500 men and 200 packhorses, left Camp Union. Another 200 men, under Colonel William Christian, were to gather at Camp Union and to depart for the mouth of the Kanawha on September 25 or 26.[45] From Lewisburg, Lewis' army followed the Old Buffalo Trail, which ran along present U.S. Route 60 to Ansted and then wound over a mountainous course by way of Rich Creek, Twenty-Mile Creek, Gauley River, Bell Creek, and Kelly's Creek to the Kanawha River, which it followed to the Ohio.[46]

When Lewis arrived at the mouth of the Kanawha on October 6, he found a message from the governor awaiting him, ordering him to join his army to Dunmore's about twenty-five miles from Chillicothe. Lewis' men were highly displeased that they should leave the mouth of the Kanawha undefended, knowing that it

[44] Dunmore to Andrew Lewis, July 24, 1774, Draper MSS, 3QQ141; Thwaites and Kellogg, eds., *Dunmore's War*, pp. 97-98.

[45] William Russell to William Preston, August 16, 1774, Draper MSS, 3QQ78; Arthur Campbell to William Preston, August 19, 1774, *ibid.*, 3QQ80; John Brown to William Preston, August 22, 1774, *ibid.*, 3QQ81; William Preston to Arthur Campbell, August 25, 1774, *ibid.*, 3QQ82; Arthur Campbell to William Preston, August 26, 1774, *ibid.*, 3QQ83; Anthony Bledsoe to William Preston, August 28, 1774, *ibid.*, 3QQ85; William Russell to William Preston, August 28, 1774, *ibid.*, 3QQ86; William Russell to William Preston, August 28, 1774, *ibid.*, 3QQ86; James Robertson to William Preston, September 1, 1774, *ibid.*, 3QQ88; Michael Woods to William Preston, September 3, 1774, *ibid.*, 3QQ88; William Christian to William Preston, September 3, 1774, *ibid.*, 3QQ89; William Christian to William Preston, September 7, 1774, *ibid.*, 3QQ92; Andrew Lewis to William Preston, September 8, 1774, *ibid.*, 3QQ93; William Fleming to Nancy Fleming, September 4, 1774, *ibid.*, 2ZZ1; William Fleming to Nancy Fleming, September 7, 1774, *ibid.*, 2ZZ2. See also Thwaites and Kellogg, eds., *Dunmore's War*, pp. 156-94.

[46] Colonel William Fleming's Orderly Book, Draper MSS, 2ZZ72; Thwaites and Kellogg, eds., *Dunmore's War*, pp. 323-25.

lay along a favorite Shawnee route into Augusta, Botetourt, and Fincastle counties.[47] While he was yet encamped at Point Pleasant, however, Lewis became engaged in the greatest battle ever fought on the West Virginia frontier and the only engagement of Dunmore's War.

Cornstalk, the Shawnee chief, was well aware of the advance of both Dunmore's and Lewis' armies. He proposed to attack Lewis before he could join Dunmore and then, if successful, to cut Dunmore's army of about 1,000 men to pieces as it passed along the Hocking Valley. In implementing his strategy, Cornstalk led his warriors—some 800 to 1,100—to a densely forested area on the banks of the Ohio opposite Point Pleasant. During the night of October 9 he quietly crossed the river to the West Virginia side. About dawn the Indians fired upon Valentine Sevier and James Robinson, two of Lewis' men who were out hunting turkeys. They, along with hunters from other companies, hurried back to camp with reports that Indians were in the vicinity.

Andrew Lewis immediately ordered out two parties of 150 men each, under Charles Lewis and William Fleming, to scout along the Ohio and Kanawha rivers. About sunrise the Indians, whose numbers included Shawnees, Delawares, Mingoes, Ottawas, and others, concentrated a heavy attack upon Charles Lewis' men and mortally wounded young Lewis. Now realizing the magnitude of the attack, Andrew Lewis sent out another force under Colonel John Field, but Field also met his death. By then Fleming's men had given way, and Fleming himself had suffered severe but not mortal wounds.

From dawn until noon the battle raged. Cornstalk's voice could be heard above the din of battle, urging his warriors to destroy their foes. Reinforced by companies of Augusta and Botetourt troops, the whites forced the Indians to give ground but were unable to deliver a decisive blow. At this juncture, Isaac Shelby directed a flanking movement along the east bank of Crooked Creek, a small stream flowing parallel with the Ohio.

[47] William Fleming to Adam Stephen, October 8, 1774, Draper MSS, 2ZZ11; Thwaites and Kellogg, eds., *Dunmore's War*, p. 237.

Believing that reinforcements were arriving for Lewis, the Indians placed the bodies of their fallen men in the Ohio River and during the night retired to the north bank of the river. The battle of Point Pleasant had cost Lewis forty-six men killed and eighty wounded. The Indian losses could not be ascertained.

Defeat brought Cornstalk face to face with a decision of crucial importance—whether to continue the fight against the whites to the bitter end or to sue for peace. He returned to his villages on the Pickaway Plains and placed the issue squarely before his people, proposing that they either kill all the women and children and fight until all their men were dead or that they ask for peace. The Shawnees decided for peace, and Cornstalk sent Matthew Elliott, a white man, to seek a conference with Lord Dunmore.

Having heard nothing from Lewis, but believing that Lewis had sufficient men to take care of himself, Dunmore had meanwhile left a garrison of a hundred men at Fort Gower and set off with the remainder of his army for the Indian towns. When he was within fifteen miles of the villages, he was met by Cornstalk's emissaries. Dunmore agreed to listen to their requests for peace, and, hastily forming an encampment known as Camp Charlotte, began negotiations with the chiefs. On the same day, Lewis placed Fleming in charge at Point Pleasant and with a hundred men left to join Dunmore. On his way he met a messenger who informed him that Dunmore had already concluded an agreement with the Indians. Lewis' men were yet bent upon attacking the Indian towns. Dunmore, however, with John Gibson and fifty men, hurried to Lewis' headquarters and persuaded the men to return to Point Pleasant.

The Treaty of Camp Charlotte was only a tentative agreement formulated to govern Indian-white relations until a definitive treaty could be negotiated. By its terms the Indians agreed to give up prisoners whom they had taken in their attacks upon the whites, to surrender Negroes, horses, and other valuables which they had seized, and to refrain from hunting south of the Ohio. To guarantee compliance, they delivered hostages to Dunmore. Finally, they agreed that there should be a general conference at Fort Dunmore, or Pittsburgh, the following spring for the purpose of working out details of a definitive treaty.[48]

Meanwhile, Dunmore ordered a strengthening of frontier defenses. He left a garrison of seventy-five men under John Connolly at Fort Dunmore. For the protection of the Kanawha and Greenbrier settlers, he ordered William Russell to build a fort at the mouth of the Kanawha to replace the small stockade which had earlier been constructed by Andrew Lewis. This defense, known as Fort Blair, was "a small palisaded rectangle, about eighty yards long, with blockhouses at two of its corners and cabins for barracks within."[49] These two forts together with Fort Fincastle at Wheeling were to remain the major bulwarks in the defense system of the West Virginia frontier.

At long last—six years after the Treaties of Hard Labor and Fort Stanwix had cleared away the claims of the Cherokees and the Six Nations—the Indian menace seemed to have been eliminated for West Virginia's Allegheny settlements. But twenty more years were to elapse before transmontane West Virginia would be free of danger from the Indians. Immediately on the horizon lay the Revolutionary War with some of the most bloody experiences the Allegheny pioneers would ever remember.

[48] William Ingles to William Preston, October 14, 1774, Draper MSS, 3QQ121; Isaac Shelby to John Shelby, October 16, 1774, *ibid.*, 7ZZ2; John Floyd to William Preston, October 16, 1774, *ibid.*, 33S44-49; Thwaites and Kellogg, eds., *Dunmore's War*, pp. 257-59, 266-77; Caruso, *Appalachian Frontier*, pp. 133-38.

[49] Virgil A. Lewis, *First Biennial Report of the Department of Archives and History of the State of West Virginia* (Charleston, W. Va., 1906), pp. 237-38.

Chapter Five

British at the Back Door

News of the momentous events in Boston in the spring of 1775 momentarily diverted the attention of the Allegheny pioneers from matters of frontier security. Despite their isolation and their preoccupation with their own problems, settlers in the backcountry had followed with lively interest accounts of the political and ideological conflicts which had for several years troubled relations between Britain and her American colonies. In general, West Virginia pioneers, like most other frontier residents, reacted to events with intense enthusiasm for the American cause. Adam Stephen, whose estate, "Bower," was located near Martinsburg, undoubtedly spoke for many of his western compatriots when he declared that "for my part before I would submit my life, liberty, and property to the arbitrary disposal of a corrupt, venal aristocracy, the wanton and effeminate tools of power, I would set myself down with a few hundred friends upon some rich and healthy spot, six hundred miles to the westward, and there form a settlement, which, in a short time would command attention and respect."[1] During Dunmore's War Daniel Morgan and scores of his fellow militiamen avowed that they would aid their "brethren in Boston" if hostilities should erupt there.

Support for the American cause in western Virginia seemed so overwhelming that Richard Henry Lee declared that the six frontier counties (Hampshire, Berkeley, Frederick, Dunmore, Augusta, and Botetourt) would provide 6,000 fighting men. Moreover, said Lee, these frontiersmen had developed "amazing hardihood" from years spent in the woods as hunters and Indian fighters and had acquired such "dexterity" with the Kentucky rifle that they scorned any target closer than 200 yards or larger than an orange.[2]

The westerners were quick to match professions of enthusiastic support with energetic action. In April, 1775, upon hearing reports that Governor Dunmore had seized the powder in the Williamsburg magazine and stored it aboard a British vessel lying in the James River, more than 1,000 men, including 600 good riflemen, from the frontier counties gathered at Fredericksburg and were dissuaded from marching against the governor only by the timely intervention of George Washington.

The opportunity for these impatient sons of the frontier to engage in military action, however, was not long in coming. On June 14, 1775, the Second Continental Congress voted to raise ten companies of expert riflemen for the aid of Massachusetts, two of which were to be furnished by Virginia. To meet this request, Virginia authorities asked the local committees of safety of Berkeley and Frederick counties to provide one company each. Upon the recommendation of the county committees and the advice of Horatio Gates, a resident of Berkeley County and later the hero of the battle of Saratoga, Washington named two veterans of Dunmore's War, Hugh Stephenson of Berkeley County and Daniel Morgan of Frederick County, to command the companies. Scores of men sought to enlist, and, despite the high degree of selectivity, both companies were filled within a week. The recruits, mostly young men in their early twenties, were required to equip themselves with rifles, tomahawks, scalping knives, and other accouterments.

After some delay due to difficulty in obtaining suitable rifles, the two companies set out, Morgan from Winchester on July 15 and Stephenson from Shepherdstown on July 17. Apparently the two commanders had agreed to join forces at Frederick, Maryland, but Morgan, eager to be the first to arrive in Cambridge and realizing that joint entry would give credit to Stephenson, who outranked him, broke his promise to wait for Stephenson and hurried on northward. He arrived at Cambridge on August 6, five days ahead of Stephenson. Their companies were the first troops from south of the Potomac to join Washington's army.[3]

1 Quoted in Freeman H. Hart, *The Valley of Virginia in the American Revolution, 1763–1789* (Chapel Hill, N. C., 1942), p. 85.

2 Don Higginbotham, *Daniel Morgan: Revolutionary Rifleman* (Chapel Hill, N. C., 1961), pp. 19-20.

3 *Ibid.*, pp. 20-24; Millard Kessler Bushong, *A History of Jefferson County, West Virginia* (Charles Town, W. Va., 1941), pp. 27-29.

Transmontane settlers, unfortunately, could spare little time sympathizing with the Bostonians, for unprecedented dangers lurked at their very door. From such strongholds as Detroit and Niagara the British were in a position to launch devastating attacks upon the vulnerable Allegheny frontier. The provisional Treaty of Camp Charlotte, which had afforded a brief respite from Indian forays, might prove exceedingly fragile once the western tribes comprehended the full implications of the breach between Britain and her colonies.

Dunmore immediately endeavored to turn conditions on the frontier to British advantage. The general peace with the western tribes which he had hoped to attain at the conference scheduled for the spring of 1775 would no longer serve Britain's interests. He therefore instructed Connolly, who visited Williamsburg in February, to release Mingo prisoners detained at Fort Dunmore and to seek to make the Indians allies of the British. In June Connolly succeeded in obtaining pledges of friendship from the Delawares and a few of the Mingo chiefs. In July Dunmore added to the dangers confronting the Allegheny pioneers by ordering the disbanding of the garrisons at Fort Dunmore, Fort Fincastle, and Fort Blair and the evacuation of the posts.[4]

Frontier residents made frantic appeals for protection to both the Virginia authorities and to the Continental Congress. On August 7 the Virginia Convention responded to their entreaties by ordering Captain John Neville and a hundred men from Winchester to Fort Dunmore, which was again given its older name, Fort Pitt. Fort Blair had been burned some weeks previously by marauding Shawnees. Even before the action of the Convention, the House of Burgesses, at its final session, had named a commission consisting of Thomas Walker, Andrew Lewis, James Wood, John Walker, and Adam Stephen to confer with tribal chiefs with a view to obtaining their neutrality. Wood visited the Indian villages at great personal risk and succeeded in arranging a conference at Fort Pitt for September. The Treaty of Pittsburgh, which was signed in October,

[4] William Russell to William Preston, June 12, 1775, Draper MSS, 4QQ19; Reuben Gold Thwaites and Louise Phelps Kellogg, eds., *The Revolution on the Upper Ohio, 1775–1777* (Madison, Wis., 1908), pp. 12-20.

1775, was largely a victory of the Virginia commissioners. The Continental Congress had in the meanwhile divided frontier areas into three Indian departments and had included Virginia in its central department. Although Lewis Morris, Thomas Walker, and James Wilson, the commissioners for the central department, attended the proceedings at Pittsburgh, they acted as little more than observers. It was Virginia's commissioners who wrung from the major tribes north of the Ohio, including the Shawnees, Delawares, Mingoes, Senecas, Wyandots, Pottawattomis, and Ottawas, agreements which made the Ohio River the boundary between the Indian country and the areas open to settlement and promises that the Indians would remain neutral in the contest between the colonies and Britain.[5]

The full significance of the Treaty of Pittsburgh could not be immediately apparent, but for nearly two years following the agreement the Indians honored their promises. Only occasional isolated instances of hostility marred the interlude of peace. The Senecas were so strict in their neutrality, refusing to allow either belligerent to cross their lands, that they may have actually prevented the British from using Fort Niagara for mounting an attack upon Fort Pitt. The relatively quiescent state of the Allegheny frontier produced by the Treaty of Pittsburgh and the occupation of Fort Pitt by colonial troops permitted an uninterrupted advance of settlers into the transmontane parts of West Virginia and Pennsylvania. With additional protection afforded by small private forts and stockades, of which at least forty were constructed between 1769 and 1777, the Allegheny area of West Virginia was in a better defensive position in 1777 than it had been at the beginning of the war.[6]

The first serious threat to the West Virginia settlements grew out of a scheme known to westerners as "Connolly's Plot." After abandoning Fort Dunmore, John Connolly hastened to join Lord Dunmore aboard a British man-of-war off Yorktown. There

[5] Thwaites and Kellogg, eds., *Revolution on the Upper Ohio*, pp. 20, 23n, 25-127; Thomas Perkins Abernethy, *Western Lands and the American Revolution* (New York, 1937), p. 141; Solon J. Buck and Elizabeth Hawthorn Buck, *The Planting of Civilization in Western Pennsylvania* (Pittsburgh, Pa., 1939), p. 182.

[6] Thwaites and Kellogg, eds., *Revolution on the Upper Ohio*, p. xiv; Virgil A. Lewis, *First Biennial Report of the Department of Archives and History of the State of West Virginia* (Charleston, W. Va., 1906), pp. 217-49.

he laid before the governor a plan which so impressed Dunmore that he asked Connolly to present it to General Thomas Gage in Boston. With Gage's approval, Connolly proposed to journey to Detroit, where he would gather a force of British and Indians, together with the necessary arms and supplies. Then proceeding by way of Lake Erie, he would capture Fort Pitt. Connolly hoped to win support from settlers of the backcountry by promises of generous land grants. If they did not succumb to his blandishments, he proposed to destroy Fort Pitt and Fort Fincastle and to join forces with those of the governor at Alexandria. Unable to travel to Detroit by way of Quebec and the Great Lakes because of Benedict Arnold's capture of Montreal, Connolly, in disguise, set out via Virginia and Maryland. Unfortunately for the success of his venture, John Gibson, a Pittsburgh trader with whom Connolly had corresponded prior to his journey to Boston, put the West Augusta committee of safety on the alert. The committee, in turn, spread the alarm. A potential danger to the frontier settlements of the Alleghenies was averted when on November 20, 1775, Connolly and two companions were arrested near Hagerstown, Maryland, and imprisoned.

Although Connolly's plan to drive a wedge between the northern and southern colonies failed, Loyalism on the upper Ohio was sufficiently widespread to cause considerable apprehension. Numerous pioneer leaders, including Alexander McKee, Simon Girty, and Matthew Elliott, openly espoused the British cause and made their way to Detroit, while others were suspected of British sympathies. Hundreds of other settlers, fearful of the consequences of the war or genuinely attached to the mother country, gave evidence of their feelings. In southwestern Pennsylvania and the northern part of present West Virginia they created such a "frantic scene of mischief" that Colonel Zackwell Morgan of Monongalia County enlisted 500 men for quelling their disturbances.[7]

[7] Zackwell Morgan to Edward Hand, August 29, 1777, Draper MSS, 3NN65, 66; John Gibson to Edward Hand, October 22, 1777, *ibid.*, 3NN182; James Chew to Edward Hand, October 23, 1777, *ibid.*, 1U124; Edward Hand to a Committee of Congress, December 21, 1777, *ibid.*, 3NN85-88; Thwaites and Kellogg, eds., *Revolution on the Upper Ohio*, pp. 136-42; Reuben Gold Thwaites and Louise Phelps Kellogg, eds., *Frontier Defense on the Upper Ohio, 1777–1778* (Madison, Wis., 1912), pp. 52-53, 142-45, 184-87.

The suppression of Loyalist activity did not entirely allay the settlers' apprehension of a British thrust from Detroit. Almost from the outset of the war they heard persistent reports that the British commandant at Detroit was pressing Indian tribes northwest of the Ohio to join the British in attacks upon the Allegheny settlements and that he had made progress in luring the Wyandots and Ottawas away from their neutrality. This intelligence prompted the Continental Congress to discuss the possibility of an attack upon Detroit, but more immediate problems prevented such an expedition. Virginia, however, sought to bolster frontier determination by extending once again her defense lines to the Ohio. In the early summer of 1776 Matthew Arbuckle built Fort Randolph, a strong stockade with blockhouses and cabins, to replace Fort Blair, and he and his men remained at the fort as its garrison.[8]

Virginia added depth to her border defenses in West Virginia by stationing militia at some of the most important private forts and by placing scouts at strategic places along the trails over which Indian war parties traveled. Without such protection to their homes and families, militia were loath to take up duty at positions along the outer defense perimeter. John Stuart warned that "should our people pen themselves in little Forts as formerly they did it will be the Readyest method of having themselves Distroyed." Upon his recommendation, a fort was built at Lewisburg and militia were placed at Arbuckle's old fort on Muddy Creek, on Indian Creek, and at Donnally's Fort. In addition, scouts were assigned positions at the pass along Little Meadow River and the Warrior's Ford, along the head of Gauley River, at the mouth of the Greenbrier, and at the head of Paint Creek.[9] Similar arrangements were made on the upper Ohio. Detachments of militia were stationed at several points along the river from Fort Pitt to the mouth of Fishing Creek, but to give added protection to the Monongahela settlements, com-

[8] Thwaites and Kellogg, eds., *Revolution on the Upper Ohio*, pp. 143-45, 158-59, 185n; Lewis, *First Biennial Report of the Department of Archives and History . . . of West Virginia*, p. 238.

[9] John Stuart to William Fleming, August 2, 1776, Draper MSS, 3ZZ1; John Stuart to William Fleming, August 10, 1776, *ibid.*, 3ZZ2; William Fleming to John Stuart, August 24, 1776, *ibid.*, 3ZZ3; Thwaites and Kellogg, eds., *Revolution on the Upper Ohio*, pp. 179-84.

panies encamped at the heads of Dunkard Creek, a tributary of the Monongahela, and Middle Island Creek. Both were key points on the Scioto–Monongahela Indian trail, which led from the Shawnee towns in Ohio to the middle Monongahela Valley.[10]

Despite these precautions, small bands of Indians, many of them Mingoes, managed to elude the scouts and from the fall of 1776 to the summer of 1777 attacked isolated settlements from Kentucky to West Virginia's Northern Panhandle and deep into the Monongahela Valley. In March, 1777, the council of Virginia voted to dispatch a punitive expedition into the Indian country, but George Morgan, whom Congress had appointed Indian agent for the Middle Department, feared that such a campaign might escalate into a general Indian war and induced Congress to restrain Virginia. When Virginia yielded, Congress assumed a more positive role in frontier defense by sending Brigadier General Edward Hand to Fort Pitt on June 1, with orders to coordinate all defense measures on the upper Ohio.

Even before Hand arrived at Fort Pitt, the British government had instructed Henry Hamilton, its governor and commandant at Detroit, to convene a grand council of the Indians northwest of the Ohio for the purpose of inducing them to abandon their neutrality. The plan to make the Indians active allies was part of the general British military strategy for 1777, by which expeditions from Canada, Oswego, and New York, led by John Burgoyne, Barry St. Leger, and William Howe, respectively, would join forces in the Hudson Valley and cut off New England from the rest of the colonies. Hamilton's assignment envisioned only diversionary activities which would augment the chances of success of the major operation. In June, Hamilton assembled chiefs representing the Ottawa, Huron, Chippewa, Miami, Wyandot, Mingo, Shawnee, and Delaware tribes. He won over the Chippewa and Ottawa chiefs and some of the Wyandots and Mingoes, but was unable to obtain commitments from the

[10] Dorsey Pentecost to David Shepherd, September 4, 1776, Draper MSS, 1SS15; Dorsey Pentecost to William Harrod, October 16, 1776, *ibid.*, 4NN28; Dorsey Pentecost to Patrick Henry, November 5, 1776, *ibid.*, 13S190-91; Thwaites and Kellogg, eds., *Revolution on the Upper Ohio*, pp. 195-96, 207-208, 212-14.

Delawares and Shawnees, whose lands lay closest to the dreaded Virginia "Long Knives."[11]

Friendly Indians and missionaries lost little time in carrying reports of Hamilton's coup to commanders of the forts along the Ohio. On July 25, Nonhelema, a sister of Cornstalk and a trusted friend of the whites, informed Matthew Arbuckle that the Shawnees had been planning a friendly visit to Fort Randolph when they learned of the agreement at Detroit. They had then altered their plans and gone into a tribal council at Chillicothe. According to Arbuckle's information, the western tribes planned to destroy Fort Randolph and Fort Henry, formerly Fort Fincastle, at Wheeling, either by storming those defenses or starving out their occupants, and then striking at the settlements to which the forts gave cover. Three days later David Zeisberger, the Moravian missionary, warned Hand at Fort Pitt that all the western tribes, with the exception of the Delawares, were likely to become allies of the British.[12]

Reports from the Indian country became increasingly ominous. In early August Moravian missionaries warned Hand that the Indians were preparing a major attack upon the West Virginia frontier, but that they had been unable to learn its exact target. Hand immediately ordered Colonel David Shepherd, the lieutenant of Ohio County, to leave his own fort at the forks of Wheeling Creek and to take charge of Fort Henry, which at that time had no regular garrison. He further directed Shepherd to assemble at Fort Henry all the militia companies between the Ohio and Monongahela rivers. In response to Shepherd's call, eleven companies gathered at Fort Henry, but when the end of August came and no attack had occurred, Shepherd concluded that reports of an assault were either unfounded or the attack was not planned for Fort Henry. He permitted nine of the companies to return home, leaving only two, the local company under Captain Samuel Mason and the supply company

11 Thwaites and Kellogg, eds., *Frontier Defense on the Upper Ohio*, pp. 7-13, 36-37, 40; Buck and Buck, *Planting of Civilization in Western Pennsylvania*, pp. 186-87.

12 Matthew Arbuckle to William Fleming, July 26, 1777, Draper MSS, 1U68; David Zeisberger to Edward Hand, July 29, 1777, *ibid.*, 1U69; Thwaites and Kellogg, eds., *Frontier Defense on the Upper Ohio.* pp. 25-29.

from the Beech Bottom fort, twelve miles north of Wheeling, under Captain Joseph Ogle. Altogether less than sixty men remained on duty at Fort Henry.

Hardly had the nine companies departed when the blow fell. During the night of August 31 about two hundred Wyandots and Mingoes, accompanied by a few Delawares and Shawnees, crossed the Ohio to the vicinity of the fort. They concealed themselves in a cornfield, where they formed two long columns extending from Wheeling Creek to the Ohio River. Between the columns six Indians acted as decoys. The first intimation of their presence came about sunrise on September 1. Andrew Zane, John Boyd, Samuel Tomlinson, and a Negro left the stockade to search for horses belonging to Dr. James McMechen, who planned to leave that day for either the Monongahela or settlements east of the Alleghenies. The six Indians fired upon the party and killed Boyd. Zane escaped by leaping over a cliff, which tradition insists was seventy feet high. The Indians permitted Tomlinson and the Negro to escape, knowing that they would sound the alarm at the fort and bring some of its defenders outside the walls.

The Indian strategy worked perfectly. Captain Mason, believing there to be only a few Indians in the vicinity, sallied out of the fort with fourteen men. The Indians drew the rescuing party some distance from the fort and then fell upon its members and cut them to pieces. The cries of the militiamen brought a second detachment of twelve men under Ogle to their aid, but this force suffered a similar fate. Of the twenty-six men who left the fort, only three, including Captains Mason and Ogle, escaped death.

For three days and three nights the Indians besieged Fort Henry, whose garrison now numbered only thirty-three men. Although they failed in their efforts to storm its gates, the Indians left behind a scene of desolation when they retired across the Ohio River. According to Ebenezer Zane, "they burnt all the houses &c. without the Garrison to the number of about 25 and destroyed all the Cattle Horses &c in the settlement[.] thus a great proportion of the inhabitants were left without a bed to

lay on a morsel of bread or milk to feed their families, or even
many of them without a garment to clothe themselves the alarm
having been given soon after daylight in the morning and the
women and children retreating to the fort for safety without
taken even a garment to cover them[.]"[13]

The assault upon Fort Henry proved but the prelude to an
autumn and winter of unprecedented horror for the Allegheny
frontier. As early as July 15 Hamilton had dispatched fifteen
bands of Indians, each including one or two white men, to the
frontiers. Within six months they had delivered to the commandant 73 prisoners and 129 scalps, many of them taken in
transmontane West Virginia. Although Cornstalk, their principal
chief, remained friendly to the Americans, many Shawnees
joined these raiding parties.[14]

The Indian depredations were conducted with frightful
audacity, making "forting" the normal mode of life throughout
the Alleghenies. Parties of Indians who appeared in the Greenbrier area on September 11 displayed typical boldness when
they stormed the house of James Graham, which stood within
three hundred yards of Van Bibber's Fort, killing three persons
and taking another prisoner. On the upper Ohio another band
surprised a small group of settlers near Van Meter's Fort on
Short Creek and killed one of them. On October 13 a woman
was scalped within 150 yards of Coon's Fort on the West Fork
of the Monongahela. Numerous other persons perished or fell
captive during the winter of "the bloody year of the three sevens"
under circumstances which raised doubts as to whether even the
forts offered sufficient protection to induce the inhabitants to

[13] [Alexander Scott Withers], Queries Submitted to the Consideration of Colonel
Ebenezer Zane of Ohio, Tavenner-Withers Papers, Duke University Library. I
have followed Zane's account of the attack on Fort Henry rather than the traditional narrative of Joseph Doddridge, who was only eight years old at the time
of the attack. See also Reminiscences of Dr. Joseph Doddridge, Draper MSS
6NN123-26; Recollections by John Hanks, *ibid.*, 12CC138; Mrs. Joseph
Stagg, *ibid.*, 12CC236-37; and Mrs. Lydia Cruger, *ibid.*, 2S148-51. These accounts
are reproduced in Thwaites and Kellogg, eds., *Frontier Defense on the Upper Ohio*,
pp. 54-68. The version given in Alexander Scott Withers, *Chronicles of Border
Warfare*, ed. Reuben Gold Thwaites, new ed. (Cincinnati, Ohio, 1903), pp. 219-
26, 228, is based upon an account by Noah Zane, son of Ebenezer.
[14] Buck and Buck, *Planting of Civilization in Western Pennsylvania*, pp. 185-86.

remain on their lands. Many families along the exposed Ohio border fled eastward, and the garrison at Fort Henry agreed to remain only until relief might arrive.[15]

Scouting parties sent out from the forts on the Ohio also operated under heavy risk. The most disastrous incident involving a scouting mission was known as "Foreman's Massacre." Forty-six men under Captains William Foreman, William Linn, and Joseph Ogle, set out from Fort Henry on September 26 to reconnoiter as far south as Captina Creek. At the mouth of Grave Creek, where they expected to obtain canoes, they found the inhabitants gone and the fort in ashes. The party decided to encamp for the night and to return to Fort Henry the next morning. On the journey back, Linn, an experienced frontiersman, led his men along the crests of the hills, but Foreman, dismissing any danger of attack on so large a force, kept to the riverbank. At McMechen's Narrows, about midway between Moundsville and Wheeling, Indians ambushed the party, killing Foreman and twenty of his men and capturing another.[16]

General Hand had sought to forestall the bloody events of the fall and winter of 1777 by sending an expedition against the Indian towns, particularly those of the Wyandots and the hated Pluggy's Town confederacy. At the end of July he issued a call for 2,000 men, the minimum number considered necessary to intimidate the tribes and secure peace on the frontiers. Hand ordered recruits from western Virginia to rendezvous at Fort Henry, Fort Randolph, and Fort Kerns, the last at present Morgantown. In spite of the cooperation of Governor Patrick Henry, Hand was able to raise only half the required number of

[15] David McClure to Edward Hand, September 8, 1777, Draper MSS, 1U93; John Van Bibber to William Fleming, September 11, 1777, *ibid.*, 3ZZ10; David Shepherd to Edward Hand, September 15, 1777, *ibid.*, 1U94; Zackwell Morgan to Edward Hand, September 18, 1777, *ibid.*, 1U98; Thwaites and Kellogg, eds., *Frontier Defense on the Upper Ohio*, pp. 76-79, 83-85, 93, 129-32, 135. For conditions at Fort Henry, see James Chew to Edward Hand, October 10, 1777, Draper MSS, 4ZZ12.

[16] David Shepherd to Edward Hand, September 27, 1777, Draper MSS, 6ZZ9; John Van Meter to Edward Cook, September 28, 1777, *ibid.*, 6ZZ10; Daniel Mc-Farland to Edward Hand, September 30, 1777, *ibid.*, 6ZZ11; Recollections of Rachel Johnson, *ibid.*, 2S280-81; Petition of John Cullins, *ibid.*, 2E67; Thwaites and Kellogg, eds., *Frontier Defense on the Upper Ohio*, pp. 106-12; Withers, *Chronicles of Border Warfare*, pp. 228-30.

men. Monongalia, Ohio, and Yohogania counties relied upon volunteers to fill their quotas, seldom a successful method when homes and families were thereby left exposed. In Botetourt County, where methods of raising its quota were left to William Fleming, the county lieutenant, the six-months' term of enlistment stipulated by Hand discouraged recruiting. Only relatively unendangered Hampshire County filled its assigned quota.[17]

Discouraging as were the failures of the counties to supply their quotas for the proposed expedition, Hand's decision to postpone the move until the following spring seems not to have been definitely made until after his visit to Fort Henry in the fall of 1777. On November 2, after viewing the destruction at Fort Henry, Hand wrote his wife that he despaired of "being able to do anything effectual this season. If I can assist the inhabitants to stand their ground, and wait the event of our success to the Northward," he said, "I shall now deem myself doing a great deal." Acting upon this assessment of the situation, Hand ordered 150 militia stationed in each of the frontier counties during the winter months.[18]

Meanwhile, an incident at Fort Randolph added immeasurably to the danger confronting the trans-Allegheny pioneers. Early in November, Cornstalk, accompanied by two other Indians, arrived at the fort, ostensibly to inform Matthew Arbuckle that the Shawnees had, against the chief's desires, insisted upon joining the British and that Cornstalk, as a friend to the Americans, felt obligated to tell Arbuckle that he could no longer restrain his warriors from attacking the whites. Arbuckle suspected the truth of Cornstalk's story and detained him at Fort Randolph until he could obtain the advice of General Hand as to the course he should pursue. On November 9, Elinipsico,

[17] Patrick Henry to Edward Hand, July 27, 1777, Draper MSS, 18J26; Edward Hand to William Fleming, August 12, 1777, *ibid.*, 1U80; Zackwell Morgan to William Harrod, August 15, 1777, *ibid.*, 4NN58; Zackwell Morgan to Edward Hand, August 25, 1777, *ibid.*, 3NN154-55; David Shepherd to Edward Hand, August 28, 1777, *ibid.*, 1U87; Edward Hand to George Washington, November 9, 1777, *ibid.*, 15S113; Edward Hand to Patrick Henry, November 9, 1777, *ibid.*, 3NN62-63; Thwaites and Kellogg, eds., *Frontier Defense on the Upper Ohio*, pp. 30-33, 42-44, 48-50, 154-55.

[18] Edward Hand to Patrick Henry, November 9, 1777, Draper MSS, 3NN62-63; [Congressional] Commissioner to Edward Hand, 3NN21-23; Thwaites and Kellogg, eds., *Frontier Defense on the Upper Ohio*, pp. 146, 154-55, 238-40.

Cornstalk's son, visited Fort Randolph in order to ascertain the fate of his father. He, too, was held. The killing of two hunters by Indians the following day convinced most of the militia at the fort of Cornstalk's duplicity. Enraged, they demanded retribution, and in spite of Arbuckle's efforts to prevent them, headstrong militiamen killed the old chief, Elinipsico, and their companions.[19]

For most settlers the prospects of Shawnee retaliation for Cornstalk's death appeared too horrible to contemplate. Swayed by the pleas of Colonel William Preston and an urgent petition of the Greenbrier residents, Governor Patrick Henry recommended additional defensive measures, which were approved by the council on February 19, 1778. They envisioned the ranging of scouts into the Indian country, the strengthening of stockades for the security of the settlers, the erection of a post at the mouth of Elk River, and the addition of fifty Botetourt militia to the garrison of Fort Randolph. On the other hand, the council sought to appease the Indians by calling upon the settlers to assist in bringing the killers of Cornstalk and his companions to justice, but this was no more than a futile gesture.[20]

Problems of frontier defense were complicated by the shortage of arms and ammunition. In July, 1776, Captain George Gibson and Lieutenant William Linn of the Virginia militia, with fifteen men, had made their way from Fort Pitt down the Ohio and Mississippi rivers to New Orleans, where they hoped to purchase a supply of gunpowder. Spanish officials permitted them to buy 12,000 pounds, but insisted that the transaction be conducted in such a manner as to preserve at least the illusion of Spanish neutrality. It was decided that Gibson should remain in New Orleans in deference to the desire of the Spanish authorities

[19] Matthew Arbuckle to Edward Hand, November 7, 1777, Draper MSS, 3NN78, 79; Narrative of John Stuart, *ibid.*, 6NN105-12; Deposition of John Anderson, William Ward, and Richard Thomas, *ibid.*, 3NN80; Edward Hand to Samuel McDowell, December 5, 1777, *ibid.*, 3NN67; Edward Hand to Patrick Henry, December 9, 1777, *ibid.*, 3NN69-71; Thwaites and Kellogg, eds., *Frontier Defense on the Upper Ohio*, pp. 149-50, 157-63, 175-77.

[20] H. R. McIlwaine and Wilmer Hall, eds., *Journals of the Council of the State of Virginia*, 3 vols. (Richmond, Va., 1931-1952), II, 86-87; Patrick Henry to William Fleming, February 19, 1778, Draper MSS, 15ZZ17; Patrick Henry to William Preston and William Fleming, March 27, 1778, *ibid.*, 15ZZ23; Thwaites and Kellogg, eds., *Frontier Defense on the Upper Ohio*, pp. 205-209, 240-41.

to appear neutral. Linn, with fifty-three men, took charge of the powder and in May, 1777, safely landed 9,000 pounds of the precious cargo at Fort Henry. Not only did Linn's feat relieve the shortage of gunpowder on the upper Ohio frontier, but it probably had a significant bearing upon the failure of the Indians to reduce Fort Henry in September, 1777.[21]

The need for arms and ammunition, made all the more acute by the Indian depredations of the winter of 1777–1778, prompted the only offensive move made by General Hand against the Indians. In February, 1778, Hand set out with some 500 men, drawn largely from Westmoreland, for the mouth of the Cuyahoga River, where the British had reportedly established a powder magazine. The progress of the expedition was so impeded by floods in Beaver River that the men had to confine their efforts to raiding two towns of the Delaware Indians. Three Indians were killed—a man, a woman, and a boy—but the only booty taken by Hand's men consisted of two squaws. The disappointed settlers derisively dubbed Hand's excursion into the Indian country the "Squaw Campaign."[22]

In June, 1778, David Rogers and about forty men from the Monongahela Valley set out, on orders of Governor Henry, "on an Embassy to New Orleans to negotiate Business of Importance" to Virginia and her western settlers. Rogers hoped to repeat the fruitful mission of William Linn. Like Linn, Rogers obtained a supply of gunpowder, as well as medicines and other needed articles. On October 4, 1779, as it was returning up the Ohio River, Indians led by the Girty brothers attacked the party, killing Rogers and seizing the five batteaux which carried the goods.[23]

21 Dorsey Pentecost to William Harrod, January 28, 1777, Draper MSS, 4NN46; Zackwell Morgan to William Harrod, May 7, 1777, *ibid.*, 4NN54; Thwaites and Kellogg, eds., *Revolution on the Upper Ohio*, pp. 226-29, 252-53.

22 Edward Hand to William Crawford, February 5, 1778, Draper MSS, 3NN95; Edward Hand to David Shepherd, March 7, 1778, *ibid.*, 3NN100; Recollections of Samuel Murphy, ibid., 3S28-32; Thwaites and Kellogg, ed., *Frontier Defense on the Upper Ohio*, pp. 201-202, 215-22.

23 Hampshire County Legislative Petitions, November 3, 1786; Patrick Henry to Edward Hand, January 15, 1778, Draper MSS, 3NN199; Thwaites and Kellogg, eds., *Revolution on the Upper Ohio*, p. 232n; Don Bernardo de Galvez to Thomas Jefferson, 1780, Lawrence Kinnaird, ed., *Spain in the Mississippi Valley, 1765–1794*, American Historical Association *Annual Report, 1945*, 4 vols. (Washington, D. C., 1949), I, 375-76; Randolph C. Downes, *Council Fires on the Upper Ohio:*

During the summer of 1778 the Indians poured bitter vengence upon the West Virginia frontier. To what extent their attacks were specifically reprisals for the murder of Cornstalk, however, is not clear. On May 16, about 300 Indians, mostly Wyandots and Mingoes, appeared before Fort Randolph and demanded its surrender. Captain William McKee, who had charge of the fort during a temporary absence of Matthew Arbuckle, refused to surrender or to send men out to battle. The Indians thereupon spent the remainder of the day killing nearly all of the 150 cattle which grazed outside the walls of the fort. As evening came on, they changed their tactics and pretended that they really wanted peace. McKee clutched at even this slender straw and sent Nonhelema, also known by her baptismal name of Katy, outside the fort to read the Indians a proclamation of Governor Henry which expressed the desire of Virginia for peace with the Indians. The Indians feigned approval of the governor's message and promised to withdraw across the Ohio.

McKee's close observation of the movements of the Indians, however, soon disclosed that they were stealing up the Kanawha toward the Greenbrier settlements. On May 18 McKee dispatched two men to warn the Greenbrier residents, but, finding Indians on both sides of the Kanawha, they hastened back to Fort Randolph. Believing that a messenger must be sent to the Greenbrier inhabitants at all costs, McKee called for volunteers. John Pryor and Philip Hammond courageously offered to undertake the dangerous mission. Disguised as Indian warriors by the artistry of Nonhelema, they overtook the Indians at Meadow River, only twenty miles from Fort Donnally. They succeeded in passing the Indians without being detected and about sunset reached that little outpost of the Greenbrier frontier. The alarm was immediately sounded, settlers hastily herded into the fort, and water barrels filled in anticipation of attack.

A Narrative of Indian Affairs in the Upper Ohio Valley until 1795 (Pittsburgh, Pa., 1940), pp. 255-56. Rogers' widow, Mary, who later married John Jeremiah Jacob, a well-known Methodist minister of West Virginia, was granted a tract of land in recognition of Rogers' efforts. Hampshire County Legislative Petitions, December 9, 1797.

The Indians struck about dawn. The defenders, numbering some twenty-five men and about sixty women and children, put up a vigorous fight until about three o'clock in the afternoon. By that time Matthew Arbuckle and Samuel Lewis arrived with sixty-six men from Camp Union. Creeping up to the rear of the fort, the relief party opened a devastating fire upon the Indians, forcing them to scatter in all directions. All of the rescuers, almost miraculously, then entered the fort safely. The Indians soon returned to the attack, but within a short time they lost seventeen men. Unwilling that their numbers should be further decimated, they broke up into small parties and confined their depredations to small-scale attacks upon isolated farmsteads. In contrast to the casualties sustained by the Indians, the defenders of the fort lost only four men.[24]

As in similar instances, the assault upon Fort Donnally produced its share of local heroes, but none of the fort's defenders gained more glory than Dick Pointer, a Negro slave belonging to Andrew Donnally. When Indians broke into the yard of the enclosure and attempted to ram the door of the house, Pointer placed large water barrels against the door. He then exerted his own strength against the Indians, "who had nigh forced open the Door, and by that means gave time to the inhabitants who were collected there to arm themselves and defeat the attempts of those Invaders." Numerous witnesses bore testimony to Pointer's crucial role in saving the fort. Years later, in 1795, many of the grateful survivors supported the aging Negro when he addressed a moving appeal to the Virginia

---

[24] Matthew Arbuckle to Edward Hand, June 2, 1778, Draper MSS, 18J76; David Zeisberger to George Morgan, June 9, 1778, *ibid.*, 3NN120-21; Arthur Campbell to Charles Cummings, June 10, 1778, *ibid.*, 18J77; William McKee to Edward Hand, June 21, 1778, *ibid.*, 3NN210-13; Notes of Hugh Paul Taylor, *ibid.*, 32S13-18; Account of John Stuart, *ibid.*, 6NN112-18; Louise Phelps Kellogg, ed., *Frontier Advance on the Upper Ohio, 1778–1779* (Madison, Wis., 1916), pp. 64-65, 73, 82-86, 98. On May 18, 1784, Hammond and Pryor asked the General Assembly for a grant of land in compensation for their services, which would "also be an Excitement to others to decline no Dangers in the Service of their Country when they find the same will be amply rewarded." John Stuart, lieutenant of Greenbrier County, and Colonels Andrew Donnally, Samuel Brown, and Andrew Hamilton verified statements of Hammond and Pryor regarding their 200-mile journey and their participation in the defense of Fort Donnally. Greenbrier County Legislative Petitions, June 12, 1784. See also James Wade's Statement, Draper MSS, 12CC26.

General Assembly requesting that he "in the decline of life shall be at public expense liberated, and enjoy by the bounty of the legislature that freedom he has long sighed for."[25]

If Virginia's defensive measures seemed inadequate, it must be remembered that she had to spread her military strength over a vast frontier extending from central Kentucky to the forks of the Ohio. Moreover, the remote Kentucky settlements were as hard pressed as those of West Virginia. After failing in an assault upon Boonesborough in March, 1777, Chief Blackfish and about 300 Shawnees spent the summer in central Kentucky, keeping all of the stations in a virtual state of siege. The dispatch of Colonel John Bowman and a hundred men to Fort Harrod in August and another fifty in September induced Blackfish to retire across the Ohio, but he left behind him a desolate land with "no bread, no salt, no vegetables, no fruit of any kind, no ardent spirits, nothing but meat." By January, 1778, when Daniel Boone and thirty men visited the Blue Licks on Licking River for the purpose of obtaining a supply of salt, the defense capability of the Kentucky settlements had reached a dangerously low point. When Boone, who was out hunting, was seized by a party of Shawnees, he led his captors to his men at the salt spring, knowing that such a move would likely prevent the Indians from attacking the nearly defenseless stations. During his captivity, however, Boone learned of another planned attack upon Fort Boonesborough. He knew that he must take the risks incident to an effort to escape and warn the settlers of the impending assault. Thanks to Boone's courage, Boonesborough withstood an attack by 400 warriors followed by a siege that lasted for nine days.[26]

Nor, in the interest of proper perspective, should it be overlooked that the frontiers of other states from New York to the

[25] Greenbrier County Legislative Petitions, November 12, 1795; Notes of Hugh Paul Taylor, Draper MSS, 32S13-18; Account of John Stuart, *ibid.*, 6NN112-18; Kellogg, ed., *Frontier Advance on the Upper Ohio*, pp. 69-70, 72-73; Withers, *Chronicles of Border Warfare*, pp. 243-44.

[26] Ray Allen Billington, *Westward Expansion: A History of the American Frontier*, 3d ed. (New York, 1967), pp. 177-79; Thomas D. Clark, *A History of Kentucky*, (Lexington, Ky., 1954), pp. 53-55; Charles Gano Talbert, *Benjamin Logan: Kentucky Frontiersman* (Lexington, Ky., 1962), pp. 50-67.

Carolinas shared the horrors visited upon the West Virginia and Kentucky settlements. In New York, General St. Leger, with an army of 1,700 men, including both Tories and Indians, was ordered to move from Oswego along the Mohawk to a junction with Burgoyne's army, which was advancing down Lake Champlain. After an unsuccessful seventeen-day siege of Fort Stanwix, St. Leger retired to Oswego, but the American relief expedition of 800 men under General Nicholas Herkimer was ambushed at Oriskany by 400 Indians and a small detachment of Tory rangers. The battle, much of it hand-to-hand combat featuring the use of musket, tomahawk, and knife, raged for hours. Although Herkimer took a heavy toll of his attackers, his own losses included about 200 casualties and dozens of prisoners, and he himself was mortally wounded. In June, 1778, Colonel John Butler with 1,000 Indians and Tories fell upon the 5,000 residents of the Wyoming Valley in Pennsylvania, killing 360 of them and leaving scores of others to die of exposure and starvation.[27]

Most of the terror-stricken frontiersmen of West Virginia and Kentucky knew that there would be no significant abatement in the dangers to which they were exposed until the seats of British power in the West were broken. As long as Detroit, in particular, remained in British hands, the frontier would not provide the margin of safety needed to induce settlers to stand their ground or encourage prospective immigrants to resume the march westward across the Alleghenies. The Continental Congress, however, was so burdened by the military needs of other fighting fronts that it was unwilling to authorize any major expedition against British posts in the West.

As had so often happened before, the most significant—and in this case the most spectacular—blow against the British and Indians was struck by Virginia. During the winter of 1777–1778 young George Rogers Clark prevailed upon the Virginia legislature to permit him to undertake an expedition against Indians in the Illinois country. A successful venture, Clark believed, would weaken the British influence with western Indians, enable

27 Billington, *Westward Expansion*, p. 180; John Richard Alden, *The American Revolution, 1775–1783* (New York, 1954), pp. 136–39.

the Americans to make freer use of the Mississippi, and enhance Virginia's claims to the Northwest. Clark gathered about 150 men from the Monongahela Valley and added twenty more, one of whom was Simon Kenton, from the Kentucky settlements. On June 26, 1778, he set out from Fort Massac, ten miles below the falls of the Ohio, with 175 seasoned riflemen. Proceeding overland rather than by the more widely traveled rivers, Clark reached Kaskaskia on July 4 and took the British completely by surprise. He repeated his success at Cahokia, while Father Gibault, a priest from Kaskaskia, carried the news of Clark's victories to Vincennes and accepted the surrender of that post. Clark readily gained the support of the French *habitants,* who were informed of the recently concluded alliance between the United States and France. Moreover, most of the Indians of the upper Mississippi and even a few of the Ohio tribes responded to either Clark's bravado or to his distribution of presents by proclaiming friendship with the United States.

Clark's accomplishments were threatened when Governor Hamilton set out from Detroit in October with 500 British and Indians for the purpose of recapturing the Illinois outposts. In December Hamilton seized Vincennes, but unusually heavy rains prevented his moving on the other forts. When Clark learned, through a trader, that Vincennes had fallen, he acted quickly. Displaying once again the decisiveness and reckless audacity which had brought his original successes, he set out immediately for Vincennes with 172 men. For 180 miles the little party traveled through mud and rain, and for the last twenty miles they waded icy waters, often up to their shoulders. But their determination was rewarded, and at dusk on February 23 they stole into Vincennes. Although he had only thirty-three able-bodied men and was low on provisions, Hamilton resisted the attack, but after a night of battle, he surrendered. The triumphant Clark sent the British soldiers, including the governor himself, to Virginia as prisoners of war.[28]

Meanwhile, the disastrous incursions upon the frontiers had at

[28] Good brief accounts of Clark's expedition are in Billington, *Westward Expansion,* pp. 181-83; Thomas D. Clark, *Frontier America: The Story of the Westward Movement* (New York, 1959), pp. 112-19.

last forced Congress to act. After investigating conditions at Fort Pitt, it named General Lachlan McIntosh to succeed Hand and ordered the Eighth Pennsylvania, the part of the Thirteenth Virginia then in the East, and two new regiments, yet to be raised, to the frontier. In June the Board of War instructed McIntosh to move against Detroit with 3,000 regulars, augmented with not more than 2,500 Virginia militia. The governor and council of Virginia, however, opposed the expedition. Virginia's opposition, coupled with the needs of other battlefronts, induced Congress to alter its plans. On July 25 it voted to postpone the attack upon Detroit and instead to assemble 1,500 regulars and militia at Fort Pitt for the purpose of destroying the towns of the Indians.

Virginia's opposition to the strike against Detroit apparently stemmed in part from a belief that George Rogers Clark could capture that stronghold, thereby rendering the McIntosh expedition unnecessary, and from fears that a successful move by McIntosh might detract from the state's claims to the Northwest. But Virginia authorities were also besieged with wails of distress from the northwestern counties, particularly after the attacks on Fort Randolph and Fort Donnally, and with pleas for immediate retaliation against the Indians. When the expedition planned by McIntosh proved slow in getting started, Governor Henry responded sympathetically to the cries of the frontier and authorized a punitive force of 600 men, who would strike into the Indian country by way of the Kanawha and Fort Randolph. The council, however, disallowed the plan.

At last, in October, after many delays, McIntosh's army began its advance. It moved down the Ohio to the mouth of Beaver Creek, where the troops built a large post known at Fort McIntosh. In November McIntosh with 1,200 men pressed on to the Tuscarawas River in the land of the Delawares and built Fort Laurens. The effectiveness of this outpost, however, was largely nullified by the expiration of militia enlistments in December and by the inadequacy of its supplies. Although it was reduced to the necessity of appealing to the Delawares for food to sustain the garrison during the winter and was besieged by British-led Indians in March, Fort Laurens survived, but its weaknesses made it anything but a major bastion of frontier defense. McIntosh's campaign thus failed almost entirely to accomplish its purpose of chastising the Indians.[29]

Nevertheless, the successes of George Rogers Clark, the probable effects of the French alliance upon the outcome of the war, and McIntosh's preparations for invasion of the Indian territory combined with attacks upon the Iroquois led by General Daniel Brodhead, the new commandant at Fort Pitt, and John Sullivan to weaken the power of the Six Nations and to elevate American prestige to its greatest heights since the outbreak of the Revolution. In the fall of 1779 the situation had so improved that delegations of Wyandots and some Shawnees journeyed to Fort Pitt for the purpose of arranging a peace. Although the West Virginia frontier continued to experience Indian incursions, attacks diminished somewhat in frequency and intensity.

Unfortunately, American prestige did not rest upon a solid basis, and the apparent advantages which the Americans held proved highly ephemeral. When the Girtys apprehended the David Rogers party en route from New Orleans to Fort Pitt in October, 1779, they learned, through letters which Rogers was carrying, just how tenuous were the footholds which George Rogers Clark had established in the Illinois country. Disclosures of the weakness of the American position had immediate effects upon the Indians. The Wyandots, who a few months previously had courted American favor, renewed their alliance with the British, and in February, 1781, even the Delawares deserted the Americans for the British.[30] With the defection of the Delawares, American influence over western tribes reached its nadir.

Hoping to stave off an attack by the Delawares, General Brodhead began to assemble an army to strike at the Indians before they could gather their forces. In April, Brodhead, with about 300 men, about equally divided between regulars and

---

[29] William Fleming to Patrick Henry, July 19, 1778, Draper MSS, 2U37; William Christian to Arthur Campbell, September 10, 1778, *ibid.*, 9DD18; William Christian to William Fleming, September 10, 1778, *ibid.*, 2U45; Kellogg, ed., *Frontier Advance on the Upper Ohio*, pp.115-16, 134-37; Downes, *Council Fires on the Upper Ohio*, pp. 212-15, 217-27; Buck and Buck, *Planting of Civilization in Western Pennsylvania*, pp. 190-92.

[30] Downes, *Council Fires on the Upper Ohio*, pp. 251-56; Buck and Buck, *Planting of Civilization in Western Pennsylvania*, pp. 192-96.

militia, moved against the Delawares, destroying their towns of Coshocton and Lichtenau, killing fifteen warriers, capturing twenty prisoners, and taking much plunder. The militia, however, refused to engage in further chastisement, and Brodhead was obliged to withdraw. The expedition returned to Wheeling, where the plunder was sold and the money divided among the participants.[31]

Problems of frontier defense were further complicated by the shifting of the major theater of war to the South, where British armies had overrun large parts of Georgia and the Carolinas by 1780. Virginia's plans, for example, to establish a post of communications between the Greenbrier settlements and Fort Randolph at Kelly's Creek, about twenty miles below the falls of the Kanawha, were delayed until 1780 as a result of the Indian incursions during the summer of 1778 and the demands of the armies on other military fronts. The needs of the East may also have been responsible for the abandonment of Fort Randolph in 1779 and its subsequent burning by the Indians.[32]

The summer of 1781 might have proved especially disastrous for the West Virginia settlements had it not been for the Indians' knowledge that George Rogers Clark was assembling a large expedition for an attack upon Detroit. During the winter of 1780–1781 Clark made plans to advance upon Detroit with an army of 2,000 men, gathered from the Virginia backcountry. Despite his energetic preparations, Clark was unable to raise the necessary men. Few counties cared to jeopardize their defenses by relinquishing a part of their militia, and enthusiasm among the militiamen themselves was singularly lacking. Officers of Berkeley County declared that it would be impossible to

[31] Buck and Buck, *Planting of Civilization in Western Pennsylvania,* p. 196.

[32] The post at Kelly's Creek was proposed in 1778 but rejected in the belief that limited manpower could best be employed by stationing militia at the Greenbrier posts. William Fleming to William Preston, June 16, 1778, Draper MSS, 4QQ177; William Preston to William Fleming, *ibid.,* 2U29; Andrew Lewis to Joseph Crockett, August 10, 1780, *ibid.,* 50J55; Kellogg, ed., *Frontier Advance on the Upper Ohio,* pp. 93-94; Louise Phelps Kellogg, ed., *Frontier Retreat on the Upper Ohio, 1779–1781* (Madison, Wis., 1917), p. 243; McIlwaine and Hall, eds., *Journals of the Council of the State of Virginia,* II, 111; Petition of Greenbrier Inhabitants, September 19, 1781, W. P. Palmer and others, eds., *Calendar of Virginia State Papers and Other Manuscripts,* 11 vols. (Richmond, Va., 1875-1893), II, 468-69.

raise 275 men in that county, predicting that "those whose Turn it now is to go from this County will suffer any punishment rather than obey our orders for their march." Greenbrier officers requested that since their total strength was only 550 men and the county was exposed to "the daily inroads of the Indians, they be given a postponement in filling their quota of 146 men." The exemption of some 600 or 700 men from Berkeley, Frederick, and Hampshire counties was regarded by Clark as "too great a stroke to recover," a blow made all the heavier by Clark's belief that the militia of those counties "would have marched with cheerfullness, had they not been encouraged to ye contrary." Finally, Clark could expect no aid from Ohio and Monongalia counties, it being said that the 300 men whom they had provided for the earlier expedition against the Moravian towns had participated in that expedition only to avoid serving in any force moving against Detroit.[33]

Clark had other difficulties in recruiting. Although his proposal had the support of both Governor Thomas Jefferson and Washington, local conditions sapped the expedition of its strength. Brodhead, who had been instructed by Washington to provide Clark with as many men as possible, proved generally unsympathetic to the project. Western Pennsylvanians, embittered over the long boundary dispute with Virginia, declined to join Clark's expedition, although the council of the state specifically granted them permission to do so. Even after he assembled 400 men at Wheeling, Clark's force suffered such depletion from desertions that he was forced to leave Fort Henry on August 8 without waiting for a detachment of about 100 Westmoreland men under Archibald Lochry.

Clark's plan suffered its coup de grace in an attack upon Lochry's party, which followed some days behind the main force. About twenty miles below Cincinnati, a large band of Indians led by Alexander McKee and Joseph Brant, the Mohawk

<hr />

[33] Philip Pendleton, *et al.*, to Thomas Jefferson, January 25, 1781, Palmer and others, eds., *Calendar of Virginia State Papers*, I, 461; Andrew Donnally, Samuel Brown, and Andrew Hamilton to Thomas Jefferson, January 29, 1781, *ibid.*, pp. 468-69; George Rogers Clark to Thomas Jefferson, March 27, 1781, *ibid.*, p. 597; George Rogers Clark to Thomas Jefferson, May 23, 1781, *ibid.*, II, 117; John Gibson to Thomas Jefferson, May 30, 1781, *ibid.*, p. 131.

chieftain, fell upon Lochry's force and killed or captured every member. Such a catastrophe was too great for Clark to overcome.[34]

Clark's inability to recruit a force sufficient to strike at Detroit was in some respects symptomatic of the war weariness which had spread over substantial portions of the West Virginia frontier. Indeed, the trans-Allegheny pioneers had been subjected to a kind of total war, which had spared neither men, women, nor children. Moreover, the incessant requisitions for beef, grain, and other commodities and payment in ever-depreciating paper currency required continuing sacrifices which many farmers were reluctant to make. Andrew Woodrow of Hampshire County declined appointment as commissioner under the provision law on the ground that paper money had totally ceased to pass and that he could give the people no assurance that they would be paid a fair value for supplies. Woodrow declared that nothing could be obtained without compulsion. The provisions in the county were fast spoiling, and those who had wagons refused to carry them without being paid for their labor in specie or its real value.

Similar attitudes prevailed in other part of West Virginia. Although wheat and other commodities were more abundant and cheaper along the Monongahela than in counties east of the Alleghenies, settlers in Monongalia County had by May, 1780, "been so disappointed in giting their cash for articles they have spared" that they would part with nothing more. Even the practice of procuring goods for the public use upon pledges of credit of leading citizens was now of no avail. Andrew Donnally found Greenbrier residents of like mind. Writing in March, 1781, he declared that the depreciation of the currency had been "so rapid that no one will freely credit the Public for Provision or other necessities."[35]

Such conditions were primarily responsible for the wave of Loyalism—or perhaps, more accurately, war weariness—which

[34] Buck and Buck, *Planting of Civilization in Western Pennsylvania,* pp. 196-97.

[35] Andrew Wodrow [Woodrow] to William Davies, September 15, 1781, Palmer and others, eds., *Calendar of Virginia State Papers,* II, 438; John Evans to Philip Bush, May 9, 1780, *ibid.,* I, 348; Andrew Donnally to Thomas Jefferson, March 27, 1781, *ibid.,* p. 601.

swept over parts of West Virginia in 1780. With the exception of Tory plots, which had centered around Fort Pitt and which had attracted some residents of the Monongahela Valley in the fall of 1777, the West Virginia frontier had been until then but little affected by Loyalist propaganda. The areas of West Virginia where disaffection reached its most serious proportions during 1780 and 1781 were east of the Allegheny Front and principally in Hampshire County. Even there, Colonel Garret Van Meter wrote Governor Jefferson, discontent stemmed largely from "the execution of the late Acts of Assembly for Recruiting this states [*sic*] Quota of Troops to serve in the Continental Army, and the Act for supplying the Army with Clothes, Provisions & Waggons."

Resentment burst into resistance when an official went into Hampshire County to collect taxes. "A certain John Claypole said if all the men were of his mind, they would not make up any Cloathes, Beef, or Men, and all that would join him shuld turn out. Upon which he got all the men present, to five or six and Got Liquor and Drank King George the third's health, and Damnation to Congress." Warrants were issued for Claypool and his associates, and the sheriff, with a guard of about fifty men, set out to arrest them. When they reached the scene of the disorder, they found Claypool and about sixty or seventy men prepared to offer resistance. Faced with such opposition, the sheriff decided that discretion was, after all, the better part of valor. He refrained from making the arrests when Claypool agreed to turn himself in at a later time, a promise which Claypool did not keep.

Armed opposition, the chief object of which was "to be clear of Taxes and Draughts," flared up in other parts of Hampshire County. On May 22, 1781, Colonel Elias Poston sent an urgent plea to Frederick County for 300 men, declaring that the "lives and fortunes" of patriotic Hampshire Countians were in danger. On the preceding day the militia had been fired upon and two of them taken prisoner at the mill of John Brake, whose home on the South Fork of the South Branch had frequently served as a meetingplace for the insurgents. Worse still, Claypool was now rumored to be assembling an army of a thousand men in the

Lost River area. Poston declared that nothing less than the dispatch of troops under General Daniel Morgan, who was then in Frederick County, could quiet the disorders in Hampshire County, since Claypool was "so much connected, as well as related" to so many people of the county that it would be impossible to assemble a force in the area to take up arms against him.

Four companies of infantrymen from Frederick County and other recruits under Daniel Morgan dispersed the rioters. Forty-two of them, including Claypool, either surrendered or were captured. Most of the leaders, however, fled over the mountains upon the approach of Morgan's army. Claypool and several of his associates prayed the governor for pardon, declaring that "the petitioners living in an obscure and remote corner of the State, are precluded from every Intelligence of the State of affairs, either by Public Papers or from Information of Men of Credit and Veracity, and at the same time infested by the wicked Emmissaries or pretended Emmissaries of the British who travel through all parts of the Frontier, and by Misrepresentations and false news poisoned the Minds of the Ignorant and credulous Settlers." The petitioners, believing the tax of eighty-two pounds paper money on every three hundred pounds of their property as valued in specie, a bounty for recruits for the Continental Army, and the act for providing clothing for the army were excessive levies, had simply sought to defend what the unpatriotic "wretches called their Liberty and property."

Claypool's defense elicited considerable sympathy. Peter Hog pointed out to the governor that Claypool was the father of five sons who were connected by marriage "with the most considerable Families on those waters, and the strongest friends to our present Constitution, and to prosecute him with rigour, whilst the ringleaders have evaded Justice by flight, and those in similar circumstances of Guilt are pardoned, would probably sour the minds of his numerous connexions, and perhaps by reguarded by them as pointed and partial." Other citizens of Hampshire County vouched for Claypool as an "Honest Peacable well meaning man." Even Daniel Morgan rose to his defense. Morgan called attention to the isolation and ignorance of the people of Hampshire County, but added that the requirements of humanity dictated leniency, since Claypool had a wife and fourteen children, "chiefly small," dependent upon him.[36] Most of the participants were pardoned, and several later served in American armies.

On October 19, 1781, a few months after the disorders in Hampshire County had been quieted, Lord Cornwallis surrendered the British army at Yorktown, thereby ending the war in the East. No prospect of a cessation of hostilities in the West, however, brightened the gloomy autumn days for the trans-Allegheny settlers. Only a month before the collapse of the British position in eastern Virginia, a large band of Indians set out from Sandusky with plans to attack Fort Henry. Friendly Moravian missionaries warned the Wheeling area of the imminent attack and enabled the residents to prepare for an assault. Unfortunately, the hostile Indians learned of the warning and they forced both the Moravian missionaries and the Christianized Indians to move from their towns along the Tuscarawas to Sandusky. From time to time during the winter the Indians returned to their towns to gather corn, which they had left standing in the fields. On such visits they were sometimes accompanied by hostile Indians, one group of which struck at the settlements in Washington County, Pennsylvania, in February, 1782.

Knowing that any raid at that time of year must have originated from the towns along the Tuscarawas, about a hundred Washington County militia, led by Colonel David Williamson, set out to destroy the supposedly deserted villages. On March 7 they descended upon the town of Gnaddenhutten, where they learned, quite by accident, of the presence of some of the Indians who had participated in the attack upon the Washington County

[36] Buck and Buck, *Planting of Civilization in Western Pennsylvania,* p. 189; Garret Van Meter to Thomas Jefferson, April 11, 1781, Palmer and others, eds., *Calendar of Virginia State Papers,* II, 28-29; Garret Van Meter to Thomas Jefferson, April 14, 1781, *ibid.,* pp. 40-41; Garret Van Meter to Thomas Jefferson, April 20, 1781, *ibid.,* pp. 58-59; Elias Poston express to County Lieutenant of Frederick, May 22, 1781, *ibid.,* pp. 113-14; Garret Van Meter to Thomas Jefferson, June 16, 1781, *ibid.,* pp. 163-64; Petition of John Claypole [Claypool], *et al.,* 1781, *ibid.,* pp. 682-83; Peter Hog to Thomas Nelson, August 21, 1781, *ibid.,* pp. 284-85; Undated Hampshire County Petition, *ibid.,* II, 683; Daniel Morgan to Benjamin Harrison, February 10, 1782, *ibid.,* III, 57-58.

settlements. They abandoned their original intention of taking the friendly Indians to Fort Pitt as captives, and in their anger, voted, with only eighteen nays, to kill every Indian present, friendly or hostile. The following morning nearly a hundred Indians, who had spent the night confined in the church, engaged in singing and praying, were killed, women and children along with the men, and the yet unharvested crops were destroyed.

Once again frontier settlers of West Virginia faced the horrors of Indian vengeance. General William Irvine, who had succeeded Brodhead as commandant at Fort Pitt, endeavored to strengthen the defense posture on the upper Ohio by reorganizing the remaining Continental troops stationed there and by repairing the fort.[37] Even so, morale among the trans-Allegheny settlers sank disastrously. Between April 1, 1781, and March 1, 1782, the Tygart Valley settlements suffered three attacks, and the Buckhannon settlers left their homes. Even more exposed were the Monongalia County settlements, and John Evans, the county lieutenant, predicted that most of the residents would leave unless militia were sent to protect them. Some relief was afforded by the arrival on March 26, 1782, of a company of Hampshire County militia. The Tygart Valley settlers, however, objected strenuously to the departure of the Hampshire militia from their own county for Monongalia County, declaring that residents of the latter could "hardly subsist themselves" and that between them and the Tygart Valley there was "no Fort nor Inhabitant for 'fifty-five computed miles, and several Indian paths [were known] to cross that way.'" Declaring that twenty men at the latter place were worth more than fifty at the former, Samuel Brown, lieutenant of Greenbrier County, asked that the guard customarily placed at the mouth of the Kanawha be stationed instead at the mouth of the Elk.[38]

Meanwhile, Irvine sought to calm the fears of the frontiersmen and to avert any massive reprisals for the massacre at Gnaddenhutten by assembling a volunteer expedition to march

[37] Buck and Buck, *Planting of Civilization in Western Pennsylvania*, pp. 197-98.

[38] Benjamin Wilson to Benjamin Harrison, March 1, 1782, Palmer and others, eds., *Calendar of Virginia State Papers*, III, 82; John Evans to Benjamin Harrison, March 9, 1782, *ibid.*, pp. 89-90; Joseph Nevill to Benjamin Harrison, March 21, 1782, *ibid.*, p. 105; Samuel Brown to Benjamin Harrison, February 16, 1782, *ibid.*, p. 65.

against the Indian towns. At the end of May, about 500 mounted men, with Colonel William Crawford as their leader, set out for the Wyandot town of Sandusky. The attackers found the town deserted, but on June 4 they engaged a large party of Wyandots in battle. The arrival of reinforcements for the Indians threw the militia into a panic, and Crawford ordered a retreat. The routed frontiersmen fled in great disorder, but more than 300 returned home safely on June 12. A large number of them, however, including Crawford, were captured. As retaliation for the murder of the residents of Gnaddenhutten, the Indians treated Crawford to a hideous death by slow roasting.[39]

A few weeks later a large party of Wyandots, Delawares, and Shawnees set out for Wheeling. The Shawnees, alarmed by reports that George Rogers Clark was about to attack their towns, deserted their allies. Despite their withdrawal, the remainder of the attacking force, consisting of more than 200 Wyandots, Delawares, and British, under the command of Joseph Brant, hastened on to Wheeling. Their approach was discovered by John Linn, a scout, whose timely warning enabled the inhabitants to take shelter either within the stockade of Fort Henry or in the house of Colonel Ebenezer Zane, which stood forty yards from the fort.

On September 10 the Indians laid siege to Fort Henry. Unfortunately, the Wheeling residents had not prepared for a sustained attack. Part of the supply of military stores had been placed at Zane's house, and a quantity sufficient only for a limited defense had been taken into the fort. On the other hand, the riflemen who remained at Zane's house were able to subject the Indians to a crossfire which made their assault upon the enclosure extremely hazardous.

Failure in their efforts to storm the fort proved exceedingly frustrating to the Indians. More than once they must have heaped verbal abuse upon the commandant at Detroit, who had refused to supply them with cannon. Then there came what must have appeared as a stroke of fortune. A small boat moving upstream and laden with cannonballs for Fort Pitt put ashore at Wheeling. The little craft and its cargo promptly fell into the hands of the

[39] Withers, *Chronicles of Border Warfare*, pp. 328-34.

Indians. The ingenious warriors improvised their own cannon by hollowing out a log and filling it with cannonballs. They then aimed it at Fort Henry. The charge killed several persons and wounded numerous others—all Indians.

The defenders of Fort Henry were by this time having their troubles. Gunpowder was running low, and not a man could be spared for a hazardous dash to Zane's house, where the supplies were ample. At this critical juncture, according to one of the most persistent legends of the West Virginia frontier, Betty Zane, the sister of Ebenezer, displayed uncommon heroism. She sped to Zane's house, obtained the precious gunpowder, and then once again braved the enemy fire to deliver it to the fort's defenders. The defense of the fort was so spirited that after three days of failure the Indians gave up the siege, and about half of them retired beyond the Ohio.[40]

The remainder of the Indians, numbering about a hundred, headed north to Rice's Fort, on Buffalo Creek, at present-day Bethany. The little stockade, which normally gave protection to about a dozen families, had only six defenders, and one of them was killed soon after the Indians attacked. In what was certainly one of the most remarkable of all frontier engagements, the remaining five men held out against a twelve-hour attack in which they killed several Indians and wounded numerous others.[41]

The sieges of Fort Henry and Rice's Fort marked the last massive attacks upon the West Virginia frontier during the Revolutionary War. A few weeks after the assaults upon the forts, Sir Guy Carleton, the British commander-in-chief, instructed the officers at all of Britain's western posts to desist from further attacks upon the frontiers. The expectations of West Virginia pioneers that they might now be left to peaceful pursuits, however, were ill-founded. Twelve more bloody years were to elapse before the trans-Allegheny regions would be entirely free of the Indian menace.

[40] *Ibid.,* pp. 355-59.

[41] Joseph Doddridge, *Notes, on the Settlement and Indian Wars, of the Western Parts of Virginia & Pennsylvania, from the Year 1763 until the Year 1783 Inclusive, together with a View, of the State of Society and Manners of the First Settlers of the Western Country* (Wellsburgh, [W.] Va., 1824), pp. 281-87.

Chapter Six

The Alienation of the Land

One of the great ironies of the history of the Allegheny area is that most of the land which had been won at such painful cost from the British and the Indians should have fallen not into the hands of the pioneers who had shed their blood and spent their treasure in gaining it but into the clutches of speculators, many of whom never set foot in the mountains. Most of the grandiose and imaginative schemes of pre-Revolutionary years did not survive the war, but in their places were scores of lesser ventures, which in their cumulative effects had a most vicious and enduring influence upon the history and development of the Allegheny region. Nowhere were these influences more pronounced than in West Virginia. But before examining these postwar dealings, it is necessary to trace briefly the later phases of the ante bellum speculations in Allegheny lands.

The most spectacular of the proposals affecting West Virginia, the establishment of Vandalia, was nearing reality when the gathering clouds of war rained disappointment upon the hopes of the colony's promoters. Seeking to salvage what they could, members of the Indiana Company, who had merged their claims with the Vandalia project, followed the advice of Benjamin Franklin and took steps to disassociate their interests from those of the Vandalia Company. On September 21, 1775, nine of its twenty-two members, including such influential shareholders as William Trent, George Morgan, George Croghan, and Robert Callender, met at Pittsburgh and adopted resolutions whereby the boundaries of the Indian grant would be surveyed, squatters on the lands, dispossessed, a land office opened, and the jurisdiction of Virginia over the area recognized. Although Samuel and Thomas Wharton and other powerful promoters of the Vandalia scheme at first opposed the action of the Indiana group, they eventually yielded to the persuasions of Franklin and accepted a plan which vested technical ownership of the Vandalia claims in three trustees and placed the management of its affairs in the hands of the Indiana Company. On January 25, 1776, five days after the opposing factions reached agreement, George Morgan was instructed to take charge of a land office, and squatters were warned that they must either purchase lands, not to exceed 400 acres, at $50 per hundred or face eviction by January 1, 1777.[1]

The Vandalia group, particularly Morgan, Franklin, and the Whartons, was very likely behind the attempt in the summer of 1776 to create a fourteenth commonwealth to be known as West-sylvania. Trans-Allegheny residents were urged to hold meetings in August for the purpose of determining whether to petition Congress for statehood or to establish a new state by their own authority and then send delegates to Congress. Although apparently no constitutional convention ever met, residents did submit a petition to Congress in August. They pointed out the difficulties inherent in the disputed jurisdiction of Virginia and Pennsylvania, in the Croghan and the Indiana and Vandalia claims, and in the locations of the seats of government of both Pennsylvania and Virginia across nearly impassable mountains and some four or five hundred miles distant. Then, lifting their arguments to a philosophical basis, they declared that they had "emigrated from almost every Province of America" and had "imbibed the highest and most extensive Ideas of Liberty." Therefore, they refused to be annexed to either Virginia or Pennsylvania and to be robbed of the lands and the country to which they, as the first occupants, were entitled by the "Laws of Nature and of Nations." Significantly, the boundaries set forth for Westsylvania coincided exactly with those of Vandalia except that Westsylvania would have excluded the area west of the mouth of the Scioto and would have included all of Penn-sylvania west of the Fort Stanwix line. The proposed state would have embraced all of trans-Allegheny West Virginia.

[1] George E. Lewis, *The Indiana Company, 1763–1798: A Study in Eighteenth Century Frontier Land Speculation and Business Venture* (Glendale, Calif., 1941), pp. 163-88; Max Savelle, *George Morgan: Colony Builder* (New York, 1932), p. 86.

Powerful forces, however, opposed the creation of a new commonwealth. With the Declaration of Independence at hand and a need for unity among the thirteen states, Congress had no intention of antagonizing two of its most important commonwealths by depriving them of western lands to which they held claim. Even though David Rogers, the representative from the District of West Augusta in the Virginia House of Delegates, favored the Westsylvania scheme, other Virginians, including John Neville, John Campbell, John Gibson, and the majority of the West Augusta committee, fought the proposal. Edmund Pendleton, who served as president of the Virginia Committee of Safety prior to the formation of the new state government in July, 1776, attributed the Westsylvania movement entirely to the Indiana and Vandalia promoters and George Croghan. Pennsylvanians who had no connection with the land companies, such as Arthur St. Clair, a champion of the proprietary interests, were also hostile to the Westsylvania project.[2]

Virginia authorities reacted swiftly and vigorously to the claims set forth by the Indiana Company. When the company announced that George Morgan was establishing a land office, the Virginia representatives in Congress called upon Thomas Wharton, the company's vice president, in Philadelphia and informed him in no uncertain terms that the Indiana claim lay within territory which belonged to Virginia by terms of her charter and by purchase from the Indians in the Treaty of Lancaster of 1744. Moreover, they told Wharton, a Virginia law of 1754 forbade any purchase of Indian lands by individuals.

The Virginia Convention dealt yet another blow to the hopes of the Indiana and Vandalia companies. Acting on behalf of the Ohio Company, George Mason, on June 24, 1776, offered a resolution, supported by liberals concerned for the rights of small farmers and adopted by the Convention, declaring that "all persons actually settled on any of the said lands ought to hold the same without paying any pecuniary or other consideration whatever to any private person or persons (pretending to

[2] Thomas Perkins Abernethy, *Western Lands and the American Revolution* (New York, 1937), pp. 176-77; Solon J. Buck and Elizabeth Hawthorn Buck, *The Planting of Civilization in Western Pennsylvania* (Pittsburgh, Pa., 1939), pp. 170-71.

derive title from Indian deeds and purchases) until . . . the validity of the title under such Indian deeds or purchases shall have been considered and determined on by the Legislature of this country." At the same time, it warned that "no purchase of lands within the chartered limits of Virginia shall be made under any pretense whatever, from any Indian tribe or nation, without the approbation of the Legislature."[3]

Confident that the Indiana claimants lacked a defensible case, the government of Virginia sent commissioners to Pittsburgh in the spring of 1777 for the purpose of taking depositions regarding the company's title. Among those summoned to appear was George Morgan, who began his testimony on March 10. Already, when it had become apparent that Virginia was likely to reject its claim, the company's lawyers had recommended challenging the validity of any jurisdiction which Virginia might assert on the basis of the Treaty of Lancaster. Fearing that its previous registration of its claims in Williamsburg might be construed as *ipso facto* recognition of Virginia authority, the Indiana group also took the precaution of recording its claims in Pennsylvania as well. Although the evidence gathered at Pittsburgh was inconclusive, the Indiana claimants were apprehensive over the course of events and proposed that their case be heard by an impartial tribunal. Virginia authorities flatly refused to allow others to adjudicate such an important matter, but they did agree to a hearing for the Indiana group by the General Assembly.[4]

Reluctantly, but not without some optimism that its memorial would receive a sympathetic hearing, the Indiana Company decided to present its case to the Virginia General Assembly. Carter Braxton, in his 1776 plan of government for Virginia, had recognized the validity of both the Treaty of Fort Stanwix and the Indiana grant. Other leading conservatives, including Edmund Pendleton and James Mercer, as well as Dr. Thomas Walker and members of the Loyal Company, favored recognition

---

[3] Lewis, *Indiana Company*, pp. 200-201, 204; Charles H. Ambler and Festus P. Summers, *West Virginia: The Mountain State*, 2d ed. (Englewood Cliffs, N. J., 1958), pp. 87-88; Abernethy, *Western Lands and the American Revolution*, pp. 189-90.

[4] Lewis. *Indiana Company*, pp. 202-10.

of the Indiana grant. Trusting to such friends, the Indiana Company hoped for favorable action by the General Assembly in 1777 and did not present petitions to Congress.

The optimism of the land company, however, proved ill-founded. The General Assembly was controlled by liberals of the Thomas Jefferson–Richard Henry Lee variety, who did not share the views held by many conservatives with respect to the company. As a result, the General Assembly heard the pretensions of the Indiana Company discussed several times on the floor during 1777 but did not reach a decision regarding its claims. Indeed, resolutions of January 22, 1778, which declared that backcountry lands should be sold with the purpose of establishing a sinking fund for the discharge of the state debt and that any survey entry made there prior to the time when Virginia might set up a land office would be void, cut at the very roots of the Indiana claim. The outlook for the Indiana Company was not brightened by the Loyalism of Joseph Galloway, who fled to England, or the pacifism of Thomas Wharton, who was taken into custody, branded an enemy of the United States, and stripped of his property in 1777.

After numerous delays, the General Assembly invited all persons who claimed grants from the Indians within the boundaries of Virginia to present their cases to the legislature in May, 1779. Dismayed at the implications of Virginia's assertion of authority, the Indiana Company had little choice except to comply, and, after careful preparation, dispatched William Trent to Williamsburg. Trent argued that the Indiana grant was legal under English law, that on at least two occasions the General Assembly had recognized the Treaty of Fort Stanwix on which the Indiana grant was based, and that the Virginia law of 1776, which in effect invalidated claims based upon Indian grants, was *ex post facto*.

Trent's arguments were ably answered by George Mason, who feared that validation of the Indiana grant would jeopardize the claims of the Ohio Company. Mason maintained that Virginia's jurisdiction rested upon the purchase of the lands from the Six Nations in 1744 and that even if the Indians had not sold the lands at that time they had lost their rights by 1768, having been driven from them during the French and Indian War. Moreover, Mason declared, failure of the Indiana Company to record the deed in Augusta County or in the general court of Virginia invalidated it. Finally, Mason denied the Indiana Company and the "Suffering Traders" any right to special consideration for their losses at the hands of the Indians, and declared that even should such compensation be desirable, the petitioners should seek it from Pennsylvania rather than from Virginia.

On June 9, 1779, the House of Delegates, by a vote of 50 to 28, rejected the Indiana claims. It reaffirmed Virginia's rights to all lands embraced within her charter, denied the validity of any titles acquired by individuals through purchase from the Indians, and declared that all such purchases, past and future, were void. Three days later the Senate upheld the action of the House of Delegates by refusing even to hear the Indiana plea.[5]

Stung by the crushing defeat at the hands of the Virginia legislature, the Indiana associates seized upon a provision of the July, 1776, draft of the Articles of Confederation, which gave Congress jurisdiction over western lands and empowered it to determine state boundaries. On September 14, 1779, George Morgan and William Trent presented similar petitions seeking confirmation of the claims of the Indiana and Vandalia companies, respectively. The Vandalia group offered to pay Congress slightly more than 10,460 pounds, the amount originally agreed upon with the British government, and to guarantee settlers their rights.

Virginia's representatives in Congress countered with a "Statement of Facts" in which they denied the jurisdiction of Congress over the Indiana case. Despite Virginia's opposition, Congress on October 8, 1779, chose a committee to hear the petitions of both the Indiana Company and the Vandalia promoters. On October 27, however, the committee reported that it was unable to distinguish between the questions of Virginia's jurisdiction over the lands and the merits of the Indiana claim. Consequently, it recommended that, considering the incomplete

[5] *Ibid.*, pp. 219-22; Abernethy, *Western Lands and the American Revolution*, pp. 217-27.

state of the confederation, Virginia and every other state in similar circumstances suspend for the duration of the war the sale, grant, or settlement of any land unappropriated at the time of the Declaration of Independence.

Angered by the Congressional assumption of authority, the Virginia House of Delegates appointed a committee consisting of Patrick Henry, George Mason, and Robert Munford to draw up a remonstrance, which would deny Congressional authority and assert "the rights of this Commonwealth to its own territory." The final draft of the statement, approved by both the House of Delegates and the Senate and forwarded to Congress on December 14, declared that any attempt by Congress to claim sovereignty over the territory "would be a violation of public faith, introduce a most dangerous precedent, and establish in Congress a power which in process of time must degenerate into an intolerable despotism." The United States, the remonstrance went on, had no territory except "in right of some one individual state in the Union" and under the proposed Articles of Confederation "no state could be deprived of territory for the benefit of the United States."[6]

Following Virginia's strong assertion of states' rights, the fate of the claims of the land companies became enmeshed in the broader question of the cession of western lands to Congress by the states. On September 6, 1780, Congress requested the states to cede their lands. Four months later, on January 2, 1781, the Virginia General Assembly complied with the request by relinquishing all claims to territory northwest of the Ohio River, estimated at approximately 60,000,000 acres. This land was to be put into a common fund, with all private Indian deeds to be declared void. Virginia also insisted that Congress must guarantee her title to her lands south of the Ohio.

At this juncture Morgan indicated a willingness to arbitrate the Indiana claim, but James Madison closed the door to such a solution, declaring that Virginia "could not reconcile with the sovereignty and honor of the state an appeal from its own jurisdiction to a foreign tribunal, in a controversy with private individuals." Rebuffed again, Morgan heeded the advice of Benjamin Franklin, Thomas Paine, and other nationalists and took the Indiana case to the Confederation Congress. At the direction of their state's legislature, New Jersey's representatives in Congress sponsored Morgan's request, and despite strenuous objections by Virginia, Congress referred the Indiana and Vandalia claims to its Committee on Western Lands.

On November 3, 1781, in a report which implied that Congress possessed sovereignty over western lands, the committee dealt a severe setback to Virginia's position. It recommended rejection of the terms of the cession of Virginia's lands as "incompatible with the honor, interests, and peace of the United States, and therefore altogether inadmissable." Moreover, it upheld the validity of the Indiana grant on the ground that the lands had been purchased with the knowledge of the Crown and the governments of Virginia and New York in accordance with the "usage and custom" of the time. It also recognized the validity of the Vandalia grant, but since such a large grant was considered "incompatible with the interests, government and policy of these United States," it recommended that members of the Vandalia Company who were citizens of the United States should lose their rights but be reimbursed for their actual expenses by new grants of land.

Believing that the committee report violated the provision of the Articles of Confederation that "no state shall be deprived of territory for the benefit of the United States" and that its findings represented undue influence by the land companies, Arthur Lee of Virginia moved that consideration of the report be postponed until Congress could determine the relationship of each member with land companies which had sought to deny the territorial rights of any state. Lee's motion failed to pass.

The Virginia delegates now placed the issue in the hands of the state's General Assembly. That body appointed a committee consisting of Thomas Jefferson, George Mason, Edmund Randolph, Arthur Lee, and Dr. Thomas Walker to set forth Virginia's position. The fervor with which they enunciated Virginia's views, reiterating her good faith in entering the Confederation and pointing out the dangers inherent in efforts to deprive her of her territory, convinced Congress that a compromise was essential to preserve the Confederation. On March 1, 1784, Congress accepted the cession of Virginia's western lands on terms which left the state in possession of the territory south of the Ohio River, including trans-Allegheny West Virginia.

Despite the fact that Congressional acceptance of the Virginia cession was tantamount to abandonment of the theory, so persistently propounded by the Indiana and Vandalia companies, that sovereignty over land south of the Ohio had shifted from Britain to Congress, the Indiana claimants presented yet another memorial to Congress. Once again Virginia brought heavy pressures to bear upon Congress, and that body, undoubtedly weary of the whole affair and beset by a multitude of problems of great urgency, refused to consider the Indiana petition.[7]

If the Indiana venture was not yet dead, its demise was close at hand. But its old archenemy, George Mason, did not lower his guard. Fearing that adoption of the Constitution might result in the establishment of a strong supreme court and that the Indiana Company might bring suit against Virginia, Mason urged the Virginia Convention of 1788 to insist upon an amendment to the Constitution by which the federal judicial power should not extend to any case where "the cause of action shall have originated before the ratification of this Constitution."

Mason's fears were well-founded. On August 11, 1792, the Philadelphia attorney Benjamin H. Morgan instituted a suit known as *William Grayson et al.* v. *the Commonwealth of Virginia*. Once again Virginia fought vigorously an attempt by the Indiana Company to sequester her territory. On December 3, 1793, her legislature adopted resolutions denying the suability of a state in a federal court and by implication the right of the Supreme Court to hear the Indiana suit and refused to allow the commonwealth's attorney general to heed a summons to appear in behalf of the state. On December 6 the General Assembly sent copies of the resolutions to the governors of other

[7] Lewis, *Indiana Company*, pp. 234-65.

states and to the representatives of Virginia in Congress.

Most other states concurred in Virginia's attitude regarding the suability of a state in the federal courts, and Virginia's representatives in Congress, aided by those of Georgia, which had just suffered a setback in the case of *Chisholm* v. *Georgia,* had little difficulty in mustering sentiment for an amendment to the Constitution. In 1798 the Eleventh Amendment, forbidding a citizen to sue a state of which he was not a resident, was added to the Constitution, and following its adoption the Supreme Court dismissed the Indiana case for lack of jurisdiction.[8]

The Ohio Company also suffered reverses during the Revolutionary War years. Prior to the outbreak of the war its members had rejected moves by George Mercer to merge its interests with those of the Grand Ohio Company, and, with George Mason as its foremost spokesman, it had continued to press its claims. Transaction of its business, however, was hampered by the possession by Englishmen of six of the twenty shares into which its assets were divided. Hoping to salvage what he could of the company's interests, Mason petitioned the General Assembly on November 20, 1778, to make individual grants to members of the company residing in Virginia and Maryland in proportion to their shares in the original 200,000-acre grant. Denied this request, the Ohio Company entered a somewhat languid period. After 1779 it held no meetings, and, with the death of George Mason in 1792, it ended virtually all of its activities.[9]

By 1778 the often vague claims of the land companies constituted a serious threat to the thousands of settlers who, prior to the establishment of a land office or the legal machinery for granting lands in Virginia, had streamed across the Alleghenies. Fearing eviction from their homes should the claims of the land companies later be upheld by the government of Virginia, these "squatters" exerted such pressures upon the Convention that it enacted legislation on May 14, 1776, which promised preemption rights to the settlers when the lands should be made available

[8] *Ibid.,* pp. 271-93.

[9] Kenneth P. Bailey, *The Ohio Company of Virginia and the Westward Movement, 1748–1792: A Chapter in the History of the Colonial Frontier* (Glendale, Calif., 1939), pp. 269-81.

for sale. In October, 1777, the General Assembly set the amount of land which a preemptor might acquire at 400 acres, but at the same time it made him liable for the payment of taxes pending the acquisition of his title.[10]

Fortunately for the preemptors, the General Assembly was controlled during these years by liberal elements sympathetic to their condition. Led by such men as Thomas Jefferson, Richard Henry Lee, George Mason, George Wythe, and Patrick Henry, and supported by John Taylor, John Tyler, Sr., and James Madison, the liberals successfully staved off efforts by conservatives such as Carter Braxton, Benjamin Harrison, Archibald Cary, and Edmund Pendleton to validate the claims of the land companies. In 1778 the liberals sought to establish a land office, believing that such a move would cripple the position of non-resident speculators who sought lands within Virginia's borders, avoid further confusion in western land titles, and provide a source of revenue with which to bolster the state's sagging credit. But the conservatives feared that the sale of western lands would draw off the population of the East and depreciate land values, as well as undermine the claims of the Indiana Company, with whose members many conservatives were in some way allied. Their opposition, coupled with that of military authorities, who saw in the proposed measure a drain upon available manpower, defeated the land office bill.

The setback for the settler, nevertheless was temporary. His disappointment over the failure to secure enactment of a land office bill was mitigated by a resolution of the General Assembly on January 24, 1778, that no further entries or surveys should be made in the transmontane areas until the state had set up a land office and that persons who settled on the lands thenceforth should have preemption rights to no more than 400 acres of land. Moreover, the new session of the legislature, which convened in the fall of 1778, was favorably disposed toward the

[10] *The Proceedings of the Convention of Delegates held at the Capitol in the City of Williamsburg in the Colony of Virginia, . . . May, 1776* (Richmond, Va., 1816), p. 63; William Waller Hening, comp., *The Statutes-at-Large: Being a Collection of All the Laws of Virginia from the First Session of the Legislature in the Year 1619*, 13 vols. (Richmond, Va., 1809-1823), IX, 349, 355-56.

settlers and passed a resolution denying the legality of unauthorized purchases of land from the Indians. This action
constituted a direct assault upon the rights of the Indiana
Company.[11]

The liberals—and through them the small western farmer—
achieved signal successes in the summer of 1779. On June 22
they secured enactment of a bill, sponsored by George Mason,
creating a land office and coupled it with a measure for settling
claims to unpatented western lands. The new legislation vali-
dated surveys made by accredited county surveyors or their
deputies prior to the act of January 24, 1778, and recognized
entries made in the trans-Allegheny region prior to 1763, provided that they did not exceed 400 acres, and any outstanding
claims of officers and soldiers under Dinwiddie's proclamation of
1754. The law had the effect of confirming the Loyal Company
and the Greenbrier Company in about 200,000 and 50,000 acres,
respectively, of their original grants, subject to approval by the
Court of Appeals. On the other hand, it nullified the Ohio
Company grant, since the company's surveyors had not been
accredited by the county surveyors, most of whom were connected with the Loyal and Greenbrier companies.

The act also provided that settlers who had taken up their
lands prior to January 1, 1778, might obtain 400 acres at a
nominal price and preemption rights to another 1,000 acres
at the usual price of forty pounds per hundred acres. Settlers
who arrived between January 1, 1778, and the passage of the
land office act might acquire 400 acres at the customary price,
but no provision was made for those who might make settlements later.

To expedite the adjustment of western land claims, the new
legislation divided the transmontane counties into four districts
and directed the governor to appoint for each a four-man commission whose decisions would be final. After all outstanding
claims had been settled, the remaining lands were to be sold
at forty pounds the hundred acres, a price which in depreciated
paper currency was roughly the equivalent of the old colonial

[11] Abernethy, *Western Lands and the American Revolution,* pp. 217-21.

charge of ten shillings the hundred, since quitrents were abolished and lands were conveyed in fee simple.[12]

Both the land companies and the settlers took a keen interest in the selection of commissioners. Andrew Lewis, whose family was among the prime movers of the Greenbrier Company, was dismayed that William Preston showed reluctance at being one of the commissioners. Writing to Preston on August 4, 1779, Lewis asserted his belief that Preston was probably the only person named by the governor who had a "clear and just knowledge" of the business and implored Preston "for God sake do not decline that necessary service." Lewis anticipated that most of the business of the commissioners for the district would lie in Greenbrier County, and while he warned Preston that he would likely be "a mongst [*sic*] the number of those that may give you trouble," he believed that in the long run he could lessen the problems.

The enormous political influence of the Loyal and Greenbrier companies and the possibility of their control of the commissioners aroused the apprehension of the settlers. On February 25, 1783, Alexander McClanahan and Michael Bowyer of Augusta County wrote to Governor Benjamin Harrison protesting the appointment of John Stuart, Charles Cameron, Thomas Hughart, and Thomas Adams as commissioners to settle claims in the district embracing Augusta, Botetourt, and Greenbrier counties, alleging that some of them were personally interested in the lands or had close family ties with other claimants. They suggested two attorneys, Andrew Moore and Archibald Stewart, as more suitable for such duties.[13]

Prominent Greenbrier residents, including Samuel Brown, Archer Mathews, John Stuart, John Anderson, Andrew Donnally, William Hunter Cavendish, and Peter Lewis, also lodged protests. Fearing that their money would be "grappled away" by lawyers, they asked that a meeting scheduled at Greenbrier

---

[12] Hening, comp., *Statutes-at-Large . . . of Virginia*, X, 35-37.

[13] Lewis to Preston, August 4, 1779, Draper MSS, 5QQ5; Alexander McClanahan and Michael Bowyer to Benjamin Harrison, February 25, 1782, W. P. Palmer and others, eds., *Calendar of Virginia State Papers and Other Manuscripts*, 11 vols. (Richmond, Va., 1875-1893), III, 75.

Court House on April 15, 1782, be postponed until the county court could select such persons for commissioners as would be qualified judges and until residents living at a distance could be summoned. Colonel William Fleming informed the governor that the commissioners for Montgomery, which included part of West Virginia, and Washington counties anticipated violence and requested that they be accompanied by the sheriff and an escort of militia.[14]

Although the trans-Allegheny settlers generally hailed the new land legislation with enthusiasm, they were well aware of new problems which it created. Of immediate concern was the requirement that settlers who held lands from the Greenbrier and Loyal companies must pay their composition money within six months or have their lands revert to the companies. Declaring that because of the great "scarcity of Money it is evident the lands will revert," a group of prominent Greenbrier residents, who held their lands from the Greenbrier Company, endeavored to secure repeal of the disturbing clause.[15]

Still another serious threat lay ahead for the Greenbrier residents. In May, 1783, the Court of Appeals declared the grants of both the Greenbrier and Loyal companies valid. Many settlers, hoping perhaps to weaken the claim of the former, had sought title to their lands from the commissioners who adjusted the claims and had paid all commissioner's, clerk's, surveyor's, and register's fees. Under the court ruling, however, they were obligated to pay the Greenbrier Company three pounds for each hundred acres and interest thereon. Unfortunately for their case, many of these settlers, at the urging of Andrew Lewis, the agent of the Greenbrier Company, had sent a petition to

14 Thomas Adams to [Benjamin Harrison], March 27, 1782, Palmer and others, eds., *Calendar of Virginia State Papers*, III, 111; William Fleming to Benjamin Harrison, September 4, 1782, *ibid.*, p. 289.

15 Greenbrier County Legislative Petitions, November 18, 1782. Signers of the petitions included, among others, Andrew Donnally, William Renick, James Alexander, Michael See, John See, Michael Keeney, John Keeney, John Stuart, John Archer, William Morris, George See, George Yocum, Leonard Morris, John Jones, John Alderson, John Van Bibber, and Peter Van Bibber. At least three of the petitioners, William Morris, Leonard Morris, and John Jones, were living in the Kanawha Valley at the time, but they may have yet held claims in the Greenbrier area.

the governor and council in 1773 asking that they might hold their lands under the Greenbrier Company. However, they later declared that they had done so only as means of protecting their lands from the claims of the officers and soldiers, which then threatened them. Nearly three hundred residents, professing not to know "what handle hath Since been made of the said petition" before the governor, the legislature, or the Court of Appeals, stoutly maintained that "nothing but the danger which then threatened" could have induced them to take such a step. Fearing now that they might become "the unhappy Sufferes of the Misconstructions of the Court of Appeals," they reminded the General Assembly of their expense and inconvenience in defending their titles before the commissioners and begged that "we may not become a prey to those who hath never been Instrumantal either in Settling or aiding us."[16]

The Greenbrier and Loyal companies fought all efforts of settlers to avoid dealing with their agents and to obtain lands directly from the state. In a long review of their history, the two companies in November, 1795, informed the General Assembly that they had "constantly kept Collectors employed" and that debtors of "upright minds" had continued to make payments, but that others, "encouraged to hope they might evade the Payments altogether by some influential characters in that country," had "used every method to obstruct Payment." The companies declared that they had no objection to the many acts which had postponed payment and did not wish to disturb the titles of settlers who paid within a reasonable time. They complained, however, that acts of 1783 and 1784 which forbade forfeitures of settlers' lands for nonpayment of sums due the companies had inspired the residents to defy the companies and even to sell the lands and move away. The Greenbrier and Loyal companies ended their appeal to the General Assembly by declaring that the two acts violated the federal Constitution by impairing contracts and the Virginia constitution by being *ex post facto* in nature. Once again they asked that the tracts held by settlers stand as security for payment for the lands and

[16] Greenbrier County Legislative Petitions, June 13, 1783.

accumulated interest or be forfeited by them if payment were not made to the companies.[17]

Nor were the Greenbrier residents the only West Virginians threatened by the land companies. In 1802 settlers in the northwestern counties were confronted with a resurrection of the Indiana Company claims and a court test directly involving about sixty persons and indirectly affecting some 20,000 to 30,000 families living in the disputed area. Many of the earliest settlers had been aware of the Indiana claims and had not sought to acquire titles to their holdings, but after the General Assembly had voided private purchases of land from the Indians and set up a land office they had relied upon its "discernment and good faith" and had purchased their lands from the state. In a petition widely circulated in Monongalia, Harrison, Randolph, Ohio, and Wood counties, hundreds of residents took the view that the Virginia government was bound "by every tie of Justice & good faith" to defend and protect the titles which the settlers had legally obtained.[18] Declaring their belief that it was "a Fundamental princible [*sic*] in all well organized governments that alegiance, and protection, are Reciprocal," they asked the General Assembly to appropriate from the public treasury whatever sums might be necessary for defending the rights of the settlers in the suit brought by the Indiana Company.[19]

George Jackson, a prominent Clarksburg attorney, who led the fight against the Indiana Company, set forth arguments which seemed to most pioneers to be incontrovertible justification of their rights to their lands. Jackson maintained that the settlers had given "bona fide satisfaction" for their lands and paid annually large sums in taxes into the state treasury, "whereas it is not pretended by the claimants [the Indiana Company] that *they* have ever paid one shilling to the commonwealth, either

---

[17] *Ibid.*, November 23, 1795. For attitudes of the two companies concerning payment by settlers, see also Thomas Walker to William Preston, May 9, 1783, Draper MSS, 5QQ118.

[18] Monongalia County Legislative Petitions, December 6, 1804. For attitudes of the first settlers, see James Chew to George Morgan, May 18, 1777, Palmer and others, eds., *Calendar of Virginia State Papers*, I, 287-88; Depositions taken by the Commissioners, March 10, 1777, *ibid.*, pp. 279-82.

[19] Harrison County Legislative Petitions, February 7, 1803.

as purchase money, or for Taxes." Nor, continued Jackson, had the company "expended one farthing in defense against Indian hostility, which never entirely ceased until the year 1795, nor made any effort or incurred any expenses in holding possession against that enemy, whose mode of warfare and savage cruelties compelled every man who resided within the aforesaid boundaries, for almost thirty years, to be, not only the provider for his family, but . . . likewise to become an active and vigilent soldier."[20]

Despite the numerous petitions and the utmost exertions by Jackson, the General Assembly declined to underwrite the expense involved in defending the settlers against the Indiana Company. Thrust back upon their own resources, at a mass meeting in Clarksburg on January 3, 1805 residents of Harrison County resolved to raise the necessary money by popular subscription. When the method proved inadequate, they petitioned the General Assembly to lay an additional 25 percent levy upon all lands within the Indiana grant and to use the revenue for the defense of settlers' rights in their suit with the Indiana company.[21] Rejection of the company's case, however, made such action unnecessary.

Meanwhile, large numbers of land titles in the Eastern Panhandle were called into question. Virginia's land legislation of 1779 had empowered the state to sell waste and unappropriated lands and to abolish "servile, feudal, and precarious" tenure within its borders. Under this law, Virginia attempted to confiscate the Fairfax estate and began to sell tracts from the holding. In 1791 Denny Martin, the heir of Lord Fairfax, moved to protect his interests by instituting an ejectment suit against David Hunter, who had received a patent to his lands from Virginia in 1788. In 1794 the Virginia District Court at Winchester upheld Martin's rights and ordered the ejectment of Hunter.

Later, in 1810, after John Marshall and a group of associates had acquired title to the "waste and ungranted" lands of the Fairfax estate, Hunter took his case to the Virginia Court of

[20] *Ibid.*, December 4, 1804.
[21] *Ibid.*, December 4, 1805.

Appeals. This tribunal, over which Judge Spencer Roane, an archenemy of Marshall, presided, reversed the decision of the lower court. Ultimately the case reached the United States Supreme Court, of which Marshall was Chief Justice. In an opinion delivered by Justice Joseph Story, but approved by Marshall, who did not sit on the case, the Supreme Court ruled that the treaty of 1783 protected the claims of Fairfax and his heirs. The Virginia Court of Appeals, however, maintained that the Supreme Court did not have appellate jurisdiction in the case and refused to execute the decision of the federal court. Finally, in 1816, in the celebrated case of *Martin* v. *Hunter's Lessee,* the United States Supreme Court declared that it did have jurisdiction because the case involved a treaty to which the United States was a party. Once again, it upheld Martin's rights.[22]

The battles waged by West Virginia settlers against the land barons were, to be sure, in part pragmatic responses to efforts to dispossess them of their lands, but they were also rooted in philosophical considerations. Whether as a result of the frontier experience, the long contests with land speculators, or the egalitarian ideas of the Revolutionary period, many pioneers had developed an essentially democratic belief that a man should hold no more land than he could use. Joseph Doddridge, the noted authority on the trans-Allegheny social history of Virginia and Pennsylvania, recalled that his father felt such a sense of guilt at obtaining preemption rights to a tract of land adjoining his property that, despite its strict legality, he gave it to a servant boy whom he had reared.[23]

Ironically, the most insidious and exploitative forms of speculation were made possible by the Virginia land legislation of 1779. By making preemption rights and military warrants transferable, the law opened the way to a spirited traffic in trans-Allegheny lands. Speculators purchased land warrants for a fraction of

---

22 For a brief account, see Ambler and Summers, *West Virginia,* pp. 110-11.

23 Joseph Doddridge, *Notes, on the Settlement and Indian Wars, of the Western Parts of Virginia & Pennsylvania, from the Year 1763 until the Year 1783 Inclusive, together with a View, of the State of Society and Manners of the First Settlers of the Western Country* (Wellsburgh, [W.] Va., 1824), p. 243.

their value and ultimately acquired hundreds of thousands of acres in West Virginia. In doing so, they impeded the settlement of the area by small farmers.[24]

During the last two decades of the eighteenth century speculation in West Virginia lands, as well as vast acreages in southwest Virginia and Kentucky, became almost a mania. By 1805 at least 250 persons or groups, often in a bewildering fabric of interlocking combinations, acquired grants of 10,000 acres or more. Records of grants lying entirely or predominantly in the Allegheny sections of West Virginia show that during these years 101 grantees acquired holdings ranging from 10,000 to 25,000 acres; 64, from 25,001 to 50,000 acres; 41, from 50,001 to 100,000 acres; and 44, more than 100,000 acres. Of the latter group, five grantees—Henry Banks, James Welch, Robert Morris, Wilson Cary Nicholas, and George K. Taylor—each claimed princely domains in excess of 500,000 acres.[25]

One of the most acquisitive of the postwar speculators was Henry Banks. A member of the merchandising firm of Hunter, Banks and Company, whose business house was located immediately across the street from the Virginia state capitol in Richmond, Banks obtained scores of military warrants in return for merchandise or small cash considerations. In addition, the firm had its own claims against the government of Virginia. During the Revolutionary War it had supplied large quantities of cloth, canvas, lead, shot, tea, steel, and other articles to the Virginia armed forces. Moreover, as "owner and ship's husband to many vessels," it had suffered the loss, through destruction

[24] Abernethy, *Western Lands and the American Revolution*, pp. 228-29; Hening, comp., *Statutes-at-Large . . . of Virginia*, X, 60.

[25] In arriving at these figures, large speculative combines have been counted only once, even though individual members may have owned 10,000 acres or more in their own right. Individual grantees have been counted only once and have been placed in a category where their major interests seemed to lie. The figure 10,000 acres is wholly arbitrary. Unquestionably, many persons who possessed less than that amount engaged in land speculation. On the other hand, families were large, and in many instances 500 to 1,000 acres for each child would not have left many acres to spare from a 10,000-acre tract. All figures are derived from transcripts of land grants in the Office of the Auditor of the State of West Virginia. Originals are in the Virginia State Library, Richmond, Virginia. Listings may be found in Edgar B. Sims, *Sims' Index to Land Grants in West Virginia* (n. p., 1956), passim.

or capture by the British, of a number of its merchantmen, which had been pressed into the defense of Virginia by Governor Thomas Jefferson. After years of failure to obtain compensation, Banks, in June, 1795, expressed a willingness "to invest a greater part of the whole claim in Land Warrants, and perhaps the whole," but he made it clear that he wanted "at least 500,000 acres."[26]

Through these means, Banks acquired 528,779 acres in Greenbrier, Harrison, Kanawha, Monongalia, and Randolph counties between 1783 and 1801. In addition, substantial parts of the 100,887 acres which he held in Montgomery and Wythe counties and of the 200,000 acres in Russell County, which he owned jointly with Richard Smith, lay in present West Virginia. Some of his most desirable lands, however, he shared with Philip Barbour and included 362,954 acres taken up along the Ohio River in Jefferson County, Kentucky.[27]

Rich merchants in other eastern cities also dealt heavily in West Virginia lands. Conspicious among them were Bernard and Michael Gratz, who within a few years of their arrival in America in 1754 and 1758, respectively, from Langersdorf, Germany, were presiding over one of the most successful mercantile establishments in Philadelphia. The Gratz brothers

[26] Henry Banks to Executive of Virginia, December 22, 1787, Palmer and others, eds., *Calendar of Virginia State Papers*, IV, 371-72; Henry Banks to Governor and Council of Virginia, May 22, 1791, *ibid.*, V, 307; Henry Banks to Governor of Virginia, June 4, 1795, *ibid.*, VIII, 252; Henry Banks to Governor of Virginia, May 28, 1796, *ibid.*, p. 371.

[27] Greenbrier County Land Grants, I (1779–1820), passim; *ibid.*, II (1787–1824), passim; *ibid.*, III (1793–1805), passim; *ibid.*, IV (1796–1820), passim; *ibid.*, V (1800–1858), 569; *ibid.*, VI (1820–1864), passim; Harrison County Land Grants, I (1785–1786), passim; *ibid.*, IV (1793–1800), passim; *ibid.*, V (1800–1816), 24, 29-30; Kanawha County Land Grants, I (1790–1812), 106-107, 263-64; Monongalia County Land Grants, I (1782–1785), passim; *ibid.*, II (1785–1786), passim; *ibid.*, III (1786–1788), passim; Randolph County Land Grants, I (1788–1851), 87-95, 416-17; *ibid.*, II (1796–1861), 10, 20-21. For descriptions of lands that Banks held jointly with others, see Montgomery County Land Grants, I (1784–1798), 176-80, 479-82, 485-87, 491-512, 517-18; Bath, Wythe, Russell, and Botetourt County Land Grants, I (1772–1825), 207, 216. Plats for the Kentucky surveys and for 246,373 acres that Banks held in Monongalia, Harrison, Greenbrier, and Montgomery counties may be found in Plats of Surveys for Henry Banks, MS volumes in possession of Joseph M. Holt, Lewisburg, West Virginia (Photostats in the Office of the Auditor of the State of West Virginia). Plats for 45,332 acres in Greenbrier County are in Henry Banks Survey, 1787, Miscellaneous Manuscripts, Box CII, West Virginia Department of Archives and History Library.

had a long record of land speculations, which included interests in the Indiana Company and in the Illinois and Wabash schemes. After the establishment of the Virginia Land Office, they acquired 148,820 acres in tracts lying entirely or largely within West Virginia. Another Philadelphia house, that of Antoine and Barthelemy Terrasson, a branch of their father's firm of John Terrasson of Paris and Lyon, France, acquired 59,000 acres in Monongalia and Harrison counties. Samuel and Robert Purviance, Baltimore merchants who had emigrated from Ireland, controlled 69,994 acres in Ohio and Monongalia counties. Numerous other merchants of eastern cities acquired land warrants worth thousands of acres through the normal trade relations between trans-Allegheny settlements and the Atlantic seaboard.[28]

Local merchants in West Virginia towns also evinced keen interest in lands. Typical of these speculators was Thomas Laidley, who purchased furs, bearskins, and deerskins at his store in Morgantown and sent them by packhorse to Richmond, where he converted them into land warrants. Between 1786 and 1804 Laidley obtained warrants for 25,775 acres in Monongalia County.[29]

Aside from the activities of Henry Banks, however, the speculations of eastern merchants were almost eclipsed by those of public officials. Probably West Virginia's best known land-

[28] Descriptions of lands owned by the Gratz brothers are in Greenbrier County Land Grants, I (1779–1820), 181, 262-65; Monongalia County Land Grants, III (1786–1788), 162, 312-13; Montgomery County Land Grants, I (1784–1798), 153-59, 163-70, 181-90, 194-99, 215-23, 230, 293-99, 311, 313, 331; Randolph County Land Grants, I (1778–1851), 52-60; Ohio County Land Grants, I (1779–1787), 216-25. Lands of the Terrasson brothers are described in Monongalia County Land Grants, III (1786–1788), 469-79, 515-24; Harrison County Land Grants, II (1786–1788), 273, 305. For lands held by the Purviances, see Monongalia County Land Grants, I (1782–1785), 250-56, 258-61, 333-35, 465-66, 468, 470-89; *ibid.*, II (1785–1786), 410-14, 445-47, 459-62, 522; Ohio County Land Grants, II (1787–1796), 237, 300-303. An account of the Purviance brothers is in J. Thomas Scharf, *The Chronicles of Baltimore: Being a Complete History of "Baltimore Town" and Baltimore City from the Earliest Period to the Present Time* (Baltimore, Md., 1874), pp. 125-28, passim.

[29] James Morton Callahan, *History of the Making of Morgantown, West Virginia: A Type Study in Trans-Appalachian Local History* (Morgantown, W. Va., 1926), p. 82. For Laidley's holdings, see Monongalia County Land Grants, II (1785–1786), 501-502; *ibid.*, III (1786–1788), 12, 15, 18-21; *ibid.*, IV (1788–1796), 323; *ibid.*, V (1796–1806), 508, 560, 565.

holder was George Washington, who, between 1772 and 1784, obtained 33,210 acres in nine tracts along the Ohio and Kanawha rivers. Much of his land was acquired through purchase of military warrants issued to veterans of the French and Indian War. De Witt Clinton, the New York politician, obtained 272,000 acres along the tributaries of the Guyandotte and on Coal River and Paint Creek. Timothy Pickering, former quartermaster general of the United States, held 31,000 acres along the Little Kanawha and on Middle Island Creek. Long before he became secretary of the treasury under Thomas Jefferson, Albert Gallatin visited West Virginia and selected lands, which ultimately aggregated about 184,786 acres. Most of Gallatin's lands, which were located in Harrison, Kanawha, Monongalia, Greenbrier, and Randolph counties, were held with Savary de Valcoulon. Also included among the highly placed national figures who acquired lands in West Virginia was John Beckley, the first clerk of the House of Representatives, who, with a group of associates, claimed 259,074 acres in the Greenbrier region, along Elk River, and on New River.[30]

None of these land barons approached the scale of operations of Robert Morris, the Philadelphia financier. Morris held 1,300,000 acres on the Big Sandy, Tug, and Guyandotte rivers, 200,000 acres on the Greenbrier, Gauley, and Birch rivers, and a modest 30,038 acres on the branches of the Monongahela in Harrison County. Some of his Big Sandy lands were shared

[30] For Washington's grants, see Fincastle County Land Grants, I (1772–1833), 524. Detailed descriptions of his holdings are in Roy Bird Cook, *Washington's Western Lands* (Strasburg, Va., 1930) pp. 43-68, 75-99; Edgar B. Sims, *Making a State* (Charleston, W. Va., 1956), pp. 128-36. Clinton's holdings are noted in Montgomery County Land Grants, I (1784–1798), 561, 564. Pickering's lands are described in Harrison County Land Grants, I (1785–1786), 202-205; Ohio County Land Grants, I (1779–1787), 182-84, 192-94, 233, 267-68, 315. For Gallatin's holdings, see Harrison County Land Grants, I (1785–1786), 62-63, 131, 143-54, 157-59, 184-88, 214-16, 224-25, 237-40; *ibid.*, II (1786–1788), 158-59, 209, 268-69, 548; *ibid.*, III (1788–1817), 102, 221-22; Kanawha County Land Grants, I (1790–1812), 39-42, 44-46, 48-49, 71, 466, 468-70, 472-73; *ibid.*, II (1815–1861), 68; Monongalia County Land Grants, III (1786–1788), 540; *ibid.*, IV (1788–1796), 102, 156; *ibid.*, V (1796–1806), 197, 283; Randolph County Land Grants, II (1796–1861), 12. A brief sketch of John Beckley is Raymond V. Martin, Jr., "Eminent Virginian—A Study of John Beckley," *West Virginia History*, XI (October, 1949-January, 1950), 44-61. Beckley's lands are described in Greenbrier County Land Grants, II (1787–1824), 54, 96, 98; *ibid.*, III (1793–1805), 21-39.

with Wilson Cary Nicholas, Virginia assemblyman, governor, congressman, and United States senator, who had personal holdings of over 1,100,000 acres in Montgomery, Russell, and Wythe counties and 50,000 acres in Greenbrier County, all obtained while he was a member of the Virginia General Assembly.[31]

A closer examination of Morris' activities provides insights into the connections among some of the great speculators. One of Morris' associates in his Kentucky enterprises, Levi Hollingsworth, held 188,472 acres in Pendleton County and 10,000 acres in Ohio County. In addition, Hollingsworth was a partner of Dorsey Pentecost in the acquisition of 170,750 acres in Montgomery County. Pentecost, in turn, provided a link which tied together other speculative groups. In Kentucky, he joined forces with Robert Morris, Levi Hollingsworth, and the Gratz brothers, who supplied land warrants, while Pentecost located desirable tracts. Well entrenched politically—he served as a justice in both Bedford County, Pennsylvania, and Virginia's District of West Augusta—Pentecost was also involved in the West Virginia interests of Hollingsworth, the Gratz brothers, and the Purviances.[32]

Members of the Virginia General Assembly also caught the land fever. At least 52 members of the House of Delegates or the Senate received grants exceeding 10,000 acres during the last quarter of the eighteenth century. Of this number, 22, with grants totaling 2,764,461 acres, represented West Virginia constituencies. Moreover, several of these men were allied with nonresident land speculators. Cornelius Bogard of Randolph County and Edward Jackson of Harrison County shared 100,000 and 50,000 acres, respectively, of the 565,412 acres of James Welch. George Clendenin of Greenbrier County was associated

[31] Greenbrier County Land Grants, III (1793–1805), 206, 241-42, 289, 328, 547, 558, 560, 563; Bath, Wythe, Russell, and Botetourt County Land Grants, I (1772–1825), 196, 198-99, 201, 215; Harrison County Land Grants, III (1788–1817), 379-81, 390-93; Montgomery County Land Grants, I (1784–1798), 555.

[32] Pendleton County Land Grants, I (1789–1799), 226-27, 573, 576, 582, 586, 588, 590, 592, 594; Ohio County Land Grants, I (1779–1787), 145-54; Montgomery County Land Grants, I (1784–1798), 9-152, 311, 331, 338-39; Monongalia County Land Grants, I (1782–1785), 250-56, 258-61, 333-35, 465-66, 468, 470-80; Abernethy, *Western Lands and the American Revolution*, p. 263.

with John Beckley, who received all of his 28,893 acres in that county while Clendenin was in the House of Delegates. William McCleery, a Monongalia County delegate, was a partner of Samuel and Robert Purviance in 30,875 acres in that county. Still others, such as Peter Hull, Sr., and William McCoy, Jr., of Pendleton County, apparently engaged in little speculation on their own, but were agents of large nonresident landowners. One member of the House of Delegates, Henry Banks, although a resident of Richmond, actually represented Greenbrier County on the basis of his landholdings there.[33]

The rampant speculation reduced land titles in West Virginia, many of them already of dubious validity, to utter chaos. Much of the difficulty grew out of Virginia's land system, which permitted settlers and purchasers of land warrants to locate their tracts before making actual surveys. The result was a patchwork of irregularly shaped tracts, many of which did not include a single permanent marker. Although grantees were required to recognize prior claims based upon settlement rights, the confusion was actually confounded when the speculators superimposed their claims upon those of the settlers. Both groups assailed the land law of 1779, which, in the words of William Prentiss, the agent of one large speculator, "opened the door to every species of *mistakes, fraud & Imposition*" and victimized

---

[33] The twenty-two representing West Virginia districts were John Pierce Duvall, George Jackson, William G. Payne, John Preston, Francis Preston, George Arnold, Henry Banks, William McCleery, Daniel Morgan, Thomas Wilson, Moses Chapline, Hezekiah Davisson, John Jackson, Thomas Laidley, Thomas Pindall, Archibald Woods, George Clendenin, Cornelius Bogard, John Davis, Edward Jackson, Abner Lord, and Charles Simms. For a list of West Virginia delegates to the General Assembly and Banks' political ties to Greenbrier County, see Virgil A. Lewis, *Second Biennial Report of the Department of Archives and History of the State of West Virginia* (n. p., n. d.), pp. 103-52. Holdings of Bogard, Clendenin, and McCleery are shown in Randolph County Land Grants, I (1788-1851), 373-74; Kanawha County Land Grants, I (1790-1812), 100, 111, 173, 302; Harrison County Land Grants, IV (1793-1800), 189, 502; Greenbrier County Land Grants, II (1787-1824), 54, 96, 98; *ibid.*, III (1793-1805), 21-39, 396, 543, 545, 579, 581, 583, 586, 588; *ibid.*, IV (1796-1820), 2, 29, 31, 38, 65, 238, 297, 424, 547, 550; *ibid.*, V (1800-1858), 143-45, 192-93, 223; Monongalia County Land Grants, II (1785-1786), 410-14, 445-47, 459-62, 522. For McCleery's interests, see also Monongalia and Harrison County Surveys, pp. 78-83, Cunningham Papers, West Virginia University Library. Activities of a resident land agent are noted, for example, in Memorandum, July 29, 1808, McCoy Family Papers, West Virginia University Library.

both the honest settler and the upright land dealer.[34]

Despite their large acreages, many speculators found that after they subtracted prior grants they had little except poor and inaccessible lands. John D. Sutton, who in 1798 visited the Elk Valley for the purpose of locating and recording titles to seven 1,000-acre tracts which had been purchased by his father, found on one of the tracts only forty acres of bottom land, the rest being "highland . . . of little consequence." Worse still, he wrote his father, "it may be as well to mention once for all that we could find no lines to any of the tracts."[35] An even more disheartening experience confronted Benjamin Haskell, William Walter, and John Warren, who in 1796 bought two 100,000-acre tracts from Alexander Wolcott and Austin Nichols for fifteen cents an acre. They later discovered that prior claims totally consumed one of the tracts. From the other, they realized only 15,000 to 20,000 acres, and even then only after bitter court battles which lasted seven years. Their agent lashed out at unscrupulous land jobbers, describing them as men of "debased principles [who] have combined for the purpose of dishonorable gain, and have fattened on the vitals of the state, and by cheating the unsuspecting out of large sums of money when these speculators knew that most of the lands were either covered with prior Grants or on Mountains inaccessible [*sic*] and of no Value whatever."[36] In 1837 John Hoye had entirely lost sight of a 20,000-acre tract in Harrison County and was enlisting the aid of Thomas Haymond in locating it. As late as 1853, an heir, Charles Hoye, was still trying to determine whether the elder Hoye had owned lands in Jackson County.[37] With such shadowy titles, many speculators found it virtually impossible to dispose of their lands.

Even when titles were relatively clear, the unattractiveness and inaccessibility of many holdings presented problems for their owners. When Henry Morris, the heir to Levi Hollings-

[34] Greenbrier County Legislative Petitions, December 20, 1826.

[35] C. H. Ambler, ed., "The Diary of John D. Sutton and Kanawha County Land Grants," *West Virginia History*, IV (April, 1943), 185, 196.

[36] Greenbrier County Legislative Petitions, December 20, 1826.

[37] John Hoye to Thomas Haymond, June 16, 1837, Haymond Family Papers, West Virginia University Library; T. W. Hiron to Neamish [*sic*] Smith, May 13, 1853, George W. Smith Papers, West Virginia University Library.

worth's 137,245 acres in Pendleton County, sought information concerning his lands, William McCoy, Jr., informed the Philadelphian: "As to the quality of those lands I cannot say much, there is almost every variety except *Good*—and most of it can never be valuable except for timber." McCoy expressed the belief that some of the lands in the Allegheny Mountains might be used for grazing and some of the tracts adjoining small farms might be sold, but he declared that he himself would not give Morris $500 for all his lands. In response to an inquiry by Morris, McCoy wrote, perhaps facetiously: "I do not know which of the Tracts is called Angel's Rest! nor how near the moon it may be. Some of it as near perhaps as any other part of Terra Firma, for I believe it includes the highest peak of the *highest* part of the Alleghany." In case Morris wished to see the lands for himself, McCoy advised travel by horseback, "inasmuch as no Stage rout approaches nearer than 40 miles of this place & the balance of the journey must be made on horseback or in a balloon."[38]

In order to sell isolated and relatively undesirable lands, many owners adjusted their prices in accordance with the value of particular plots and extended credit to purchasers. Francis Deakins instructed the agent who looked after his Preston County holdings to visit a number of "Dutch people" living in the Ketocton area, who were reportedly interested in leaving. Try to persuade "one or two of the most influential men to Ride with you," Deakins told the agent, and "you may get a large party made up to follow you & take lands—you Can let them know you expect others and them that goes first will get the Choice." He recommended that the journey be made as late as possible in May in order that the party might see the glades in bloom. Deakins also sought to attract purchasers for the lands by laying out a town, called Salem, and by donating lots for a schoolhouse and a church.[39]

Other speculators were unwilling to make concessions to

[38] William McCoy, Jr., to Henry Morris, December 7, 1832, McCoy Family Papers.
[39] Memorandum of Sales, January 24, 1854, McCoy Family Papers; Francis Deakins to John Gallaspie, July 10, 1804, and Plat of Salem, Deakins Family Papers, West Virginia University Library; Francis Deakins to E. Butler, April 2, 1803, Ewin Family Papers, West Virginia University Library.

purchasers and insisted that lands must be laid off in such a manner that the buyers must take poor lands along with the good. T. G. McCulloh of Chambersburg, Pennsylvania, instructed his agent not to sell plots to neighboring farmers unless they were willing to take both good and bad lands. "Select parcels," he told the agent, "I would not sell unless for as much as the whole would be worth." Joseph Miller of Philadelphia observed that some persons who wished to buy choice tracts from his Harrison County lands "probably think I would sell at any price, in order to get rid of it as quickly as possible, which is not correct." Instead, he was convinced that "it would be better to sell at a low rate, and lay the land off regular, than a high price, and pick small patches of the best land, and leave the worst which would become unsaleable."[40] The insistence that purchasers relieve the speculators of substantial parts of their uninviting lands in many instances prevented sales of any kind.

Still other holders of large tracts chose to retain their lands in the expectation that they would appreciate in value. Henry Morris, whose holdings were described as "so opposite to Good," trusted that "as the Resources of the 'Old Dominion' were developed by time and internal improvement they may be more valuable." Ashton Richardson of Wilmington, Delaware, inquired of Thomas Haymond, the surveyor of Harrison County, whether "there is any canals or rail roads, projected or likely to be made in that country; and if there is any trade of importance down the [Little] Kenawa." At the same time he voiced the hope that "the progressive improvement of that country may have affected its value as it has in many other states." William Read of Philadelphia, who owned tracts in Harrison County, optimistically predicted in 1838 that "the improvements making on the Mongahela [*sic*] in Penna. to be extended to the Va. line will no doubt add Value to the lands."[41]

Without question, the evils of Virginia's land system and of

40 T. G. McCulloh to William McCoy, Jr., July 19, 1836, McCoy Family Papers; Joseph Miller to Luther Haymond, August 13, 1835, Haymond Family Papers.
41 Henry Morris to William McCoy, Jr., August 19, 1833, McCoy Family Papers; Ashton Richardson to Thomas Haymond, October 25, 1836, Haymond Family Papers; William Read to Luther Haymond, September 18, 1838, *ibid.*

the land law of 1779, in particular, fell most heavily upon the yeoman farmer. Rights acquired by settlement, payment of the required legal fees, and certificates from the commissioners for settling western land titles did not per se assure the occupant undisputed possession of his property. Nor did they guarantee that he would be spared, perhaps many years later, costly and inconvenient legal battles with the speculators. Residents of Ohio and Brooke counties complained to the General Assembly in 1800 that for twenty years they had "felt altogether secure in their titles, Until the eagle-eyed speculators came forward and claimed every Improvement except the first," and "actually laid Treasury Warrants on a number of places" where rights had been established. Memorialists from Nicholas County, threatened in a like manner, excoriated a land system, which "after expelling a man from what he fondly hoped was his freehold and his home, consigns to his tardy but successful rival, and often to the merciless speculator, a property acquiring its chief value from the sweat of his brow, and the labour of his hands, without remuneration or recompense to the sufferer for that labour and industry."[42]

Typical of the fate which overtook many settlers was that which befell Levi Nutter of Harrison County. Nutter settled on what he believed to be wasteland and cleared sixty acres and made other improvements. After living on the land for eleven years, he found that it was part of a large tract claimed by Joseph Sims of Philadelphia. Nutter contracted with Archibald McCall, Sims' agent, for the purchase of five hundred acres, which were to be surveyed and valuated by Thomas Haymond, the county surveyor. When Nutter made his first payment, he found that Sims had failed to pay taxes on his tract and that it had been forfeited to the Literary Fund. Unable to purchase the land directly from the Literary Fund, Nutter was forced to appeal to the General Assembly for special legislation which would enable him to buy from the state lands which he had long believed that he already owned.[43]

[42] Ohio County Legislative Petitions, December 3, 1800; Kanawha County Legislative Petitions, December 12, 1817.
[43] Wood County Legislative Petitions, February 3, 1832.

The pernicious effects of the land system were even more in evidence in the French Creek community in Upshur County. Between 1808 and 1816 immigrants from Massachusetts, Connecticut, and Vermont settled in the French Creek area. Among them were members of the prominent Phillips, Alden, Young, Gould, and Gilbert families. In 1816 the Hampshire County, Massachusetts, Missionary Society took cognizance of the vitality of their settlement and sent Asa Brooks, a Congregational minister of Halifax, Vermont, to serve as pastor of the community's church. Several years later it was discovered that the titles to some of the lands purchased by the New Englanders were defective. The settlers now faced the appalling prospect of having to repurchase their lands, and, in addition, any improvements which they had made. The French Creek residents thereupon instituted legal proceedings, for, in the words of Robert Young, one of the leaders of the community, "as a number of Deferent persons Clam'd this same land it was needfull we should know the Real owner." Shortly afterward, two of the rival claimants, Daniel Boardman of New York City and Robert McCall of Philadelphia, each entered ejectment suits against Young, Asa Brooks, and other residents.[44]

Because of court dockets crowded with other land cases, the lack of a surveyor's report on the disputed lands, and demands by the French Creek residents that a new survey be made, the ejectment suits dragged on for years. Moreover, the entire problem was complicated when McCall brought suit against Boardman in 1826 for recovery of 8,000 acres of land. The French Creek settlers by that time were contending that the lands belonged to neither Boardman nor McCall but to Standish Ford and John Reed under a still older patent. Ford and Reed, Philadelphia speculators, however, were currently involved in an ejectment suit of their own, in which still other tenants charged that the Ford and Reed grant had been based upon a forged plat and certificate of survey and that the lines of the tract had

[44] Robert Young to Daniel Boardman, June 9, 1825, Daniel Boardman Papers, West Virginia University Library; Daniel Boardman to James Pindall, April 28, 1825, *ibid.* For an account of early French Creek, see Maurice Brooks, "A Community Records Its History," *West Virginia History*, XVII (April, 1956), 252-54.

been determined illegally by the surveyor of another county.[45]

Although the French Creek residents ultimately gained title to their lands, the long years of litigation produced a demoralizing effect among them. Writing to Daniel Boardman in 1825, Robert Young declared, "I have had a great deal of troble [*sic*] relating to those suits my expenses and troble I think has been double the worth of the hundred acres of land I live on." Other residents, too, said Young, were discouraged and "there has been but a little Done to profit Sence your suit was commenc'd." After urging Boardman to be generous with the settlers, who had by that time received many invitations to locate elsewhere, Young reminded the New York claimant that the "land on French Creek is altogether up land and the part that is settled is very uneven Virginians will not Settle on it they want Bottom Land but the New England people will cultavate the mountains, and this is the onely [*sic*] way to settle this tract of land." Finally, Young pleaded with Boardman to at least bestow upon Asa Brooks the land which the minister claimed.[46]

The confusion in land titles was inevitably carried over into Virginia's taxes on real estate. One of the 100,000-acre tracts acquired by Haskell, Walter, and Warren was also assessed in the names of Richard Smyth and Henry Banks and was "sold 3 times over on one Tax" as delinquent land. The agent of the former declared, "I was disposed to pay the Taxes If I knew what we owned, if any." At the same time, the names of residents who held prior claims which wiped out the other 100,000-acre tract purchased by Haskell, Walter, and Warren were not listed at all on the tax books. The delinquent tax list for Monongalia County in 1814, typical of those of many other counties, reveals that in that year sixteen speculators with lands totaling 355,183 acres had tax arrearages amounting to $328.81. Included among them were Henry Banks, Standish Ford and John Reed, John Hopkins, Archibald McCall, James Swan,

[45] James Pindall to Daniel Boardman, September 5, 1821, Daniel Boardman Papers; James Pindall to Daniel Boardman, October 6, 1822, *ibid.*; James Pindall to Daniel Boardman, August 11, 1823, *ibid.*; William Hacker to Daniel Boardman, May 4, 1826, *ibid.*
[46] Robert Young to Daniel Boardman, June 9, 1825, *ibid.*

Barthelemy Terrasson, and Robert Troop. It is perhaps significant that in all sixteen cases speculators had lands marked "not found" and that the owners were listed either as "nonresidents" or "residence not known."[47] In this manner, hundreds of thousands of acres were forfeited to the Literary Fund and thereby deprived the state of the modest taxes, which they, as wild lands, would otherwise have yielded.

West Virginia's Allegheny residents quickly realized that the land law of 1779, so democratic in its intent but so harmful in its effects, had combined with speculative greed to produce disastrous conditions. "When we compare the present condition of our section of the country, labouring under the evils of a spare [sic] population, insufficient for the development of its natural resources—unequal to the opening of roads through an extent of territory as yet unoccupied," declared a group of Nicholas Countians in 1817, there could be no doubt that the reason for the retardation lay in "the proverbial uncertainity of our land titles."

Numerous proposals were set forth for alleviating the situation. Residents of Nicholas County urged legislation which would require persons claiming wastelands to have them surveyed before making any sales and to compensate any settlers, who might be evicted, for their improvements. They argued that such a law would increase population, lessen emigration, provide additional taxes, stimulate agriculture, and attract capital for industrial enterprises. Passage of the recommended legislation, they asserted, was the "only efficient mode by which this interesting section of the country can be regenerated." When the changes were effected, they declared, "the Ohio River, the great channel, as well as the reservoir of emigration to the west, [which] carries by our doors along the whole length of our border, that inexhaustible current of population which is fertilizing the country more remotely west," would no longer lure settlers to circumvent the Allegheny sections of West Virginia.[48] Wood Countians advocated a law making it mandatory upon

---

[47] Greenbrier County Legislative Petitions, December 20, 1826; Delinquent Tax List, 1814, Monongalia County Court Records, West Virginia University Library.
[48] Kanawha County Legislative Petitions, December 12, 1817.

"every old claimant to ascertain his boundaries and manifest his claims or forfeit his rights thereto. And to make every innocent improver who shall have resided on the land three years or upwards under such an adverse title a compensation for all useful improvements thereon before such Improver shall be ousted from his possessions."[49]

Although West Virginia pioneers readily grasped the immediate implications of the Virginia land system and the resultant speculation, they could hardly have foreseen the ultimate consequences of the shortsighted policies. The sparse population and lack of internal improvements were the result of geographical conditions as well as of the land system. Without the vicious land policies, which prevailed in southwestern Virginia and Kentucky as well as in West Virginia, a strong, self-reliant, and determined yeomanry, guided by capable leaders, might have gone far in overcoming natural handicaps and in dealing successfully with economic, educational, and political problems which troubled mountainous areas. The tragedy of the system was that it deprived West Virginia of substantial numbers of these sturdy yeoman, who chose to settle where land titles were secure and opportunities somewhat greater. At the same time, much of the land—and the wealth—of West Virginia fell into the hands of absentee owners, whose major concern was profit on their investments and whose interest in the problems of the area was exceedingly limited. Finally, the land system laid the basis for an economic exploitation in the late nineteenth and the twentieth centuries such as few areas of the United States have experienced. Armed with laws which placed no restraint upon their greed, the speculators—the economic royalists of the post-Revolutionary generation—planted the seeds which in the mid-twentieth century bore bitter fruit in the form of Appalachia.

[49] Wood County Legislative Petitions, December 9, 1816.

Chapter Seven

Compromising with Nature

Seldom have environmental factors more profoundly shaped the life of a people or exerted a more enduring influence upon them than in the Allegheny Highlands. Their effects were particularly evident in the mountainous areas of West Virginia. There geographical features such as topography, rivers, forests, and soils determined in large measure the response of the settler to his problems of survival, the relationship of much of the state to the mainstream of late eighteenth- and early nineteenth-century American migration, and the stability or fluidity of the early settlements.

As elsewhere in the Alleghenies, West Virginia's rugged, forested terrain with its abundance of animal life for food and clothing, its infinite variety of fruits, berries, and nuts, and its unlimited supply of wood for building cabins and use as fuel offered its own peculiar kind of sustenance and stubbornly resisted the pioneer's efforts to mold his own environment. The forests receded with painful slowness before his expanding fields, and wild beasts, to which they gave cover, long remained a threat to livestock. In such an environment, hunting and food gathering at first took precedence over farming, and even after farms were well developed pioneer habits persisted.

Far from resenting the impositions of nature, the pioneer took to its prescriptions with alacrity. When Leonard Schnell, a Moravian missionary, visited a settlement near the headwaters of the South Branch of the Potomac in 1749, he preached to a congregation made up almost entirely of women and children, because the men, even though it was Sunday, were away hunting bears. Settlers in the Ohio Valley portion of the Alleghenies spent much of their time in hunting, very often bagging a hundred or more bears or deer during a single season. Believing that pelts were very good in every month in which the letter "r" appeared, they spent much of their time from early fall until late spring in the woods, and according to Francois Michaux, the noted traveler, developed a "fondness . . . for this kind of life . . . injurious to the cultivation of their lands." Michaux's observation was borne out by Joseph Doddridge, who remembered that long after the frontier was gone the men of western Virginia were seized at certain times of the year with a strange restlessness which was not allayed until they had completed a successful hunting expedition.[1]

The methods by which the earliest pioneer met the elementary needs of food, shelter, and clothing reflected his close alliance with the forest. Nothing gave more striking evidence of his dependence upon the forest than his cabin. His first home was a structure, often windowless, built of unhewn logs. He chinked the cracks with grass and mud and covered the cabin with a roof of clapboards about four feet long, which he fastened into place with heavy poles laid crosswise. A chimney of mud, sticks, and stones, of the "cat and clay" variety served the fireplace, which occupied most of one end of the building. Although the houses were "almost always in agreeable spots" with "charming views," their smallness and "wretched appearance," observed one traveler, seemed to belong to a country "in which wood is procured with the greatest difficulty."[2]

The interior of the cabin was as crude as its external appearance. There was often no floor except the earth itself, and the furnishings—tables, chairs, and beds—were rudely fashioned from slabs of native wood. A ladder might lead to a loft, which was ordinarily used for storage and for sleeping quarters for

[1] William J. Hinke and Charles Kemper, eds., "Moravian Diaries of Travels through Virginia," *Virginia Magazine of History and Biography*, XI (October, 1903), 121; Joseph Doddridge, *Notes, on the Settlement and Indian Wars, of the Western Parts of Virginia & Pennsylvania, from the Year 1763 until the Year 1783 Inclusive, Together with a View, of the State of Society and Manners of the First Settlers of the Western Country* (Wellsburgh, [W.] Va., 1824), p. 123; F. A. Michaux, *Travels to the Westward of the Allegany Mountains, in the States of Ohio, Kentucky, and Tennessee, and Return to Charleston, through the Upper Carolinas; . . . Undertaken in the Year X, 1802 . . .* (London, 1805), p. 132.

[2] Michaux, *Travels to the Westward of the Allegany Mountains*, pp. 132-33. See also Thaddeus Mason Harris, *The Journal of a Tour into the Territory Northwest of the Alleghany Mountains; Made in the Spring of the Year 1803 . . .* (Boston, 1805), pp. 15, 58-59.

younger members of the family. Spartan though they were, not every family possessed even these meager comforts. John Stewart, a Methodist circuit rider traveling the Little Kanawha Circuit in 1817–1818, was welcomed to one home which had neither chairs, table, bedstead, nor floors, and where to do courtesy to the minister, the owner "set out the iron bake-oven, and putting a lid on it, gave it to the preacher for a seat while they gathered about him to hear the news or receive such instruction as he had to give." When bedtime came, "one of the family claimbed [sic] up to the loft, threw down a quantity of robes, taken from the wild animals of the forest. These were spread on the ground floor on each side of a spacious fireplace, and soon parents, children, and the preacher were fast asleep."³

Accounts by other travelers show that the conditions described by Stewart were by no means rarities. Francis Asbury, the famed Methodist circuit rider and bishop who visited scores of residences over a period covering about a quarter of a century, wrote that he preferred "a plain, clean plank to lie on, as preferable to most of the beds, . . . and the floors are worse." Anne Royall, while spending the night at a house near Salt Sulphur Springs, fell victim to fleas, perhaps a not too uncommon experience.⁴

For food and clothing the first settler relied heavily upon his prowess as a hunter. With little effort he could provide his table with venison, bear meat, turkey, and small game, which in season his wife might supplement with wild fruits, nuts, berries, and an assortment of "greens." Corn from his semicleared fields completed the fare and became with bear meat the great staple of what during most of the year was a highly monotonous diet. Moravian missionaries who included the area in their itinerary in 1749 found bear meat in every house on the South Branch.⁵ Clothing, too, such as the hunting shirts and leggings of the

³ John Stewart, *Highways and Hedges; or, Fifty Years of Western Methodism* (Cincinnati, Ohio, 1872), pp. 35-36.

⁴ [Francis Asbury], *Journal of Rev. Francis Asbury, Bishop of the Methodist Episcopal Church,* 3 vols. (New York, n. d.), II, 37; Anne Royall, *Sketches of History, Life, and Manners, in the United States* (New Haven, Conn., 1826), p. 31.

⁵ Hinke and Kemper, eds., "Moravian Diaries of Travels through Virginia," XI (October, 1903), 122.

men, was made of skins taken from wild animals. Henry Smith, a Methodist circuit rider who preached to a congregation about fifteen miles from Clarksburg in 1794, reported his amazement when "I looked around me and saw one old man who had shoes on his feet. The [local] preacher wore Indian moccasins; every man, woman, and child besides, was bare-footed. Two old women had on what we called short-gowns, and the rest had neither short nor long gowns. This was a novel sight to me, for a Sunday congregation."[6]

If in outward appearances early West Virginia pioneers seemed much alike, the keen observer would have detected significant differences among them. Large numbers of the settlers were of that class which Frederick Jackson Turner designated pioneer farmers, but others were permanent settlers reduced by the exigencies of environment to a near-savage level of existence. The pioneer farmer lived principally by hunting and by grazing livestock on the natural vegetation of the country and limited his cultivation of corn and garden vegetables only to what he needed to supplement the bounties of forest and pasture. He seldom devoted much effort to improving his cabin or clearing additional acres. Nor did he become greatly agitated about land titles, since he ordinarily sought only the usufruct of the land and moved on when its bounties began to diminish. David Crouch, in describing his father, caught the spirit of this restless individual. The elder Crouch "wanted to live on the grass & the range. As soon as the range was gone, he wanted to move." He moved from the South Branch to the Tygart Valley in 1770, then to the Yadkin, and from there back to the Tygart Valley. Before death overtook him he moved three more times, finally stopping along the banks of the Ohio in Kentucky.[7]

There is evidence that the pioneer farmer made up an unusually large proportion of the early settlers of the Alleghenies. Francois Michaux estimated that one-half the settlers in the Ohio Valley were temporary residents. Although Michaux's figures are probably too high, there can be little doubt that the population of Allegheny areas of West Virginia

---

[6] Quoted in Wade Crawford Barclay, *Early American Methodism, 1769–1844,* 2 vols. (New York, 1949), I, 87.
[7] Statement of David Crouch, Draper MSS, 12CC225.

was highly mobile. Of 371 persons who received grants along the Monongahela, Cheat, and West Fork rivers on the basis of settlement rights established between 1769 and 1784, 156 obtained their lands by purchasing the rights of settlers who had preceded them and who had presumably moved. Ohio County survey books reveal that 80 of 321 persons who acquired rights based on settlements made along the upper Ohio between 1769 and 1777 assigned their rights to others.[8] Although the confusion of land titles undoubtedly drove some of these settlers to emigrate, it is likely that many of them merely succumbed to their wanderlust.

Alongside the pioneer farmer, but often not readily distinguishable, was the permanent settler. Unlike his restless neighbor, the latter had a vision of what time and industry might do for his virgin acres. The increasing reliance upon the cultivation of the soil is probably reflected in the size of West Virginia farms. Although the Virginia land law of 1779 recognized 400 acres as a reasonable amount for a farmer-grazier, most West Virginians, perhaps because of the terrain, did not acquire that amount. Of 287 landholders in Brooke County in 1799, 206 had less than 300 acres, and only 29 had more than 500. In the upper district of Ohio County, 293 of the 382 landowners held less than 300 acres, but again only 29 exceeded 500. The same proportions were exhibited by Lord Fairfax's rent rolls. In 1762 only 10 of 56 tenants on his South Branch Manor and 7 of 31 lessees on the Patterson's Creek Manor held more than 300 acres.[9]

Most settlers cultivated only a small part of their lands. Hands were scarce, and wages were out of proportion to the prices

[8] Michaux, *Travels to the Westward of the Allegany Mountains*, p. 192. For the figures on the Monongahela Valley and its tributaries, see Monongalia County Land Grants, I (1782–1785), passim; *ibid.*, II (1785–1786), passim. Upper Ohio Valley statistics are derived from Ohio County Survey Book, 1779–1786, passim; *ibid.*, 1786–1797, passim; *ibid.*, 1790–1859, passim, Ohio County Court Records, Microfilm in West Virginia University Library. Descriptions of pioneer farmers are in Michaux, *Travels to the Westward of the Allegany Mountains*, p. 135.

[9] Brooke County Land Tax Books, 1799, Brooke County Court Records, Microfilm in West Virginia University Library; Ohio County Land Tax Books, 1814, Ohio County Court Records, Microfilm in West Virginia University Library; Fairfax Rental List, South Branch Manor, South Branch Valley MSS, and Survey of Patterson's Creek Manor of Lord Fairfax by Joseph Neavill, November 20, 1762, Transcript in West Virginia Department of Archives and History Library.

received for agricultural products. Consequently, the pioneer cleared only as much land as he and his family could till. Along the Ohio this often amounted at first to only eight or ten acres. As late as 1834, farms in Monongalia and Harrison counties, described in Luther Haymond's survey books and probably typical of those in other mountainous parts of West Virginia, varied from three to eighty acres under cultivation, the average being about twenty-five. On the other hand, some settlers quickly set the plow to sizable holdings. Along the Ohio River, below Captina Creek, Michael Cresap, with hired help, had a substantial part of his thousand acres of "first rate bottom" in crops in 1802. At Belleville on Lee Creek George Avery, an immigrant from Connecticut, had seventy acres in corn, fifty in wheat, and a large meadow. John Wells' farm below the mouth of Fish Creek required the help of eight or nine hands at harvest time. But perhaps most impressive of all was the estate of Harman Blennerhassett near Parkersburg, which was one of the finest in the entire trans-Allegheny region.[10]

In frontier agriculture corn was king. Settlers planted it in fields not entirely clear of stumps and used only the hoe in its cultivation. Yet it throve, the average yield along the Kanawha, for example, being from fifty to eighty bushels an acre, with a hundred or more not at all uncommon. As early as 1755 corn grown in the Greenbrier region was pronounced the best in the colony of Virginia. For years it remained the chief crop in West Virginia's Eastern Panhandle, and for nearly a quarter of a century after settlement began there it was about the only crop grown along the Ohio River.

The reasons for the universality and popularity of corn are not difficult to fathom. Not only could it be planted before the land had been completely cleared, but it could be ground into meal with the simplest of devices. Moreover, it could be

[10] Michaux, *Travels to the Westward of the Allegany Mountains,* p. 132; Luther Haymond's Second Field Book, 1834, Monongalia and Harrison County Surveys, Cunningham Papers, Microfilm in West Virginia University Library; F[ortescue] Cuming, *Sketches of a Tour to the Western Country, through the States of Ohio and Kentucky; A Voyage down the Ohio and Mississippi Rivers, and a Trip through the Mississippi Territory, and Part of West Florida, Commenced at Philadelphia in the Winter of 1807, and Concluded in 1809* (Pittsburgh, Pa., 1810), pp. 99-100, 109-12.

prepared for the table in innumerable ways, the most popular forms being mush, grits, hominy, roasting ears, and journeycakes. Equally important, corn fitted perfectly into a system of agriculture which placed emphasis upon the raising of cattle and hogs.[11]

Within a few years the permanent settler turned to the cultivation of other grain crops such as wheat, rye, oats, barley, and buckwheat, the latter being especially well adapted to the higher elevations of Preston and Greenbrier counties. Next to corn, wheat was the most important grain crop, but it was usually not planted for at least three years after the land had been cleared and until the tree stumps had been removed. In new soil it grew too rank and shed its seed without forming an ear. Besides, in planting it had to be scattered by hand and "shoveled" or harrowed into the ground. Nevertheless, wheat prospered in most parts of West Virginia, particularly in the Potomac region and in the Monongahela Valley. On the level mountaintops of the Greenbrier country it yielded from thirty to forty bushels an acre. Because of their greater value, isolated mountain farmers often grew wheat, rye, oats, and buckwheat for cash crops and reserved their corn for their own use.[12]

Hemp and flax were also important crops on the West Virginia frontier, the former being raised chiefly as a money crop. As early as 1734 John Smith operated a grist and hemp mill at Smithfield in Berkeley County. For years large quantities of hemp were raised along the upper Potomac and on the South Branch of the Potomac and shipped downstream to cities and

[11] C. H. Ambler, ed., "The Diary of John D. Sutton and Kanawha County Land Grants," *West Virginia History,* IV (April, 1943), 194; Douglas Southall Freeman, *George Washington: A Biography,* 7 vols. (New York, 1948–1957), II, 121; Hu Maxwell and H. L. Swisher, *History of Hampshire County, West Virginia* (Morgantown, W. Va., 1897), p. 317; Michaux, *Travels to the Westward of the Allegany Mountains,* p. 133.

[12] Anne Royall, *Sketches of History, Life, and Manners,* pp. 69, 71; Ambler, ed., "The Diary of John D. Sutton and Kanawha County Land Grants," p. 194; Michaux, *Travels to the Westward of the Allegany Mountains,* p. 134; Maxwell and Swisher, *History of Hampshire County,* p. 316; Zadok Cramer, *The Navigator; Containing Directions for Navigating the Monongahela, Allegheny, Ohio, and Mississippi Rivers; With an Ample Account of These Much Admired Waters, from the Head of the Former to the Mouth of the Latter; And a Concise Description of Their Towns, Villages, Harbors, Settlements, &c. . . . .* (Pittsburgh, Pa., 1814), pp. 14-15.

towns along the Atlantic Coast. Although their cultivation was somewhat neglected in some parts of the Monongahela Valley, Francis Deakins advertised in 1804 that the Cheat Valley, where part of his extensive landholdings were located, was "remarkably Healthy & lands fertile, particularly in Grass flax & Hemp." Unlike hemp, flax was raised primarily for domestic consumption. When linen fibers were mixed with woolen, the result was linsey-woolsey, one of the most popular fabrics of pioneer times.[13]

Although most of the Allegheny area, unlike eastern Virginia, was ill-adapted to the cultivation of tobacco, pioneers did not entirely neglect the popular weed. As early as 1790 residents along both the South Branch and Patterson's Creek raised "considerable quantities of Tobacco," as did farmers of the lower Shenandoah Valley. In 1805 a number of the prominent citizens of the Kanawha Valley pronounced that region as "well adapted to the cultivation of tobacco" and asked that a tobacco inspector be established at Charleston. Earlier, in 1789, settlers along the Monongahela Valley, expecting "to experience the advantages of transporting their produce by water to market through the Channel of the Mississipi [sic]," asked that a tobacco inspector be located at Morgantown.[14]

Along with his increased attention to the cultivation of the soil, the pioneer placed heavy reliance upon the raising of livestock. He often chose the site for his dwelling at the mouth of a small hollow and turned his animals into the little valley behind his house to graze. In this way "the mountains hemmed in the cattle, so they co'dn't get over." Many farmers, if their locations permitted, sought the rich natural grasses which grew in the glades of the Alleghenies.[15]

Although there were variations in emphasis, most early pioneer

[13] Robert L. Bates, "Middleway, A Study in Social History," *West Virginia History,* XI (October, 1949-January, 1950), 25; John Wrigh[t] to William Fox, May 17, 1810, Fox Family Papers, West Virginia University Library; James Adam to Battaile Muse, May 20, 1783, Battaile Muse Papers, Duke University Library; Francis Deakins to John Gallaspie, July 10, 1804, Deakins Family Papers; Maxwell and Swisher, *History of Hampshire County,* p. 316.

[14] Hampshire County Legislative Petitions, October 19, 1790; Kanawha County Legislative Petitions, December 9, 1805; Monongalia County Legislative Petitions, October 21, 1789.

[15] Statement of Jacob Lawson, Draper MSS, 12CC251.

stockmen showed little inclination to specialize in animal husbandry. Typical of prosperous Eastern Panhandle farmers was
Thomas Hite of Berkeley County, who at the time of his death
in 1779 had sixteen horses, fifty-one cattle, and twenty-eight
sheep. Michael See, who lived on the South Branch of the
Potomac, in 1796 had eight horses, twenty-four cattle, six hogs,
and twenty-one sheep. In 1795 the estate of Edward Pindall of
Monongalia County included five horses, twelve cattle, and nine
sheep.[16]

As time passed farmers placed increasing value upon cattle
and hogs, partly because of the ease with which they could be
marketed. Very early they began the practice of making long
drives from the Potomac, Greenbrier, and Monongahela valleys
to such eastern cities as Washington, Baltimore, and Philadelphia.
Francis Deakins declared in 1804 that most of the beef arriving
at Washington, Baltimore, and Alexandria markets originated in
the Cheat and Monongahela valleys. In 1785, if not earlier,
Isaac Zane and George Green of Wheeling were driving cattle
to Detroit and "bringing back a great pile of money." On a
later journey, when they were returning with fourteen packhorses loaded with skins and furs, they were killed by Indians.
Many stockmen along the Ohio drove their cattle and hogs eastward by way of the Kanawha Valley. The road along the
Kanawha, wrote Anne Royall in 1823, "is alive from morning
till night, with people, horses, cattle, but principally hogs:
myriads of hogs are driven this way annually, to the east. They
commence driving in September, and from that [time] till
Christmas, you can look out no time in the day without seeing
a line of hogs."[17]

Without question, the South Branch of the Potomac was the

[16] Appraisement of the Estate of Thomas Hite, September 6, 1779, Rigsby
Papers, MSS in the possession of Leon Louisa Rigsby, Catlettsburg, Kentucky
(Microfilm in University of Kentucky Library); Appraisement of the Estate of
Michael See, April 13, 1796, South Branch Valley MSS; Appraisement of the Estate
of Edward Pindle [Pindall], November 14, 1795, Estates, 1799 [1795]–1829,
Monongalia County Court Records.

[17] Royall, *Sketches of History, Life, and Manners*, pp. 52, 71; Francis Deakins
to John Gallaspie, July 10, 1804, Deakins Family Papers. Depositions of John
Hanks and John Crawford, Draper MSS, 12CC138 and 12CC160, respectively,
throw light on the trade between the upper Ohio and Detroit.

cattle-raising section par excellence of West Virginia and perhaps of the entire Allegheny area. Cattlemen there are said to have originated two widely adopted techniques in animal husbandry. They neither sheltered nor housed their cattle, but placed them in open fields of from eight to ten acres and fed them twice daily on unhusked corn. They also developed the practice of cutting the stalks of corn off near the ground and then stacking them in the fields where the crop was grown.[18] With such winter forage and the use of the glades of the Alleghenies in the summer, they abandoned the practice of the pioneer farmer of allowing his livestock to fend for itself.

Hoping to reap the full advantage of their rich limestone soils and their nutritious natural grasses, South Branch cattlemen soon began to give thought to the improvement of their stock. Shortly after the American Revolution, Matthew Patton of Pendleton County purchased blooded English cattle from Gough and Miller, the Maryland and Virginia importers. Although "large, somewhat coarse and rough, with very long horns," the Patton cattle, a cross between the common stock and the English breeds, proved far superior to their predecessors. Within a few years Patton and members of his family moved to the Kentucky Bluegrass region, where the "Patton stock" became favorities with cattlemen for their milking qualities, their great size, and their excellence for crossing with the common stock of the area. For these reasons, South Branch stockmen, like those of Kentucky, continued to prefer the longhorns even after the shorthorn cattle craze had swept the country. In 1808, when ordinary stock was selling at two to four pounds per head, improved cattle in the South Branch Valley brought as much as ten pounds.[19]

[18] U. S., Bureau of the Census, *Agriculture of the United States in 1860; Compiled from the Original Returns of the Eighth Census* (Washington, D. C., 1864), p. cxxx,

[19] Frankfort (Ky) *Franklin Farmer*, II (February 9, 1839), 169. For a description of the Patton cattle and their impact upon the western livestock business, see Otis K. Rice, "Importations of Cattle into Kentucky, 1785–1860," *Register of the Kentucky Historical Society*, XLIX (January, 1951), 36-38. See also List of Cattle Sold to Solomon Fisher, January, 1808, Fox Family Papers; Appraisement of the Estate of Michael See, April 13, 1796; Appraisement of the Estate of Edward Pindle [Pindall], November 14, 1795; Pendleton County Legislative Petitions, December 15, 1815; Hampshire County Legislative Petitions, December 7, 1815.

During the early nineteenth century the South Branch became a major link in the nation's west-to-east cattle business. Many of the most prominent cattlemen of the Ohio Valley, including members of the Renick, Inskeep, Patton, Gay, and Sanders families, had emigrated from the South Branch Valley and continued to keep close contacts with stockmen there. Michaux noted as early as 1802 that western cattlemen sent droves of from two to three hundred cattle to the Potomac region, "where they sell them to graziers . . . who afterwards fatten them for the markets of Baltimore and Philadelphia." By 1822 many of "the most worthy, respectable and influential persons" residing along the South Branch were "extensively engaged in the business of grazing cattle in the Allegany Glades" and were employing herdsmen to care for the animals which they sent to graze there during the summer months. By that time, too, residents of the Greenbrier area were, according to Anne Royall, taking "great pains in the art of rearing cattle," having found their soil better adapted to grass than to grain.[20]

Sheep-raising, for many years limited primarily to meeting family needs, was hindered in the Allegheny regions by the numerous packs of wolves which roamed the woods. Voicing a complaint common among pioneers, Monongalia Countians declared in 1798 that, despite the bounty on wolves, they continued to lose large numbers of sheep, which, they said, "Deprives us of the Chance of Manufacturing our Wearing Aperral—[as] those Ravenous Vermin Destroys both Sheep and young hogs." Residents of Hampshire County experienced "such devastation" from wolves that sheep-raising was hardly profitable. In 1808, with American trade with Europe disrupted by the Embargo and the Napoleonic Wars, Hampshire County farmers appealed to the General Assembly for relief, declaring that "at a time like this when the situation of our country calls so loudly for the encouragement of domestick manufactories of every kind the pressure of this inconvenience is doubly felt." They asked that

[20] Michaux, *Travels to the Westward of the Allegany Mountains,* pp. 235-36; Cuming, *Sketches of a Tour to the Western Country,* p. 117; Paul C. Henlein, *Cattle Kingdom in the Ohio Valley, 1783–1860* (Lexington, Ky., 1959), pp. 2-3; George Calmes to John Pearce and Vause Fox, April 25, 1822, Fox Family Papers; Royall, *Sketches of History, Life, and Manners,* p. 71.

the bounty on wolves be increased as a means of insuring "the destruction of that noxious animal."[21]

As the menace from wolves diminished, stockmen gave greater attention to sheep-raising. In the Northern Panhandle the completion of the National Road to Wheeling in 1818 also gave impetus to the industry. In 1825 the area between Harmon's Creek and Wheeling Creek, which was some twenty-five miles in length and five miles in width, provided pasturage for five to six thousand lambs.[22]

Perhaps the lowliest of all forms of animal husbandry was the raising of hogs. Long after other types of agriculture had emerged from their primitive beginnings, hog-raisers continued the custom of turning their animals loose to feed on the mast in the woods or upon whatever else they could find. Because of this practice, they often incurred an odium not visited upon other farmers. The Virginia legislature was constantly besieged with petitions from the chartered towns asking laws to prevent hogs from running at large. Morgantown residents complained that some owners had as many as forty or fifty hogs loose in the streets, but they intimated that there would be no serious objection were the number per family only three or four. In December, 1797, nearly two hundred petitioners, including numerous cattlemen, who occupied rich lands along the South Branch, besought the General Assembly to enact a law forbidding hogs from running at large on the South Branch Manor. They branded the practice a nuisance and declared that they were helpless against it because of their inability to procure sufficient fence rails to enclose their lands.[23]

Hog-raisers dependent upon the mast, many of them from the poorer economic strata of society, looked upon any restrictive laws as highly discriminatory class legislation. Residents of the South Branch Manor who lived some distance from the river

[21] Monongalia County Legislative Petitions, December 7, 1798; Hampshire County Legislative Petitions, December 8, 1808; Greenbrier County Legislative Petitions, December 20, 1803; Harrison County Legislative Petitions, December 24, 1807.
[22] William Vause to Vause Fox, May 5, 1825, Fox Family Papers.
[23] Hampshire County Legislative Petitions, December 7, 1797; Monongalia County Legislative Petitions, December 22, 1807; Ohio County Legislative Petitions, December 8, 1803.

rightly claimed that the mast was essential to their economic welfare. They argued that persons who had no lands of their own and those who cultivated lands on the share with landowners, which was "a very common case on the manor," would be unable to raise enough hogs to support their families. Moreover, they declared, "a very undue Influence will be throwen in to the hands of the Landholders on the river who having large pasture Lands can raise what Hogs they please and despose of them to there [*sic*] less fortunate neighbours on there [*sic*] own terms." The legislature harkened to their pleas and rejected requests to force owners to enclose their stock. A similar objection was voiced by residents of the town of Franklin, who, faced with a petition to prevent their stock from running at large, declared that the range, which was so convenient to the town, was especially necessary to the poor.[24]

With the shift from a woods economy to an agricultural base, and particularly after the plow supplanted the hoe, the horse assumed major importance on the pioneer farm. Not only was he needed as a draft animal, but he was essential to the transportation of furs, skins, and farm products to market. As early as 1748 James Rutledge had a "Horse Jockey" about seventy miles above the mouth of the South Branch. By 1797 only twelve of 316 Pendleton County families were without horses, and the average number per family was from two to four. George Rexroad, at the time owned eighty-four horses and was evidently a dealer with considerable business. About the same situation prevailed in Monroe County, where in 1804 some 800 taxpayers owned 2,045 horses. When Anne Royall first visited the Greenbrier region, "there were not a dozen horses that could be called handsome in the whole bounds," but with attention to breeding, there were in 1823 numerous animals remarkable for both their size and their beauty. In the Northern Panhandle of West Virginia the large and muscular Shylock colts made a "considerable sound" among farmers.[25]

---

[24] Hampshire County Legislative Petitions, December 7, 1797; Pendleton County Legislative Petitions, December 2, 1800.

[25] John C. Fitzpatrick, ed., *The Writings of George Washington from the Original Manuscript Sources, 1745–1799*, 39 vols. (Washington, D. C., 1931-1944), I, 10; Pendleton County Assessment Book of James Ewin, 1797, West Virginia University

Despite the improvements in agriculture, there remained many sections of the Alleghenies where farming methods changed but little. Peter H. Steenbergen, John Lewis, and Lewis Summers, in seeking incorporation of the Mason, Cabell, and Kanawha Agricultural Society, declared in 1840 that "with some exceptions the tillage of the cleared lands [in trans-Allegheny West Virginia] has not advanced beyond the first rudiments in husbandry." Pointing to the beneficial effects of government support to agriculture in such countries as England and France and of agricultural societies in other states, they urged the establishment of a state board of agriculture which would study Virginia's agricultural problems and disseminate information of value to the state's farmers. They also recommended the setting up of four experimental farms in the state, one of which would be located at the mouth of the Kanawha River.[26]

In addition to his livestock, wheat, and tobacco, the pioneer soon found other products which could be converted into cash or traded for articles which he could not produce for himself. Apples and peaches from his growing orchards were made into readily marketable brandy, cider, and cider royal. Ginseng, or "sang" as the pioneer called it, abounded in the hills and was in great demand in eastern seaboard cities, where it was an important commodity in the China trade. Maple trees, growing by the thousands on the hillsides, provided sap from which sugar was extracted, affording the pioneer not only sweetening for his own table but another article with cash value. By custom, the proceeds from the sale of such articles as butter, cheese, wool, and feathers were turned over to the womenfolk, who used them to purchase coffee, tea, and other luxuries which added to the comfort and even the grace of the pioneer home.[27]

Once he had surmounted the problems of mere survival and had diversified the economic base upon which his livelihood rested, the enterprising settler began to give thought to more

---

Library; Personal Property Tax List, 1804, Monroe County Court Records, Microfilm in West Virginia University Library; Royall, *Sketches of History, Life, and Manners*, p. 71; William Vause to Vause Fox, May 5, 1825, Fox Family Papers.

[26] Mason County Legislative Petitions, December 23, 1840.

[27] Cramer, *Navigator*, p. 15; Cuming, *Sketches of a Tour to the Western Country*, p. 114; Royall, *Sketches of History, Life, and Manners*, pp. 56, 71-72.

substantial living quarters. His crude log cabin gave way to a house constructed of hewn logs, with the cracks filled with stones and clay and with a roof made of shingles "nicely laid on." Glass panes adorned the windows, replacing the oiled paper which served the original cabin—if, indeed, it had had any windows at all. Squared stone blocks made possible a more satisfactory chimney, and puncheons or even planks provided a smooth floor. In some parts of the state the double log house, with its two rooms divided by a central breezeway, or "dog-run," was popular. Other pioneers preferred to add lean-tos to the house in order to provide additional space for a growing family.[28]

By this time the pioneer was ready for some of the material comforts and even a few of the luxuries of life. To satisfy these yearnings, he sent surpluses from his farm and products of the forest by packhorse to eastern towns or by flatboat or canoe downstream to the western river towns, where he traded his goods for a variety of articles. In many parts of the state, however, itinerant merchants, sensing a profitable business, made their way to the settler's very door. Along the Ohio River, vendors from Pittsburgh and Wheeling passed up and down stream in canoes laden with numerous small wares and accepted in payment butter, hemp, brandy, flour, and other farm products. In 1807 Fortescue Cuming observed a "floating store" which had taken on a cargo at Wheeling for the downriver traffic. This craft was "a large square flat, roofed and fitted with shelves and counter, and containing a various assortment of merchandise, among which were several copper stills, of which use is now made throughout the whole western country for distilling peach and apple brandy." The store's two owners acted as both boatmen and merchants and established rapport with their customers by first inviting them to "partake of a dram" with them.[29]

Among the merchants of the Greenbrier and Monroe County areas was Andrew Beirne, an immigrant from County Roscommon, Ireland. In 1795 Beirne began business as a peddler, transporting his wares overland by wagon from Philadelphia.

[28] Harris, *Journal of a Tour into the Territory Northwest of the Alleghany Mountains*, p. 15; Cuming, *Sketches of a Tour to the Western Country*, pp. 134-35.
[29] Michaux, *Travels to the Westward of the Allegany Mountains*, p. 135; Cuming, *Sketches of a Tour to the Western Country*, p. 98.

Much of his payment took the form of ginseng, cattle, and pelts, but he also accepted virtually any salable farm product. A graduate of Trinity College in Dublin, Beirne possessed a pleasing personality and unusual business acumen. He prospered beyond all expectations, was ultimately elected to the Virginia state senate and then to Congress, and at the time of his death was reputedly worth a million dollars.[30]

The success of Andrew Beirne testifies to the pioneer's deep desire for the trappings of civilization. The records of one merchant in the Greenbrier-Monroe area show that in 1784 he retailed a wide assortment of articles including fine linen, calico, Holland, silk for bonnets, cambric, velvet, broadcloth, check, Durant, stock mohair, scarlet cloaks, and apron strings; buttons, needles, and thread; salt, pepper, chocolate, ginger, pepper boxes, and coffee; teapots, coffeepots, cruets, soup plates, cups and saucers, knives, and tumblers; and guns, barlow knives, padlocks, jackknives, and saddles. A further analysis of his sales reveals that twelve families bought silk handkerchiefs; eleven families, shoe buckles; three, knee buckles; six, inkpots or inkstands; twenty-one, looking glasses; fifteen, knives and forks; nineteen, ribbons of various kinds; five, razors; and twelve, quantities of rum, ranging from one pint to four gallons, with the exception of one customer, Garret Green, who traded his entire stock of seventy pounds of ginseng and certain credits established with the merchant for forty gallons of rum.

One of the most significant aspects of this merchant's transactions for 1784—and the same was true of many other early businesses—was that they were conducted almost entirely without money. Although his total sales were slightly in excess of 906 pounds, the merchant received a little less than 18 pounds, or less than 2 percent of his income, in cash. The article most frequently offered in payment for his goods was ginseng, of which he accepted 5,178 pounds and for which he allowed his customers two shillings sixpence per pound. Ginseng thus ac-

[30] Edward T. White, "Andrew Beirne and Oliver Beirne of Monroe County," *West Virginia History,* XX (October, 1958), 16; Edward Fife to Thomas Fife, July 7, 1816, Wilson and Stribling Family Papers, West Virginia University Library; Royall, *Sketches of History, Life, and Manners,* pp. 36-38; Ruth Woods Dayton, *Greenbrier Pioneers and Their Homes* (Charleston, W. Va., 1942), pp. 206-208.

counted for nearly 640 pounds, or over 70 percent, of his receipts. He also took a variety of other roots, particularly snakeroot, as well as saltpeter, corn, rye, tallow, and brimstone.

Careful examination of the operations of the merchant, however, indicates a more complex business life than that of a mere exchange of goods between a retailer and his customers. With money almost nonexistent in the area, the merchant performed a kind of elementary banking function by permitting customers to discharge obligations to third parties by arranging for the latter to draw upon credits which the debtors established with the merchant. Of 129 accounts listed on the books for 1784, 50 showed either charges or credits involving third persons.[31]

Another account book for the same Greenbrier-Monroe area provides graphic documentation of an advancing economy. In 1783 this merchant, too, accepted large quantities of ginseng, which accounted for 197 pounds of his total receipts of 299 pounds. Ten years later he took no ginseng. Instead, eleven customers paid their accounts entirely with cash, and fifteen others used money for part of their payments. But along with the customary payment in brandy, wheat, barley, and saltpeter, the merchant received numerous other articles and services, including a waterwheel, cooperage, masonry, "weatherboarding the house," and "the hire of . . . Negroes [at] 6 dol[lars per] month." The trend away from a high degree of self-sufficiency and toward a greater specialization in labor was perhaps even more discernible in the account book of a Greenbrier merchant, who during the years between 1799 and 1814 received payment in such services as spinning, shaving shingles, smithing, shoemaking, clearing ground, mowing, saddlery work, fulling, and stilling.[32]

The economic growth of trans-Allegheny West Virginia was seriously impeded by the shortage of money, which during the post-Revolutionary War years was so acute that the collection of taxes became virtually impossible. Monongalia Countians

[31] Unidentified Private Account Book, 1783–1785, Monroe County Court Records.

[32] Unidentified Private Account Book 1783–1810, Monroe County Court Records; [James Alexander?], Greenbrier County Ledger, 1800 [1799]–1814, West Virginia Department of Archives and History Library.

complained in 1782 that "Specie cannot be rais[d] in this Country as there is (Comparatively speaking) none amongst us," and asked that they be permitted to pay a special tax levied upon them in kind. Five years later they still experienced such a scarcity of specie that they were prevented from "paying an Equal proportion of the General taxes." They specifically pointed to the poll tax as a burden and blamed it for the removal of many settlers either down the Ohio or into Pennsylvania. About the same time some eighty Ohio County residents, including some of the most prominent families in the county, contended that all the specie in their county would not cover one-fourth of the taxes for one year and asked that they might be allowed to pay their taxes in products such as hemp, flour, or tobacco. They even asked that a warehouse he built somewhere on the Ohio River to receive these products. An even more serious situation prevailed in Greenbrier County, where the sheriff, Andrew Donnally, declared in 1782 that not only was there no money in the county but that the payment of taxes in "commutables" was useless because of a lack of a wagon road for transporting the products.[33]

The transition from a woods to a diversified agrarian economy occurred at widely disparate rates in Allegheny West Virginia. Maturation took place most rapidly in the Eastern Panhandle, in the Greenbrier-Monroe area, along the upper Ohio, and in parts of the Monongahela and Kanawha Valleys. But even in these sections primitive ways of life long remained intermingled with more complex forms, and in many of the more isolated and mountainous areas an enervating retardation placed an almost indelible stamp upon a large part of the population. A New England missionary described the houses along the upper Kanawha in 1817—more than forty years after settlements had first been established—as "mere hovels, to which the dwellings of the poorest labourers of the northern states, seem like little palaces." Moreover, he continued, "the furniture and arrangement, in some, the inside of which I saw, bore a just proportion to their

[33] Monongalia County Legislative Petitions, November 12, 1782; *ibid.,* October 26, 1787; Ohio County Legislative Petitions, October 26, 1786; Greenbrier County Legislative Petitions, June 11, 1784.

appearance without." On both sides of the Kanawha River he found a "considerable number of these poor ignorant settlers," who, in spite of their illiteracy and lack of comforts, displayed a cheerful and generous nature. "Poverty personified," declared the sympathetic missionary. Elbridge Gerry, Jr., who journeyed eastward from Marietta via Salem and Clarksburg in 1813, reported conditions equally primitive. Indeed, travelers' accounts so frequently point to a lassitude among many of the early residents of the mountainous regions that there can be little doubt that many settlers had yielded to the often overpowering forces of environment and failed to catch the vision of a more sophisticated life which motivated many of their fellow pioneers.[34]

Some pioneers who distinguished themselves as hunters and Indian fighters in the advance of the frontier never successfully adapted to a stabilized, agrarian society. Typical of such persons were the Wetzel brothers of Ohio County. From the time of their arrival on Wheeling Creek, reputedly in 1770, until "the conclusion of peace with the indians," the Wetzel family "lived in a State of warfare on the Frontier, continuously, spending the greater part of every Season in hunting and destroying the enemy without paying any or little attention to their own private affairs." Most of their scouting was done on a voluntary basis, and "they could neither receive pay or pensions from their country." The Wetzel brothers—Martin, Jacob, Lewis, and John —in seeking pensions from the state in 1803, declared that it was well-known that they and their father had "rendered more Service, and provided more protection to the Frontier than any family that ever lived on it and more to their own present detriment." By constantly traversing the wilderness they had "with their own hands taken and destroyed thirty two or thereabouts indians at different times of hostility, & mostly in individual engagements."

The brothers declared that because of the mode of life "in which they were raised, . . . none of them learned trades, or any other method of Supporting themselves except laboring on a

---

[34] Isaac Reed, *The Christian Traveller, in Five Parts, including Nine Years and Eighteen Thousand Miles* (New York, 1828), p. 34; Claude G. Bowers, ed., *The Diary of Elbridge Gerry, Jr.* (New York, 1927), pp. 121-23.

farm." But the wounds which they had sustained in battling the Indians now prevented their farming. Lewis, who had been "shot thro the breast from side to side," was "wholly disabled to labor." Jacob had "one arm broken and [the] other disjointed"; Martin had been "shot thro each hip each side & thro his shoulder"; and John had his arm broken both above and below the elbow. All of them, the brothers said, were thus unable to do any labor.[35]

Although few families could match their record, the Wetzels had many kindred spirits in trans-Allegheny West Virginia. With an environment which proved highly unresponsive to his hand and with forty years—nearly two generations—of sustained warfare with the Indians, the Allegheny pioneer could hardly have been other than slow in returning to more sophisticated ways of life. Most of the mountain pioneers, however, were motivated by the same human desires as the remainder of the country, and thanks to their valiant efforts the wilderness was conquered and nature became a partner rather than an enemy.

[35] Wood County Legislative Petitions, December 8, 1803.

Chapter Eight

Mountaineer Ways and Folkways

In 1861, when he began scouting activities in the Kanawha Valley, General Jacob D. Cox found "little farms in secluded nooks among the mountains, where grown men . . . had never before seen the American flag, and whole families had never been further from home than a church and country store, a few miles away." Luther Haymond, a member of a prominent Clarksburg family, declared that he was well past twenty-one years old before he ventured beyond the bounds of three Monongahela Valley counties.[1] The isolation which these observations bespoke, unrelieved by a transcendent system of education, preserved customs and ways of thinking which the settlers carried with them into the Alleghenies and in time accentuated traits and practices which might otherwise have been discarded or modified.

The loneliness incident to life in mountainous areas gave rise to an interest in others that often evoked excessive inquisitiveness and to a friendliness upon which numerous travelers commented. Even in the crudest cabin the wayfarer was hospitably received, provided with food, and offered accommodations for the night. On the other hand, the insatiable curiosity of the pioneer's family frequently taxed his patience. Anne Royall declared that any stranger who stopped at a house in the Greenbrier region was bombarded with questions: "What may be your name? where are you going? from whence you came? and whether you are married? and have you any children? and whether your father and mother be alive?"[2]

Because of his loneliness, the mountain pioneer welcomed opportunities for social gatherings. Weddings were especially festive occasions. On the morning of the wedding day attendants and friends of the bridegroom assembled at his house. They accompanied him to the bride's house, arranging to reach it just before noon, a popular hour for frontier weddings. Pranksters saw to it that the progress of the wedding party was impeded by trees felled across its path, snares of tangled vines, and other obstructions. Sometimes they fired guns, covering the party with smoke, startling the horses, and giving the gallant young men an opportunity to prove their chivalry to the ladies in the procession.

When the company was about a mile from the bride's house, two young men were chosen to "run for the bottle," a container filled with alcoholic refreshments and in the possession of the bride's father. This dash, often over a course obstructed by trees and dense undergrowth, involved a test of horsemanship. The victor in the race returned to the approaching party with the bottle, which he first presented to the bridegroom and then passed along so that each of the members could partake of its contents.

Following the marriage ceremony the bride's family set before the guests a dinner as sumptuous as farm and forest could provide, with ample servings of beef, pork, fowl, bear, and venison and an assortment of fruits and vegetables. German settlers usually chose four young men and four young women to serve the meal. One of their duties was to prevent anyone from stealing the bride's shoe from her foot. Should they fail to protect her, they were assessed a fine of a dollar or a bottle of wine, and the bride was not permitted to dance until her shoe had been recovered. The dancing began soon after dinner was over and lasted until morning.

About nine o'clock, while the festivities were in full swing, a

---

1 Jacob D. Cox, *Military Reminiscences of the Civil War,* 2 vols. (New York, 1900), I, 85; Luther Haymond Diary [1809–1830], West Virginia University Library.

2 William J. Hinke and Charles Kemper, eds., "Moravian Diaries of Travels through Virginia," *Virginia Magazine of History and Biography,* XI (October, 1903), 122; John Stewart, *Highways and Hedges; or, Fifty Years of Western Methodism* (Cincinnati, Ohio, 1872), pp. 35-36; Anne Royall, *Sketches of History, Life, and Manners in the United States* (New Haven, Conn., 1826), pp. 47, 59. An account with adverse comments upon the friendliness of West Virginians is F[ortescue] Cuming, *Sketches of a Tour to the Western Country, through the States of Ohio and Kentucky; A Voyage down the Ohio and Mississippi Rivers, and a Trip through the Mississippi Territory, and Part of West Florida, Commenced at Philadelphia in the Winter of 1807, and Concluded in 1809* (Pittsburgh, Pa., 1810), p. 135.

group of young ladies led the bride to her bed in the loft. Young men then escorted the bridegroom thither. The merrymakers did not forget the newlyweds, but from time to time during the night carried "Black Betty," or the bottle of spirits, and quantities of food up to them. Nor did they neglect their own thirst. They frequently called for "Black Betty" and drank toasts to the bride and bridegroom and wished them strong and healthy children.

There yet remained the infare, the phase of the wedding celebration which took place at the bridegroom's home. Once again the wedding party rode forth, with a repetition of the prankish behavior of the wedding day, including another run for the bottle, filled for this occasion by the bridegroom's father. Another round of feasting and dancing awaited the guests before the festivities were concluded.[3]

Construction of a cabin for the newly married pair provided yet another occasion for socializing. Once the site had been selected, a "fatigue party" arrived to cut down the trees, haul the logs to a designated spot, make the clapboards for the roof, and prepare the puncheons for the floor. By evening the foundation was laid. The next morning the actual raising began. While four skilled cornermen notched and placed the logs, other workers laid the floor or built the chimney. Thanks to the pioneer dexterity with the axe, the cabin was quickly brought under roof, and by the end of the third day was ready for occupancy and the housewarming.[4]

Most of the first churches and schoolhouses were the result of similar common endeavor, and even after better buildings were in demand, the habit of cooperation survived. According to tradition, while the men of the Lewisburg area were building the Old Stone Church in 1796, their womenfolk carried the sand for their mortar by horseback from the Greenbrier River, four miles away. Women of the French Creek community made

---

[3] Joseph Doddridge, *Notes, on the Settlement and Indian Wars, of the Western Parts of Virginia & Pennsylvania, from the Year 1763 until the Year 1783 Inclusive, together with a View, of the State of Society and Manners of the First Settlers of the Western Country* (Wellsburgh, [W.] Va., 1824), pp. 128-34; Samuel Kercheval, *A History of the Valley of Virginia*, ed. Oren F. Morton, 4th ed. (Strasburg, Va., 1925), pp. 61-62.

[4] Doddridge, *Notes, on the Settlement and Indian Wars, of the Western Parts of Virginia & Pennsylvania*, pp. 134-37.

their contribution to the construction of the Presbyterian church there about 1823 by spinning flax and making linen, which was taken by horseback to Staunton and traded for nails and glass. Contributions to the construction of the Clarksburg Presbyterian Church took a somewhat different form. Waldo P. Goff gave "$20 in goods," Daniel Wilson ten sheep, Hiram Lincoln $10 in plank at his mill, and John Garrett $12.50 in shingles.[5]

An essential part of the work of clearing land for farms and public structures and one which required cooperation among pioneer families was the logrolling, which usually began in February and lasted for about six weeks. In preparation for this event, the owner of the land cut the trees, removed the branches, and then cut notches about ten feet apart along the tops of the remaining logs. At each of the notches he placed a dry limb, which he ignited so that it would burn for a time. After repeating the latter process morning and night for about a week, he had burned the log into manageable lengths. On the day of the logrolling, the men of the neighborhood gathered, equipped with handspikes made of dogwood and about five feet long. They slid the handspikes under the log so that they could get holds on each side and then carried the log to the heap where it was to be burned. To be able to "pull down" other men in a logrolling contest was a mark of prestige. Often the host at a logrolling served a dish known as bergoo, a kind of potpie made of vegetables and wild meats, such as squirrel, turkey, and venison. It was a dull and lazy neighborhood that did not have ten or twelve logrollings in the early spring.[6]

Less strenuous but no less exciting than the logrolling was the corn shucking. At the appointed time, men came with the sleds and oxen and heaped the corn, which had been "snapped," into great stacks. In some cases the shucking was accelerated by placing a jug of apply brandy or other spirits at the bottom of

[5] U. S., Work Projects Administration, Historical Records Survey, *Inventory of the Church Archives of West Virginia: The Presbyterian Churches* (Charleston, W. Va., 1941), pp. 61, 109; Clarksburg Presbyterian Church Records, 1798–1803, West Virginia University Library.

[6] Everett Dick, *The Dixie Frontier: A Social History of the Southern Frontier from the First Transmontane Beginnings to the Civil War* (New York, 1948), pp. 125-27; George W. Atkinson, *History of Kanawha County, from Its Organization in 1789 until the Present Time* (Charleston, W. Va., 1876), p. 103.

the stack. The man who found the jug not only had the privilege of drinking first but also the right to kiss "the best lookin' gal" in attendance. The corn shucking ended with a frolic—singing, square dancing, and drinking.[7]

In the fall, too, the making of sorghum molasses often brought neighbors together. The operation provided work for everyone in the family, either in the cane field, in feeding fresh stalks to the mill, in clearing the mill grinders of pulp, or stirring the boiling juice. Children were kept busy gathering wood for the fire, which was made in a furnace of field stones and clay. Even the mule or ox did his part by turning the mill. Finally, there was the "lasses lickin'," in which each person was provided with a small wooden paddle to scrape the leavings from the boiling pan. Then followed games, singing, and storytelling. As always, young couples enjoyed the occasion for it was said, "as everybody knows and expects, 'they's a sight o' courtin' ben did at 'lasses lickin's.' "[8]

With women, quilting parties were favorite occasions. While the men were engaged in house raisings, logrollings, and corn shuckings, the women pieced quilts and prepared meals. In some instances the women completed from three to five quilts, with designs of "circles, semi-circles, curved and straight lines, diamonds, hearts, and every imaginable shape and form."[9]

Funerals provided more solemn occasions for neighborhood gatherings. Because of the lack of ministers in many isolated areas, the dead were laid to rest with the simplest of ceremonies. But proper respect required that services by a minister be held at the first opportunity. Accordingly, there developed the custom of holding a second funeral when a minister made his rounds, which might be weeks, months, or even years, later. Services consisted of a sermon, a procession to the grave, the singing of hymns, and a floral offering. Persons of unusual standing in a community were frequently accorded special marks of respect. When Asa Brooks, a pastor of the Clarksburg Presbyterian Church, died in 1834, residents met "to take into consideration

---

[7] U. S., Work Projects Administration, Writers' Program, *West Virginia: A Guide to the Mountain State* (New York, 1941), p. 470.

[8] *Ibid.*, pp. 415-16.

[9] Atkinson, *History of Kanawha County*, p. 104.

the measures most proper . . . in paying the last honors" to him. They decided not only to suspend all business in the town for three hours and to invite all citizens to the funeral but also asked that they "wear crape on the left arm for one month, as a testimony of their respect for the deceased."[10]

Wherever pioneers gathered, except under the most grave circumstances, sports featuring tests of skill or strength excited interest. Running, jumping, and wrestling were popular with both men and boys. In wrestling, combatants sometimes gouged out eyes, bit off ears and otherwise maimed their opponents. Some sports, such as throwing the tomahawk and shooting matches, had considerable practical value. In throwing the tomahawk, young lads learned to ascertain the number of turns which it would take in a given distance and to imbed it in a tree from almost any position. Marksmanship, encouraged in every young boy, improved with the hunting of raccoons and turkeys or "barking" a squirrel and enabled the youth of twelve or thirteen years to perform important services as a fort soldier during Indian attacks. Under normal circumstances, the pioneer, possessed of amazing accuracy with the rifle, preferred to shoot from a rest and "at as great a distance as the length and weight of a barrel of a gun would throw a ball on a horizontal level."[11]

One of the oldest and most picturesque of sports in the Alleghenies was the ring tournament held in the South Branch Valley. With an elaborate ceremony and an ancient ritual, the tournament involved tests of skill and precision. For the occasion, three arches were erected and placed sixty feet apart. From each a ring one and one-half inches in diameter was suspended. Contestants, "knights" on horseback, galloped beneath the arches and attempted to collect the rings on the tip of a needlepointed lance seven to nine feet long. Each "knight" rode the course three times. Those who collected all nine rings, or perhaps the five who collected the most, participated in the second round in which rings three-fourths of an inch in diameter were used. Winners of this round then vied with each other in an attempt

---

[10] U. S., W. P. A., *West Virginia*, p. 142; Clarksburg Presbyterian Church Records, 1798–1903, December 23, 1824.

[11] Doddridge, *Notes, on the Settlement and Indian Wars, of the Western Parts of Virginia & Pennsylvania*, pp. 156-59.

to collect rings only one-half inch in diameter. The winner of the last course had the right to select the queen of the tournament. This popular sport has survived into the mid-twentieth century.[12]

The monotony of pioneer life was also relieved by a variety of political and religious gatherings. Services of local church congregations were supplemented by protracted meetings, church conferences, and camp meetings. With the growth of county government, court days brought the excitement incident to cases of assault and battery, defamation of character, and even murder. They also brought wrestling bouts, feats of strength and marksmanship, drinking, gambling, and fighting. Elections evoked equal interest and the same kinds of diversion.

As colorful and exciting as the experiences themselves were the pioneer's stories and songs. Told and retold before the cabin fires on long winter evenings and at neighborhood gatherings, they constituted a significant part of the frontier folklore which was passed from generation to generation. Abounding in detail and filled with adventure, many of the narratives bore striking resemblance to the wanderings of Ulysses or to *Pilgrim's Progress*. But the frontier mind was also creative, and many stories bore the unmistakable stamp of pioneer exaggeration. When Luther-Haymond journeyed from Clarksburg to Baltimore in 1830 he kept a diary, which was characterized by exaggeration and "profanity." Haymond later regretted the "profanity," but explained that the diary had actually been written for the entertainment of his friends, who, like himself, had never been far from home. Many popular songs of the mountain frontier dealt with the exploits of mythical heroes, whose feats attested the well-known propensity of the pioneer for extravagant statement. Others, in the tradition of much folk music, were concerned with personal tragedy and were often referred to as "love songs about murder."[13]

The pioneer could recognize a tall tale for what it was, but stories of ghosts and witchcraft he did not dismiss so lightly.

---

[12] U. S., W. P. A., *West Virginia*, pp. 141-42, 338-39.

[13] Doddridge, *Notes, on the Settlement and Indian Wars, of the Western Parts of Virginia & Pennsylvania*, pp. 159-60; Luther Haymond Diary.

Witches were believed to be responsible for strange and incurable diseases, especially among children. They were reported to have also changed men into horses and ridden them to their frolics or to their haunts. Fortunately, the settler had means of breaking witches' spells. One method was to draw a picture of the witch on a board or tree stump and to shoot the picture with a bullet containing a bit of silver. The witch herself would then be cast under a spell, which would be removed only by borrowing some article from the family afflicted by her enchantment. Because of such beliefs, many old women suspected of witchcraft were sometimes unable to borrow virtually anything from their neighbors.

Livestock and dogs were believed to be the most frequent victims of witchcraft. Failure of cows to give milk was often attributed to witches, who were said to have milked them by putting a new pin through a new towel and hanging it above their door and then using a secret incantation to transfer the milk from the cow to the towel. Animals suspected of being bewitched were burned on the forehead with a branding iron. Should witchcraft result in the death of an animal, its remains were burned to ashes. By this means the spell was cast upon the witch. German ironmakers in the Eastern Panhandle of West Virginia sometimes cast live dogs into their furnaces as a means of preventing witches from interfering with their production.

The mysteries of the supernatural sometimes excited an entire neighborhood. Typical of pioneer reaction to reports of occult happenings was the stir created by the ghost at Middleway in Jefferson County in 1794. The strange occurrences began when an unidentified stranger, who had been given lodging at the home of Adam Livingston, an industrious and prosperous farmer, died under mysterious circumstances. During his death throes the visitor called for a priest, but Livingston, being opposed to Catholicism, had no intention of inviting a priest into his house, and the stranger died and was buried without the last rites of his church. After that the most awesome happenings began to take place at the Livingston house. Coals jumped from the fireplace and danced about the floor. A rope stretched itself across the road in front of the house and then mysteriously disappeared. Invisible horses galloped around the house. Finally, there came invisible scissors, snipping day and night and cutting up clothing, blankets, saddles, bridles, and boots and eventually clipping off the heads of Mrs. Livingston's flock of ducks. After that, Livingston abandoned his home to the unseen visitors and to the curious crowds. His health began to fail, and his friends began to fear for his sanity. But a dream in which Livingston saw a saintly figure in flowing robes and an interpretation of the dream by a clergyman led the distraught man to confer with a Catholic priest, who later visited Middleway and held mass for the deceased stranger. Thereupon the spirit was exorcized, and life at Middleway returned to its usual routine.

There was a little known sequel to the strange happenings at Middleway. In 1798 Laurence S. Phelan, a Catholic priest from Hagerstown, Maryland, visited Adam Livingston, and, after an investigation, concluded that the supernatural was in no way involved. Noting that an Irishman named Gorman, an alleged adulterer with a wife in Ireland, had been blamed by many persons, Phelan charged that Livingston's wife, Mary, was herself the ghost and that in the "infamous plot" she "with the assistance of some other knavish hussies of the neighbourhood" had taken advantage of an old man "simple in appearance." Mary Livingston, in a tone of deep umbrage, replied to Phelan's charges. The trouble yet remained in the Livingston family, she declared, and was aided by priestcraft. It had, she said, secluded her from her family and "the embraces of an affectionate husband" and made her "an object of public contempt." She suggested that the purpose of the allegations made against her was to frighten her into relinquishing her "lawful third of Adam Livingston's estate."[14]

The significance of superstition in the lives of pioneers would be difficult to exaggerate. Numerous everyday occurrences

---

[14] Doddridge, *Notes, on the Settlement and Indian Wars, of the Western Parts of Virginia & Pennsylvania,* pp. 161-63. For the ghost at Middleway, see Robert L. Bates, "Middleway, A Study in Social History," *West Virginia History,* XI (October, 1949-January, 1950), 13-20; Martinsburg *Potomak Guardian,* August 29, September 12, 1798.

were invested with the utmost importance. If a black cat crossed one's path, bad luck was certain to ensue, unless, of course, one walked backward across the cat's path. The breaking of a mirror foretold seven years of bad luck. However, if the broken pieces were placed in running water, the ill fortune would pass within seven hours. A bird flying into the house was regarded as an omen of a death in the family. Should a girl tear her dress the first time that she wore it, someone would lie about her before nightfall. Scores of similar beliefs captured the minds of pioneers and were taken with more than a grain of seriousness until well into the twentieth century.[15]

For a highly superstitious people, dreams and visions were filled with special meaning. Dreams were often considered omens of good fortune of forewarnings of danger or tragedy. Ministers, who lived in the midst of battle between the forces of good and evil, often interpreted dreams as evidences of God's favor or as devices used by the Devil to turn them from their work. No dream was too inconsequential to excite speculation regarding its meaning, and none was dismissed without due regard for its implications.[16]

Although the vast majority of the Allegheny pioneers were hard-working, warmhearted, and God-fearing people, the rugged hills and isolated valleys offered welcome retreats for individuals impatient of the restraints imposed by the mores of society or contemptuous of the law. In 1785 Ohio County officials sought permission to extend their authority over the part of Yohogania County which had been cut off from Pennsylvania on the ground that numerous citizens of the former county had been "injured & abused by Refractory persons" who lived there and who committed "Riots, assaults, Batteries, &c. . . . under the Specious

---

[15] U. S., W. P. A., *West Virginia*, pp. 142-43.

[16] Typical examples of interpretations of dreams are in the Diary of John Jeremiah Jacob, reproduced in Marjorie Moran Holmes, "The Life and Diary of John Jeremiah Jacob" (M.A. thesis, Duke University, 1941), pp. 365-67; William Warren Sweet, *Religion on the American Frontier; The Baptists, 1783–1830: A Collection of Source Materials* (New York, 1931), pp. 144-45; Journal of John Smith . . . on the Greenbrier Circuit, July 4, 1787, to July 8, 1788, pp. 21-22, Garrett Biblical Institute. For this study I have used a typescript of Smith's journal, graciously lent to me by the Reverend Lawrence Sherwood of Oakland, Md.

pretext that the process of the Law Cannot Reach them." A similar situation prevailed in the Big Sandy area, "a wild, mountainous, half-civilized region" where "deep glens, and mountain gorges, and dense, unbroken forests, made it the home of a daring, reckless race of individuals, . . . the horse thief, and gambler, and counterfeiter." Even in the Monongahela Valley were people described by Bishop Francis Asbury as "of the boldest cast of adventurers," who had little regard for "the decencies of civilized society."[17]

Allegheny pioneers were probably, on the whole, neither notably better nor worse than those in other frontier areas. From the very beginning of settlement public opinion was a strong deterrent to antisocial behavior, and in time acceptable standards of conduct were buttressed by legal and religious support.

One of the most common failings of the pioneer was his propensity for intoxication. For convenience in marketing, he usually converted his corn and rye into whiskey and his peaches and apples into brandy and cider. He ordinarily reserved a portion of his distillations for his own use, and in their consumption he not infrequently transcended the bounds of moderation. Moreover, grog shops and taverns kept copious supplies of intoxicants other than those produced locally. In 1818 the inventory of William Stevens of Monroe County consisted of 270 gallons of common whiskey, 15½ of French brandy, 10 of Maderia wine, 19 of gin, 36 of bounce, 33 of rum, 3 of common wine, 30 of rectified whiskey, and 24 of peach brandy. One of his most popular offerings was sangaree, a glass of which cost only slightly less than a full meal. No part of pioneer West Virginia, or of the Alleghenies generally, escaped the problem of intoxication. "It is a matter of grief," Francis Asbury wrote of Morgantown in 1788, "to behold the excesses, particularly in drinking, which abound here." Churches frequently censured members for inebriation, and in 1787 the Greenbrier Baptist

[17] Order Book, 1778–1786, for August 1, 1785, Ohio County Court Records; James B. Finley, *Sketches of Western Methodism: Biographical, Historical, and Miscellaneous, Illustrative of Pioneer Life*, ed. W. P. Strickland (Cincinnati, Ohio, 1855), p. 387; [Francis Asbury], *Journal of Rev. Francis Asbury, Bishop of the Methodist Episcopal Church*, 3 vols. (New York, n. d.) II, 37

Church felt constrained to warn the wife of its elder against "the Sin of Drunkeness."[18]

During the early nineteenth century, efforts at controlling the use of intoxicants were directed toward temperance rather than abstention. Moderate drinking had social, legal, and even religious sanction. In 1833 eight of the twelve churches in the Greenbrier Baptist Association had active temperance societies, but in response to a query from one of its churches as to whether "entire abstinance from ardent Spirits [was] essentially necessary to constitute a *test* of fellowship," the association answered unanimously in the negative. The following year it reaffirmed its position. Not until 1848 did the association "most affectionately and urgently request every brother and sister connected with churches associated in this body, to abstain entirely from the sin of intoxicating liquors as a drink." Not until 1850 was one of its churches, the Raleigh Church at Beckley, constituted "on the plan of total abstinence from all intoxicating drinks as a beverage." And, finally, it was not until 1852 that the association took a prohibitionist stand and urged members to sign petitions to the Virginia General Assembly requesting it to enact legislation forbidding the manufacture and sale of intoxicants.[19]

The courts apparently were little concerned with intoxication, except in cases where other charges, such as assault and battery, involved drunkenness. Instead, they concentrated upon other aspects of the liquor problem, particularly illegal distilling and retailing liquors without a license. Between 1789 and 1810 the Monongalia County court, for example, heard fifteen cases involving illegal distilling but only two listing intoxication. Only one case out of 205 in Ohio County between 1796 and 1820 was based upon charges of intoxication. On the other hand, thirteen

---

[18] Private Account Book of Stevens, Alexander, and Company, 1817–1818, Monroe County Court Records; Asbury, *Journal*, II, 37; The Minutes of the Greenbrier Baptist Church [1781–1835], for January 29, 1791, and August 27, 1808, Baptist Historical Collection, West Virginia Department of Archives and History Library.

[19] Records of the Greenbrier Association of Baptists [1825–1868], pp. 98-110, 170-71, 184, 300, 332, 375, Baptist Historical Collection, West Virginia Department of Archives and History Library.

of forty-seven cases in Monroe County between 1806 and 1811 sprang from retailing liquor without a license, and in the latter year five persons were indicted for selling "cider oil" contrary to law. Between 1797 and 1820 retailing liquors without a license took third place among the offenses tried in Brooke County.[20]

Next to drinking and intoxication, the frontiersmen seemed most disposed to fighting. Undoubtedly, the two often went together. The pioneer was acutely sensitive to any disparaging remark or imagined affront, and his code of justice and honor called for satisfaction. The most common procedure was to settle a matter forthwith by a "mode of single combat . . . dangerous in the extreme. Altho' no weapons were used, fists, teeth, and feet were employed at will; but above all, the detestable practice of gouging, by which eyes were sometimes put out, rendered this mode of fighting frightful indeed."[21]

When physical revenge was impossible or undesirable, justice was left to the slower processes of the courts. "The more I have reflected upon the treatment that I received from [Hugh] Phelps on monday last," wrote George Dunlevy of Snakeville in Wood County to Attorney James Wilson of Parkersburg, "the louder my feelings call for and demand satisfaction." For that purpose, Dunlevy requested Wilson to institute a suit in the district court at Morgantown against Phelps for "Trespass assault & Battery Damage $5000." In 1817 William Williamson of Ohio County was sued by Humphrey and Mary Younger for defamation of the latter's character. Williamson admitted "speaking the slanderous words," but explained that "from his state of intoxication" at the time he remembered nothing of the occasion. Although he admitted that he knew "nothing derogatory to the character of Mary Younger, and that the words were spoken without any colour of truth," his indiscretion cost him twenty dollars in damages to the plaintiff.[22]

---

[20] Statistics are based upon Subject Indexes to Monongalia, Ohio, and Brooke County Court Records, West Virginia University Library, and Minute Books, 1804–1821, for September 10, 1811, Monroe County Court Records.

[21] Doddridge, *Notes, on the Settlement and Indian Wars, of the Western Parts of Virginia & Pennsylvania*, pp. 171-72.

[22] George Dunlevy to James Wilson, April 19, 1805, Wilson and Stribling Family Papers; Minute Books, 1815–1819, for May 26, 1817, Ohio County Court Records.

Damages awarded by the courts, however, did not always assuage wounded pride. George Jackson, a Harrison County delegate to the Virginia General Assembly, angrily complained to the governor in 1791 that actions of the Harrison County Court during a recent slander suit in which he was the plaintiff had cost him his seat in the legislature. According to Jackson, the sheriff of the county had carried to the jury during the course of the trial a quantity of ardent spirits concealed in a teakettle. Thus refreshed, the jury then proceeded to make merry over Jackson's case. It found a verdict in his favor, but awarded him only seven shillings damage. The finding, Jackson said, had been used against him in the ensuing election campaign by enabling his enemies to spread the report that the character of Harrison's County delegate in the legislature was worth only seven shillings.[23]

Especially anathema to the Allegheny pioneer was thievery, for which he had "a kind of innate, or hereditary detestation." Before the establishment of legal institutions, settlers usually dealt with a thief by whipping him and running him out of the community. If the value of the stolen article were very great, the offender often received the Law of Moses, or forty stripes save one laid upon the bareback. For less valuable articles, he very likely escaped with the United States flag, or thirteen stripes. In spite of the repugnance of the crime, cases involving theft occupied much of the time of the county courts. Between 1789 and 1810 the Monongalia County Court heard forty-five cases variously labeled larceny, larceny constituting a felony, petit larceny, grand larceny, robbery, and common theft. About one-fifth of the cases in Ohio County between 1796 and 1820 grew out of larceny, robbery, and horse theft.[24]

A less frequent, but often more serious, crime was arson.

[23] Letter of July 5, 1791, W. P. Palmer and others, eds., *Calendar of Virginia State Papers and Other Manuscripts,* 11 vols. (Richmond, Va., 1875-1893), V, 339-40.

[24] Doddridge, *Notes, on the Settlement and Indian Wars, of the Western Parts of Virginia & Pennsylvania,* pp. 170-71. The incidence of theft and larceny among court cases in Monongalia and Ohio counties was determined by examining Subject Indexes to Monongalia and Ohio County Court Records. See also Minute Books, 1815–1819, for April 16, 1816, April 26, 1817, May 26, 1817, November 5, 1831, Ohio County Court Records; Minute Books, 1804–1821, passim, Monroe County Court Records.

About 1806 incendiaries applied the torch to property of George Avery, who owned a flourishing farm at Lee Creek near Parkersburg. Losses included a barn with two thousand bushels of grain, several stacks of grain, and horse-operated grist and saw mills. Because of lack of evidence, the culprits were never convicted. Resentment and superstition appear to have inspired some charges of arson. Jane McLaughlin, a "Spinstress," was accused of burning the barn of James and Mathew Ralston of Monroe County, but was cleared of the charges. But Milly, a slave belonging to David Robe, did not fare so well. Her crimes included not only burning her master's barn but also attempting to kill his son and administering medicine, any one of which was a capital offense. Milly was tried at a special called session of the Monongalia County Court and sentenced to death by hanging on September 1, 1798. Her accomplice in the burning of the barn, a slave of Barsheba Ferguson, was burned in the hand and given thirty lashes.[25]

More than any other crime, murder was capable of outraging frontier sensibilities, and it usually evoked the death penalty. The incidence of murder appears not to have been unusually great, but its perpetration drew the scorn of the pioneer even when the victim was a slave. In 1818 Robert Curry of Monroe County was arraigned for "felloniously wickedly & with malice aforethought" beating his Negro boy, Sam, with a cowhide "in and upon the head breast back belly sides & other parts of the body" during which Curry gave Sam "several mortal strokes wounds & bruses."

One of the most spectacular murders in frontier West Virginia occurred at Clarksburg on the night of November 8, 1805, when Abel Clemmons killed his wife and eight children with an axe. The incident aroused the entire Monongahela Valley. Joseph Campbell, publisher of the *Monongalia Gazette* at Morgantown, immediately issued a special broadside entitled *Murder—Horrible Murder!* A few months later he provided the public with a

---

[25] Cuming, *Sketches of a Tour of the Western Country*, p. 112; Minute Books, 1804–1821, for November 29, 1806, Monroe County Court Records; James Morton Callahan, *History of the Making of Morgantown, West Virginia: A Type Study in Trans-Appalachian Local History* (Morgantown, W. Va., 1926), p. 125.

complete account of the event in a publication which included not only Clemmons' confession but also a letter which he wrote his brother the day before he was hanged and the exhortation of the judge who tried and sentenced Clemmons. The account of the Clemmons murder became a "horror classic" of the frontier and was reprinted many times.[26]

Other pioneer residents were hailed into court when they attempted to augment the limited supply of specie and paper money with issues of local manufacture. Counterfeiting, however, required skill and materials which few settlers possessed. While it would be unwise to generalize concerning its incidence, it was probably more prevalent in those areas where towns and considerable public traffic made the passing of spurious currency likely.[27]

Seldom was the dichotomy between professed standards and actual conduct more striking than in the case of gambling. Among pioneer men cardplaying, cockfighting, and horseracing provided outlets for sportive instincts. Although they were denounced by most churches, they continued to thrive. With the use of lotteries approved by laws as a means of raising funds for both schools and churches, enforcement of laws against gambling and gaming appears to have been in many areas desultory, to say the least. Moreover, the ambivalent attitude regarding the various forms of gambling produced confusion in the public mind.

Mores regarding gambling varied with localities. In 1797 both Charles Town and Smithfield featured horseraces with elaborate rules and sizable purses. As early as 1808 Wheeling had a racetrack and purses up to sixty dollars. On the other hand, the owners of a faro bank and betters on horseraces in Monroe County were arrested, and John Vance of Ohio County was summoned to show cause why he should not be prosecuted for "having unlawfully played at a place of public resort in the

26 Subject Indexes to Monongalia, Ohio, and Brooke County Court Records; Minute Books, 1804–1821, for April 14, 1818, Monroe County Court Records; Boyd B. Stutler, "Early West Virginia Imprints," Separate from the *Papers* of the Bibliographical Society of America, XLV (Third Quarter, 1951), 2-3.

27 Minute Books, 1815–1819, for April 17, 1815, Ohio County Court Records; Minute Books, 1804–1821, for April 26, 1819, Monroe County Court Records.

County of Ohio at a certain game called Rölette."[28]

Two of the most common breaches of approved behavior, and ones which drew the fire of both church and legal authorities, were Sabbathbreaking and profanity. The number of court cases involving the former, however, was relatively small, indicating a tendency on the part of the law-enforcement officials to leave the matter to church regulation. Church authorities, on the other hand, did not hesitate to discipline members who were guilty of infractions of rules regarding the keeping of the Sabbath, which was considered a day of rest for older folk and a time for play for children.[29]

One of the most grievous instances of Sabbathbreaking, in the eyes of Henry Dans Ward, the rector of St. John's Episcopal Church in Charleston, was the practice of saltmakers along the Kanawha of operating their furnaces on Sunday. Ward warned John D. Lewis, one of the salt manufacturers, against "keeping up the furnace heat on Sundays" and also offered "a word of duty to the laboring class, the slaves." But Ward's advice went unheeded. Within two years, however, the saltmakers had "ruined themselves by making too much salt." Then, wrote Ward, undoubtedly convinced that sin carried its own punishment, "where formerly the black smoke from engines & furnaces . . . darkened the heavens . . . now the face of the skies was clear, and no sign of the blackness of darkness arose from the furnace or engine, far or near, on the whole route[.]" Ward's "heart was glad, and [he] rejoiced in the happy valley & the delightsome land."[30]

The courts appear to have taken a more active part in efforts to curtail profanity. In October, 1778, the Ohio County Court,

---

[28] *Wheeling Repository*, October 15, 1808; Shepherdstown *Potowmac Guardian, and Berkeley Advertiser*, July 11, September 12, October 11, 1791; Shepherdstown *Impartial Observer: or Shepherd's-Town, Charles-Town, & County Advertiser*, September 13, 1797; Minute Books, 1804–1819, for September 11, 1809, and April 17, 1810, Monroe County Court Records; Minute Books, 1831–1837, for October, 1831, Ohio County Court Records; Subject Index to Brooke County Court Records.

[29] Doddridge, *Notes, on the Settlement and Indian Wars, of the Western Parts of Virginia & Pennsylvania*, p. 173; Records of Presbyterian Church, Clarksburg [1832–1894], for April 6, April 17, June 7, 1841, West Virginia University Library.

[30] Rev. Henry Dans Ward Journal [1843–1862], West Virginia University Library.

for example, fined nine persons as "Common Swearers." But, as in the vase of Sabbathbreaking, the major burden fell upon the churches. In its actions against offenders, the Fords of Cheat Baptist Church was typical of many others. When Thomas Evans, already suspect because of his doctrines, was found guilty of "prophane swearing," he was "secluded from the privileges and fellowship" of the church. The same church excommunicated David Scott "for Cursing and Blasfemous Swearing and not keeping his place in the Church . . . Untill God in his Mercy shall be pleased to work a Reformation in his soul."[31]

Although both sought to strengthen morality and to reduce crime, churches and legal authorities did not always work in harmony. As a part of a denomination which had led the fight for separation of church and state in Virginia, it was ironic that the Greenbrier Baptist Church should endeavor to extend its authority into areas clearly within the realm of civil law. Holding that it was "unscriptural" for one church member to engage in litigation with another, the Greenbrier church on several occasions intervened in such matters as the adjustment of land disputes and cases of defamation of character. On at least one occasion, the church leaders set themselves in opposition to legal processes. Joseph Parker, ordered to explain his failure to attend church, finally appeared and apologized. Parker, in the words of the church records, "got Entangled in Debt and the Sheriff has a [warrant] Against his Body, is not willing to be taken, and so is keeping out of the way untill he can make Out some way to discharge his lawful Debt & when that is accomplish'd he talks of tending meetings more Strictly [and] the Church taking it into Consideration had granted his request."[32]

Both church and legal authorities regarded the family as a bulwark against crime and delinquency. The Greenbrier Baptist Church in 1787 investigated reports that one of its prominent

[31] Order Book, 1778–1786, for October, 1778, Ohio County Court Records; Forks of Cheat Baptist Church Records, 1775–1830, for February, 1789, and June, 1804, Typescript in West Virginia University Library.
[32] Minutes of the Greenbrier Baptist Church [1781–1835], for April 23, July 28, 1787, August 28, 1802, March 25, 1815.

members was guilty of "Several transgressions Such as seperating from his wife [and] undecent behaviour." Convinced that the charges were true, the church excommunicated the accused member "for putting away his wife," but it also excluded her on charges of fornication. Some commentary upon local mores may be implied in the indictment of Elijah Dunn in Monroe County in 1818 "for marrying & taking to wife his former wife's sister."[33]

On the other hand, the very isolation of many parts of the Allegheny sections of West Virginia threatened to undermine marriage as an institution. Dozens of petitions to the legislature evinced deep concern for the lack of ministers legally qualified to perform marriage ceremonies. In 1802 residents of the Laurel Hill section of Monongalia County complained that they had no minister within thirty or forty miles who was authorized to solemnize matrimonial rites and asked that two men recommended for magistrates be appointed to perform this necessary service. The only alternative, they said, was "an unlawful Marriag Which your Worships will not Countenance, And it has become the general Custom Rather than go so far." In 1811 a group of Ohio Countians asked that a Presbyterian minister residing nearby in Pennsylvania be empowered to perform marriage ceremonies in Virginia. Still other residents of Ohio County complained that they were forced to journey over into the Northwest Territory in order to have marriages legally celebrated.[34] Persons living in the interior sections of the state, however, did not have recourse to ministers residing in surrounding states.

Although crime, evil, and wrongdoing gave frontier areas a notoriety and a reputation for contemptuousness for law and order, there can be little doubt that the vast majority of the Allegheny pioneers, as illustrated by the numerous petitions for ministers to legalize marriages, deplored lawlessness and

[33] *Ibid.*, December 27, 1787, February 23, March 25, September 27, 1788; Minute Books, 1804–1819, for April 14, 1818, Monroe County Court Records.

[34] Monongalia County Legislative Petitions, December 8, 1802; Ohio County Legislative Petitions, December 17, 1811; *ibid.*, December 11, 1801; Kanawha County Legislative Petitions, December 5, 1822; Wood County Legislative Petitions, December 2, 1800.

moral depravity. Lapses in approved personal and public conduct, they believed, could be prevented only by the founding of churches, the establishment of schools which would promote moral as well as intellectual development, and the support of local governments close to and reflecting the will of the moral and upright residents of a developing area.

Chapter Nine

Repairing Broken Constitutions

The common belief that the wilderness was conquered by men and women of unusual physical strength and robust health is without solid foundation. Instead, the difficulties which lay across the path of civilization were overcome by pioneers whose physical vigor was sapped by privation, disease, exposure, and debilitating seasonal ailments. Such an accomplishment by no means diminishes—rather, it enhances—the heroism of the conquerors.

With frequent need for medical attention, but often far removed from competent aid, the early settler became, of necessity, his own physician. For knowledge of anatomy and the causes and nature of diseases he substituted experimentation, superstition, and the advice of others who had borne similar bodily afflictions. Consequently, his approach to medical treatment leaned heavily toward specifics. For drugs from which to compound his medicines, he scoured the hills and vales for roots, barks, and herbs, some of which proved their efficacy, others of which endangered his very life. Fortunately, most of the remedies devised by Allegheny pioneers were of that class which Dr. Joseph Doddridge described as "harmless substances, which do wonders in all . . . cases in which there is nothing to be done."[1]

Prominent among pioneer afflictions, but probably more common in the lowlands than among the higher elevations, were malarial diseases. Symptoms of these fevers—known by various names, including intermittent fever, remittent fever, ague, dumb ague, shaking ague, and chill fever—varied with individuals. Some experienced alternating chills and fevers on the same day. Others had chills one day and fevers the next. Still others showed symptoms of a rhythmic character peculiar to themselves. Except when the disease took the form of the dumb ague, which was marked by "an abscess of the liver and a stupefying fever," it was seldom fatal, but it left its victims weak and susceptible to other ailments.[2]

In treating both remittent and intermittent fevers, the pioneer made generous use of hot drinks to induce sweating but carefully avoided cold liquids or fresh air. For intermittent fevers he favored drinks made from barks of cherry, dogwood, and poplar, "digested in whiskey, or decoction of Boneset." Remittent, or bilious, fever, "a regular Summer and Fall disease," elicited a more radical approach in which "the patient was generally vomited with Lobelia, after which he was purged with infusion of white walnut bark, and sweated with copious draughts of warm elder-blossom tea." Offering its readers a more sophisticated remedy for the ague, the Pittsburgh *Gazette* in 1787 recommended a mixture of "flour of brimstone" and lemon juice dissolved in a glass of rum or port wine to be taken as the seizure came on. In 1803 Dr. Gideon Forsythe introduced into the Wheeling area the use of Peruvian bark and calomel in the treatment of malarial fevers and enjoyed such success "as to render him quite popular."[3]

Early medical practitioners, however, were by no means in agreement as to the most effective treatment for malarial disorders. The few local doctors disagreed violently over methods of dealing with "a malignant bilious remittent fever" which prevailed in the Parkersburg area from 1821 to 1824. Drs. Riggs and Holliday urged the use of "stimulants and support," but Dr. Safford regarded the disease as "sthenic in character and requiring active depletory and antiphlogistic treatment." A devotee of the distinguished Dr. Benjamin Rush, Safford used the lancet freely. He " 'cleared the ship, fore and aft,' and if

[1] Joseph Doddridge, *Notes, on the Settlement and Indian Wars, of the Western Parts of Virginia & Pennsylvania, from the Year 1763 until the Year 1783 Inclusive, together with a View, of the State of Society and Manners of the First Settlers of the Western Country* (Wellsburgh, [W.] Va., 1824), pp. 150-51.

[2] R. Carlyle Buley, *The Old Northwest: Pioneer Period, 1815–1840*, 2 vols. (Bloomington, Ind., 1951), I, 244-45; Solon J. Buck and Elizabeth Hawthorn Buck, *The Planting of Civilization in Western Pennsylvania* (Pittsburgh, Pa., 1939), p. 341.

[3] Doddridge, *Notes on the Settlement and Indian Wars, of the Western Parts of Virginia & Pennsylvania*, p. 153; E. A. Hildreth, *A Contribution to the History of Medicine, with a Biography of Deceased Physicians in the City of Wheeling, for the Last 100 Years* (Wheeling, W. Va., 1876), p. 8; Buck and Buck, *Planting of Civilization in Western Pennsylvania*, p. 341.

this seemed insufficient to enable her to outride the storm, he did not hesitate to throw overboard a part of the cargo." He was so certain of the necessity of blood-letting that he "employed a number of deputies," whom he trained and sent about the country to perform this essential service.[4]

A much more common complaint, particularly among men who worked and hunted much of the time in cold, wet deerskin moccasins and leggings, was rheumatism. Perhaps the most widely used treatment lay in bathing the swollen and aching joints with oil and baking it in before an open fire. For this reason, hunters often slept with their feet to the fire. The oils preferred were those of rattlesnakes, geese, wolves, bears, raccoons, groundhogs, and skunks. Petroleum, called "Seneca oil" and regarded as "an infallible specific," came into somewhat general use in mountainous regions of northwestern Virginia and western Pennsylvania after Bushrod Creel began to collect seepages from his Hughes River farm in 1810. Other victims sought to effect cures by bathing in water dipped from an open stream before sunrise on Ash Wednesday. Or, if the pains were in their feet, they might simply turn their shoes bottom side up before going to bed. Still other remedies called for cohosh, bloodroot, or the bark of leatherwood. Their use was often accompanied by a "regular Indian sweat," brought about by wrapping the sufferer in a blanket, crouching him over a red-hot stone, and then pouring cold water over the stone in order to produce a heavy vapor of steam. Then he was put to bed and sponged off with cold water. One veteran rheumatic, after undergoing the "Indian sweat," declared that "he experienced the most complete and glorious relief of his torturing pains, and slept soundly that night, the first for many weeks."[5]

Along with rheumatism, winter months brought pleurisy,

---

[4] *Transactions of the Medical Society of the State of West Virginia, Instituted April 10, 1867* (Wheeling, W. Va., 1870), p. 163.

[5] Doddridge, *Notes, on the Settlement and Indian Wars, of the Western Parts of Virginia & Pennsylvania*, p. 152; Buck and Buck, *Planting of Civilization in Western Pennsylvania*, p. 341; Charles H. Ambler and Festus P. Summers, *West Virginia: The Mountain State*, 2d ed. (Englewood Cliffs, N. J., 1958), p. 433; U. S., Work Projects Administration, Writers' Program, *West Virginia: A Guide to the Mountain State* (New York, 1941), p. 140; Hildreth, *Contribution to the History of Medicine*, p. 7.

coughs, colds, and pulmonary disturbances. Pleurisy was accompanied "with such a state of exalted action in the circulatory apparatus that [it] called for the use of active depletory measures," which afforded an opportunity to "the most sanguine practitioner to satisfy his ardent craving for blood." Indeed, bleeding was universally approved as a treatment for pleurisy, and, as Dr. Doddridge observed, the danger lay not in using the lancet too freely but in using it too sparingly, in which case the patient might be left with a spitting of blood or even consumption.

Many cough syrups were built around formulas in which spikenard or elecampane were the principal ingredients, but Virginia snakeroot was considered an effective remedy regardless of the nature of the cough. Pioneers also placed great faith in dried Indian turnip mixed with honey, but they knew that unless the Indian turnip had been scraped from the top downward the mixture would have no effect. Teas made from horehound, catnip, and bear's-paw root also enjoyed great favor as cures for colds, but the latter was so bitter that the patient needed a "good nerve" to drink it.[6]

The *Agricultural Almanac*, sold in Charleston by James M. Laidley, offered its readers a recipe which it claimed was an "almost infallible remedy" for colds and coughs, provided it was taken in time. This "sovereign balsamic cordial for the lungs," it was said, had been known to cure colds that had "almost been settled into consumption, in less than three weeks." The valuable "receipt" called for a mixture of one teaspoonful of flaxseed, "two penny worth" of licorice, and four ounces of sun raisins in two quarts of water. These ingredients were to simmer over a slow fire until the mixture had been reduced to one quart, whereupon four ounces of powdered brown sugar candy and a tablespoonful of vinegar or lemon juice was to be added. A pint of the preparation was to be taken before bedtime and additional quantities imbibed when the cough was troublesome.[7]

[6] Doddridge, *Notes, on the Settlement and Indian Wars, of the Western Parts of Virginia & Pennsylvania*, p. 152; Hildreth, *Contribution to the History of Medicine*, pp. 6-7; U. S., W. P. A., *West Virginia*, pp. 139-40.

[7] *Agricultural Almanac for the Year of Our Lord, 1830* (Charleston, W. Va., [1830]), p. 26.

Specific remedies for "Inflammations of the Chest" leaned heavily toward steaming, demulcent liquids, and rubefacients. Vapor inhalations preferred were those making use of whiskey or hot water, while comfrey, spikenard, sassafras pith, and slippery elm furnished the principal ingredients of the soothing drinks. Stubborn cases, in which there was difficulty in breathing, often responded to the application of poultices made of horse-radish or mustard.[8]

Asthma and consumption were never taken lightly, and in their treatment the pioneer often grasped at straws. The *Potomak Guardian* offered despairing victims hope by recounting the experience of an aged dissenting minister, who, when he was about twenty years old had been "reduced to the last extremity in a Consumption," so that even his closest friends "had taken their last leave of him." When the young man was at the point of death, a long-absent relative who had served as a ship's doctor returned and offered advice which save the consumptive's life. The physician prescribed the smoking of tobacco and the swallowing of the saliva as it formed. This simple remedy worked and was now offered to others who were in their last stages of the affliction and who had tried every other treatment available.[9]

Among young children, the croup, often called the "bold hives," was common. Severe cases sometimes resulted in death. Although steam inhalations were sometimes used, the most popular remedy for this spasmodic laryngitis was made from the juice of roasted onions or garlic. Believing an ounce of prevention to be worth a pound of cure, however, many pioneers sought to ward off attacks of croup by placing black silk cords around the necks of children susceptible to the affliction.[10]

Concern over contagious diseases varied according to their severity. Believing many of the communicable diseases to be inevitable, some parents deliberately exposed their children to those considered to be of minor significance. In diseases

---

8 Hildreth, *Contribution to the History of Medicine,* p. 6.

9 Martinsburg *Potomak Guardian, & Berkeley Advertiser,* January 19, 1797.

10 Doddridge, *Notes, on the Settlement and Indian Wars, of the Western Parts of Virginia & Pennsylvania,* p. 148; U. S., W. P. A., *West Virginia,* p. 140.

characterized by skin eruptions, such as measles and chickenpox, treatment was directed toward bringing out the rash. For this purpose, a variety of brews, including the saffron tea, whiskey, and "nanny tea," so widely used in other frontier areas, was concocted by early West Virginia settlers.

None of the contagious diseases occasioned greater dread than the smallpox. When Neal's Station near the mouth of the Little Kanawha was threatened with "hourly danger" from Indian attack in 1793, Captain Cornelius Bogard and a number of the men serving as its garrison who had not had the smallpox chose to leave the fort and those whom it protected to their fate rather than expose themselves to the ravages of the disease which had broken out there. Vaccination against smallpox was not available to most isolated settlers, and many of them would undoubtedly have evinced qualms concerning its use had immunization been within reach. On the other hand, an outbreak of the disease in Martinsburg in 1799 was followed by "a general inoculation for the Small Pox (by an almost unanimous consent of the inhabitants)," and the town was spared the ravages which occurred elsewhere. By the early nineteenth century vaccination was common in the towns and on the larger plantations. Between 1821 and 1831, for instance, Dr. Lee Griggs, a general practitioner at Charles Town, vaccinated at least eighty-seven persons of whom seventeen were Negro slaves.[11]

Another dreaded pioneer affliction was dysentery. Marked by an acute inflammation of the intestines and a high fever, it took a considerable toll in human life. In seeking to alleviate its distressing symptoms, the settler placed his faith in "oak ooze," mayapple root and walnut bark, slippery elm bark tea, and bitter elm bark, the latter regarded as a specific for the ailment. To assist these internal medications, hot fomentations were placed upon the abdomen of the sufferer.[12]

Less enervating but supremely annoying were the numerous

---

[11] [Cornelius Bogard] to Unidentified Addressee, October 29, 1793, W. P. Palmer and others, eds., *Calendar of Virginia State Papers and Other Manuscripts*, 11 vols. (Richmond, Va., 1875-1893), VI, 612; Buck and Buck, *Planting of Civilization in Western Pennsylvania*, p. 343; Dr. Lee Griggs' Account Book, 1821–1831, West Virginia Department of Archives and History Library.

[12] Hildreth, *Contribution to the History of Medicine*, p. 8.

skin troubles with which the pioneer was afflicted. The treatment of erysipelas, or St. Anthony's fire, which resulted from a hemalytic streptococcic infection, required the blood of a black cat. Consequently, in many areas it was difficult to find a black cat with both its ears and its tail, since most of them had sacrificed those appendages to the cause of medicine. The itch, "a very common disease in early times," often responded to an ointment made of brimstone, or sulphur, and lard. For simple skin rashes, bathing in dew or in a mixture of honey and buttermilk was considered efficacious. Chapped lips might be healed by kissing the middle rail of a five-rail fence. Treatment of corns, produced by ill-fitting shoes, required patience and sometimes ingenuity. The *Agricultural Almanac* recommended nightly applications of the prickly pear, or garden cactus, but warned readers to place the mucous side rather than the thorny side next to the corn. The publication assured its readers that cures would be effected with a week or less, for experience had placed the remedy "beyond doubt."[13]

To mitigate the pain of a felon, or whitlow, the pioneer was willing to resort to almost any remedy which promised relief. Joseph Godfrey, an early resident of the Wheeling area, had a thumb swollen "one inch larger around than his wrist, and so exceedingly painful and tender as to prevent sleep or rest for four days and nights." Since no doctor was available, Godfrey consulted Colonel Ebenezer Zane, who frequently dispensed medical aid and advice. Zane manipulated the thumb and advised Godfrey to go to bed early without his supper. This Godfrey did, and from four o'clock in the afternoon until six o'clock the next morning he slept soundly. After repeating the procedure for three days, Godfrey found the tenderness gone and the swelling entirely eliminated. Although other factors were unquestionably at work, Godfrey was apparently unaware of them. Most treatments for felons consisted of the use of salves. One salve was made by wrapping a piece of rock salt about the size of a butternut in a cabbage leaf or a piece of brown paper,

[13] Doddridge, *Notes, on the Settlement and Indian Wars, of the Western Parts of Virginia & Pennsylvania*, p. 153; U. S., W. P. A., *West Virginia*, p. 140; *Agricultural Almanac . . . , 1830*, p. 25.

Thomas Hughes, Indian fighter of Harrison County, made from a verbal description given by Adam Flesher

by Joseph Diss Debar

Typical Allegheny pioneers

Pioneer women, between the Great Kanawha and Little Kanawha rivers, 1847

by Joseph Diss Debar

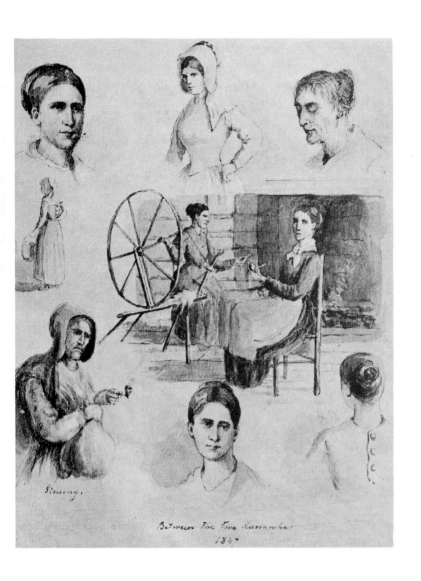

Simong.

Between The Two Laurens
1847

Erection of a log house, showing cornermen and facilities for lifting logs into position

by Joseph Diss Debar

Pioneers burning dry logs   *by Joseph Diss Debar*

Pioneer farm, showing crops planted among remaining tree stumps

by Joseph Diss Debar

Pioneer kitchen, used for cooking, eating, living, and sleeping

by Joseph Diss Debar

Bear trap, used in capturing the numerous bears which roamed the Alleghenies

by Joseph Diss Debar

Wheeling in the 1840's, showing the National Road and the famed suspension bridge

Historic residence in Monongalia County, probably that of John Evans, a local military and political leader

"Harewood," home of Samuel Washington, built at Charles Town in 1770

Alexander Campbell, Disciples of Christ minister and founder of Bethany College

Dr. John McElhenney, pastor of the Lewisburg Presbyterian Old
Stone Church

A religious encampment in a forest

Bethany College

Saltworks on the Kanawha River

moistening it with water, placing it in embers and roasting it for about twenty minutes, removing it and powdering it, and then mixing it with a hard soap.[14]

Stubbornly resisting remedies which the pioneer had at his disposal were inflammations of the eye. A typical case was that of William Vause, a cattle dealer, who was forced to postpone indefinitely a business journey into the South Branch Valley. The delay, Vause explained, was necessary in order "to have the inflammation taken off my Eye, by which a worse one was produced, a similar spot appeared on other eye also on the opposite corner of the same one, which threatened to deprive me of sight altogether." As a result, said Vause, "it became necessary for me to Reduce myself by bleeding and purging, and live very low, confining myself finally, to a dark room, and when out to shade my eyes from the light."

A similar difficulty confronted Jacob Young, a Methodist minister in West Virginia's Northern Panhandle. "When I would look at the Bible," Young declared, "it would look like half a dozen Bibles." In his effort to effect recovery, Young ran the gamut of recommended cures. He first tried, without success, a ten-day regimen of "local and general depletion." He consulted the best doctors available locally, but with no better result. At last, in desperation, he visited a local Quaker-reared doctor, who had fallen upon evil ways. The physician diagnosed Young's illness and noted the mistakes in previous treatments. "The pair of nerves that support the eye-balls, have given way, and can no longer discharge their functions," the doctor told Young. The result was that "the fluid that ought to be carried off lodges there, and causes inflammation." The Quaker added, "thy physicians have been blistering, cupping, salivating, and starving thee, and all have had a tendency to make the disease worse." Although the doctor was by no means optimistic about Young's recovery, he prescribed a treatment remarkable for its mixture of common sense and superstition. According to Young, he "prepared a wash for my eyes, gave me some medicines to take inwardly, and a white powder, to be dissolved in dew, or

[14] Hildreth, *Contribution to the History of Medicine*, p. 8; *Pittsburgh Magazine Almanac for 1824* (Pittsburgh, n. d.) [no pagination].

rain water." He instructed the minister to "go home and live generously, drink no slops, but good tea and coffee, sweetened with loaf-sugar; eat good, well-cured ham and beef-steak, well-cooked," and to eat often but not too much at a time. He further advised Young to take as much exercise as he could "well endure," to work with his sons in the field, and to see the physician again in about ten days. By that time the doctor's sage prescriptions had produced their effects, and Young "could see across a ten-acre field pretty clearly." Remedies for ophthalmia most commonly made use of stramonium, or the dried leaves of the jimson weed, and goldenseal, or yellow root.[15]

In spite of the ignorance and superstition which clouded medical practice, the pioneer at times displayed keen perceptiveness concerning the sources of his health problems. The Quaker doctor who treated Jacob Young understood the connection between proper diet and health. George Calmes also recognized this relationship when he wrote concerning his sick wife that "she has Improv'd in health as Lucy has [been] wanting a Cook more than a docter." Although he did not suspect the mosquito and erroneously attributed the disease to the "offensive odor of decaying vegetation," the pioneer perceived a connection between malarial complaints and the numerous ponds and marshy areas. Large numbers of residents along the Monongahela River objected to plans to construct locks and dams on that stream on the ground that the improvements would create backwaters which would become stagnant in summer and endanger their health. The pioneer observed, too, that typhoid, intermittent and remittent fevers, and diarrhea and dysentery frequently followed floods in the Ohio River and its tributary streams. Moreover, the early settler was aware of the importance of pure air to health. Henry Ruffner, who had spent many years as president of Washington College in Lexington, Virginia, returned to his native Kanawha Valley "with the hope of repairing a constitution broken by 30 years of constant labor in a literary

[15] William Vause to Vause Fox, May 5, 1825, Fox Family Papers; Jacob Young, *Autobiography of a Pioneer; or, The Nativity, Experience, Travels, and Ministerial Labors of Rev. Jacob Young; with Incidents, Observations, and Reflections* (Cincinnati, Ohio, [1857?]), pp. 420-21; Hildreth, *Contribution to the History of Medicine*, p. 7.

institution." He cleared a farm on top of a mountain near Charleston, and after ten years' residence there found his health entirely "renovated."[16]

Along with the endemic and epidemic diseases, the West Virginia pioneer had to deal with other menaces to health and safety. A major hazard was snakebite. Although the rattlesnake and copperhead were the only poisonous snakes generally found in the state, snakebite was always taken seriously, and a variety of cures was enlisted in overcoming its effects. Of the internal remedies, white plantain boiled in milk was perhaps the most highly regarded, but a decoction made from the walnut fern was also widely acclaimed. Joseph Doddridge placed little faith in internal cures, since they were neither emetics or cathartics nor sudorifics; but he conceded that they did no harm. Most cases of snakebite were treated by cupping and sucking the wounds or by making deep incisions which were filled with either salt or gunpowder. Some pioneers preferred an "Indian cure," which consisted of a poultice made from a strong smelling plant of fibrous black roots resembling the Virginia snakeroot.

Superstition also entered into the treatment of snakebite. One method consisted of capturing the snake, cutting it into pieces about two inches long, placing the pieces on the wound to draw out the poison, and then burning them to ashes as a kind of revenge. One victim then had his entire leg encased in chestnut bark, and a brew made by boiling chestnut leaves was repeatedly poured over the leg. Then some of the boiled chestnut leaves were bound to it. The latter process was repeated several times a day.

Burns and scalds called for external applications, the most important of which were poultices of Indian meal, scraped potatoes, roasted turnip, and slippery elm bark. The *Agricultural Almanac* recommended dipping a cloth in tar and applying it to the affected area. Declaring that this remedy provided

[16] George Calmes to John Rogers, August 2, 1831, John Rogers Papers, West Virginia University Library; *Transactions of the Medical Society . . . of West Virginia*, p. 163; Hildreth, *Contribution to the History of Medicine*, p. 22; Monongalia County Legislative Petitions, December 19, 1826; Henry Ruffner, "The Kanawha Country," Henry Ruffner Papers, Historical Foundation of the Presbyterian and Reformed Churches.

"almost certain relief from the most violent pain," it urged that tar be kept "in the house by every family having young children."[17]

The pioneer had to treat, often with the most limited resources, a variety of wounds which he sustained in everyday life and at the hands of the Indians. Because of the lack of doctors and of persons skilled in using the lancet, he escaped for a time the bleeding and depletory actions commonly employed after medical practice became more sophisticated. Instead, in treating his wounds, he drew freely upon his repertoire of poultices, with some preferences perhaps for those made from slippery elm bark or flaxseed. A typical case was that of Thomas Mills, who in 1784 was brought to Fort Henry at Wheeling with fourteen wounds inflicted by Indian rifles, a broken leg, and numerous lacerations. Since no doctors were at the fort, Mills was treated by Mrs. Ebenezer Zane and Mrs. Isaac Williams, who applied poultices of slippery elm bark and jimson weed to his wounds. Not only did Mills survive, which at the time was believed impossible, but both of his legs were saved. It was said that had regular army surgeons attended him, they would have amputated both legs.[18]

As the density of settlement in frontier West Virginia increased, especially after 1800, there occurred "an enlargement of the nosological list," brought about largely by the appearance of several epidemic diseases. In the winter of 1813–1814 a mysterious illness known as the "cold plague" swept eastward from Trumbull County, Ohio, and caused many deaths in transmontane West Virginia. Its symptoms were sudden chills and great pulmonary congestion. At Wheeling Dr. Martin Luther Todd treated it with tonics and stimulants and "also used, with happy effect, brewer's yeast."[19]

In 1832 the dreaded Asiatic cholera, carried up the Ohio River by steamboat, spread eastward into trans-Allegheny West

---

[17] Doddridge, *Notes, on the Settlement and Indian Wars, of the Western Parts of Virginia & Pennsylvania*, pp. 148-51; *Agricultural Almanac . . . , 1830*, p. 25.

[18] Doddridge, *Notes, on the Settlement and Indian Wars, of the Western Parts of Virginia & Pennsylvania*, p. 152; Hildreth, *Contribution to the History of Medicine*, p. 5.

[19] Hildreth, *Contribution to the History of Medicine*, pp. 5, 8, 22; Young, *Autobiography of a Pioneer*, p. 308.

Virginia. At Wheeling the mortality rate among those contracting the disease was from 50 to 60 percent. Dr. M. H. Houston, the hastily appointed city health officer, urged that litter in the marketplace, on the streets, and in the low grounds be covered with lime and a solution of sulphate of iron. Ignoring his advice, the town council ordered litter carted up and thrown over the riverbank, "with the result of inducing in a few days 39 deaths, in the neighborhood of its deposit." Treatment for cholera victims varied, but the use of calomel, opium, and capsicum produced best results. Many persons sought to ward off the disease by "wearing a large burgundy pitch plaster over the stomach and abdomen." At St. Albans, on the Kanawha River, the disease affected almost every family, "with several Cases of the Severest Sort which . . . proved fatal." As late as 1834 Joseph Capehart, a resident of the town, declared that the cholera or a similar scourge was still "Sweeping many of our fellow beings from the Shores of times and landing them in a long and lasting eternity."[20]

Physicians appeared in frontier areas as soon as there were sufficient concentrations of population to warrant the practice of their profession. By 1800 the Potomac settlements were served by a number of practitioners, including Adam Stephen, William McMechen, John Briscoe, John McCormick, and Robert Henry. By that time Absalom Baird, Thomas Bond, Solomon Brown, and Silas Lord had all apparently begun practice in Morgantown, and before another decade had passed at least four other physicians were at work in the area. Gideon Forsythe, who in 1803 became the first doctor in Wheeling, was joined before the close of the War of 1812 by Thomas Tonner, Martin Luther Todd, James H. Rolfe, Jess Wilson, and J. Wishart. On the other hand, Dr. Jesse Bennet, who established a practice at Point Pleasant in 1797, was the only physician within a radius of fifty miles.[21]

20 Hildreth, *Contribution to the History of Medicine*, p. 23; Joseph Capehart to George W. Smith, July 13, 1833, George W. Smith Papers; Joseph Capehart to George W. Smith, August 20, 1834, *ibid.*

21 Roy Bird Cook, *The Annals of Pharmacy in West Virginia* (Charleston, W. Va., 1946), p. 8; James Morton Callahan, *History of the Making of Morgantown, West Virginia: A Type Study in Trans-Appalachian Local History* (Morgantown, W. Va., 1926), pp. 118-19; Hildreth, *Contribution to the History of Medicine*,

Training and qualifications of pioneer physicians varied widely. During the early years there were "no means, legal or otherwise, of preventing any bold man, young or old, from offering his services to the public as Physician or Surgeon, regardless of his qualifications, and pursuing his avocation with an effrontery and presumption, directly proportioned to his ignorance." Declaring that "in many parts of the State there are persons professing to have Skill and administering medicines, who from a want of knowledge in their profession often impose upon the Credulous to the great danger of the health of those who employ them," a group of Monongalia Countians in 1800 asked the legislature to establish "some tribunal" which would license those who practiced medicine.[22]

Most of the Allegheny region's early doctors gained their medical knowledge by the apprenticeship method and combined the practice of medicine with other callings, often the ministry. At least five Monongalia County doctors received their preliminary training at the hands of Dr. Charles McLane, a Morgantown physician. In 1832 another of the town's practitioners entered into an agreement with the Reverend Peter Laishley by which he promised to instruct Laishley "in the Science of Medicine on the Old & reformed systems" to the extent of the former's ability and "to confer upon him Diplomas agreeable to the constitution of our Society, as soon as he is worthy to receive it."[23]

On the other hand, populous towns attracted doctors whose training was as good as the times afforded. Dr. Wishart, who arrived in Wheeling in 1808 with a medical degree from the University of Pennsylvania and "experience in Country, likewise in City and Hospital Practice," confidently announced his ability to give satisfaction to the people. Joshua Morton, who established a practice at Wheeling in 1816, held a medical degree

pp. 7-17; Land and Licensing Books, Ohio County Court Records, Microfilm in West Virginia University Library; Dorothy Poling, "Jesse Bennet, Pioneer Physician and Surgeon," *West Virginia History,* XII (January, 1951), 111.

[22] *Transactions of the Medical Society . . . of West Virginia,* p. 150; Monongalia County Legislative Petitions, December 23, 1800.

[23] Callahan, *History of the Making of Morgantown,* p. 119; Agreement between John [?] and Peter T. Laishley, June 16, 1832, Peter T. Laishley Papers, Microfilm in West Virginia University Library.

from Harvard. It was said of him that "if he had *time* to consider any intricate case his diagnosis would be correct." Another University of Pennsylvania graduate, Dr. James Clemans, who arrived in Wheeling in 1819, set up his own chemical laboratory and "was a constant reader of medical periodicals, both foreign and domestic." Jesse Bennet, the pioneer physician at Point Pleasant, studied under both Drs. Benjamin Rush and William Shippen at Philadelphia, and in 1794, prior to his moving to the Ohio River town, performed a successful cesarean section and ovariotomy upon his wife.[24]

Although some of the abler doctors established extensive practices, most pioneer physicians in West Virginia probably did not find the medical profession highly remunerative. After riding miles in rain and snow, the doctor often had to render his services in exchange for country produce or without payment of any kind. Because of the great scarcity of money, Jesse Bennet acquired a variety of articles, including a pair of shoes, two large tubs and a bucket, a plow beam, a gunstock, bedsteads, and a cradle. Even though he practiced in a relatively thickly settled and prosperous place, Dr. Lee Griggs accumulated during ten years in the Charles Town area outstanding accounts amounting to $4,632.92 at the time of his death. Griggs listed many of those indebted to him as "insolvent," "dead and insolvent," and "good for nothing." Rather interestingly, Griggs on May 18, 1827, worked out a prepaid medical plan with Joseph Daugherty. According to the arrangement, Griggs would provide medical services to Daugherty and his family for fifteen dollars a year, with Daugherty "finding the medicines." This fee did not include any "accouchement" of Mrs. Daugherty, for which Griggs was to receive his standard fee of ten dollars.[25]

Many self-styled physicians resorted to the use of the same roots, barks, and herbs which the pioneer knew so well. At Martinsburg, John Tincklin, "alias Doctor Jack," announced in 1795 that "from a long and continuous enquiry into the nature and utility of the different ROOTS and HERBS," he had "long

[24] Wheeling *Repository*, June 16, 1808; Hildreth, *Contribution to the History of Medicine*, p. 9; Poling, "Jesse Bennet, Pioneer Physician and Surgeon," pp. 105-107.
[25] Poling, "Jesse Bennett, Pioneer Physician and Surgeon," pp. 111-12; Dr. Lee Griggs' Account Book, 1821-1831.

since acquired the knowledge of assisting" persons suffering from fits, poisons, mortifications, consumptions, rheumatic pains, sore throats, measles, itch, colds, ulcerous infections, pleurisy and "almost every disease incident to the human body."[26]

The arrival of well-trained physicians was accompanied by an increase in the drugs and remedies available to the ill. As early as 1798 Dr. Alex Sanderson was supplying residents of the Charles Town area with red vermilion, red lead, and elixir of paregoric. At Wheeling Gideon Forsythe opened an apothecary shop, a practice emulated by most of his successors. Lee Griggs' stock of medicines, included cathartics and emetics, digitalis, calomel, spirits of niter, laudanum, quinine, bitters, vitriol, epsom salts, camphor, cinchona, liniment, antimony, ammonia and magnesia.[27]

For residents of isolated areas, the small general store was likely to be the source of medicines not indigenous to their localities. In 1784 a Monroe County merchant offered his customers alum, brimstone, camphor, copperas, asofoetida, and mustard. A small village store at Kanawha Falls, whose customers came from a radius of thirty miles or more, retailed copperas, camphor, sweet oil, paregoric, opedeldoc, alum, brimstone, beeswax, castor oil, Lee's pills, calomel, jalap, and asofoetida. A much larger assortment rested on the shelves of Francis Tiernan and Company at Guyandotte in 1822 and included opium, Peruvian bark, Glauber salts, gum tragacanth, aloes, rhubarb, ipecac, tartar emetic, salts of tartar, oil of vitriol, elixir of vitriol, white vitriol, aqua fortis, spirits of hartshorn, syrup of squills, sugar of lead, Bateman's drops, Godfrey's cordial, Anderson's pills, cologne water, and spring and thumb lancets. In addition to the usual offerings, John Rogers of Morgantown stocked antibilious pills, extract of mustard, spruce, itch ointment, tooth powder, lip salve, ague water, toothache drops, patent lozenges, and corn plasters.[28]

[26] Martinsburg *Potomak Guardian, & Berkeley Advertiser*, March 2, 1795.

[27] Cook, *Annals of Pharmacy in West Virginia*, p. 13; Hildreth, *Contribution to the History of Medicine*, p. 7; Dr. Lee Griggs' Account Book, 1821–1831. See also Jacob Hite's Account for Medicines, Rigsby Papers.

[28] Unidentified Private Account Book, 1783–1785, Monroe County Court Records; Unidentified Kanawha Falls Account Book, 1829–1831, West Virginia

Aware of the paucity of doctors and the pioneer's tendency to treat his own ailments, Dr. Henry Rogers, who opened a pharmacy at Charleston in 1824, assembled a home medicine chest. In order that the ministrations of medicine might be as scientific as possible, he placed in each kit apothecary's scales and weights, a lancet, a "Glyster Pipe" and bladder, and a spatula. Even then, he cautioned users that "in all cases where there are doubts as to a disease, or the proper remedy, the advice of a physician should be obtained."

Rogers' well-stocked chest provided epsom salts, castor oil, rhubarb, jalap, sweet oil, cream of tartar, Seidlitz powders, soda powders, senna, and flour of sulphur for use as purgatives and tartar, ipecac, and antimonial wine as emetics. For cholera and biliousness, he included calomel and Lee's Pills and for colic in children, spirits of lavender and essence of peppermint. The prevalence of malarial diseases and the need for tonics received recognition in the inclusion of Peruvian bark. For adults, the recommended dosage was "(when given for ague and fever) a tea spoonful every hour during the intermission, and when there is NO fever." If it was used as a tonic, a teaspoonful three or four times a day was sufficient. Should the sufferer experience loss of appetite, night sweats, and "inward fever," Rogers recommended elixir of vitriol. Another "useful and convenient tonic" designed to improve the appetite, strengthen the stomach, and promote digestion might easily be made by boiling a "handful" of chamomile flowers in a quart of water and taking a wine glass full three or four times a day.

Rogers prepared his customers to cope with other afflictions and discomforts. There were antimonial wine for the croup and syrup of squills, licorice balls, and elixir of paregoric, the latter to be taken "when it is required to allay cough, produce sleep, and compose the patient"; sugar of lead, cream of tartar, to be used with flour of sulphur, and Turner's cerate for skin eruptions; precipitate ointment for the itch; spirits of camphor and spirits of hartshorn for sprains, bruises, and fainting; eye water for eye inflammations; and borax for sore mouth. As "a

---

Department of Archives and History Library; Charleston *Western Courier*, October 8, 1832; John Rogers' Accounts Payable Ledger, 1816, John Rogers Papers.

grateful cordial," he added spirits of lavender, which, taken ten to a hundred drops on a lump of sugar or in water, he recommended for colic and stomach disorders and "for low spirits, and in nervous affections."[29]

Seriously handicapping the progress of medicine was the popular antipathy toward autopsies and post mortem exploration of the human body. The lack of cadavers induced Gideon Forsythe of Wheeling to arrange for the surreptitious exhumation of an old Negro woman who died there in 1807. Unfortunately for the doctor, his employees placed the body in the river after he had completed his examination. When the body, "sawn and hacked to pieces," was subsequently discovered and when the dastardly act was traced to "the savages of the Doctor's shop," the residents of Wheeling rose up in arms. There was such a fear of similar treatment, it was said, that many families were afraid to entrust their departed members to the graveyard.[30]

For those who preferred nature's own remedies, combined with social pleasantries, there were the numerous mineral springs of the Alleghenies. Each of the watering places had its own peculiar attributes and its loyal clientele. By the 1830's it was customary for well-to-do families, in which there was any real or imagined affliction, to make a grand tour of the springs in what frequently amounted to an invigorating social whirl. The waters of Sweet Springs, noted for their "briskness," were considered particularly efficacious in the treatment of dyspepsia, but if there were much gastric irritation or "evident phlogosis of the liver" as manifested by a parched skin or other symptoms, the use of the water must be accompanied by one or two small bleedings, the taking of a blue pill at night, and either epsom salts or calcined magnesia in the morning. The waters were especially helpful for females of "a nervous habit of body." They were recommended for both drinking and bathing for persons enfeebled by confinement. For drinking, the water was

[29] [Henry Rogers], *Directions for a Family Medicine Chest, Put up and Sold by Henry Rogers, Chemist and Druggist, Charleston, Kanawha County, [West] Virginia* (Charleston, W. Va., [1830]), pp. 2-9, passim; Cook, *Annals of Pharmacy in West Virginia*, p. 20.

[30] Wheeling *Repository*, December 31, 1807.

to be taken early in the morning, again between twelve and one o'clock, and again before dinner, but none at teatime.

The waters of Red Sulphur Springs were considered especially useful in the treatment of consumption, scrofula, jaundice and "other bilious affections," dyspepsia, chronic dysentery and diarrhea, rheumatism, gout, dropsy, neuralgia, scurvy, ringworm, and itch, and had "long been celebrated as a vermifuge." If the patient left Red Sulphur Springs in a worse condition than when he arrived, either the disease had progressed too far for effective treatment or the sufferer had been guilty of some "imprudence." The waters were also considered an excellent tonic, and visitors were reported to have gained from one to two pounds a day for several successive days. For best results, the use of the waters must be accompanied by a vegetable diet, moderate exercise, and a calm mind. It was said that those who drank the waters for their diuretic or purgative qualities were sometimes taken, after about ten days, "with a sensation of fullness in the head," but this feeling was regarded as a favorable sign and an indication that the patient was on the road to recovery if he would exercise "perseverance and prudence."[31]

The favorite of all the state's watering places was White Sulphur Springs, which drew visitors from all over the South. Interest in the springs first developed in 1772 when a pioneer woman, crippled with rheumatism, visited the waters and bathed in a trough hollowed from a large tree trunk. After a few weeks of regular baths and copious drinking of the water, she left her bark bathing cabin with her health allegedly perfectly restored. Soon other pioneers with their families began to visit the springs and to erect tents or log cabins to house themselves during their sojourn.

By the 1830's the resort had become famous and an elegant center of fashion. Cottages were built and laid out in rows,

---

[31] Joseph Martin, *A New and Comprehensive Gazetteer of Virginia, and the District of Columbia* (Charlottesville, Va., 1835), pp. 393-95, 398-400, 402-403; William J. Hinke and Charles Kemper, eds., "Moravian Diaries of Travels through Virginia," *Virginia Magazine of History and Biography*, XI, (October, 1903), 121; [Francis Asbury], *Journal of Rev. Francis Asbury, Bishop of the Methodist Episcopal Church*, 3 vols. (New York, n. d.), II, 58-59; Hampshire County Legislative Petitions, November 23, 1816.

among which were Virginia Row, Georgia Row, Paradise Row for newlyweds and young ladies, and Wolf Row for bachelors. Society at the springs was delightfully cosmopolitan. "From the East," it was said, "you have consolidationists, tariffites, and philanthropists; from the Middle, professors, chemical analysts, and letter writers; from the West, orators and gentlemen who can squat lower, jump higher, dive deeper, and come out drier, than all creation besides; and from the South, nullifiers, Union men, political economists, and statesmen." But from all parts of the country came "functionaries of all ranks, ex-candidates for all functions, and the gay, agreeable, and handsome of both sexes," whose purpose in coming was "to see and be seen, to chat, laugh, and dance, and each to throw his pebble on the great heap of general enjoyment."

Such an atmosphere undoubtedly contributed to the psychological uplift of the patrons of the springs, but there were also the physical benefits so widely acclaimed. A young Philadelphian, writing under the pen name of Peregrine Prolix, who visited the springs in 1834, declared that it was popularly believed that the waters cured "Yellow Jaundice, White Swelling, Blue Devils and Black Plague; Scarlet Fever, Yellow Fever, Spotted Fever and fever of every kind and colour; Hydrocephalus, Hydrothorax, Hydrocele and Hydrophobia; Hypochondria and Hypocrisy; Dispepsia, Diarrhea, Diabetes, and die-of-anything; Gout, Gormandising and Grogging; Liver Complaint, Colic, Stone, Gravel and all other diseases and bad habits, except chewing, smoking, spitting and swearing." Contributing to the efficacy of the waters, which contained sulphurated hydrogen and other ingredients, was "a very strong infusion of fashion," described as "an animal substance," whose quality was not readily ascertainable but which was said to be on the increase.[32]

To be sure, the vast majority of West Virginia pioneers soon found themselves cut off, because of economic conditions, from whatever advantages the springs may have had. Moreover, competent physicians long remained beyond the reach, both physically and financially, of a vast segment of the population.

[32] Peregrine Prolix, *Letters Descriptive of the Virginia Springs: The Roads Leading Thereto and the Doings Thereat*, 2d ed. (Philadelphia, 1837), pp. 31-33.

For residents deprived of the benefits of the springs and the healing abilities of well-trained doctors, the relief offered by commercially prepared drugs and patent medicines was the most to be hoped for in the way of external aid. But in isolated areas, which predominate in much of West Virginia and the Alleghenies generally, tradition and time-honored usage die slowly, and long after new and better treatments were available, residents clung tenaciously to folk remedies handed down from generations long past. Many such remedies survived well into the twentieth century and even yet constitute a part of the home treatments practiced in remote areas of the mountains.

Chapter Ten

The Midnight of Ignorance

In the spring of 1845 a colporteur for the American Tract Society, accompanied by a young lawyer named Francis H. Pierpont, journeyed into "the country among the mountains" around Fairmont for the purpose of distributing a stock of books. His experience was, for the agent, "like a translation from sunlight into darkness—from a high civilization into one of ignorance and superstition, with here and there a family of wealth and refinement." He found whole families who did not know the alphabet and visited as many as fourteen houses in succession in which there was not even a Bible. Pleading for the establishment of a free public school system in the proposed state of West Virginia, a delegate to its First Constitutional Convention, in January, 1862, declared that he knew men and women who had never seen a schoolhouse.[1]

The widespread illiteracy, so graphically described by such observers, was common throughout the Alleghenies, but the seeming unconcern regarding education appears to have been at least partly of mountain origin. The first settlers of West Virginia, for example, were apparently literate and interested in establishing schools. A schoolmaster was among the persons killed by Indians in the Greenbrier region in September, 1755. Thomas Opp taught a German school at or near Brandywine in Pendleton County prior to the summer of 1758, and in 1760 Frederick Upp held a school on the South Fork of the South Branch in the same county. By 1762 Shepherdstown had both a German and an English school.[2]

Even the first trans-Allegheny pioneers shared the concern for education. Records of early transmontane schools are almost nonexistent, but indirect evidence suggests that they were more numerous than might at first appear. By 1783 a schoolhouse was built at the forks of Cheat River on lands belonging to

William Stewart. In 1784 a merchant in the Monroe County area allowed Thomas Edmonstone two pounds eight shillings in merchandise for "Scholing and Scholars." From 1787 until 1790 Israel Donelson taught a school in Ohio County. Shortly after his arrival from Fauquier County in 1790 Jesse Rector opened a subscription school at Buzzard's Glory near Pruntytown, where he is said to have first flown an American flag over a West Virginia schoolhouse. The description of William Morris' lands on Kelly's Creek indicates that a school existed near present Cedar Grove in the Kanawha Valley by 1798.[3]

Faced with the formidable task of conquering a wilderness— and often subdued themselves by its inexorable demands— generations immediately following the first settlers of the Alleghenies were often forced to push educational interests into the background while they battled for survival. By the time that many of them were in a position to give serious thought to educational matters, they had begun to question the value of "book-learning" in a society in which the knowledge and skills deemed most essential could be acquired in the home, on the farm, in the forest, or in association with one's neighbors. These were the "dark ages" in the educational history of West Virginia, and out of them developed a popular apathy toward education which persisted until well into the twentieth century.

Fortunately, even during these discouraging years a small minority of the settlers sought to keep the lamps of learning trimmed and burning. Through their efforts, the first common schools were established. These schools were of the subscription type and were popularly known as "Old Fields" schools. They were evidence of the spirit of cooperation often found among pioneer families and were supported entirely by the resources

[1] [John Cross], *Five Years in the Alleghanies* (New York, 1863), pp. 57-58; Charles H. Ambler, Frances Haney Atwood, and William B. Mathews, eds., *Debates and Proceedings of the First Constitutional Convention of West Virginia, 1861–1863*, 3 vols. (Huntington, W. Va., n. d.), II, 1033.

[2] "Preston's Register"; Charles H. Ambler, *A History of Education in West Virginia from Early Colonial Times to 1949* (Huntington, W. Va., 1951), p. 3.

[3] Monongalia County Land Grants, I (1782–1785), 11; Unidentified Private Account Book, 1783–1785, Monroe County Court Records; Ambler, *History of Education in West Virginia*, pp. 3, 113-14; Kanawha County Land Grants, I (1790–1812), 150.

of the subscribers. Available only to those children whose parents could afford to pay tuition, they at first reached only a small proportion of the youth of school age, leaving the vast majority of them without opportunity for formal instruction.

The initiative in starting a subscription school often came from a schoolmaster, who offered to teach in return for cash, country produce, and "bed and board" in the homes of his patrons. Once the settlers had decided to employ the teacher, the contracting parties drew up an agreement setting forth the number of children to be taught, the rates of tuition and how it was to be paid, the length of the term, and the subjects in which instruction was to be offered. At the same time the parents arranged for quarters for the school, which, if a school-house were not available, might be held in a barn, a loft, or one of their homes. Typical of these contracts was one governing a school in Jackson County in 1849. Indicating a semiliteracy on the part of the writer—perhaps the schoolmaster himself—it read: "Hiram Thomas proposes to teach an English School with the exception of arithmetic and that as far as the single rule of three on elk fork of mill creek the said Thomas agrees to teach regular hours and pay good attention to each schollar for which we the undersigned gree to pay said Thomas at the rate of two dollars for sixty days, in good merchantable produce delivered at Geo. B. Wolf's."[4]

Although most of these early subscription schools were of extremely poor quality, a few measured up to the highest standards. Of the latter variety was the Union School, opened apparently at Summit Point in Jefferson County in 1794. Prime movers in the establishment of the school were Battaile Muse, John McPherson, William Castleman, and Thomas Kennan, all prominent residents of Jefferson County, who served as its board of trustees. In a businesslike manner, the trustees on July 24, 1794, drew up two agreements, which laid down in con-siderable detail the policies under which the school would operate.

The first of the contracts was between the trustees and Joseph

---

4 Ambler, *History of Education in West Virginia*, pp. 2-3, 6; Subscription School Contract [1849], George W. Smith Papers.

H. Jones, whom they engaged to teach for the ensuing twelve months at a salary of 50 pounds Virginia money. Jones agreed to teach reading, writing, and arithmetic to thirty pupils, if that number could be obtained. During the summer the schoolday was to begin at seven o'clock in the morning and last "to an hour by the Sun," with a noon recess from twelve until two o'clock, but in winter months instruction should take place from "a half after 8 to twelve and from One to such time as may be convenient for the Children to get home." The contract called for vacations of one week each at Easter, Whitsuntide, and Christmas, but aside from six days' absence allowable for illness, Jones was to make up any other days lost "by his own neglect." In all matters Jones agreed to be "regulated by the Trustees and to adopt such modes and regulations as they shall think fit."

In the second contract the trustees set forth their own obligations, both collectively and severally. They agreed that McPherson should provide board for the schoolmaster, for which he would be paid eighteen pounds, and that Muse should have built on his lands at their joint expense "a School House Twenty Feet Square of Hewed Logs with a Shingled Cover Planked above and below," with the property assigned to the trustees. Each trustee agreed to pay his proportionate share of the sixty-eight pounds needed for the schoolmaster's salary and board, with amounts to be based on the number of children whom he sent to school. Pupils other than the fourteen children of the trustees were charged ten dollars per year each. Finally, the trustees bound themselves to meet every three months at the school in order "to examine the conduct of the Teacher" and to transact any other business.[5]

The Union School proved highly successful. By 1796 Jones had contracted to teach "the English Grammatically, Writing, Arithmetic in whole numbers, Fractions both Vulgar & Decimal, the Extractions of the roots, Duodecimals & Book keeping after the Italian method," with pupils instructed in these subjects "according to their abilities." Later the trustees provided schoolmaster with "a Dwelling House Kitchen & Stable House," which, along with increases in salary, were inducements to

[5] Articles—1794, Battaile Muse Papers.

capable instructors. The trustees, however, maintained close supervision of the school and made it clear to subscribers that in any agreements which they made they were bound to the trustees and not to the teacher.[6]

Such facilities as those provided by the Union School trustees were clearly the exception in pioneer West Virginia and were possible only in such sections as the lower Shenandoah and Potomac River basins, where there existed a stable society with large numbers of well-to-do farmers and townspeople. It should be remembered, in the interest of perspective, that at the very time the Union School was established settlers in the trans-Allegheny regions were not yet free of the Indian menace and had little time for cultural matters.

The presence of large numbers of illiterate and ignorant citizens hardly offered a solid basis upon which to build the republican form of government or to effect the democratic processes so widely advocated during the Revolutionary era. Believing education to be the *sine qua non* of enlightened popular government, Governor Thomas Jefferson in 1779 proposed to the Virginia General Assembly a plan which would have divided each of the state's counties into hundreds and set up a free public school in each. Jefferson's plan would have assured every child in the state at least three years of schooling at public expense, with each child's advancement beyond that point dependent upon his initial progress. The plan also provided for a corps of adequately trained teachers. Jefferson's sagacious proposal failed to win the approval of the legislature, thus leaving Allegheny settlers to lift themselves out of their intellectual abyss.[7]

In 1796 the General Assembly passed the Aldermanic Law, which incorporated some features of Jefferson's plan. The act permitted, but did not require, county courts to provide for the election of aldermen, who might establish and supervise tax-supported public schools within their jurisdictions. For several

[6] Articles of Agreement, August 4, 1796, *ibid.;* Articles of Agreement, August 31, 1798, *ibid.;* Articles of Agreement, November 9, 1801, *ibid.;* Subscription Paper to Union School for 1802, *ibid.*

[7] See, for example, Dumas Malone, *Jefferson, the Virginian* (Boston, 1948), pp. 280-85.

reasons, county courts failed to authorize such elections. The reasons stemmed in part from an abatement of the public enthusiasm for education which had prevailed during the Revolutionary era, as well as from the commonly held belief among persons of affluence, many of whom were members of the county courts, that the wealthy would be saddled with the costs of educating the poor. Many of the opponents of the aldermanic system disdainfully noted that some of the strongest advocates of general education were members of the evangelical churches. The latter, particularly the Methodists and Baptists, dominated religious life in West Virginia.[8]

Continued agitation for aid in educating the indigent, however, bore fruit with the creation of the Literary Fund by the legislature in 1810. In this legislation, Virginia provided opportunities comparable to those of other states, such as Pennsylvania, which passed similar acts between 1800 and 1810. Set up solely for the purpose of providing elementary education for needy children, the fund was administered by a board consisting of the governor, lieutenant governor, treasurer, attorney general, and president of the state Court of Appeals. Administration of funds in the counties rested with commissioners, numbering from five to fifteen, appointed by the county courts. Although the school commissioners theoretically held broad power over finances, choice of teachers, determination of the number of poor children to receive aid, and selection of schools which their wards might attend, in practice they were compelled to attune their efforts to local conditions. Their limited funds did not permit them to build schools, they could not have staffed them in many western counties if they could have built them, and they had no authority to compel any poor child to attend school. As a consequence, they worked with existing subscription schools and used persuasion rather than force with their charges.[9]

Despite the restrictions placed upon it, the Literary Fund produced something of a transformation in common-school education in frontier areas of West Virginia. The typical mountain school during the first half of the nineteenth century

[8] Ambler, *History of Education in West Virginia*, pp. 37-38.
[9] *Ibid.*, pp. 18-26.

was a subscription school formed by parents of the requisite means, to which were added children whose tuition was paid by the Literary Fund. In many localities, where there were insufficient numbers of paying children for a school, the addition of the tuition of poor children augmented funds to a point where a school might be established. Such was the case in Greenbrier County, where by 1825 schools had, "by the aid of a few indigent children to make up a sufficient number, been established in almost every section of the county," and especially in those parts where the population was thin and scattered. Harrison County, then comprising a large part of the upper Monongahela Valley, reported in 1831 that "schools have been established in settlements where none existed before, and where none could conveniently have been established, except by the aid of the fund, and by this means education has been made accessible to all."[10]

Despite the opportunities made possible by the Literary Fund, school attendance remained extremely low in many parts of West Virginia. Statistics for the early nineteenth century are meager, but there is reason to believe that not more than 40 percent of the children in mountainous areas were in school in 1840. One of the reasons for nonattendance stemmed from parental aversion to making use of the Literary Fund, since an acknowledgment of poverty was the criterion upon which it paid tuition. Only gradually did they overcome their reluctance to make use of the fund. Twelve years after the inception of the Literary Fund, Brooke County commissioners reported that "the prejudices and mistaken pride" of parents and guardians of needy children were only partially removed, but in Monongalia County most parents were "becoming reconciled to the great object of the legislature in providing for the education of the poor." As late as 1839, however, in sparsely populated Logan County there were islands of resentment.[11] On the other hand,

[10] *Governor's Letter, Transmitting a Statement of the Accounts of the Literary Fund, for the Year Ending 30th September, 1825* (Richmond, Va., 1825), p. 26; *Second Auditor's Report on the State of the Literary Fund, and Proceedings of the School Commissioners, in the Different Counties, for the Year Ending September 30, 1831* (Richmond, Va., 1831), p. 25.

[11] *Communication from the President and Directors of the Literary Fund, Touching the Primary Schools* (Richmond, Va., 1823), pp. 6, 9; *Second Auditor's Report on the State of the Literary Fund for the Year 1840, and Proceedings of the School*

many parents undoubtedly feigned a reluctance to accept charity as an excuse for keeping their children at home. To deal with such persons, the Brooke County commissioners proposed that they be given authority "to use coercive measures with the parents and guardians of such poor children as ought to be educated."[12]

Economic hardship undoubtedly prevented many families from sending their children to school, even when their tuition was paid by the Literary Fund. In 1825 the commissioners of Brooke, Harrison, and Monongalia counties suggested to the superintendent of the Literary Fund that they be permitted to use part of their money for purchasing shoes and clothing for indigent children in order that they might attend school. Two parts of mountainous Nicholas County had so many poor children in 1836 that schools could not be established, even with aid of the Literary Fund. Fayette County in 1840 claimed many sections in which the majority of the children were "proper subjects for the state's bounty."[13]

In many parts of West Virginia, particularly in mountainous regions, children were often deprived of schooling because the population was too sparse to support education. Residents of Mason County, for example, were in 1822 "so much dispersed as to render it impossible, in many parts, to locate a school, so as to accomodate a sufficient number of scholars." Faced with a similar problem, Nicholas County school commissioners advanced the proposal that children in isolated areas be boarded in the homes of families who lived near a school in the hope that "it might be the means of making valuable citizens of some, who will otherwise become profligates, and a disgrace to their country and society." School authorities in Pocahontas and Randolph counties noted that the families who were the poorest

---

Commissioners in the Different Counties, for the Year Ending September 30, 1839 (Richmond, Va., 1840), p. 27.

[12] *Communication from the President and Directors of the Literary Fund, . . .* [1823], p. 6.

[13] *Governor's Letter . . . 1825*, pp. 24, 27, 30; *Second Auditor's Report on the State of the Literary Fund, for the Year 1837, and Proceedings of the School Commissioners in the Different Counties, for the Year Ending September 30, 1836* (Richmond, Va., 1837), p. 26; *Second Auditor's Report on . . . the Literary Fund . . . 1840*, p. 24.

and most incapable of supporting schools were also settled in the most inaccessible places. Because of the difficulty in making up a sufficient number of pupils to establish schools in isolated areas, many counties were unable to spend the pittance which was made available to them from the Literary Fund.[14]

Another major cause of low attendance lay in the utilitarian concept of education almost universally held by pioneers. /From their point of view, education should be along highly practical lines, with training which would equip their offspring for a way of life similar to their own. Attracted by the idea that the child learned by doing, they set their children to work at dozens of farm and household tasks which not only prepared them for making a livelihood but at the same time contributed to the productivity and self-sufficiency of their own farms.) Such knowledge was deemed of more importance than "book-learning," and if many pioneers were forced to make a choice for their children they chose the practical route to an education.) With this philosophy, the pioneer regarded absence from school very lightly. Typical of this attitude was the explanation of one parent from Bullskin in Jefferson County, who explained to the schoolmaster that his son's absence was not due to "the want of health," but that "as I had him to help secure our harvest I also have Concluded to continue him at home to help sow." As soon as that work had been completed, he promised that he would "cheerfully & thankfully" send the boy to school.[15]

The need for the labor of children on the farms and the lack of money of most pioneer families combined to keep school terms short. In many sections of the Alleghenies schools were in session only during the winter months. Statistics for twenty-one of twenty-three West Virginia counties show that in 1831 children whose schooling was financed by the Literary Fund attended school for less than seventy-five days. In eight of the counties, they attended less than fifty days. Of the twenty-five counties and towns in Virginia in which poor children attended

---

[14] *Communication from the President and Directors of the Literary Fund, . . .* [1823], p. 8; *Governor's Letter . . . 1825*, p. 33. See also Report of the Wood County School Commissioners, 1827, West Virginia University Library.

[15] Daniel Collett to Joseph H. Jones, August 16, 1796, Battaile Muse Papers.

school on the average of more than one hundred days in the year, only one—Ohio County—was in the Allegheny section of West Virginia. Since, without the support of tuition paid for poor children, there were in many areas insufficient funds for keeping schools in session, the attendance of the poor children is undoubtedly an accurate indicator of the length of school terms in West Virginia at that time.[16]

One of the most pressing problems confronting education in West Virginia, as in all frontier communities, and one which undermined some of the benefits of the Literary Fund, was the shortage of qualified teachers. Although ministers or farmers with some pretense to learning sometimes kept schools, most of the early schoolmasters were itinerant teachers. In many parts of the Alleghenies however, there were no teachers at all. In 1830 parts of Hardy County, for example, were entirely without schools because of the inability to procure teachers. As late as 1840 "the want of a sufficient number of suitable teachers" was still one of the most urgent problems of Harrison County. Even when teachers were available, they often refused to go into isolated communities. Moreover, the remuneration was often so low that, as the Monroe County commissioners reported, "qualified persons do not find it to their interest to become teachers."[17]

No one was more concerned about the teacher shortage in the mountainous areas of the state than James Brown, the superintendent of the Literary Fund. Noting that many college-trained teachers preferred to establish private schools rather than open instruction to all children, Brown proposed that county school commissioners enter into agreements with parents of poor children, who, unaccustomed to wealth, would be sent to academies in order to qualify as teachers for common schools. He also recommended "the selection of females of competent

[16] *Second Auditor's Report on . . . the Literary Fund . . . 1831*, pp. 15-16. The Ohio County commissioners noted that the influx of industrial workers to Wheeling added large numbers of poor children to their rolls, *ibid.*, p. 31.

[17] *Ibid.*, p. 24; *Second Auditor's Report on . . . the Literary Fund . . . 1837*, p. 25; *Second Auditor's Report on the State of the Literary Fund, for the Year 1839, and Proceedings of the School Commissioners in the Different Counties, for the Year Ending September 30, 1838* (Richmond, Va., 1839), p. 27.

qualifications, as preferable to male teachers, for the younger portion of the children."[18] Indeed, by 1840 several West Virginia counties were already employing women teachers. Ohio County reported that its women instructors, "characterized for piety and intelligence," had been able to impart "a correct tone . . . to the morals of their female pupils" and had provided instruction "in such particular branches of education" as the latter would need in making homes and rearing families.[19]

Even where teachers were available, their qualifications were often of a low order. Many were judged primarily by their ability to maintain strict discipline and elicit politeness from their pupils, which frequently required little more than the brawn necessary to wield birch and hickory withes and cow the larger boys into submission. (In an age when a major goal of education was the inculcation of moral principles in the pupils, school commissioners gave more attention to the moral attributes of their teachers than to their intellectual acquirements.) In 1825 the Nicholas County authorities boasted that they had "in every instance, procured teachers of correct and upright morals." Even in sparsely populated Pocahontas County, where teachers were scarce, the instructors were "mostly men of moral character."[20]

The intellectual attainments of most early schoolmasters fell far short of their moral qualifications. Reports of the county school commissioners in West Virginia indicate that large numbers of the instructors suffered serious academic deficiencies. Those of Harrison County were described as "generally men of good moral character, but not to be called men of high literary acquirements." Kanawha County instructors were deemed "capable of instructing in the common rudiments of education,"

[18] *Second Auditor's Report on the State of the Literary Fund, for the Year 1836, and Proceedings of the School Commissioners, in the Different Counties, for the Year Ending September 30, 1835* (Richmond, Va., 1836), p. 3; *Second Auditor's Report on . . . the Literary Fund . . . 1840,* pp. 4-5.

[19] *Second Auditor's Report on the State of the Literary Fund, for the Year 1841, and Proceedings of the School Commissioners in the Different Counties, for the Year Ending September 30, 1840* (Richmond, Va., 1841), p. 34.

[20] Ambler, *History of Education in West Virginia,* pp. 7-8; *Governor's Letter . . . 1825,* p. 31; *Second Auditor's Report on . . . the Literary Fund . . . 1831,* p. 32.

but a large part of those of Ohio County were branded as "very incompetent." Most of the teachers of Logan County in 1837 —and undoubtedly those of most other counties—had no education beyond that of the common school.[21]

With little formal education themselves, parents who financed the subscription schools often displayed little discrimination in the choice of a teacher. Commissioners in Morgan County complained of the "facility with which incompetent teachers get employment from the people generally." In Mason County their selection was said to depend upon "the whim of the neighbourhood in which they are employed." Yet in most areas the choice was undoubtedly between a school taught by anyone who offered his services and no school at all.[22]

The prevailing view, however, was that any school was better than none at all. This philosophy was shared by James Brown, who declared that instruction *"ought never to be withheld because better cannot be procured.* The teacher himself may *spell* and *read* very imperfectly, still the boy of moderate genius and industry will *learn, from the books* put into his hands, to do both with comparative facility and correctness." His mingling in society would eventually correct his mispronunciation, and he might in time be able to teach his master.[23] Referring in part to West Virginia teachers, Brown noted that "there is a very considerable number, especially in the thinly settled and mountainous parts of the state, whose qualifications are by no means of as high an order as they should be, and the employment of whom can only be justified on the ground that, ignorant as they are, they can at least teach the children to read," an accomplishment which the recipients of support from the Literary Fund would otherwise never attain. It was, said Brown,

---

[21] *Second Auditor's Report on . . . the Literary Fund . . . 1837,* p. 22; *Second Auditor's Report on the State of the Literary Fund, for the Year 1834, and Proceedings of the School Commissioners, in the Different Counties, for the Year Ending September 30, 1833* (Richmond, Va., 1834), p. 23; *Governor's Letter . . . 1825,* p. 31; *Second Auditor's Report on the State of the Literary Fund, for the Year 1838, and Proceedings of the School Commissioners in the Different Counties, for the Year Ending September 30, 1837* (Richmond, Va., 1838), p. 27.

[22] *Second Auditor's Report on . . . the Literary Fund . . . 1831,* p. 29; *Second Auditor's Report on . . . the Literary Fund . . . 1839,* p. 26.

[23] *Second Auditor's Report on . . . the Literary Fund . . . 1838,* p. 4.

"a choice between a glimmering of the light of knowledge and the midnight of ignorance."[24]

Most of the common schools of the Allegheny sections of West Virginia limited instruction to spelling, reading, writing, and arithmetic. The most widely used textbooks in these subjects were Webster's, Cobb's, and the United States spellers, the English Readers, American Primer, and Pike's and Smiley's arithmetics. In the relatively few localities where history and geography were taught the most popular texts were Webster's, Goodrich's, and Grimshaw's histories of the United States, histories of Greece and Rome, and Olney's, Smith's, and Wood-bridge's geographies. There was virtually no uniformity in the textbooks used. In 1838 fourteen counties reported forty-nine different texts in use. Seven of the fourteen listed the Bible and the New Testament as texts, indicating not only the strong emphasis upon moral training but perhaps also the scarcity of other books.[25]

Although there were some commonly used techniques, methods of instruction varied as widely as the textbooks. In keeping with the primary purpose for which they were established, early schools placed heavy emphasis upon reading. Almost universally, schoolmasters approached this subject by way of the alphabet and spelling out words. Once they had summoned their pupils to their books in the morning, most early masters heard a succession of classes which stood before the teacher's desk during recitation. Believing implicitly in the efficacy of competition among pupils, these masters frequently employed the "head and foot" method in their classes.

Procedures for study elicited disagreement among oldtime teachers. Some preferred that pupils preparing for a recitation study silently, but others favored lip movements or even oral reading by students at their seats. They may have believed that the latter method offered some guarantee that the pupils were not squandering their time. That it was distracting is

---

[24] *Second Auditor's Report on . . . the Literary Fund . . . 1840*, p. 4.

[25] *Second Auditor's Report on . . . the Literary Fund . . . 1837*, p. 2; *Second Auditor's Report on . . . the Literary Fund . . . 1839*, pp. 41-43. Some commissioners complained of the small allotment for books and papers. *Second Auditor's Report on . . . the Literary Fund . . . 1836*, p. 25.

borne out by a letter from James M. Smith, a pupil in a Point Pleasant school in 1847. Writing to an uncle, the youth declared "I am very well satisfiete with my school only that he keeps to much of a open school lets them studys their lessons out loud[.]" The youngster informed his uncle that he was getting along with his grammar "verry well," had gone through the arithmetic to the rule of three, and expected to get "through the arrithmatic twist against this session is out."[26]

Some of the same conditions which hampered the operation of the Literary Fund in the Allegheny area also impeded the establishment of free public schools. The possibility of free public instruction appeared on the educational horizon in 1829 when the Virginia legislature enacted a law providing for the division of counties into districts and the setting up of free public schools in each. In any district in which the inhabitants subscribed, through voluntary contributions, three-fifths of the amount needed to erect "a good and sufficient schoolhouse of wood, stone or brick," the county school commissioners might subscribe the remaining amount, provided it did not exceed 5 percent of their annual quota from the Literary Fund. They might also appropriate from their funds $100 "for the employment of a good and sufficient teacher" for any schools thus established. The only West Virginia county to set up free schools under the provisions of the law was Monroe. The county was divided into thirty-one districts, and in 1829 the first free public school in West Virginia was opened at Sinks Grove. The following year two additional schools were established. These schools The absence of broad popular support and overspending by enrolled any white child between the ages of eight and sixteen. school commissioners brought about the abandonment of the free schools in 1836 and a reversion to the practice of drawing upon the Literary Fund for support for indigent children.[27]

[26] Ambler, *History of Education in West Virginia,* p. 9; William Griffee Brown, *History of Nicholas County, West Virginia* (Richmond, Va., 1954), pp. 225-27; James M. Smith to George W. Smith, October 1, 1847, George W. Smith Papers.

[27] *Second Auditor's Report on the State of the Literary Fund, and Proceedings of the School Commissioners, in the Different Counties, for the Year Ending September 30, 1832* (Richmond, Va., 1832), p. 28; *Second Auditor's Report on . . . the Literary Fund . . . 1837,* p. 25; Ambler, *History of Education in West Virginia,* pp. 43-45.

It is worthy of note that only two other Virginia counties—Washington and Franklin—attempted to set up free public schools under the provisions of the act of 1829. The failure of the free school movement in the early 1830's lay partly in the lack of any statewide system of public taxation for educational purposes or any responsible framework of school administration. In many mountainous counties the sparsity of population and the inadequate machinery for effective local school administration further hampered progress toward a system of universal free public schools. Adding to these hindrances was the aristocratic view, held by numerous leaders in the Potomac section of West Virginia as well as influential persons in the Tidewater and Piedmont, that free public schools simply saddled "the liberal and the just" with the burden of educating the children of the "parsimonious and niggardly."

In general, Allegheny settlers remained apathetic toward education during the 1830's. There is no evidence of strong grassroots agitation for the establishment of free public schools. One looks in vain, for example, through hundreds of petitions of West Virginia residents to the General Assembly prior to 1840 for a single plea in behalf of common school education. Instead, the people appear to have been concerned almost entirely with material benefits—roads, bridges, ferry franchises, clarification of land titles, and tax relief—which the legislature might confer upon them.

The failure of the common folk of Virginia to exert their growing political influence in behalf of a secularized system of public education provided Protestant clergy with an opportunity to press for a church-dominated educational structure. Foremost among the West Virginia clerical leaders of the early 1830's was Alexander Campbell, head of the Disciples of Christ Church, who during the Virginia Constitutional Convention of 1829–1830 advocated publicly supported schools operated under church supervision. The strongest pressures for church control, however, centered in eastern Virginia. Dr. John Holt Rice, the famed Presbyterian minister, exerted great influence through his editorship of *The Virginia Evangelical and Literary Magazine*. Pleas for a religiously oriented educational system also sprinkled the pages of the widely respected *Southern Literary Messenger*. A somewhat broader view underlay the recommendations of the Institution of Education of Hampden-Sydney College and the ideas of the college's president, Dr. Jonathan D. Cushing. In an address before the Virginia Historical and Philosophical Society in 1832, Cushing advocated a plan of education designed to strengthen and mature all the human powers—physical, intellectual, and moral—and bring them into "the highest degree of improvement, and the most perfect symmetry of which they are susceptible."[28]

In 1839 Governor David Campbell, whose roots in education-conscious Washington County had made him a crusader in the field of education, urged the General Assembly to reorganize the state's educational structure and to take immediate steps to augment the Literary Fund to $200,000, erect and maintain 8,000 schoolhouses, and employ 4,000 teachers, the expenses of which should be borne in part by local taxation. The governor's plea, which emphasized widespread illiteracy, shook the complacency of the General Assembly and at least forced it to consider the educational status of the commonwealth.

During the course of its deliberations the legislature heard a report from Dr. Benjamin M. Smith, a resident of Danville, who had recently returned from Prussia. While admitting that there were aspects of the Prussian educational system unsuited to a republic, Smith believed that numerous features were worthy of emulation by the Old Dominion. Among them were the Prussian concept that education of the masses was a state duty, the use of only state-trained teachers, and an emphasis upon the practical, especially upon science, citizenship, and agriculture. Smith also urged that schools be free of any stigma of pauperism and that education, even at the university level, be available to all. The Smith report, together with the disclosure of the 1840 census that illiteracy in Virginia, already at the 60,000 mark, was increasing, induced the legislature in 1841 to authorize additional compensation for teachers of poor children. Even more important, it asked the president and directors of the

[28] Ambler, *History of Education in West Virginia*, pp. 44-45; Sadie Bell, *The Church, the State, and Education in Virginia* (Philadelphia, 1930), pp. 260-61.

Literary Fund to make recommendations for a school system "best adapted . . . to secure the benefits of education to the people of this commonwealth."[29]

Seizing upon this opportunity, proponents of a free school system held a series of meetings, the most important of which met at Clarksburg, Lexington, and Richmond in the fall and early winter of 1841. The groundwork for the Clarksburg gathering was laid in May, 1841, when a group of the town's citizens issued a circular calling upon the people of northwestern Virginia to send delegates to a convention in September. In response to their appeal, 114 persons from sixteen counties, twelve of which were in West Virginia, met at Clarksburg on September 7 and 8. Nearly 75 percent of those present, however, represented six northwestern counties. Harrison County alone had forty-one members, and Lewis, Monongalia, Ohio, Tyler, and Wood counties each had eight or more.

The composition of the Clarksburg Convention indicates that by 1840 many political, social, religious, and journalistic leaders of trans-Allegheny West Virginia were becoming concerned about the region's educational deficiencies. Fourteen members of the convention were either serving in the General Assembly or would sit in that body before the enactment of the important public school legislation of 1846, and numerous other members held local political offices. Also active in the deliberations of the Clarksburg meeting were widely respected newspapermen such as Benjamin Bassel of the Clarksburg *Scion of Democracy* and Enos W. Newton, who less than three months later founded the influential *Kanawha Republican* at Charleston. The importance of religious influences was manifest in the convention's seating of the general agent of the American Bible Society in the West, the Reverend E. W. Sehon of Cincinnati, and in the attention which it gave to addresses prepared by Alexander Campbell and Henry Ruffner of the Disciples of Christ and Presbyterian churches, respectively.[30]

[29] Ambler, *History of Education in West Virginia*, pp. 45-46.
[30] Wheeling *Times and Advertiser*, June 1, 1841; Ambler, *History of Education in West Virginia*, p. 64n; C. H. Ambler, ed., "The Clarksburg Educational Convention of September 8-9, 1841," *West Virginia History*, V (October, 1943), 6; Virgil A. Lewis, *Second Biennial Report of the Department of Archives and History of the State of West Virginia* (n. p., n. d.), pp. 139-40.

The major address during the convention, prepared by Alexander Campbell but read for him in his absence, skillfully blended the views of Jeffersonian liberals and Christian idealists. Campbell declared that experience had proved that many of the worthy poor would not accept aid under the humiliating conditions imposed by the Literary Fund and insisted that "we do not want poor schools for poor scholars, or gratuitous instruction for paupers; but we want schools for all at the expense of all." At the same time, he branded intellectual training without the inculcation of Christian standards of morality and ethics as calamitous. Although scathing in his condemnation of "the atheism and infidelity" of the French Revolution, Campbell nevertheless advocated no narrow sectarian control of education. Rather, he set forth the view that there was a "common Christianity" based upon piety and morality "on which all good men of all denominations are agreed" and that this "common Christianity" should lie at the base of a sound educational system.[31]

In an "Address to Our Fellow Citizens" prepared by a committee of seven, the convention dealt with a wide range of problems relating to education. Included among its recommendations were greater attention to female education, the establishment of a system of normal schools, and the publication of a "common school journal." It also urged the establishment of libraries, the award of floral crowns in recognition of merit among pupils, and the transformation of schoolhouses into genuine community centers. An uneducated citizenry, the convention declared, was the greatest threat to the republic and to the laws and political reasoning which protected private property; therefore, the self-interest of the wealthy dictated their support of general public education as the greatest bulwark against these dangers.

The second major appeal of the convention took the form of a memorial to the legislature. Deploring the system under which thousands of children were growing up "without the slightest tincture of common learning" and which left their moral training to "ignorant, coarse, and vulgar teachers," the members urged

[31] Ambler, *History of Education in West Virginia*, p. 47; Ambler, ed., "The Clarksburg Educational Convention of September 8-9, 1841," pp. 7-8.

the legislature to divide each county into school districts and to establish in each a school which would be financed in part with local levies and in part with federal and state funds. The memorial also pressed for the appointment of a state superintendent of schools with broad powers over educational matters. The district schools, to be free to all white children, must, they insisted, be made "good enough *for the rich*" in order that "they may be *fit for the poor.*"

Even though both were tabled, two proposals laid before the Clarksburg convention deserve mention. Henry Ruffner urged the creation of a system of district schools supported by a tax on property, with the initiation of the system in each district to take place when the district was able to support it. In addition, he proposed normal schools for the education of teachers. General administration of the plan would be in the hands of a state superintendent. The other proposal, offered by John D. D. Rosset of Jackson County, called for abolition of the Literary Fund and the maintenance of primary schools by direct taxation, spending of at least one-third of the school revenue on primary education, education for all white children between the ages of six and twelve, and a pension plan for teachers.[32]

The Clarksburg Convention represented a pivotal point in the educational history of West Virginia. It stirred general interest in free public education as never before in the state's history. "The ball is now in motion," wrote Enos W. Newton, "and we entertain no doubt the friends of the cause have enterprize, zeal, and energy to keep it moving." Equally significant, the convention strengthened western belief that the most urgent educational problem in Virginia was the establishment of free public schools rather than further aid to the colleges and the university. Newton believed that of the many reforms needed in the Old Dominion, "this one of primary schools, that will bring the means of a good practical education to every white child in the state, is what she wants most—it is the very foundation of all others." His views were echoed by others, including

[32] Ambler, *History of Education in West Virginia,* pp. 48-51; Ambler, ed., "The Clarksburg Educational Convention of September 8-9, 1841," pp. 8-13.

Benjamin Bassel, who declared that if there was any panacea for the ills besetting society and "the preservation of our present incomparable form of government," it rested upon the education of every child of school age.[33]

Advocates of free public schools also watched with interest the Lexington and Richmond conventions. Indeed, the Clarksburg Convention had named ten of its members to attend the former, which met on October 7, 1841. Dominated by James McDowell of Rockbridge County, the Lexington Convention modified the plan outlined by Henry Ruffner for the Clarksburg gathering. Instead of providing free schools, this proposal urged tuition reductions in proportion to need, with each family making some contribution. Alumni of Hampden-Sydney College gave the Ruffner Plan wide publicity and took the lead in arranging the Richmond Convention, which met on December 9. Under the guiding hand of Thomas Ritchie, editor of the Richmond *Enquirer,* the convention recommended a system of primary education maintained by taxation and "free to every white child of proper age." It also urged effective support for academies and colleges, which were deemed essential in providing teachers for the primary schools. Some westerners, who feared that the Richmond Convention might divert the attention of the legislature from the need for primary schools by emphasizing the plight of the colleges and the university, nevertheless conceded that its actions would keep alive the nascent interest in a free primary school system.

These educational gatherings produced no immediate results. The House of Delegates in 1842 passed a bill which embodied in its essential features the recommendations of proponents of free common schools, but the Senate rejected the measure primarily because of a provision creating the office of state superintendent. But popular enthusiasm would not permit the matter to die. James McDowell, who had in the meantime become governor, made the need for general education the burden of his message to the legislature in 1843. Ministers and officials of denominational colleges, in conventions at Richmond

[33] Charleston *Kanawha Republican,* December 11, 1841; Clarksburg *Scion of Democracy,* August 24, 1841.

in January, 1844, and August, 1845, continued to press for a system of popular education under proper moral influences. Ultimately, on December 18, 1845, another large educational gathering, made up of 213 delegates from 51 counties, convened at Richmond. About a third of the delegates were from West Virginia counties and included such men as Spicer Patrick, Allen T. Caperton, and William H. McFarland. Proceedings were directed by Governor McDowell, who presented letters from Horace Mann and other eminent educators. Although the convention proved hopelessly divided, it did agree upon the naming of a central committee to publicize the need for a revision of the state's educational system.

The clamor for change, however, soon bore fruit. On February 25, 1846, in action which was a harbinger of other advances, the legislature authorized sixteen counties and the city of Williamsburg to hold referendums on the question of establishing district free schools. Ten days later, on March 5, it revised existing school arrangements by passing an act requiring county courts to divide other counties into districts and to appoint a commissioner for each district. The commissioners, in turn, were to elect a county superintendent. The new legislation made no change in the provision of the act of 1818 which authorized tuition for poor children only. A second act of the same date offered yet another method whereby district schools might be established. If the existing system proved inadequate in any county, one-third of the qualified voters might petition the county court to hold a referendum on the matter of establishing district free schools. Should two-thirds of the eligible voters approve, the court was then required to divide the county into suitable school districts. Voters in each district would then elect a commissioner, and the commissioners for the various districts acting jointly would choose a county superintendent. Most West Virginia counties which instituted district systems did so under the first of the two acts of March 5.

Although the control of the system was in the hands of the commissioners, each subdistrict or school was administered by a board of three trustees, who passed on the academic and moral qualifications of the teachers whom they hired. Each school "precinct" was to be of such size that all children were within reach of its school, and to insure this the district commissioners were made elective by the voters of the district. Schools were to be open without charge to all white children above six years old, who would be instructed in the fundamentals and, if possible, in English grammar, geography, history, physical science, and other subjects. Both commissioners and trustees were required to visit the schools regularly and to perform other duties faithfully or be subject to penalties.[34]

The first West Virginia county to set up district free schools under the act of February 25, 1846, was Kanawha. Under this act, as amended March 10, 1847, the voters of the county on April 23, 1847, approved free public schools by a vote of 680 to 251. Powerful elements, consisting of landowners and conservatives, however, refused to accept the results of the poll, and, under an authorizing act, passed by the legislature on January 10, 1853, forced the holding of another election, which took place on May 26, 1853. Again the voters registered approval of the new system, this time by a margin of 956 to 553.[35]

The district free school system yet faced formidable opposition. In 1853 the salt firm of Dickinson and Shrewsbury, in a test case, refused to pay its school tax of $350.82. When the sheriff, James Fry, sold its property, the firm brought suit against the sheriff for trespass damages, but the court upheld the sheriff's action. Meanwhile, opponents of the system had again ap-

[34] Ambler, *History of Education in West Virginia*, pp. 51-55; Charleston *Kanawha Republican*, December 11, 1841.
[35] The distribution of the vote in 1847 is of more than passing interest. At the courthouse precinct the district free school system carried by 383 to 42, or with a majority of 9 to 1. In five of the remaining six precincts it carried with majorities ranging from 2 to 1 to more than 9 to 1. In one precinct, along the upper Kanawha, with the polling place at Jones' at present Pratt, the move failed by a vote of 7 to 105. Two possibilities loom as explanations. The upper Kanawha area was closely allied economically to the saltworks, where such producers as John Dickinson and Joel Shrewsbury vigorously opposed it. There, too, the Baptist Church was strong. Historically, the Baptists had attached little importance to education, but by this time they had a substantial Sunday school movement, which they may have deemed an acceptable substitute for district free schools. For voting statistics, see Charles H. Ambler, "Poor Relief (Kanawha County, Virginia, 1818-1847)," *West Virginia History*, III (July, 1942), 302. Figures for Sunday school enrollments are in Record of the Greenbrier Association of Baptists [1825-1868], p. 248, which shows 17 Sunday schools with 62 teachers, 433 students, and 555 volumes in the libraries.

proached the legislature. The result was that on January 14, 1853, that body reduced the amount of taxes collected in Loudoun, Fairfax, and Kanawha counties for the support of free schools. To make up the deficiency, it authorized the collection from financially able parents and guardians of a special tax of not less than 50 cents and not more than one dollar per term of three months for each pupil. The following year it set limits to the amount of school taxes and thereby severely curbed expenditures for free schools in Kanawha County.

Two other West Virginia counties instituted the district free school system. On August 7, 1847, Jefferson County, after some delay, elected school commissioners and enacted a levy, which together with subscriptions and assessments, enabled the schools to operate for a nine-month term. Even though charges of mismanagement and incompetent teaching blighted its success, its voters upheld the system in May, 1856, by a margin of nearly five to one. Ohio County put the district free school system into effect in the fall of 1848. As in Kanawha County, the system was challenged, but voters on April 26, 1848, for a second time approved the system by a ringing ten-to-one margin. By authorization of the General Assembly, the Wheeling area became an independent school district in 1849, the first in West Virginia. Residents of Ohio County approved the arrangement by a vote of 1,098 to 113.

Other counties proved less enthusiastic about district free schools. The legislature authorized Cabell and Wayne counties to vote on the question, but there is no record that they ever did so. In Marshall County, which also received authorization, on April 2, 1853, to hold elections, only one-third of the voters went to the polls, and the issue carried by such a small margin that the system was not put into effect. Brooke County in 1855 failed to obtain the necessary two-thirds majority to institute the plan, and in Mason County the vote approving the system in 1857 was challenged as fraudulent. Wood County approved the plan, with Parkersburg as an independent district, but failed to put it into effect because of the outbreak of the Civil War.

Although the way had been paved for free public education, public interest lagged far behind opportunity. Reports for the year ending September 30, 1850, show that, despite free tuition, 2,670 out of 7,013 children in Kanawha County and 1,022 out of 2,175 in Ohio County were not enrolled in school. At the same time only 225 schools of some 4,000 in the entire state were operating on the district free school basis. Moreover, less than half the poor children of Virginia were enrolled in school.[36]

The interest in education which had led to the passage of a substantial amount of district free school legislation in the 1840's subsided in the following decade. The late Professor Charles H. Ambler, the leading authority on the educational history of West Virginia, attributed part of the responsibility for failure to adopt the system to the legislation itself. He pointed out that two-thirds of the qualified voters of a county had to approve the institution of the district free school plan but that a simple majority could abolish the system. Added handicaps were the reluctance of the legislature to enact special laws needed in many instances and the limitations which it placed upon tuition and other assessments that might be levied against parents.

Ambler suggested other barriers to the adoption of the district free school idea. Sparseness of population in the mountainous areas and a middle class verging on poverty, he believed, were major handicaps. Religious conditions, such as the growth of the Sunday school enrollments, schisms within the evangelical churches which undermined much of the ecumenical outlook in educational matters, and the cautious attitude of ministers toward public affairs also slowed down the free school movement. In addition, many of the editors who had led the fight for education in the 1840's, such as John H. Pleasants and Thomas Ritchie, were no longer on the scene. Then too, comparisons between Virginia and northern states such as Massachusetts and New York in such matters as illiteracy, crime, and economic fluctuations, bred a smugness in Virginians, which convinced many of them that the state's efforts in education were sufficient.[37]

The failure of West Virginia counties to seize the opportunities presented by the legislation of the 1840's, however, suggests more fundamental reasons for the educational lag in the mountain

[36] Ambler, *History of Education in West Virginia,* pp. 56-60.
[37] *Ibid.,* pp. 60-64.

regions. The professed aversion to the stigma of poverty attached to the Literary Fund may have been less genuine than hitherto believed, and the reluctance of parents to take advantage of that beneficence may have sprung from an apathy which even they did not care to admit. Indeed, it would be a gross error to assume that the demand for educational opportunity in West Virginia or other Allegheny areas represented the voice of the frontier. Rather, the agitation for improved educational facilities in the 1840's seems to have been only a ripple on the surface, stirred by a handful of men of vision, which did not seriously disturb the placid waters of popular indifference.

Chapter Eleven

A Glimmering of the Light

Despite the low level of educational attainment during her pioneer period, West Virginia did not completely succumb to "the midnight of ignorance." Along her major streams and nestled among her hills were little frontier towns, several of which were thriving centers of learning and culture. Besides common schools of better than ordinary quality, many of these towns boasted academies, printing establishments which produced newspapers, books, and periodicals, libraries both public and private, and flourishing literary societies. With such advantages, they stood as beacons—faint though their gleam may have been—whose rays reached into the recesses of the mountains and shed "a glimmering of the light of knowledge" upon culturally improverished areas of the Alleghenies.

In late eighteenth- and early nineteenth-century America, formal instruction beyond the common school rested largely with grammar schools and academies. These institutions depended almost exclusively upon a middle-class clientele and at best attracted limited numbers of students. They prospered best where social and economic conditions were mature and where population was sufficiently concentrated to provide adequate and continuous support. Such conditions did not prevail in most sections of the Alleghenies. The sparseness of population, economic backwardness, and popular indifference to formal education which retarded the establishment of free public schools all too often undermined efforts to provide education of academic grade.

Fortunately, not all of the educational soil of the mountains was sterile. In pioneer West Virginia the social and economic conditions which proved most conducive to intellectual and cultural stimulation were found in the northern half of the state, particularly in the Potomac, Monongahela, and upper Ohio valleys, and in a belt extending from the Greenbrier region along the Kanawha to the Ohio. The Potomac Valley and the Greenbrier region developed healthy agrarian societies. The economy of the Ohio and Kanawha valleys was built upon both agricultural and industrial bases and hinged to growth along the Ohio and Mississippi. Each of these areas supported provident middle classes, whose interests and aspirations provided much of the impetus for improved educational facilities.

Leaders in the efforts to establish academies in West Virginia attributed their motives to the highest patriotism. The Republic, they believed, drew its strength from the virtues of the middle classes, and the surest way to preserve the work of the Founding Fathers was to educate the nation's citizens to middle-class ideals. Their devotion to the Republic sprang from no fanatical zeal for egalitarianism but from its promise of political, social, and economic opportunity and its protection to property and class distinctions. These advantages might be lost if the middle classes sank to the educational levels of the poor. Education was valued, therefore, not as a means of social leveling but as a necessity in providing enlightened leadership and a knowledgeable and responsible citizenry.

Such views were clearly set forth by a group of Wood Countians who in 1816 asked the Virginia General Assembly to establish Jefferson Academy. Although "placed at the verge of the ancient dominion, and hitherto regarded as orphans," they declared that they had "never lost sight of the fundamental principles of republicanism." Significantly, however, they coupled their profession of belief in the equality of men with a statement that it was "owing to adventitious circumstances alone" that distinctions had been preserved in frontier society. As "children of the revolution," they had been forced to improve their own faculties "under the sound of the War Whoop," but they had "fondly looked forward to the time when the light of science should dawn upon the rising generation." Future generations, they maintained, should imitate not only their own virtues but should duplicate the "energies of those patriots who atchieved [*sic*] our Revolution."[1]

[1] Wood County Legislative Petitions, November 22, 1816.

Of equal importance in the founding of academies in West Virginia were religious motivations. Whatever their doctrinal differences, religious leaders were agreed that education devoid of moral training was dangerous, whether at the common school or higher levels. Moreover, at a time when separation of church and state was proceeding rapidly, they saw Christian-oriented education as a formidable bulwark against Deism, which was universally detested in frontier areas. Nearly half of the academies founded in West Virginia prior to 1820 were either established by religious groups, particularly Episcopalians and Presbyterians, or presided over by prominent Protestant clergymen.

Most of the early academies of West Virginia were located in the north-central counties and in the Eastern and Northern panhandles. In 1818 ten academies were operating under charters granted by the General Assembly. With the dates of their establishment, they were: Shepherdstown, prior to 1787; Randolph, at Clarksburg, 1787; Charlestown, or Brooke, at Wellsburg, 1797; Charles Town, 1798; Lewisburg, about 1808; Monongalia, at Morgantown, 1814; Wheeling Lancastrian, 1814; Romney, 1818; Mercer, at Charleston, 1818; and Buffalo, at Bethany, 1818. A few others, such as a female seminary and Aquila M. Bolton's academy for boys at Wheeling and a grammar school and a female academy at Martinsburg, were private ventures. By comparison, Allegheny areas of Pennsylvania in 1820 had about twenty incorporated academies, most of which received some state aid. Although the number of academies in West Virginia increased about threefold by 1840, only four—Marshall at Huntington, Mercer, Lewisburg, and Union at Alderson—served southern West Virginia. Indeed, seventeen of the state's twenty-eight counties had within their borders no institution of learning higher than a common school.[2]

The dearth of opportunity for secondary education in West

[2] Charles H. Ambler, *A History of Education in West Virginia from Early Colonial Times to 1949* (Huntington, W. Va., 1951), pp. 73, 75-76, 78-80, 86-88, 107-109; Solon J. Buck and Elizabeth Hawthorn Buck, *The Planting of Civilization in Western Pennsylvania* (Pittsburgh, Pa., 1939), p. 397; U. S., Bureau of the Census, *Compendium of the Enumeration of the Inhabitants and Statistics of the United States, as Obtained at the Department of State, from the Returns of the Sixth Census* (Washington, D. C., 1841), p. 39.

Virginia stemmed in part from the desultory support given to academies and seminaries by the General Assembly, but it also resulted from the lack of any broad popular demand from mountain settlements. In his educational proposals of 1779, Thomas Jefferson had called for state-supported "colleges," in reality secondary schools, for preparing students for the College of William and Mary, which would become the state university. Forced to abandon this plan, Jefferson thereafter concentrated his interests largely upon the founding of a nonsectarian university and a system of primary schools. Subjected to only limited popular pressure to provide for education of academic grade, the legislature confined its efforts during the next half-century largely to granting charters, authorizing the use of lotteries for fundraising, and extending occasional aid from the Literary Fund.[3]

The first, and an extremely important, instance of legislative support of secondary education in transmontane West Virginia was the establishment of Randolph Academy at Clarksburg in 1787. This institution was chartered at the request of a number of prominent residents of Monongalia, Harrison, and Ohio counties, who cited the establishment of Transylvania Seminary in Lexington as precedent for legislative benevolence. In fact, the petition for Randolph Academy bears such a striking resemblance to that for the Kentucky school that there is reason to believe that Transylvania provided the inspiration for Randolph Academy. Petitioners for Randolph Academy, like those for Transylvania, professed the greatest esteem for the Tidewater college, but like the Lexington institution they sought and obtained funds that had previously been set aside for the support of William and Mary. In the case of Randolph Academy, this appropriation took the form of one-sixth of the surveyors' fees collected in the rapidly expanding frontier counties of Monongalia, Harrison, Randolph, and Ohio.[4]

That something more than an ordinary institution was envisioned for Randolph Academy is indicated by the composition

[3] Ambler, *History of Education in West Virginia*, pp. 66-70.

[4] Monongalia County Legislative Petitions, December 1, 1786; Walter Wilson Jennings, *Transylvania: Pioneer University of the West* (New York, 1955), pp. 4-9.

of its board of trustees. The governing body included outstanding residents of the four frontier counties from which the institution drew its support, among whom were George Jackson, William McCleery, John Evans, Benjamin Wilson, Nicholas Carpenter, William John, Archibald Woods, Moses Chapline, Ebenezer Zane, John Wilson, Jacob Westfall, Jr., Robert Maxwell, and John Jackson, Jr. But to these were added some of Virginia's most noted men, including Edmund Randolph, Patrick Henry, Benjamin Harrison, James Wood, George Mason, George Nicholas, and John Harvey.

Despite the eminence of its trustees, Randolph Academy's beginnings were by no means auspicious. During the months immediately following its authorization, its trustees, scattered over a large frontier area, often found it impossible to assemble a quorum for the transaction of business. To overcome this handicap, they asked the legislature to add Isaac Zane, John Haddon, Abraham Claypool, James Westfall, John Prunty, Henry Fink, Daniel Davisson, Hezekiah Davisson, Joseph Hastings, and John McCally to the board. Yet, not until February 23, 1793, did the trustees let the contract for the building, a frame structure 36 by 20 feet. More than two additional years elapsed before the institution opened it doors, in August, 1795, to students.[5]

With the Reverend George Towers, a recent immigrant from England, as its first tutor, the academy offered instruction in Latin and Greek, English, arithmetic, and geography. The income from surveyors' fees proved less than anticipated, but even so the institution "answered the Expectations of its patrons" for a number of years. This modest support enabled it to keep its fees to a minimum and to claim the lowest cost to students of any academy in the Union. In 1808 tuition and "genteel boarding," the latter including washing and lodging, required an outlay of only sixty dollars per year by students.

With a relatively fixed income, the academy fell victim to rising prices in the early nineteenth century. From 1809 to 1816 it apparently suspended operations altogether. Legislation in 1819, which cut off its income from surveyors' fees, added to

---

[5] Ambler, *History of Education in West Virginia*, pp. 75, 107-108; Harrison County Legislative Petitions, October 23, 1788.

its financial woes. With its building in "a state of rapid decay" and lacking a professor, the institution had by the mid-twenties become "dormant for want of funds." In 1826 its trustees besought the legislature "to rescue from distruction this ancient Seminary of learning." Specifically, they asked permission to raise $50,000 by lottery and to apply the money to repairs and additions to the building, to begin operation of a female seminary, and to make investments in "permanent productive stock," the income from which would be used for salaries of professors and the purchase of "Library and Philosophical Apparatus."[6] In response to the trustees' appeal, the legislature on February 11, 1828, authorized the use of a lottery, but this device did not yield the desired revenue.

Forced to rely entirely upon private support, Randolph Academy had by 1834 become moribund. Its trustees bemoaned the fact that the 24,000 residents of Harrison, Lewis, and Randolph counties now had no school "where other than the simplest rudiments of an Education is taught." In 1841 they gave the coup de grace to their nearly defunct seminary by lending their support to efforts by Clarksburg citizens to establish a new institution, which was incorporated the following year as Northwestern Virginia Academy.[7]

During its early years Randolph Academy drew some of its strongest support from the Morgantown area, which almost from its first settlement had evinced an unusual interest in educational and cultural matters. As early as 1792 Bishop Francis Asbury, the noted Methodist itinerant, recorded that he preached to a congregation in the town's "academical church." In 1803 twenty-four prominent residents of Morgantown laid before the General Assembly one of the most ambitious schemes for secondary education to originate in the transmontane counties. They asked the legislature to authorize the sale of delinquent lands in the counties of northwestern Virginia and to apply the proceeds to the establishment and support of an academy in

---

[6] Ambler, *History of Education in West Virginia*, p. 75; Harrison County Legislative Petitions, December 23, 1826.

[7] Harrison County Legislative Petitions, December 7, 1827; *ibid.*, December 17, 1834; Ambler, *History of Education in West Virginia*, p. 76.

each of the counties. Administration of the plan was to be in the hands of nine trustees in each county—four named by the legislature and five elected by qualified voters—who would be empowered to sell delinquent tracts or such parts thereof as might be necessary to discharge the tax arrearages. Unfortunately, the legislature, perhaps under pressure from landholders, refused to sanction the proposal.

The rebuff by the legislature by no means dampened the interest of Morgantown residents in education. Already they had raised money by subscription, purchased a lot, and in 1803 erected a brick building for school purposes. By 1814 this building housed two schools, "one for the teaching of the rudiments of the English language, and the other for Latin, English, and Mathematicks." In October of that year eleven residents asked the General Assembly to incorporate the latter school as Monongalia Academy and to assign to it one-sixth of the surveyors' fees collected in Monongalia County, which since 1787 had been set aside for the support of Randolph Academy. The legislature complied with their request. In 1816 the academy enrolled twenty-five students, who were instructed in the usual branches of knowledge by a tutor, who received $400 per year for his services. By 1830, thanks to funds made available from a lottery, the trustees had constructed a new and more adequate building.

These successes encouraged the trustees of Monongalia Academy to entertain even higher aspirations for their institution. In 1826 they noted that there was "no Seminary of learning in Virginia, west of the Alleghany mountains, of higher grade than a common grammar school." As a consequence, many western youths, unable to afford an education at the colleges and the university in eastern Virginia, either attended academies and colleges in Pennsylvania and Ohio or remained without further schooling. The trustees urged the legislature to establish one or two "well endowed seminaries" between the Alleghenies and the Ohio as a means of saving this "foreign expenditure" and of instilling into western youth "those patriotic and republican principles for which Virginia has long been distinguished." For several reasons, including its "moral and genteel" society, they recommended Morgantown as an ideal site for such an institution.

Although the legislature declined to act upon these recommendations, it did provide rather generous support, especially in the form of authorizations for lotteries, which during the next quarter of a century enabled Monongalia Academy to become one of the outstanding institutions of western Virginia. Its program of instruction, divided into ten classes, compared favorably with those of the best seminaries and included Greek, Latin, French, moral and intellectual philosophy, algebra, rhetoric, history, natural philosophy, geography, mathematics, English grammar, surveying, and navigation. In 1833 the trustees opened Morgantown Female Seminary, a branch of the academy but kept separate and distinct from it. Six years later the female seminary was completely detached from the academy, and, with a board of trustees made up mostly of leaders of the Methodist Church, it operated for many years under the name of Whitehall Female Seminary. This division in no way impaired the success of Monongalia Academy, and at mid-century its trustees were giving serious consideration to elevating it to a college.[8]

Some of the most stable institutions of learning were those of the Eastern Panhandle, where middle and upper classes had traditionally shown an interest in advanced education and where, significantly, the Presbyterian and Anglican churches were relatively strong. By 1822 successful academies were in operation in Shepherdstown, Charles Town, Romney, and Martinsburg. Without doubt, Shepherdstown can claim the honor of the first academy in West Virginia. The Reverend Robert Stubbs was there in 1787 as the instructor in an academy which apparently had its beginnings shortly after the close of the Revolutionary War.

Perhaps to the Reverend Moses Hoge more than to any other person belongs the credit for fostering Shepherdstown's interest in advanced education. For nearly a quarter of a century this eminent Presbyterian minister held sway over the classroom.

[8] Monongalia County Legislative Petitions, December 21, 1803; *ibid.*, October 19, 1814; *ibid.*, December 19, 1826; *ibid.*, February 4, 1831; Ambler, *History of Education in West Virginia*, pp. 80-83.

In 1792 he opened his school in which he taught Latin, Greek, and English and "some of the most useful branches of Science." By 1813 he had extended his offerings to include surveying, Euclid, rhetoric, use of globes, history, grammar, natural and moral science, composition, and elocution. His success seems to have been a major factor in the chartering of Shepherdstown Academy by the General Assembly on January 3, 1814.

Subsequent years brought further growth. In 1832 the trustees asked for bids on a new building to be "made of brick or stone with a cypress roof." This structure was to be erected on land donated several years earlier by Abraham Shepherd and was probably financed by a lottery authorized by the General Assembly in 1833. During the 1830's the academy was closely associated with the Shepherdstown Female Classical School. In addition to the customary subjects, the latter institution, under the principalship of Martha Chisholm, offered instruction in French, Italian, and Spanish, with emphasis upon the "spirit and literature" of the languages, and in drawing, painting, music and needlework.[9]

Few towns in pioneer West Virginia gave more sustained support to advanced education than aristocratic Charles Town. In 1795 eighty-one of its residents raised over 514 pounds for the erection of Charles Town Academy. With an impressive board of trustees that included Philip Pendleton, Samuel Washington, George Hite, Ferdinando Fairfax, Edward Tiffin, and other well-to-do landowners, the academy opened its doors in 1798. A unique feature of its charter was that it proposed to offer free instruction to needy students insofar as the institution's finances permitted. Its original curriculum included courses in Latin, Greek, English, French, geography, astronomy, criticism, mathematics, and natural and moral philosophy, but offerings were steadily expanded. With "newly acquired globes, an orrery, geological specimens, mechanical powers, chemical utensils, air-pumps, an electrical machine, and other important and useful articles," it claimed by 1835 to be one of the best-equipped academies in the country. On March 15, 1836, the General Assembly vested control of the institution in a joint

[9] Ambler, *History of Education in West Virginia*, pp. 73-74.

stock company. In September of that year the school opened a female department, which stressed an English education along with music, drawing, and painting.[10]

Fifteen miles west of Charles Town, at Martinsburg, an equally aristocratic society displayed similar interest in education and cultural matters. As early as 1791 John McCormick taught a grammar school in which he offered instruction in the Latin and Greek languages. On January 21, 1811, Martinsburg Academy began operation with the Reverend John B. Hoge, pastor of the Presbyterian church, in charge. Urging parents to provide their sons with a "Liberal Education," Hoge offered Latin and Greek and "such other branches of learning as are usually taught in public seminaries." In 1815 the trustees of Martinsburg Academy also became the administrative board of Martinsburg Female Academy, which opened on May 8 of that year with an enrollment limited for the time to thirty-five students.

Both Martinsburg Academy and the Female Academy prospered. The former held two sessions of five and one-half months each year. During the 1820's it had a succession of principals, each of whom seems to have had some peculiar approach to education, but Samuel M. Whann, who moved from Washington, D. C., to Martinsburg, raised it to its peak of success during his tenure from 1829 to 1836. With "so competent a teacher," an environment free from "enticements to dissipation," economical accommodations, and an enrollment of from fifty to sixty students, the trustees had good reason for pride in their institution.

During these years Martinsburg, with its wealthy and cosmopolitan citizenry, attracted no less than a dozen other educational ventures. In January, 1813, J. A. Xaupi opened a dancing school for teaching "the Ladies and Gentlemen of Martinsburg the most fashionable Dances," as well as for instruction in "Cotillion Parties and in Fencing." The popularity of Xaupi's school is indicated by an existence of more than ten years. James Maxwell, a surveyor, successfully set up a night school in which he taught not only the usual elementary subjects but also the extraction

[10] *Ibid.*, pp. 76-77; Millard Kessler Bushong, *A History of Jefferson County, West Virginia* (Charles Town, W. Va., 1941), pp. 60-62.

of roots, mensuration, and plane geometry. In 1825 Mrs. Ann Young made preparations for a school in which she proposed to teach the "different branches of Needlework" in addition to basic subjects. Two years later a young lady, recently arrived from Philadelphia, opened a "Lace School," in which she promised to teach the making of certain varieties of laces "equal to the French manufacture."

Despite its varied educational opportunities, Martinsburg suffered a waning of interest in academic and cultural matters during the late 1830's and early 1840's. Competition from nearby institutions dug deeply into enrollments at Martinsburg Academy. The Panic of 1837 created further difficulties for the institution, and even an appropriation from the Literary Fund could not entirely redeem it. In 1839 its principal pleaded with parents of the area to educate their children "to take such stations in society as the free citizens of a free country ought to occupy." But the academy failed to regain its earlier strength, and in the late 1840's it became inactive. The period of lassitude eventually passed, however, and during the middle 1850's Martinsburg reached the zenith of her ante bellum educational and cultural attainments.[11]

One other educational center of the Eastern Panhandle deserves mention. Romney, centrally located to accommodate the educational and cultural needs of South Branch residents, in 1818 became the seat of one of the Eastern Panhandle's most successful academies. The institution had as its first principal Dr. Henry Johnston, an Englishman, but it owed its greatest debts to the patronage of the Romney Literary Society and to the Reverend Dr. Henry Foote, a Presbyterian minister who served as its principal from 1826 to 1837. The academy grew rapidly and in 1832 was handsomely supported by the General Assembly, which authorized the Literary Society to raise $20,000 by lottery over a period of ten years. In 1846 the name of the institution was changed to the Romney Classical Institute, and Dr. Foote again became principal. A change from sectarian to

[11] Ambler, *History of Education in West Virginia*, pp. 90-95; Mabel Henshaw Gardiner and Ann Henshaw Gardiner, *Chronicles of Old Berkeley: A Narrative History of a Virginia County from Its Beginnings to 1926* (Durham, N. C., 1938), pp. 128-30.

secular control three years later led to the ousting of Foote, the elimination of instruction in theology, and the setting up under Foote's direction of the rival Potomac Seminary.[12]

Lagging behind Clarksburg, Morgantown, and the Eastern Panhandle were the towns of the upper Ohio Valley. The first instruction of academic grade was introduced into the Northern Panhandle in 1798 when the Reverend Joseph Doddridge, acting in behalf of the Protestant Episcopal Church, established Brooke Academy at Charlestown, later Wellsburg. Soon afterwards the trustees of the academy petitioned the General Assembly for a charter and asked approval for raising $2,000 by lottery. The legislature granted the charter in 1799 but did not sanction the lottery. Instead, it permitted the trustees to solicit subscriptions. This source of support proved inadequate, and in 1800 the trustees asked authority to levy a tax "upon store licenses and also upon county seals and law processes" in Ohio and Brooke counties. Again the legislature rejected their appeal. Not until 1842 did the General Assembly provide the institution with monetary aid, and then only a subvention of $234.92 from the Literary Fund. Despite its financial difficulties, the academy in 1843 had a faculty of five and an enrollment of about one hundred students.[13]

One of the most interesting educational endeavors in the entire Allegheny region was the result of a bequest by Noah Linsly, who devised property in Wheeling "for the education of Poor Children on the Lancastrian System." Intrigued by the Lancastrian plan, Noah Zane and Samuel Sprigg, executors of Linsly's estate, obtained legislative approval on October 10, 1841, for a charter for Wheeling Lancastrian Academy. By 1820 the trustees had constructed a two-story brick building capable of accommodating five hundred students. On December 1, 1820, the institution opened its doors.

The Wheeling Lancastrian Academy proved less successful than anticipated. Matriculations fell far short of expectations. On November 1, 1821, the school enrolled 163 students, but the trustees declared that their "competent teacher . . . could

12 Ambler, *History of Education in West Virginia,* pp. 86-87.
13 *Ibid.,* pp. 66, 78.

instruct double the number of pupils under his care." They were thus unable to reap the full benefits of the Lancastrian system, which allegedly enabled a teacher, with the aid of monitors, to instruct large numbers of students and thereby effect substantial reductions in educational costs. Moreover, the Linsly bequest provided less income than expected. Having contracted to pay the teacher $100 per quarter for the instruction of poor children, the trustees found their work "cramped for want of funds." Tuitions from paying pupils did not make up the deficit. In 1821 the trustees called upon the legislature to grant them $200 annually from the Literary Fund in order that they might "place the establishment on the original plan of the founder," but the General Assembly turned a deaf ear to their plea.

The divergence from Linsly's plan apparently involved more than the failure of the trustees to establish a self-supporting institution. Indeed, there seems good reason to question whether the school founded in 1820 could actually claim the status of an academy. In 1825 a group of Wheeling residents informed the legislature that the "Lancastrian School" was then "accomplishing the full purpose of its foundation by extending the elements of primary education to every child . . . who can be persuaded to avail themselves of its benevolent intentions." The second story of the academy building was adequate for "an extensive grammar or classical school" but was unused because of lack of funds for the salaries of teachers or professors. The petitioners asked the legislature to "establish and continue" in Wheeling "a large and respectable classical School" by granting to the trustees of Wheeling Lancastrian Academy the sum of $8,000 which might be invested in "some productive property" or an amount equal to the annual interest thereon. The trustees proposed to use this income for "the procurement & employment of teachers or Professors in a classical or grammar school to be by them established in which school shall be taught the living & dead languages, mathematics, &c." Should the legislators be unwilling to make such a grant to the Lancastrian Academy, the petitioners asked that they incorporate a classical school to be known as Wheeling Academy and to grant to it the amount requested. Their petitions and the fact that the trustees had from time to time rented the upper story of the academy building to teachers who conducted private schools indicate that at least during its early years the Lancastrian Academy was little more than a somewhat novel type of primary school.

Undismayed by legislative rebuffs to their bids for state aid, Wheeling residents in December, 1826, again appealed to the General Assembly. They now asked it to charter Wheeling Academy and to authorize it to offer instruction in English, Latin, and Greek and in such of the natural and moral sciences "as will quallify [*sic*] a student for entering any respectable college in the United States." For its board of trustees, they proposed twenty-one persons, at least a third of whom were currently trustees of the Lancastrian Academy. The memorialists declared that sentiment in favor of such an institution was so great that, had time permitted, they could have obtained the signature of every person in the county.

When this appeal, too, was rejected by the General Assembly, the trustees of the Lancastrian Academy seem to have lost interest in their institution. In 1837 a group of citizens charged them with dereliction of duty, and the grand jury investigating the allegations concurred. Declaring that the bequest of "the late highly respected Noah Linsly" was of concern to the people of Ohio County, the jurors deplored the "total neglect" of the institution's affairs and asked the court to direct the trustees to reorganize and to take steps to revive the academy along the lines set forth in Linsly's will. The investigation, however, produced no immediate change in the academy's management. Not until 1845, after many of the trustees who had been charged with mismanagement and appropriation of the institution's resources to their own use had died, was the governing board reorganized. Under the new directors, the Wheeling Lancastrian Academy entered into its most promising period during the ante bellum years.[14]

Of the privately operated grammar schools and academies, which in most instances were of short duration, none was more enthusiastically patronized than Buffalo Seminary at present

[14] Ohio County Legislative Petitions, December 5, 1821; *ibid.*, December 8, 1825; *ibid.*, December 23, 1826; Ambler, *History of Education in West Virginia*, pp. 84-86.

Bethany. In many respects it was unique. Established in 1818 by Alexander Campbell for the purpose of training ministers for disseminating the founder's religious views, the institution's classes were conducted in Campbell's residence. Campbell maintained exceedingly close relations with his students. He required them to attend family prayers morning and evening and kept close watch upon their conduct. Such restrictions, however, apparently were not oppressive, and Campbell always had more students than he could accommodate. With the assistance of his father and his sister Jane, Campbell offered English grammar and literature, natural philosophy, mathematics, and languages, including French and Hebrew. But the burden of his religious work was so heavy that he was unable to devote sufficient attention to the seminary, and after only four years of service it ceased to exist.[15]

Similar educational and religious zeal was displayed by Dr. John McElhenney, the founder of Lewisburg Academy. McElhenney, a Presbyterian minister who served as pastor of the Old Stone Church at Lewisburg for sixty-two years, opened a private academy soon after his arrival in the Greenbrier town in 1808. By the time it was incorporated in 1812, the school had "for several years past . . . been conducted with much success and credit" by the pastor. Located in the heart of an education-conscious Scotch-Irish settlement and blessed with McElhenney's dynamic leadership, the academy attracted students not only from Greenbrier and neighboring counties but even from distant states. Like Alexander Campbell, McElhenney often took students into his home, and it was perhaps owing in part to the close associations thus formed that many of them became educational and religious leaders of ante bellum Virginia. Some of McElhenney's most worthy successors after he relinquished the headship of the academy in 1824 were Northerners, but beginning in the 1830's the institution became increasingly subject to Southern influences.[16]

Meanwhile, on February 18, 1818, thirty-seven prominent

15 Ambler, *History of Education in West Virginia*, p. 117.
16 Greenbrier County Legislative Petitions, December 12, 1811; Ambler, *History of Education in West Virginia*, pp. 70-78; Ruth Woods Dayton, *Greenbrier Pioneers and Their Homes* (Charleston, W. Va., 1942), pp. 75-77.

residents of the Kanawha Valley, urging the need for "learning among men in preparing them for usefulness here and happiness hereafter," obtained legislative approval for a charter for Mercer Academy in Charleston. In 1819, even before the building was completed, the institution received its first students. Its first teacher was Henry Ruffner, a graduate of Lewisburg Academy and later president of Washington College. Ruffner took the position at the urging of Lewis Summers, a prominent lawyer and jurist; but he also had a personal zeal for education which was so strong that he donated all but five dollars of his tuition fees for the first session to the completion of the floors of the building and the construction of benches for the school. By 1823, Herbert P. Gaines, a local lawyer and newspaper publisher, had become principal. Gaines announced that he would offer instruction in English grammar, arithmetic, bookkeeping, Euclid's elements, surveying, navigation, logic, rhetoric, history, algebra, moral philosophy, and economy. He also advertised courses in law, with instruction "by lecture precisely in the mode adopted in the College of William and Mary." Latin and Greek would be available if the demand were sufficient. The following year chemistry, political economy, and natural, national, and municipal law were added, and two years later other "Collegiate branches."

During its early years the academy enjoyed substantial local support. The Presbyterian Church, although never in formal control of the institution, supplied most of its teachers, and the Charleston congregation almost consistently offered various kinds of aid. Determined "to render the Institution as respectable as any in the Western country," its trustees stressed its ability to prepare young men for colleges and universities. In short, the academy was, as Charles H. Ambler has pointed out, a first-rate pioneer log college. Although it apparently suffered from a diminution of interest during the early 1830's, the academy for nearly half a century fulfilled a major educational need of the Kanawha Valley.[17]

[17] Kanawha County Legislative Petitions, December 8, 1817. See also Charleston *Western Courier*, April 8, May 3, 1823; Charleston *West Virginia and Kanawha Gazette*, October 11, 1826; Charleston *Kanawha Register*, June 4, July 16, 1830; Charleston *Kanawha Banner*, September 16, 1831; Elizabeth Whitten

Two other academies, founded under the nourishing influences of religious interest, brightened the educational prospects of northwestern Virginia at the close of the 1830's. West Liberty Academy was the outgrowth of a subscription school begun in 1800 by Thomas Ewing, "an itinerant cobbler who mended shoes for a living and kept school for his board." Finding the little school a focus for a considerable interest in education, the Reverend Nathan Shotwell, a local Presbyterian minister, took the lead in obtaining a charter for West Liberty Academy. Pending the erection of a brick building in 1839, Shotwell, who served as principal, held classes for the sixty-five students in his own home. From the beginning the academy was coeducational, but boys and girls were segregated for instruction. Shotwell's enthusiastic leadership during its first seventeen years and a $5,000 loan from the Literary Fund enabled the institution to survive the vicissitudes which so frequently beset similar schools. Marshall Academy, founded at Huntington in 1837 and incorporated March 13, 1838, had strong support from Presbyterian, Methodist and Episcopalian laymen, several of whom served on its board of trustees. Occupying "a beautiful and healthy situation on the Ohio" and "in the midst of a moral and intelligent people," it embarked in the fall of 1838 upon its twin functions of preparing youth for college and providing teachers for the common schools.[18]

Although some early West Virginia academies enjoyed substantial support, most of them, in common with similar institutions in other frontier areas, operated on the brink of financial insolvency. Private seminaries were organized in the same manner as common subscription schools and were entirely dependent upon tuition or denominational support. Many of them were apparently short-lived. Academies chartered by the state, on the other hand, were semipublic in character. But the legislature never intended that the state should become their main support, and the most they could expect from the General

---

Williams, "Mercer Academy: A Brief History Thereof, 1819–1862," *West Virginia History*, XIII (October, 1951), 41-55; *Ambler, History of Education in West Virginia*, pp. 88-90; Address by Henry Ruffner on His Seventieth Birthday, Henry Ruffner Papers.

[18] Ambler, *History of Education in West Virginia*, pp. 95-98.

Assembly was permission to conduct a lottery, an occasional subvention from the Literary Fund, or, in the case of Randolph and Monongalia academies, assignment of a portion of the surveyors' fees from their respective areas. In 1836 it authorized county school commissioners to apply any surplus funds at their disposal to any academies within their bounds. But, when commissioners in Brooke, Kanawha, and Greenbrier counties diverted funds to Brooke, Mercer, and Lewisburg academies in 1839 and 1840, James Brown, the superintendent of the Literary Fund, rightly noted that in each case they had deprived poor children of the benefits of the common school and reprimanded them for undermining the primary purpose of the Literary Fund.[19] Except for general laws of a regulatory nature, such assistance as the academies received from the General Assembly nearly always took the form of special legislation enacted for individual institutions.

Middle classes of northwestern Virginia viewed the failure of the General Assembly to provide more adequate assistance to seminaries and academies as discriminatory in nature. In 1825 a group of Wheeling residents addressed the legislature, charging that "by the establishment of the University and the fund for the Primary Schools the richest and the poorest seem to have received a full share of your aid and support—But the middle classes those constituting the bone and nerve of a community seem alone to have been neglected by the splendid scheme of education adopted and acted upon by the Legislature for some years past." Many western residents were precluded from sending their sons to the University, since they first had to send them "abroad" to one of the few seminaries. Such an outlay was "disproportionate to the means of the yeomanry of the Country." Westerners also contended, with considerable justification, that a system of state-supported academies was essential to the success of the University.[20]

Religious support, upon which most West Virginia academies

---

[19] *Ibid.*, p. 70; *Second Auditor's Report on the State of the Literary Fund, for the Year 1841, and Proceedings of the School Commissioners in the Different Counties, for the Year Ending September 30, 1840* (Richmond, Va., 1841), pp. 24, 27, 29.

[20] Ohio County Legislative Petitions, December 8, 1825.

relied heavily, was marked by a considerable discrepancy between denominational strength and educational interest. Prior to 1840 the Presbyterians and Episcopalians provided much of the leadership in efforts to establish and maintain academies and seminaries, but numerically they were relatively weak denominations in West Virginia. The Methodists and Baptists, on the other hand, who accounted for about two-thirds of the state's churches in 1840, were slow to awaken to the importance of education. In 1838 the East Ohio Conference of the Methodist Episcopal Church, which had jurisdiction over part of northwestern Virginia, laid plans for the founding of Asbury Academy at Parkersburg. Maxwell Pierson Gaddis, a well-known Methodist minister, raised about $5,000 toward the project. After some delay, the academy was chartered on February 8, 1842, and opened to students the following autumn under the principalship of the Reverend Gordon Battelle.[21]

The Baptists were even more tardy than the Methodists in establishing schools of academic rank. In 1851 the Greenbrier Association of Baptists noted the need for "a school of a high grade" and appointed a committee to confer with the owner of the Gray Sulphur Springs concerning the acquisition of his property for that purpose. The following year the association declared that "without education we may yearly witness a lage [sic] accession to our churches, with no corresponding increase of moral power and influence." Too long, it opined, "as a denomination we have been too much accustomed to rely upon the naked power of *truth,* plainly revealed, for the diffusion and perpetuation of our distinctive doctrines and practices."[22] This recognition of the moral force of education by the Baptists heralded not only the dawn of a new day in education but also of the passing of an era in religious history.

Lacking a broad basis of either public or religious support, most West Virginia academies, particularly those in the mountainous regions, struggled along with small enrollments. In 1840 twenty-eight academies in West Virginia enrolled only

---

[21] Maxwell Pierson Gaddis, Sr., *Foot-Prints of an Itinerant* (Cincinnati, Ohio, 1855) pp. 288-89; Ambler, *History of Education in West Virginia*, p. 103.
[22] Records of the Greenbrier Association of Baptists [1825–1868], pp. 339, 366-67.

1,098 students, or an average of less than forty each. This number represented about one-fortieth of the total pupils then attending the primary and secondary schools. Inasmuch as primary schools at that time enrolled perhaps not more than 50 percent of the children of school age, these figures indicate that no more than one child in eighty was matriculated at an academy.[23] With many of these academies no better than ordinary grammar schools, secondary education in the Allegheny sections, particularly, could hardly be described as flourishing.

If education of academic grade was limited in West Virginia prior to 1840, opportunities for college training came close to being nonexistent. Hopes that Randolph Academy might develop into the William and Mary of northwestern Virginia were dashed on the hard rocks of financial instability, poor transportation, and inadequate physical facilities. Moreover, most of the educational leaders of the mountain areas directed their efforts toward the uplifting of the masses rather than the preparation of an intellectual and social elite for positions of leadership. They consistently opposed the diversion of the meager resources of the Literary Fund to any purpose other than the support of the common schools or occasional aid to financially pressed academies. Especially did they regard the University of Virginia as a bastion of aristocracy and privilege, and they waged incessant battle to prevent the appropriation of the revenue of the Literary Fund to its use.

Western attitudes toward higher education were, however, perhaps as much the expression of an emerging sectionalism as of doctrinaire thinking. In 1817 western members of the House of Delegates gave enthusiastic support to Charles F. Mercer's proposal for a broad plan of state-subsidized education, which would not only have established a system of common schools and academies but would also have created three additional state-supported colleges and a state university. Significantly, the eight-member board of public instruction which would have administered the system would have included two members each from the trans-Allegheny and Valley sections, and two of the

[23] U. S., Bureau of the Census, *Compendium . . . from the Returns of the Sixth Census,* p. 39.

three new colleges would have been in the Allegheny region. With such lure, western delegates acquiesced in the establishment of a university, but even then they endeavored to secure its location somewhere in the Valley of Virginia. The enactment of such a comprehensive scheme of education might have gone far toward allaying some of the sectional bitterness that divided eastern and western Virginia during the ensuing decades.[24] The subordination of higher education to literacy for the masses—laudable as the latter may have been—and the subversion of the common good by a shortsighted provincialism cost western Virginia heavily in enlightened political leadership during the nineteenth century.

Collegiate education in the Allegheny areas was of slow growth. By 1820 western Pennsylvania had established four colleges—Jefferson at Canonsburg, Washington, Allegheny at Meadville, and the Western University of Pennsylvania at Pittsburgh. Prior to the end of 1840 West Virginia endeavored to launch three collegiate institutions, but only two took firm root in the intellectually arid soil prevalent in much of the Alleghenies. Wheeling, whose location at the western terminus of the National Road had made it Virginia's second most populous city and a bustling commercial center of the upper Ohio Valley, was, not surprisingly, the site of the initial effort. Wheeling University, incorporated by the General Assembly on March 23, 1831, sprang from the fertile but unscrupulous mind of Dr. John Cook Bennett, who until six months earlier had practiced medicine in Ohio. A medical college was to form the nucleus of the institution, but plans also envisioned instruction in the arts and sciences.

Although physicians and leading citizens gave the university their approbation and the city and Noah Zane provided it with ten acres of land, the Wheeling community did not tender the institution adequate financial support. In December, 1831, petitioners again approached the legislature, asking that it divert to the university $15,000 in stock in the Northwestern Bank of Virginia at Wheeling, which was owned by the state. Declaring that Wheeling residents were by no means lacking in "zeal and

24 Ambler, *History of Education in West Virginia*, pp. 109-11.

patriotism," they nevertheless noted—and their observation was a significant commentary on the area's scale of values—that "any spare capital among them . . . [was] engaged in commerce, and in manufactures, and other, profitable investment." Then, passing over this materialistic orientation of popular interests, they unabashedly asked the legislature to do for Wheeling what its residents were either unwilling or unable to do for themselves. They based their appeal upon the need for state solidarity, declaring that the youth who attended colleges in nearby Ohio and Pennsylvania "discard the habits, manners, and mode of thinking characteristic of virginians, and return home with attachments weak'ned, and reverence diminished for the institutions of the commonwealth." The only means of preserving "the lofty feeling and chivalrick bearing of virginia," they argued, was to educate her youth within her borders.[25]

The General Assembly was not beguiled by the noble professions of the petitioners. It turned down their request and thereby dealt a deathblow to Wheeling University. Soon thereafter the school suspended operation, if, indeed, it ever conducted any classes. Discouraged, Bennett moved to New Albany, Indiana. There he set up Christian College, a disreputable diploma mill retailing bachelor's, master's, and doctoral degrees and medical diplomas, which was quickly disavowed by the Disciples of Christ Church with which Bennett sought to identify it.[26] In the light of Bennett's subsequent activities, the untimely demise of Wheeling University probably represented no real educational loss to West Virginia.

Like most other Allegheny colleges, the only two successful colleges founded in West Virginia prior to the end of 1840 enjoyed religious backing. Ironically, it was the Baptists who established the first such institution, Rector College, which was located at Pruntytown. But once they had become convinced of the advantages of higher education, the Baptists pursued their goal with the zeal and devotion characteristic of the denomination. Rector College owed its beginning to the Reverend

[25] Ohio County Legislative Petitions, January 27, 1831; *ibid.*, December 20, 1831; Buck and Buck, *Planting of Civilization in Western Pennsylvania*, pp. 397-98.
[26] Ambler, *History of Education in West Virginia*, p. 113.

Joshua Bradley, a Brown University graduate who founded nine churches and eight educational societies during his lifetime. Following his arrival at Pruntytown, Bradley organized the Western Virginia Education Society, which was incorporated on March 28, 1838. This organization began to solicit subscriptions for the college, and Bradley himself obtained a gift of $4,500 from Enoch Rector, a well-to-do Marietta merchant who had given up his business for the Baptist ministry. Rector's generous beneficence, together with other subscriptions and the promise of aid from the local Baptist association, enabled the college to open its doors in November, 1839, with Bradley as president and with six other faculty members and seventy students.

Rector College experienced its golden days during the 1840's under the presidency of the Reverend Charles Wheeler, another graduate of Brown University and a scholarly and inspiring teacher and administrator. In 1842, when its charter was issued, it enrolled 110 students in its academic and collegiate departments and its female seminary. Its collegiate offerings included algebra, higher mathematics, philosophy, geology, astronomy, and languages. Library facilities included not only 2,000 volumes belonging to the institution but also another 1,000 volumes in President's Wheeler's personal collection.

Toward the end of the decade Rector College began to decline. Part of the difficulty undoubtedly stemmed from an increasingly strict discipline and a rigid segregation of the sexes. A prolonged illness of Wheeler, followed by his death in January, 1851, accelerated the downward tendencies. When a fire destroyed its building in 1855, the college suffered a blow from which it never recovered.[27]

Of the colleges founded in West Virginia prior to the Civil War none enjoyed greater success than Bethany. Established at Bethany in 1840, it was located in a populous section embracing western Pennsylvania, the Northern Panhandle of West Virginia, and eastern Ohio. Even more important, its founder, Alexander Campbell, known the country over as a religious

[27] *Ibid.*, pp. 113-16; Minutes of the Western Virginia Education Society, April 13, 1840, Peter T. Laishley Papers; Minutes of the Board of Trustees of Rector College, January 11, 1844, *ibid.*

leader, debater, and publisher of the widely circulated *Millenial Harbinger,* gave the college distinction and clothed it with an interest that far transcended West Virginia. In short, the growing popularity of the Disciples of Christ and Campbell's national prominence as a religious leader guaranteed that the college would be free of dependence upon strictly local support. Moreover, Campbell's acceptance of Negro slavery gave the institution wide support in the South. Of the 2,200 students which it enrolled prior to the Civil War, 597 were Virginians, 571 Kentuckians, 210 Missourians, and 96 Tennesseans. Northern matriculates were chiefly from Ohio and Pennsylvania which provided 165 and 129, respectively.

Nor must Campbell's great personal interest in the college be underestimated as a factor in its success. The founder himself advanced $10,000 of the $16,000 needed for its first building and also provided the building site. As the college's first president, Campbell organized strong departments, each headed by a competent professor, in the manner adopted by the University of Virginia. Departments in which instruction was offered were moral philosophy, with sacred history, political economy, and evidences of Christianity; languages, including Latin and Greek, and later Hebrew; physical sciences, with chemistry, physics, zoology, and botany; natural philosophy, including astronomy, geology, mechanics, hydraulics, and pneumatics; and mathematics. Campbell staffed his departments with care, and long tenure was the rule among Bethany faculty.

As was the custom of the time, Bethany imposed a rigid discipline upon its students. Since it was founded primarily for the purpose of training ministers for the Disciples of Christ, its administration expected students to attend chapel services as a matter of duty and required them to be present for Campbell's lectures on sacred history, delivered at six o'clock each morning except Sunday. But Campbell tempered his exactions with understanding and wisdom, and both student-faculty and college-community relations in the rustic environment at Bethany seem to have been unusually happy. Campbell's ability to gauge correctly the needs of the college and its students set Bethany upon a firm course and gave it the impetus which enabled it to prosper and to become one of the state's most successful institution's of higher learning.[28]

Often working in close conjunction with academies and colleges were library or literary organizations. A number of them, including those at Harper's Ferry, Charleston, Romney, Wheeling, Wellsburg, and Lewisburg, actually served as sponsors of academies founded in their respective towns prior to 1840. Such organized interest can hardly be overestimated in considering the success of the academies. But certainly of equal importance, the library and literary societies performed an important role in elevating the intellectual tone among the citizenry who would never attend these academies.

Among the early library companies formed in West Virginia were those in the Morgantown area. The Buffalo Creek Farmers Library Company had by 1812 purchased "many books." Beginning the following year it met annually in Morgantown on the first court day in October. A similar organization, the Morgantown Circulating Library, was chartered in 1814. At that time it had accumulated "a number of well chosen books." The interest generated by the two societies was undoubtedly an important factor in the incorporation of Monongalia Academy in 1814.[29]

Equal interest was manifested by the Lewisburg Circulating Library Company. In 1822 the organization had twenty-nine members and had purchased 102 volumes, "principally excellent religious, moral, political, and historical works." The next year its members asked to be incorporated as a means of preserving their volumes and acquiring others "for the noble purpose of improving the morals and enlightening the minds of themselves, their posterity, and their fellow citizens."[30]

One of the most active literary groups in the Allegheny area was the Literary Society of Romney, first organized on January 30, 1819, as the Polemia Society of Romney. In 1822 it had more than thirty members, and on January 3, 1823, it was incorporated

[28] Ambler, *History of Education in West Virginia*, pp. 116-20.
[29] Monongalia County Legislative Petitions, December 11, 1812; *ibid.*, October 14, 1814; Ambler, *History of Education in West Virginia*, p. 80.
[30] Greenbrier County Legislative Petitions, December 4, 1823.

by direction of the legislature. During its early years it raised money by monthly levies upon its members and by this means acquired "a considerable body of ancient and modern history and other useful works in literature," for which by 1827 it had spent more than $1,000. For several years the organization endeavored in vain to obtain legislative approval for a lottery for the raising of additional funds, and in 1832 it was authorized to raise $20,000 over a period of ten years.

The recurrent appeals to the General Assembly throw considerable light upon the activities of the organization. In 1828 it sought permission to raise $25,000 for a building for a library and lecture room and for the purchase of books, maps, and scientific apparatus, with expenditures to be divided about equally between building and equipment. It also proposed to use the interest for "an annual course of popular lectures, on natural philosophy and particularly, in its application to the improvement of agriculture, manufactures, and the mechanical arts generally; and also an annual course on ethics and political philosophy." The lectures that it sponsored were open to the public.

The impact of the Literary Society upon the Romney area can hardly be overestimated. Besides its library, which in 1860 numbered more than 3,000 volumes, and its course of lectures, the organization took an active interest in the academy founded at Romney in 1818. Not only did it hold title to the academy property, but until 1846, when the institution became the Romney Classical Institute, the literary society was charged with the supervision of its activities.[31]

Of less general influence, perhaps, than the library companies were the private book collections of early West Virginia residents. While most pioneers possessed few if any books, many well-to-do farmers and town dwellers accumulated libraries which revealed both breadth of interest and discriminating taste. In 1777 John Hite of Berkeley County owned ninety-three volumes. Forty-three of them were works of distinguished English authors,

---

[31] Ambler, *History of Education in West Virginia,* pp. 86-87; Hampshire County Legislative Petitions, December 21, 1820; *ibid.,* December 17, 1822; *ibid.,* December 7, 1826; *ibid.,* December 7, 1827; *ibid.,* December 8, 1828.

including Pope, Swift, Milton, Congreve, Gay, Addison, and Steele. Besides these literary works, the collection included numerous works on history, with representative volumes on ancient, regional, and modern history. Copies of Blackstone's *Commentaries*, other volumes on law, books on arithmetic and geography, and a dictionary also indicated a concern for practical matters. Significantly, less than half a dozen books dealt with religion and philosophy.

Thomas Hite of the same county owned eighty-five volumes, whose titles revealed an interest in current literature, works of the ancients, including Horace, Virgil, and Josephus, treatises on religion and morality, and practical subjects such as geography, mathematics, and science. Less extensive, and perhaps more typical of pioneer libraries, was the collection of George Calmes of Monongalia County. The dozen or so volumes owned by Calmes included works on the history of the British Empire and of Germany, letters of George Washington, writings on religion, and copies of *Carey's General Atlas* and of *The Ohio and Mississippi Navigator*. The library of John Jeremiah Jacob, a pioneer Methodist preacher, numbered ninety-five volumes in 1808. Religious works made up the nucleus of his collection, but he owned numerous volumes on law and legal practice and a generous sampling of standard authors such as Caesar, Shakespeare, Milton, and Pope.[32]

Although most pioneer West Virginians owned few books, some indication of the reading habits of the literate citizenry may be gleaned from the titles offered for sale by the town and country stores. The inventory of William Tingle, a Morgantown merchant, consisted in 1831 of seventeen titles, among which were Blackstone's *Commentaries*, Washington's *Reports*, Powell's *Contracts*, *Law of Partnership*, Hawkins' *Pleas*, twenty Testaments, two "school Bibles," Dilworth's *Spellers*, and Greek, Latin, and French grammars. The records of a Charleston store show that twelve customers purchased books during 1823 and

[32] Appraisement of the Estate of John Hite, March 21, 1777, Rigsby Papers; Appraisement of the Estate of Thomas Hite, September 6, 1779; *ibid.;* Inventory of the Estate of George Calmes, ca. 1831, John Rogers Papers. The diary of Jacob is reproduced in Marjorie Moran Holmes, "The Life and Diary of Reverend John Jeremiah Jacob" (M.A. thesis, Duke University, 1941).

1824. Four purchasers bought school textbooks, four acquired almanacs, and two obtained Greek and Latin grammars. One customer purchased eleven titles, including Story's *Pleading,* an encyclopedia, Hamilton's *Reports,* Sullivan's *Lectures,* a volume relating to Burr's trial, the *Book of Common Prayer,* and a set of *Select Speeches* which weighed twenty pounds.[33]

In the isolated mountainous regions along the upper Kanawha and embracing portions of Fayette, Nicholas, and Kanawha counties, the demand was for still another kind of reading matter. During the years from 1829 to 1831 a merchant at the falls of the Kanawha sold eighteen almanacs, thirteen arithmetics, ten spellers, two Testaments, two geographies and atlases, one large Bible, two *English Readers,* one Law's *Crucifixion,* and one United States history. This assortment, with its emphasis upon almanacs, Bibles, and school textbooks, is probably a reliable indicator of the kinds of books found in most of the poorer homes of the Allegheny region.[34]

Any consideration of the intellectual climate of Allegheny sections of early West Virginia must take into account the pioneer newspaper. The press made its entry into West Virginia in 1790 when Nathaniel Willis emigrated from Boston and established the *Potowmac Guardian and Berkeley Advertiser* at Shepherdstown, only four years after John Scull established the first trans-Allegheny newspaper, the Pittsburgh *Gazette.* By 1830 at least forty-five newspapers had been founded in West Virginia. The towns in which they were published, together with the dates of the establishment of the first newspaper in each, were: Shepherdstown, 1790; Martinsburg, 1791 or 1792; Charles Town, 1803; Morgantown, 1804; Wheeling, 1807; Clarksburg, 1810; Wellsburg, 1814; Charleston, 1820; Harper's Ferry, 1821; Weston, 1820 or 1821; Lewisburg, 1823; Bethany, 1824; and Romney, 1829.[35]

---

[33] Inventory of the Personal Estate of William Tingle, April 12, 1811; Estates, 1799 [1795]–1829, pp. 27-28, Monongalia County Court Records; [Cabell and Trimble?] Account Book, 1823–1824, West Virginia Department of Archives and History Library.

[34] Unidentified Kanawha Falls Account Book, 1829–1831.

[35] Douglas C. McMurtrie, *The Beginnings of Printing in West Virginia, with Notes on the Pioneer Newspaper and Early Book and Pamphlet Imprints* (Charleston, W. Va., 1935), p. 6; Otis K. Rice, "West Virginia Printers and Their Work,

West Virginia newspapers not only acquainted their readers with foreign and domestic news, but their editors often took bold positions on political, social, and economic issues. Nathaniel Willis, who published the *Potomak Guardian,* as it was later called, first at Shepherdstown and then from about 1791 or 1792 until 1799 at Martinsburg, set high standards for editorial courage. A veteran of the Boston Tea Party, Willis was imbued with the principles of the Declaration of Independence and the political ideals of Thomas Jefferson. The publication of the *Potomak Guardian* in strongly Federalist territory involved Willis in numerous political fights and even in personal altercations. In 1799 Willis' archrival, young John Alburtis, established the Martinsburg *Berkeley Intelligencer,* a Federalist organ which for the next decade dominated the journalistic scene in the Eastern Panhandle. Some editors, such as Alexander Armstrong, who founded the Wheeling *Repository* in 1807, proclaimed a desire to avoid alignment on political issues, but in an era when politics was one of the most captivating and exciting topics, they found political neutrality virtually impossible.[36]

Newspapermen were attracted to a variety of social and economic crusades. Most of them supported education. John S. Gallaher, the founder of the Harper's Ferry *Free Press,* later known as the *Virginia Free Press,* lost his seat in the Virginia state senate in 1848 partly because of his aggressiveness in the fight for free public education. The Wheeling *Eclectic Observer, and Working People's Advocate,* founded in 1829 by William Cooper Howells, "a migratory, ill-paid, anti-slavery journalist" and father of William Dean Howells, devoted its columns to both general articles and labor matters and pledged support to "general education" and "equal privileges." The Charles Town *Farmer's Repository,* established in 1808 by Richard Williams and William Brown, was dedicated to the promotion of agriculture and other useful arts and was said to have been the first agricultural periodical west of the Blue Ridge. The *Kanawha Banner,*

1790–1830," *West Virginia History,* XIV (July, 1953), 299-300, 307-308, 310-12, 314, 318-21, 326, 331, 333.

36 Rice, "West Virginia Printers and Their Work," pp. 299-303, 319-20. Martinsburg *Potomak Guardian,* February 9, 1797, February 13, 20, March 27, May 8, and August 7, 1799; Wheeling *Repository,* March 5, 1807.

a Charleston newspaper, announced in its first issue in 1830 that it would sustain principles, not men, and that it would advocate the ideals of government common "in the best days of the Republic" under Jefferson and Madison, promote education, and encourage domestic manufactures.[37]

Most early newspapers faced a precarious existence. Of the forty-five newspapers established in West Virginia prior to the end of 1830, only about a dozen were then being published. The mortality rate was highest in semifrontier mountainous areas. Part of the difficulty was financial. Despite their willingness to accept such articles as wheat, oats, rye, corn, flax, tallow, beeswax, and clean linen or cotton rags in payment for subscriptions, most publishers had difficulty in collecting from subscribers. Nathaniel Willis, who in 1794 had over 700 delinquent customers, was typical of his colleagues in that he had "considerable out of door business." Dependence upon producers at Chambersburg, Philadelphia, Redstone, Baltimore, and Lexington, Kentucky, for paper often meant shortages and suspensions of publication, either temporary or permanent. Finally, the high incidence of illiteracy, especially in mountainous areas, was hardly conducive to a wide newspaper-reading public.[38]

Most pioneer printers did not confine their publication to newspapers. Nearly all of them produced other works, particularly broadsides, sermons, religious tracts, minutes of religious organizations, legal forms and an assortment of job printing. John S. Gallaher supplemented his newspaper venture with the *Ladies' Garland,* a periodical devoted to materials of a literary and miscellaneous nature of special interest to women.[39]

The prominence of religious works among early West Virginia

[37] Vernon Aler, *History of Martinsburg and Berkeley County, West Virginia* (Hagerstown, Md., n. d.), pp. 116-18; Willis F. Evans, *History of Berkeley County, West Virginia* (n. p., 1928), pp. 234-35; Wheeling *Eclectic Observer,* and *Working People's Advocate,* July 1, 1830; Allen Johnson and Dumas Malone, eds., *Dictionary of American Biography,* 20 vols. and 2 supps. (New York, 1928-1958), IX, 306; Charles Town *Farmer's Repository,* April 1, 1808; McMurtrie, *Beginnings of Printing in West Virginia,* p. 12; Charleston *Kanawha Banner,* September 10, 1830.

[38] Rice, "West Virginia Printers and Their Work," p. 338; Charlestown *Gazette,* February 17, 1815; Morgantown *Monongalia Herald,* December 23, 1820; Clarksburg *Enquirer,* January 24, 1828; Martinsburg *Potomak Guardian,* February 9, 1797; Wheeling *Repository,* August 6, 1807.

[39] Rice, "West Virginia Printers and Their Work," passim.

publications is indicative not only of the importance of religion in the lives of the pioneers but also of their reading tastes. It is not without significance that the first book published in West Virginia, *Christian Panoply*, written by R. Watson, Lord Bishop of Landaff and Regius Professor of Divinity at Cambridge University, and printed at Shepherdstown in 1797, was a vigorous attack upon Deism. Moreover, the first magazine to appear in the state, *Lay-Man's Magazine*, published by John Alburtis at Martinsburg, stressed articles of a religious and moral nature, including sermons and accounts of religious experiences.

Without question, Bethany was one of the most important centers for religious publications in the entire trans-Allegheny region. There Alexander Campbell established a press devoted exclusively to religious works. Perhaps the most notable products of Campbell's press were two periodicals, the *Christian Baptist*, established in 1823, and its successor, the *Millenial Harbinger*, founded in 1830. The latter, a monthly publication, was dedicated to "the destruction of sectarianism, infidelity, and anti-Christian doctrine and practice." Campbell's works enjoyed a wide circulation throughout the central United States. His volume of mail was so great that the government established a post office at his house and named Campbell postmaster.[40]

Wheeling, a neighboring town of Bethany, was an important center for the publication of school textbooks. During the 1820's the firm of William Davis and James F. McCarty produced several editions of Murray's *English Reader*, a widely used textbook in West Virginia schools. Albert and Edwin Picket published a variety of readers, spellers, and grammars, of which their father, a prominent educator, was the principal author. The Pickets, teachers and booksellers, later moved their operation to Cincinnati. Other publishers brought out editions of popular texts, including Noah Webster's famous *Elementary Spelling Book*.[41]

[40] *Ibid.*, pp. 304-306, 326-28; Shepherdstown *Impartial Observer: or, Shepherd's-Town, Charles Town & County Advertiser*, October 11, 1797; *Christian Baptist*, I (August, 1823), 5; *Millenial Harbinger*, I (January, 1830), 1.

[41] Rice, "West Virginia Printers and Their Work," pp. 328-30; Delf Norona and Charles Shetler, comps., *West Virginia Imprints, 1790–1863: A Checklist of Books, Newspapers, Periodicals, and Broadsides* (Moundsville, W. Va., 1958), pp. 105-106, 115-18, 164.

Interest in the pioneer period and a sense of pride in the conquest of a wilderness stimulated the writing and publication of two widely read works which were to prove of seminal importance to later studies of the Allegheny frontier. In 1824 Joseph Doddridge's celebrated *Notes, on the Settlement and Indian Wars, of the Western parts of Virginia & Pennsylvania* was published at Wellsburg. A social history of enduring significance, Doddridge's work was perhaps less exciting but certainly more accurate than Alexander Scott Withers' *Chronicles of Border Warfare*, published at Clarksburg in 1831.[42]

In spite of the substantial volume of publication, the establishment of library companies and literary societies, and the founding of academies and colleges, West Virginia in 1840 suffered an educational backwardness which was to plague most of the Allegheny region for generations to come. Nothing short of gargantuan efforts would have lifted her from the educational morass into which she had by then sunk. Such gains as were made, laudable though they were, did little more than shed "a glimmering of the light" upon an educationally darkened area.

[42] Rice, "West Virginia Printers and Their Work," pp. 316-17, 323; J. Merton England, "Some Early Historians of Western Virginia," *West Virginia History*, XIV (January, 1953), 91-96, 100-104.

Chapter Twelve

The Power of Spiritual Truths

Lord Bryce's characterization of the American South as "a land of high religious voltage" has, historically, perhaps even greater relevance to the American frontier. Certainly the description is applicable to the Allegheny frontier. The heterogeneity of its pre-Revolutionary War population, among whom the English, Germans, and Scotch-Irish were but the dominant elements, gave the region, from its beginnings, a variegated religious complexion. As in other parts of the Alleghenies, settlers who streamed into the Potomac section of West Virginia after 1730 were of Presbyterian, Lutheran, German Reformed, Dunkard, and Quaker backgrounds and dissenters from the Anglican Church, the established religious institution in Virginia.[1] Of even greater importance than this initial diversity in the religious development of the Allegheny area was the Great Awakening, whose powerful influences coincided with the advance of settlement into the mountains. This phenomenon shook the settlers loose from their old denominational moorings and gave rise to new and militant sects, which emphasized a close personal relationship with God and reliance upon the emotions as guides to spiritual truths. The new religious thought generated by the Great Awakening made rapid headway among Allegheny pioneers and resulted in a fundamentalism that has endured to the present day.

Of major significance in the religious history of the mountainous sections of West Virginia was Virginia's acceptance of religious dissent in the backcountry. Religious toleration seemed a small price to pay for the settlement of the Valley and the upper Potomac areas and the creation of a buffer population between valuable Piedmont plantations and the French and Indians. In 1738 Governor William Gooch assured the Synod of Philadelphia that Presbyterian ministers who served congregations west of the Blue Ridge would suffer no interference as long as their ministers took the oaths required of dissenters, registered their meetingplaces with the proper officials, and otherwise conformed to the provisions of the English Toleration Act of 1689. This liberality, extended to other dissenting groups, was based upon the recognition that the social and economic institutions of the backcountry were substantially different from those of the Tidewater and Piedmont and were not, like the latter, intimately bound up with the Anglican Church.[2]

In contrast with the strength of dissenting elements in the Potomac section of West Virginia, the Anglican Church was numerically weak. Only in the lower Shenandoah Valley, where the social and economic fabric was similar to that of eastern Virginia, did Anglicanism take firm root. The first Anglican congregation founded in West Virginia was Christ Church, or Morgan's Chapel, an unorganized mission established in 1740 by Morgan Morgan at Bunker Hill in the newly created Frederick parish. By 1775 Anglicans had founded five churches in Berkeley and Jefferson counties, including Mt. Zion at Hedgesville, Trinity at Shepherdstown, Trinity at Martinsburg, St. George's Chapel near Charles Town, and Calvary at Jones Spring on Back Creek. In rather typical frontier manner, these churches began as private chapels or as unorganized missions, housed in log buildings and served by lay readers. In 1772 there was also a sufficient number of Anglicans in Hampshire County to warrant consideration of sending an ordained minister from England. Although the Anglicans remained small in numbers in early West Virginia, they rapidly gained in affluence. In 1775 Philip Fithian described their church at Shepherdstown as "the most elegent Building, for a Place of Worship, that I have seen yet in this Colony."[3]

---

[1] Miles Sturdivant Malone, "The Distribution of Population on the Virginia Frontier in 1775" (Ph.D. dissertation, Princeton University, 1935), pp. 74-85; Freeman H. Hart, *The Valley of Virginia in the American Revolution, 1763–1789* (Chapel Hill, N. C., 1942), pp. 34-38; Charles H. Ambler and Festus P. Summers, *West Virginia: The Mountain State,* 2d ed. (Englewood Cliffs, N. J., 1958), pp. 107-108.

[2] Wesley M. Gewehr, *The Great Awakening in Virginia, 1740–1790* (Durham, N. C., 1930), pp. 40-42.

[3] U. S., Works Projects Administration, Historical Records Survey, *Inventory of the Church Archives of West Virginia: The Protestant Episcopal Church* (Wheeling, W. Va., 1939), pp. 25-28, 44; William Meade, *Old Churches, Ministers and*

In spite of their preponderance in numbers, dissenting denominations organized but few churches in West Virginia during the colonial period. Most active were the Presbyterians. Indeed, there is a possibility, but no conclusive evidence, that Potomoke Church, founded by the Presbyterians in 1719, may have been at Shepherdstown. By 1740 Presbyterians had established Hopewell, or Bullskin, Church near Summit Point in Jefferson County; Back Creek, or Tomahawk, Church near Hedgesville; and Tuscarora Church two miles west of Martinsburg. Five years later they organized a church at Falling Waters on the Potomac. The Donegal Presbytery, which controlled these churches, did not provide any of them with regular pastors until 1760. In that year it assigned the Reverend Hugh Vance, a graduate of Princeton, to the Tuscarora Church. Otherwise, the congregations had to rely upon occasional supplies sent out by the presbytery. The difficulty in filling its pulpit led the Hopewell Church to engage William Williams, who, although he may never have been ordained, took the oath required of dissenting ministers and was recognized by the courts of Virginia.[4]

Most German immigrants belonged to either the Lutheran or the German Reformed churches, but they organized few congregations in West Virginia. By 1748 a German Reformed dominie had visited Shepherdstown and presented a silver communion cup to the German congregation. In 1765 nine German residents organized the first Lutheran church in the region, but it had no resident minister until 1790. Until then, meetings consisting of hymn singing and preaching by laymen were held in local residences. Other German immigrants joined the Church of the Brethren, whose first congregation in West Virginia was

---

Families of Virginia, 2 vols. (Philadelphia, n. d.), pp. 281-84, 295-97, 302; Hu Maxwell and H. L. Swisher, *History of Hampshire County, West Virginia* (Morgantown, W. Va., 1897), p. 373; Philip Vickers Fithian, *Journal, 1775–1776, Written on the Virginia-Pennsylvania Frontier and in the Army around New York*, ed. Robert Greenhalgh Albion and Leonidas Dodson (Princeton, N. J., 1934), p. 182.

[4] Ambler and Summers, *West Virginia*, p. 107*n*; U. S., W. P. A., Historical Records Survey, *Inventory of the Church Archives of West Virginia: The Presbyterian Churches* (Charleston, W. Va., 1941), pp. 203-10, 214; Malone, "The Distribution of Population on the Virginia Frontier in 1775," pp. 79-82; Millard Kessler Bushong, *A History of Jefferson County, West Virginia* (Charles Town, W. Va., 1941), pp. 19-20.

established at Petersburg by Valentine and Martin Powers.[5]

Even the Quakers, substantial numbers of whom had settled in the southern parts of Berkeley and Jefferson counties, were ill-supplied with churches. They erected a church building at Hopewell on Opequon Creek in 1734 and established meetings at Back Creek in 1759, Middle Creek in 1771, and Bullskin in 1775. In the years following the American Revolution Quaker influence suffered a decline, which may have been relative rather than absolute. Quaker losses have usually been attributed to migration, but it seems more likely that the patriotic and emotional fervor which drew strength to the Methodists and Baptists may have depleted the ranks of the Quakers just as it did other long-established denominations.[6]

The frontier proved highly erosive to organized religion in the Potomac section of West Virginia prior to the Revolution, and nowhere were its effects more devastating than in the South Branch and Patterson's Creek areas. There the numerous German, Scotch-Irish, English, and Dutch settlers remained virtually without churches for more than thirty years. For people who were at heart deeply religious, this condition was a source of profound sorrow. In 1747 Germans along the South Branch complained that there was not a single German minister among them and that, in their "forsaken condition . . . they had not been to the Lord's Supper for four years for want of a minister." They were distressed that their children had not been baptized and were growing up outside the church. In their deep concern for spiritual matters, some of them occasionally gathered to hear sermons read by an old Swiss settler, Anton Richert, who himself baptized the children in his own family.[7]

At the very time that the pious and religiously sensitive settlers of the Potomac frontier were suffering from neglect by their own denominations, religious stirrings were beginning in New

[5] A. D. Kenamond, "Early Shepherdstown and Its Churches," *Magazine of the Jefferson County Historical Society*, XI (December, 1945), 39; Bushong, *History of Jefferson County*, pp. 20-21.

[6] Ambler and Summers, *West Virginia*, p. 107; Malone, "The Distribution of Population on the Virginia Frontier in 1775," pp. 75, 83-85.

[7] William J. Hinke and Charles Kemper, eds., "Moravian Diaries of Travels through Virginia," *Virginia Magazine of History and Biography*, XII (July, 1904), 55-58; *ibid.*, XI (October, 1903), 120-21.

England which ultimately brought them again into the arms of a church. The first signs of this Great Awakening appeared in the Dutch Reformed Church, particularly in the Raritan Valley of New Jersey. There during the 1720's Theodorus Frelinghuysen, a German immigrant who had developed strong pietistic feelings before leaving his homeland, conducted a revival which struck at the formalism of the church. Partly through Frelinghuysen's influence, Gilbert and William Tennent carried the revival into the Presbyterian church in New Jersey and converted large numbers of their listeners. In 1734 Jonathan Edwards employed their evangelistic methods in his church at Northampton, Massachusetts, and within six months converted more than three hundred people, or virtually the entire adult population of the town. Within the next few years revivalism engulfed the entire Connecticut Valley. In 1740 the movement reached its zenith in the North. By that time it had made important advances in the middle colonies and in Georgia. With the coming of George Whitefield the various threads were tied together and the strength of the movement was augmented.

The Great Awakening unleashed religious emotion that had been held back for generations. Its ministers broke away from customary formalism and called upon each listener to consider the state of his own soul. They confronted him with the crushing burden of his sins and pleaded with him to confess his guilt and seek forgiveness. Only by personal conversion, they warned, could the individual hope to see the glories of heaven; without such a religious experience, he was certain to witness the horrors of hell. Such direct appeals produced electrifying effects upon most congregations. Scores of stricken persons went to the mourners' benches in the hope of obtaining deliverance. Once conversion seemed assured, lamentations and cries of sorrow gave way to tears of joy and a gladness of heart that were highly infectious in a congregation.

That the Great Awakening would have a disruptive effect upon existing denominations was inevitable. It produced a schism in the Presbyterian Church, which in 1741 divided members into Old Side and New Side factions. The former stood solidly behind traditional practices and insisted upon an educated ministry. The New Side wing, on the other hand, was evangelistic and favored itineracy among its ministers. Moreover, in the face of a dearth of colleges where ministers might obtain a degree, they urged the use of log colleges, such as that established by William Tennent on Neshaminy Creek near Philadelphia, for the training of needed ministers. Not until 1758 was the rift ended. Similar disagreements troubled the Baptist Church, which split into Regular and Separate branches. Even the Anglican Church felt the effects through the activities of the Methodists, who constituted its own revivalistic wing. Yet, if the Great Awakening appeared disruptive, it also proved invigorating by infusing new religious zeal into stagnant churches. The emphasis upon emotionalism, evangelism, and personal conversion provided the impetus by which organized religion advanced into frontier areas, including the Allegheny Highlands.

Settlements along the South Branch and Patterson's Creek were probably the first in Allegheny West Virginia to feel the effects of the Great Awakening. In 1747 the plight of these upper Potomac settlers attracted the attention of the Moravians, who had themselves been affected by the upheavals in German churches in Pennsylvania. In that year their missionaries began regular itineraries during which they traversed large areas of the Maryland, Virginia, and North Carolina backcountry. In the summer months Leonard Schnell and Vitus Handrup visited the South Branch and Patterson's Creek settlements. The Moravians were coldly received at first. But eschewing any effort to press narrow sectarian views upon their listeners, the missionaries stressed the bounties of God's love and a doctrine of free grace that "tasted well" to the people. Before long, German, Scotch-Irish, English, and Dutch settlers had responded so favorably to their services that Matthias Gottlieb Gottschalk, who visited them in the spring of 1748, wrote: "In all Virginia I did not find another place like the South Branch, where I felt that the Gospel had such free course among the people."

The Moravians by no means met the religious needs of the upper Potomac frontier. Their journeys through the settlements were too brief to fulfill the demands made upon them. Gottschalk declared that any missionary sent to Patterson's Creek should remain at least a month. On the South Branch he "should erect his pulpit at least in four or five places, and take not less than two months for it, because it would be well to preach at these places several times in succession." Moreover, in order to serve all the people, the missionary should be able to speak fluently in both English and German.

Factors other than time limited Moravian success. The missionaries frequently refused to perform marriage ceremonies for couples whom they did not know or to baptize children about whose upbringing they had some question. Solomon Hedges, a justice of Hampshire County, suspecting that their reluctance arose from legal restrictions imposed upon itinerant ministers by Virginia, assured them that in that county "we do not pay any attention to the proclamation issued against you." The Moravians, who had no stated preaching places as required by law, dismissed any fears of prosecution, but remained adamant in their refusal to render the desired services.[8]

The reception accorded the Moravian missionaries emphasized two significant aspects of religion on the early Potomac frontier —the blurring of doctrinal differences among dissenting sects and the unifying influences of a great piety. In several places, members of the German Reformed Church, imbued with the thought of John Calvin and Ulrich Zwingli, worshiped with Lutherans, whose forebears had succumbed to persuasive ministers trained at the University of Halle, the center of German pietistic teachings. Whether Lutheran or German Reformed or members of numerically less important sects such as Mennonites, Dunkards, or Moravians, the Germans were as subject to religious emotion as any people in America. As one authority has noted, they formed "plastic material for the revivalist who found them receptive to a gospel which taught a direct personal relationship between Christ and the believer—the gospel of the Great Awakening."[9]

[8] *Ibid.*, XI (October, 1903), 119-22; *ibid.*, XII (January, 1904), 226-27; *ibid.*, XII (July, 1904), 56-58, 66-67.
[9] Albert Bernhardt Faust, *The German Element in the United States,* 2 vols. (Boston, 1909), I, 123; Harvey Wish, *Society and Thought in Early America: A Social History of the American People through 1865* (New York, 1950), p. 152; Kenamond, "Early Shepherdstown and Its Churches," p. 39; Maxwell and Swisher, *History of Hampshire County,* p. 375; Gewehr, *Great Awakening in Virginia,* pp. 26-27.

Scarcely less susceptible to prevailing religious currents were the Scotch-Irish. "Brought up in the Old Testament, and in the doctrine of government by covenant or compact," they were devoted to democracy in both civil and religious matters and vehemently opposed autocratic and tyrannical practices, whether in political affairs or ecclesiastical hierarchies. Moreover, the Presbyterian churches on the Potomac frontier were from their beginnings associated with the Philadelphia Synod, in which, even before the time of George Whitefield, there was an element which stressed piety and personal conversion. Reliance of early West Virginia congregations upon itinerants undoubtedly predisposed many persons toward New Side doctrines.[10]

The failure of the Moravians to plow deeply into the religious soil of the Potomac frontier left a fertile field open to other denominations. In due time, militant groups, inspired by New Light principles, entered upon the scene and pursued the settler relentlessly into and across the Alleghenies. Most successful in reaping the harvest of souls were the Methodists and the Baptists. Much less striking were the accomplishments of the Presbyterians and Episcopalians. Religious statistics for West Virginia in 1850 show that, largely as a consequence of the great post-Revolutionary interdenominational struggles, the Methodists had 281 and the Baptists 115 of the 548 churches then in the state. The Presbyterians were in third place with 61 churches, and the Episcopalians trailed far behind with only 22 churches, 10 of which were in the Potomac section.[11]

Of the two major proselyting denominations, the Baptists were at first the more aggressive in West Virginia. In 1743 a Baptist congregation which had but recently migrated there established a church at Mill Creek on the Opequon. Although temporarily dispersed during the French and Indian War, the congregation held together and in 1765 took the lead in forming the Ketocton Regular Baptist Association in Virginia.[12] The first serious efforts

[10] Frederick Jackson Turner, *The Frontier in American History* (New York, 1920), p. 103; Gewehr, *Great Awakening in Virginia*, p. 26.

[11] U. S., Bureau of the Census, *The Seventh Census of the United States: 1850, Embracing a Statistical View of Each of the States and Territories, Arranged by Counties, Towns, Etc.* (Washington, D. C., 1853), pp. 285-96.

[12] Isaac McNeel, "History of the Baptist Churches," p. 5, Typescript in Baptist

to extend the Baptist faith in West Virginia, however, were made by Separates under the leadership of Shubal Stearns, a converted New Light Congregationalist minister from Connecticut. In 1754 Stearns visited the Mill Creek Church, but the Regular Baptists there criticized his "animated preaching" and preferred charges against both Stearns and Daniel Marshall, his brother-in-law, in the Philadelphia Association. Stearns and Marshall then went to the Cacapon settlements in Hampshire County. Here, too, they found the settlers unsympathetic with their religious views.

Stearns arrived in the Potomac area hoping to conduct a successful revival and then to use the region as a base from which to spread the ideas of the Separate Baptists into the western country. His cold reception forced him to give up his plan. He then went to Sandy Creek in North Carolina and during the next few years made that area into one of the most important centers of Baptist influence in the South.[13]

The hostility encountered by Stearns and Marshall among the Potomac settlements derived from the same popular concepts which led to the severe persecution of Separate Baptists in Virginia in the 1760's. In general, the latter were identified with the lowest, poorest, most ignorant, and illiterate orders of society. Their lively meetings were condemned for taking those who most needed to labor away from their work. Their ministers, who made no pretense to learning and frequently expressed disdain for formal education, were branded as false prophets who by their methods whipped the people into a frenzy and deluded them. Refusing to recognize the right of civil authorities to regulate preaching and places of worship, they consistently violated laws requiring them to obtain licenses. Faced with such defiance, civil authorities in Virginia considered these Baptist ministers a menace to the Established Church and a threat to orderly society. Although many parts of Virginia were pyschologically prepared

Church Records, West Virginia Historical Records Survey, Box 208, West Virginia University Library.

[13] Robert B. Semple, *A History of the Rise and Progress of the Baptists in Virginia*, rev. and extended by G. W. Beale (Richmond, Va., 1894), p. 13; William Warren Sweet, *Religion on the American Frontier; The Baptists 1783–1830: A Collection of Source Materials* (New York, 1931), p. 8.

for the Great Awakening, they were not ready for the vehemence with which the Separates attacked the Anglican Church and rejected civil authority.

The religious liberty for which the Baptists battled, however, began to be regarded as a concomitant of political liberty, which had begun to pervade popular thought. Their attacks upon the Establishment and their fight against taxation for its support were decidedly in the democratic tradition. Thanks to their sincerity and to the zeal of such leaders as Daniel Marshall, Samuel Harriss, Jeremiah Moore, and James Ireland, they gradually overcame public opposition. By 1770 the worst of the persecutions were over.[14]

Encouraged by the more favorable climate which prevailed during the years immediately preceding the Revolution, the Baptists launched another assault upon the Allegheny frontier of West Virginia. About 1773 Joseph Reading and John Taylor, two self-appointed unordained ministers, visited Looney's Creek in Hampshire County and preached to "a few scattering Baptists." Here they constituted a church, which later ordained Reading as its minister. Using this church as a base, Reading and Taylor "ranged through almost every corner of the large county of Hampshire" during the next two years and established congregations on Patterson's Creek and on Lost River at the head of the Cacapon.

Such was the change in popular feeling regarding the Baptists that only once during their journeys did Reading and Taylor encounter serious opposition. The incident occurred while they were preaching at a residence in a prosperous section of the county. The owner of the house and father-in-law of the tenant who had invited them to hold services raised violent objections to the use of his property for Baptist preaching. He "roused perhaps twenty rugged young fellows, a number of whom came armed with instruments of death," whereupon "a mighty uproar soon took place in the house, with some blows from the old man on his son-in-law." Noting that a deep snow had fallen and that but few people seemed truly interested in their preaching, Reading and Taylor retired from the scene.

[14] Gewehr, *Great Awakening in Virginia*, pp. 106-37.

Fired by the zeal common to early Baptist itinerants, Taylor now determined to carry the gospel across the Alleghenies to the Tygart Valley, where about a hundred families had recently settled. In the depths of winter, with snow up to his knees, he made his way through fifty miles of trackless mountains. Much to his disappointment, he found the settlers huddled together in a little fort and only one Baptist among them—"and that one a woman." Taylor held but few meetings, "and those with a confused appearance." Discouraged, he crossed the dividing ridges to the Greenbrier Valley. He found conditions "equally gloomy" there and was "pacified" after a few meetings.

But Taylor could not overcome his concern for the transmontane pioneers. The following spring he again crossed the mountains. On his tour he visited settlements along the Cheat, West Fork, Tygart Valley, and Buckhannon rivers. As before, he found most of the people forted. In the Tygart Valley he preached to a great number of people in the woods near the fort, and they seemed "as perfectly composed as if they had no enemy in the world." Encouraged by this reception, Taylor again, in the winter of 1775–1776, sought to stir the Greenbrier inhabitants. But, he ruefully acknowledged, whether because of "the distracted state of the people, by the war, or the barrenness of my preaching, or both, I became fully convinced that if the Lord ever intended to bless that people, the time was not come, or myself was not the instrument." During the ensuing years Taylor returned to the waters of the Monongahela several times and even made two journeys into the Greenbrier settlements.

The preaching of Taylor and Reading was typical of that of other Separate Baptists. Taylor vividly described a meeting of thirty or forty Baptists in the Monongahela Glades. While Taylor was preaching, "nothing very visible" happened. When Reading's turn came, he "dwelt on the awful subject, of a Judgment to come." A young woman began to "weep and tremble." Her grandmother endeavored to stop her, but at length "began to tremble herself, as if the Judge was at the door." The effect soon spread throughout the house. Amid the "solemn groans and lamentations," one woman "dropt on her knees, in the middle of the house, with the greatest appearance of agonizing guilt," and remained there for some three hours, but "she obtained deliverance from her guilt before she left her knees." The meeting lasted a full six hours, and when it was over, the floor "was as wet with the tears of the people, as if water had been sprinkled all over it, or with a shower of rain."

During his first four years on the Allegheny frontier Taylor carried on his work without the benefit of ordination. He overcame this handicap when both the Looney's Creek Church, of which he was a member, and the church at Shenandoah directed that he be ordained. Even then, he was ordained only "in the itenerant way, and to administer ordinances where Churches were destitute of a Pastor" and called for his services, a practice that was "not uncommon for unmarried men in those days."[15]

Of more enduring significance in the extension of Baptist churches into the Alleghenies was the work of John Alderson. Like many other Baptist ministers, Alderson had almost no formal education, and his reading was confined largely to the Bible and the Baptist catechism. In 1775, shortly after he succeeded his father as a pastor of the Lynville Baptist Church in Rockingham County, he undertook the first of three journeys into the Greenbrier country. He found there "a wild, uncultivated place, in which Christ and His cross were seldom, if ever, preached." On his third visit Alderson encountered anti-Baptist feeling, but he ignored the opposition and in 1777 took up permanent residence at Alderson. Although the Greenbrier frontier was then entering the bloodiest period of the Revolutionary War, he continued his itineracy with little thought of personal safety. In November, 1781, as peace returned to the area, he organized the Greenbrier Baptist Church at Alderson. Its twelve members constituted the first Baptist church in southern West Virginia.[16]

The Greenbrier Church became the progenitor of a large number of Baptist churches. Beginning with the Indian Creek Church, whose members were made a separate congregation in 1792, Alderson had a hand in planting nine Baptist churches, scattered

[15] Sweet, *Religion on the American Frontier: The Baptists*, pp. 128-44, 147.

[16] Semple, *History of . . . the Baptists in Virginia*, pp. 424-27; Records of the Greenbrier Association of Baptists [1825–1868], pp. 100-101; Emma Frances Alderson, ed., "The Minutes of the Greenbrier Baptist Church, 1781–1782," *West Virginia History*, VII (October, 1945), 42.

from the Greenbrier region to the Ohio River, some one hundred and fifty miles to the west. Most of these churches, in turn, became parent organizations for new congregations. For example, Hopewell Church, near Ansted, whose original members had secured letters of dismissal from the Greenbrier Church, permitted some of its brethren to withdraw in 1824 to constitute Zoar Church at Kessler's Cross Lanes in Nicholas County. In time Zoar Church dismissed numbers of its own members in order that they might establish other Baptist churches on the waters of the Gauley River.[17]

The same process of extending Baptist influence by organizing new congregations as arms of existing churches was employed throughout the Alleghenies. The first two Baptist churches in the Monongahela Valley were the Simpson's Creek Church, founded at Bridgeport in 1774 by John Sutton, and the Forks of Cheat Church, organized in 1775 by John Corbly. By 1809 both of these churches counted numerous offspring among the Baptist congregations in the northern part of West Virginia.[18]

The initial successes of the Baptists among Allegheny pioneers can be attributed only in part to their identification with the Revolutionary cause in America. They gained stature because of their leadership in the fight for separation of church and state.

[17] The Minutes of the Greenbrier Baptist Church [1781–1835], July 28, 1792, June 25, 1796; Semple, History of . . . the Baptists in Virginia, p. 421; Record Book for the Zoar Church [1824–1868], April 17, 1824, Baptist Historical Collection, West Virginia Department of Archives and History Library.

[18] Semple, History of . . . the Baptists in Virginia, pp. 434, 438; McNeel, "History of the Baptist Churches," pp. 7-8. In some cases the initiative for organization of Baptist churches came from lay persons. The Kanawha Baptist Church, established near Pratt in 1796, apparently began in this manner. Several settlers in the upper part of the Kanawha Valley, including the prolific Morris family, had once lived in Culpeper County, a center of Baptist influence in Virginia since 1765. Either there or during a few years' residence in the Greenbrier area they had become Baptists. Since the Kanawha settlements were cut off from the Greenbrier Baptist Church by eighty miles of rugged land, two prominent landowners of the Kanawha Valley, William Morris and John Dickinson, agreed to give fifty acres each to Nathaniel Shrewsbury, a Baptist minister who proposed to move to the Kanawha. Shrewsbury failed to migrate at that time, but Morris persuaded James Johnston of Rockingham County to settle on the Kanawha and become the pastor of the Kanawha Baptist Church. Affadavit of John Jones, May 12, 1835; Ruth Woods Dayton, Pioneers and Their Homes on the Upper Kanawha (Charleston, W. Va., 1947), p. 15; Lyman Chalkley, Chronicles of the Scotch-Irish Settlements in Virginia Extracted from the Original Court Records of Augusta County, 1745–1800, 3 vols. (Rosslyn, Va., 1912), II, 60; Semple, History of . . . the Baptists in Virginia, p. 421.

Of equal importance was their willingness to seek out needy souls on exposed frontiers. John Taylor, John Alderson, John Corbly, and John Sutton carried their messages to outlying settlements when the perils incident to the Revolutionary War were at their greatest. Corbly's own family was killed a few miles from the Forks of Cheat Church.[19]

At the close of the Revolution, when Baptist zeal appeared to be on the wane, interest was reawakened by a revival, which began along the James River in 1783. The revival was marked by religious excesses, which were much deplored by many Baptist leaders. During services it was not uncommon for a large part of a congregation to be lying prostrate on the floor, all but unmoving. But their "screams, cries, groans, songs, shouts, and hosannas, notes of grief and notes of joy, all heard at the same time," were said to have produced "a heavenly confusion, a short of indescribable concert." Preachers who encouraged such exercises nearly always counted the most converts, but, unfortunately, many who "labored earnestly to get Christians into their churches were afterwards much perplexed to get out hypocrites."[20]

According to Josiah Osborn of the Big Levels Baptist Church, the revival reached the trans-Allegheny regions in 1786 when "the work of God broke out on the right hand and on the left through different parts of the country, and continued until 1790." Numerous members were added to the Baptist churches, but the increase in numbers was by no means equal to the accretions to Methodist societies. By 1796 the momentum of the revival was spent, and the Greenbrier Baptist Church appointed a day of prayer, "Begging our heavenly father to remove the Deadness and hardness of heart that seems to prevail among us and that a revival of religion may take place in these our Cold frozen hearts."[21]

Robert B. Semple, the historian of the Baptists in eighteenth- and early nineteenth-century Virginia, believed that, quite apart from additions to the denomination's numerical strength, the revival marked a turning point in Baptist practices. After it was

---

[19] Sweet, *Religion on the American Frontier: The Baptists*, pp. 131, 134.
[20] Semple, *History of . . . the Baptists in Virginia*, pp. 55-60.
[21] *Ibid.*, pp. 427-28; The Minutes of the Greenbrier Baptist Church [1781–1835], February 27, 1796.

over, he declared, Baptist ministers became more circumspect in their preaching, abandoning "a great many odd tones, disgusting whoops and awkward gestures." Their zeal and enthusiasm became tempered with rationalism, and they gained respectability in the eyes of the world. Thereafter "they wēre joined by persons of much greater weight in civil society."

About this time, too, there occurred a noticable blurring of differences between Separate and Regular Baptists. The earliest West Virginia Baptist associations, including the Ketocton, Redstone, and Greenbrier and their immediate offspring, were of the Regular persuasion, but their churches frequently adopted practices and techniques of the Separates. Moreover, in most frontier areas Baptists generally favored a mild form of Calvinism. With the reunification of the Regular and Separate groups in 1801, Baptists adopted a confession of faith which permitted the preaching of general atonement. In frontier areas this doctrine was far more acceptable than the strict Calvinistic tenets of predestination. Baptists remained opposed, however, to outright Arminianism and took stern measures against ministers suspected of harboring such views.[22]

Subsequent growth of the Baptists in frontier areas can be traced in part through their associations. The first churches in West Virginia were connected with the Philadelphia Association, which was formed in 1707 and made up of Regular Baptists. In 1765 the Mill Creek Church on Opequon took the lead in forming the Ketocton Regular Baptist Association, whose four original members included the Lynville Church of which John Alderson served as pastor. In 1809 the Ketocton Association included six West Virginia churches, all in the Eastern Panhandle. It was but natural that the churches of the Greenbrier region should first align themselves with this association. For convenience, however, they withdrew in 1795 and joined the New River Association. Even then, their isolated condition rendered participation in association affairs difficult. In order to remedy the situation, the Greenbrier churches for several years held "society" meetings, which "had the happy tendency towards ripening them for a

[22] Semple, *History of . . . the Baptists in Virginia*, pp. 59-60; Sweet, *Religion on the American Frontier: The Baptists*, p. 44.

separate Association." In 1801 they formed the Greenbrier Association. Because it began with only four member churches and three ordained ministers, the new organization drew criticism, but John Alderson silenced opponents by reminding them that "God did not choose the Jews because they were numerous, but because they were few in number." But the Baptist churches grew, and in 1812 seven churches in southwestern West Virginia formed the Teays Valley Association.

Churches in the northern part of West Virginia were at first members of the Redstone Baptist Association, formed in October, 1776. Eight of them withdrew from this organization in 1804 and established the Union Baptist Association. The latter ultimately included churches in about twenty counties and became the parent organization of nearly every other Baptist association in northern West Virginia. In 1835 ten of its congregations were dismissed to form the Broad Run Association, which within its first fifteen years attracted no less than forty-three churches, all in the north-central part of the state. In 1818 several churches of the Ohio Valley created the Parkersburg Association, which included more than thirty congregations in 1830.[23]

In the contest for souls on the Allegheny frontier, the Baptists held two distinct advantages. One lay in their democratic form of church organization and the other in their use of an uneducated ministry. The ideals that prompted them to fight for separation of church and state also led them to insist upon placing church authority in the congregation. Each Baptist congregation had control over its own constitution and rules of decorum, the behavior of its members, and the selection of its minister. Nor were Baptist associations theoretically superior to the congregation; the fact that churches sent "messengers" rather than delegates to association meetings underscored that point. Such independence of outside authority enabled many Baptist churches to escape the neglect and inconvenience of isolation from some remote hierarchy.

Of equal importance was the fact that the Baptists did not insist upon—indeed, they disdained—an educated ministry. Ordi-

[23] Semple, *History of . . . the Baptists in Virginia*, pp. 299, 421-23, 434, 438; McNeel, "History of the Baptist Churches," pp. 4-14, 28, 38.

narily, Baptist congregations "raised up" their own ministers. The *sine qua non* for a Baptist minister was that he receive a call from God to preach and that he provide evidence of his gifts. Such education as he had was very likely acquired after he entered the ministry. Josiah Osborn of the Big Levels Church, for example, was "scarcely able to read when he grew to manhood," but he had "a singular turn for touching the feelings." Yet, in later years he wrote and published a pamphlet entitled *David and Goliath*, which was considered one of the best treatises on baptism available in the early nineteenth century. The Baptist minister usually began his work as a licentiate, who might organize congregations, conduct meetings, and perform baptismal and marriage rites. Later, perhaps at the time he was engaged by a congregation as its pastor, he was ordained.

The typical Baptist preacher labored at his own tasks for six days a week and set aside the seventh for the work of the Lord. The farmer-preacher expected—and received—very little, if any, compensation for his services. Declaring that "it never set well on my feelings to receive pay from the people for preaching," John Taylor chose to supply his own wants and corn for his horse by cultivating a field, which he cleared from a lot of "broken land" left to him by his father. John Alderson apparently received no remuneration during his first twelve years as pastor of the Greenbrier Baptist Church, but in 1793 the congregation voted to advance him ten shillings for wearing apparel. From time to time thereafter it provided him with limited assistance.[24]

The very strengths of the Baptists, however, frequently proved also to be weaknesses. The democracy that lay at the base of their organization made their churches and associations peculiarly susceptible to internal dissension. The Mill Creek Church became involved in "a dispute almost about nothing" which stirred up "a contention that lasted several years, caused a schism in the church, and interrupted the harmony of the Ketocton Association

---

[24] Sweet, *Religion on the American Frontier: The Baptists*, pp. 36-57, 144; Walter Brownlow Posey, *The Baptist Church in the Lower Mississippi Valley, 1776–1845* (Lexington, Ky., 1957), pp. 20-25, 115-20, 155-58; Semple, *History of . . . the Baptists in Virginia*, pp. 430-31; The Minutes of the Greenbrier Baptist Church [1781–1835], April 26, 1793, March 29, 1794.

for several sessions." The recalcitrant group was excommunicated, formed an independent church, attempted to join the Philadelphia Association, and finally agreed to a solution that healed the breach. By 1833 four of the fourteen churches in the Greenbrier Association had experienced disruptive disputes arising either from doctrinal or personal causes. The Walker's Creek Church, one of the oldest in that association, suffered greatly "from the errors and irregular conduct of several prominent individuals, once Members of this church" and by 1833 had a congregation made up mostly of aged disciples "who kept the wreck afloat." Peters Creek Church in mountainous Nicholas County "became so reduced in consequence of the deleterious influence exerted by Grievous Wolves that had crept in (among which was the pastor of the Church) that she entirely lost her visibility as a Church of the Lord Jesus Christ" and completely collapsed.[25]

Baptist associations also experienced much discord. They were constantly on guard against infiltration by Arians, Seventh Day Baptists, and Pedobaptists, the latter being especially anathema. More disruptive, however, were disputes arising from extra-congregational activity. Probably no issue aroused more bitter feelings than the propriety of missionary work, which most Protestant churches in America undertook during the first quarter of the nineteenth century. Such activity engendered no serious opposition among Methodists and Presbyterians. But within a few years after the organization of the General Missionary Board of the Baptists in Philadelphia in May, 1814, the question produced irreconcilable divisions among the Baptists. Antimissionism was peculiar to the Baptists and was strongest in frontier areas where educational levels were low and people were isolated from prevailing cultural influences. Ministers with little or no education, fearful that highly trained missionaries might undermine their own positions, were conspicuous among opponents of missionary work. Theologically, the antimissionists based their arguments upon allegations that missionary activity was unscriptural, that it was Arminian in doctrine, and that it

[25] Semple, *History of . . . the Baptists in Virginia*, p. 418; Records of the Greenbrier Association of Baptists [1825–1868], pp. 102-104, 108-109; Record Book for the Zoar Church [1824–1868], June 14, 1834.

would lead to too much centralization in church government.

Of the three leading opponents of missionary work—John Taylor, Daniel Parker, and Alexander Campbell—two were intimately connected with the early history of the Baptists in frontier West Virginia. John Taylor, whose influence in Kentucky was perhaps greater than that of any other Baptist preacher of his time, served for nearly ten years as an itinerant in the Eastern Panhandle and the Monongahela Valley. In a pamphlet, *Thoughts on Missions,* published in 1819, he branded missionary societies as schemes to get money and to substitute religious aristocracies for congregational government. Alexander Campbell, a resident of Bethany and a Baptist from 1813 to 1830, used the columns of his widely circulated religious publications, the *Christian Baptist* and the *Millenial Harbinger,* to attack missionary societies, Bible societies, church constitutions, bishops, and every other practice for which he found no Scriptural sanction. Campbell's onslaughts drew a following among both Baptist ministers and laymen, who called themselves Reformers and appeared in numerous Baptist churches and associations. The third of the great opponents of missionism, Daniel Parker, set forth the ultra-Calvinistic "Two-Seed-in-the-Spirit" doctrine, which attracted some of the most extreme antimissionists.[26]

In addition to controversies over missionary work, other issues, including Bible societies, ministerial education, freemasonry, and temperance, produced dissension in several Baptist associations. In 1839 five churches of the Union Association, accusing that organization of having "departed from her constitution" and "patronized what is called 'the institutions of the day'" withdrew and established the Tygart Valley Association. Even in the Greenbrier Association, which was strongly missionary, the Indian Creek Church had in its congregation many members who opposed missionary, temperance, and other benevolent exertions. Such differences led Alexander Campbell to sever his connections with the Baptists and to form the Disciples of Christ Church.

[26] Semple, *History of . . . the Baptists in Virginia,* pp. 440-41; "Baptist Church History," Typescript, West Virginia Historical Records Survey, Box 208, West Virginia University Library; Records of the Greenbrier Association of Baptists [1825–1868], p. 97; Sweet, *Religion on the American Frontier: The Baptists,* pp. 58-76, 105-106; Posey, *Baptist Church in the Lower Mississippi Valley,* pp. 68-72.

The Elizabeth Baptist Church withdrew from the Parkersburg Association in 1821 because that organization refused to take a stand on freemasonry.[27]

In general, however, Baptists of the Allegheny sections of West Virginia gave strong support to missions and other benevolent endeavors. In 1836 the Broad Run Association endorsed the formation of "a missionary society auxiliary to the General Association of Virginia," and the following year it pledged support to the American and Foreign Bible Society of Philadelphia. It even made the unusual recommendation, in 1839, that a better translation of the Bible be undertaken as a means of reducing confusion. In action that was probably representative of attitudes among West Virginia Baptists, the Greenbrier Association, at its 1846 meeting, proposed that Baptist churches west of the Blue Ridge raise $6,000, or about fifty cents per member, for benevolent causes. Specifically, it asked $3,000 for the Western Virginia Baptist Association, $500 each for foreign missionary work, Bible societies, a Baptist college at Richmond, and a book depository at Lewisburg, and $1,000 for houses of worship at important places. Like other West Virginia Baptist associations, the Greenbrier organization took an active interest in Sunday school work, and in 1844 it had within its bounds 17 Sunday schools with 62 teachers and 433 enrollees. Its libraries aggregated 555 volumes.[28]

The lack of any strong ultraconservative movement among West Virginia Baptists can be attributed partly to a dearth of powerful leaders. To be sure, Alexander Campbell remained at Bethany, but he made Kentucky and other western areas, rather than West Virginia, the main arenas in which to wage his fight for primitive religion. John Taylor, one of the most influential antimissionists in Kentucky, left West Virginia before most of the explosive issues arose. Moreover, the ranks of Baptist ministers seem to have been in some areas substantially reduced by migration westward. With the lack of a strong central organization with authority to assign pastorates, Baptist leadership in

[27] McNeel, "History of the Baptist Churches," pp. 10, 28; Records of the Greenbrier Association of Baptists [1825–1868], p. 104.

[28] McNeel, "History of the Baptist Churches," p. 13; Records of the Greenbrier Association of Baptists [1825–1868], pp. 248, 276-77.

isolated areas of the Alleghenies was characterized by a fluidity that was hardly conducive to prolonged battles over doctrine or current issues.[29]

Moderate Baptists found themselves caught between a stern Calvinistic theology which rejected missions and other benevolent activities on the one hand and a rising tide of Arminianism, as practiced by the Methodists, on the other. John Alderson looked upon the United Baptists as a religious bulwark standing against "a torrent of opposition, from different quarters, especially the Arminians." Indeed, Arminianism, being but a short step from Baptist doctrines of general atonement, was an insidious enemy. John Smith, assigned to the Greenbrier Circuit of the Methodist Church in 1787 and 1788, characterized Josiah Osborn, a revered Baptist minister and close associate of Alderson, as "And [*sic*] Old Baptist by profession but A Methodist in principle."[30] The appeal of Arminianism explains in part why the Baptists encountered such devastating competition from the Methodists and provides one clue as to why Methodism eventually swept over pioneer West Virginia like a tidal wave.

Methodism had its beginnings in 1739 as a movement within the Church of England, under the dynamic leadership of John Wesley. The first Methodist missionaries to the colonies—three in number and self-appointed—arrived in 1766. Between 1769 and 1774, in response to appeals from colonial converts, Wesley sent eight missionaries to America. The coming of the Revolution and Wesley's steadfast Toryism, however, brought Methodism under a cloud of suspicion in America. By 1778 all of Wesley's missionaries except one, Francis Asbury, had returned to England.

Far from irreparably weakening American Methodism, the departure of the English leaders actually proved beneficial. It enabled the movement in America to cast off the stigma of Toryism and to develop largely as an indigenous growth. Through

[29] See, for example, "Baptist Church History" for an account of the Clarksburg Baptist Church, whose pastor "many years ago . . . went west [and] no successor was secured, [leaving] nothing but the grave-yard . . . where once the meetinghouse stood." See also Semple, *History of . . . the Baptists in Virginia*, pp. 334, 342, and McNeel, "History of the Baptist Churches," pp. 8, 28.

[30] Semple, *History of . . . the Baptists in Virginia*, p. 437; Journal of John Smith . . . on the Greenbrier Circuit, July 4, 1787, to July 8, 1788, p. 18.

the somewhat irregular methods of Robert Strawbridge, numerous native preachers were raised up in Virginia and Maryland. Strawbridge's "spiritual sons," including William Watters, Philip Gatch, Daniel Ruff, and Freeborn Garrettson, and numerous local preachers and exhorters with whom he worked kept Methodism alive during the Revolution. Equally significant was the contribution of Devereux Jarratt, an Anglican minister of Dinwiddie County, Virginia, whose willingness to administer the sacraments to Methodists probably prevented a serious schism in early American Methodism. Within the twenty-nine Virginia and North Carolina counties in which Jarrett labored, the number of Methodists increased from a few hundred to more than 4,000 between 1776 and 1783. At the close of the Revolution nearly two-thirds of all American Methodists were in that area.

In 1784 American Methodists established their ecclesiastical independence of the Anglican, or Episcopal, Church. Until then they were entirely a lay group within the Anglican Church. They emphasized this relationship by refraining from using the word "church" and referring to their organizations as "societies" and their places of worship as "chapels" or "meeting-houses." None of their itinerant ministers had been ordained. The war changed the relationship of the societies with the Episcopal Church and rendered impossible any strong control by Wesley over Methodist affairs in America either through dictation of the form of church organization or imposition of a church hierarchy. Asbury's insistence that these matters could be decided only by a general conference of Methodist preachers resulted in the famous "Christmas Conference," which assembled at Baltimore on Christmas Eve in 1784. The ministers present approved Wesley's designation of Thomas Coke and Asbury as superintendents and ordained twelve older preachers, first as deacons and then as elders, thereby establishing both an independent ecclesiastical organization and an ordained ministry.

The Methodist church structure which evolved during the next few years proved admirably suited to frontier conditions. In 1792 the General Conference, the supreme governing body of the church, came into existence. After 1808 the General Conference consisted of five delegates from each of the regional, or Annual, Conferences, a change in composition which provided adequate representation for frontier areas. In 1796 the Annual Conference, with definite boundaries, emerged and provided the Methodists with an administrative system which could be easily extended to cover the ever-expanding areas of settlement. In charge of each Annual Conference was a presiding elder, who had supervision over all preachers, both itinerant and located, within his district and who conducted the annual meetings.

Annual Conferences were made up of Quarterly Conferences, which, in turn, were vital to the functioning of the circuits. The key to the success of the circuit system, which was introduced from England, lay in the constancy and self-sacrifice of the traveling ministers. The most important function of the circuit rider was to coordinate the activities of local preachers, exhorters, and class leaders. These officials, particularly the class leaders, kept local groups, or classes, together and held meetings, usually weekly, in the absence of the itinerant minister. The significance of the system cannot be overemphasized in any consideration of the remarkable achievements of the Methodists in the early nineteenth century. Abel Stevens, one of the outstanding historians of early Methodism, touched the springs of their success when he stated that "the usual stationary ministers wait for the call of the people . . . ; the Methodist ministry goes forth to call the people."[31]

The earliest churches of the Potomac frontier were lineally descended from the Methodism planted by Robert Strawbridge in Frederick County, Maryland, prior to the Revolution. Among the native preachers whom Strawbridge raised up was Richard Owings, who with John Hagerty, probably introduced Methodist preaching into the Shenandoah Valley, including the Eastern Panhandle of West Virginia. In 1775–1776 several Virginia counties, including Berkeley County in present West Virginia, experienced a religious revival in which William Waters, a protégé of Strawbridge and the first American-born Methodist minister,

[31] William Warren Sweet, *Religion on the American Frontier, 1783–1840; The Methodists: A Collection of Source Materials* (New York, 1964), pp. 3-50; Abel Stevens, *History of the Methodist Episcopal Church in the United States of America*, 3 vols. (New York, [1864]), II, 219-28.

was the central figure. Within a few months Freeborn Garrettson, another associate of Strawbridge and one of the most significant of early Methodist leaders, arrived in the area and began to preach with great success. The labors of Watters, Garrettson, and others resulted in the formation of the Berkeley Circuit in May, 1778, with Edward Bailey as circuit 'rider. This large circuit included the northern part of the Valley of Virginia and all of the Eastern Panhandle of West Virginia.[32]

Also in the vanguard of Methodist leaders among West Virginia settlements was Francis Asbury himself. Asbury first visited the state in late summer of 1776, when he spent the weeks between July 18 and August 27 at Bath, or Berkeley Springs, seeking to mend his health. Even then he undertook several preaching missions into the surrounding country, often in the company of two other preachers, Richard Webster and John Hagerty. This journey was but the first of some thirty-four which Asbury made to the Allegheny frontier between 1776 and 1815. Through these travels, which kept him always in close touch with the pioneers, Asbury played a personal role in the spread of Methodism from the Potomac settlements to the Ohio River. This close association with the great Bishop Asbury goes far toward explaining the vitality of early West Virginia Methodism.[33]

By 1784 Methodism had begun to take root in several areas west of the Alleghenies, one of which was the Greenbrier Valley. In the summer of that year about half a dozen families from the more substantial landowners in the Sinks of Greenbrier organized a Methodist society. The new church, known as Rehoboth, was first served by local preachers. It flourished, and in 1785 Edward Keenan, a Catholic with strong Methodist inclinations, wrote to Bishop Asbury, requesting that a minister be sent to Rehoboth. Asbury dispatched young William Phoebus, who served the congregation for about two years.

[32] Samuel Kercheval, *A History of the Valley of Virginia*, ed. Oren F. Morton, 4th ed. (Strasburg, Va., 1925), p. 66; Lawrence Sherwood, "Methodism in West Virginia," an unpublished article which the author permitted me to read. As early as August, 1775, Philip Fithian reported that he saw a Methodist preacher "haranguing the people" at Berkeley Springs. Fithian, *Journal, 1775–1776*, p. 126.

[33] [Francis Asbury], *Journal of Rev. Francis Asbury, Bishop of the Methodist Episcopal Church*, 3 vols. (New York, n. d.), I, 143-49.

Like numerous other Methodist societies, Rehoboth Church won the membership and support of a well-to-do local resident. Shortly after the arrival of Phoebus, Edward Keenan was converted to Methodism. Keenan provided the congregation with a lot for a church building and deeded it five acres of land for a graveyard. In 1786, largely through his initiative, the members erected Rehoboth Church, an enduring landmark of Methodism in the Alleghenies. Keenan's benefices continued for the next forty years. This capacity of Methodism to appeal to men of substance, while at the same time retaining its crusading spirit, provides another clue to its success in pioneer West Virginia.[34]

The auspicious beginnings of the Rehoboth church and a rapidly growing population led to the establishment of the Greenbrier Circuit in 1787. Its organization was placed in the hands of John Smith, formerly a rider on the Redstone Circuit. To complete the circuit, which included parts of Pocahontas, Greenbrier, and Monroe counties, as well as neighboring areas of Virginia, required a journey of four weeks and services at nineteen preaching places. Smith attracted large congregations— at Rehoboth "hundreds flock'd together to hear the Word"—including a high proportion of listeners who had never before heard Methodist preaching. In July, 1788, Bishop Asbury visited the Greenbrier Circuit and at the Quarterly Meeting held at Rehoboth on July 5 and 6 ordained Smith a deacon in the first Methodist ordination west of the Alleghenies.[35]

The Methodists quickly overcame whatever advantage the Baptists had acquired by their earlier arrival in the Greenbrier area. Elder Josiah Osborn of the Baptist church at Lewisburg graphically described the distressing effects which the Methodist

---

[34] J. L. Kibler, *A Historical Sketch of Rehobeth M. E. Church, South, Monroe County, W. Va., Delivered at the Centennial Celebration, July 20, 1884,* "Methodist Shrine Edition" (Glenville, W. Va., 1960), pp. 3-6. The circumstances surrounding Keenan's conversion are illustrative of the power of early Methodism. It occurred while Keenan, Phoebus, and several others were crossing Peters Mountain on a return journey from a meeting at Pott's Creek. Their discussions of the joys of being a Christian and their singing of Methodist hymns, perhaps coupled with the primeval grandeur of the wilderness, produced such an effect upon Keenan that he was overcome and accepted Methodism even before returning to Rehoboth Church. *Ibid.,* p. 4.

[35] Journal of John Smith . . . on the Greenbrier Circuit, July 4, 1787, to July 8, 1788, pp. 13-16, 55, passim; Sherwood, "Methodism in West Virginia."

successes had upon the Baptists. At first, he said, "the people's ears, hearts, and doors were all open to receive the Word. Now the time of the singing of the birds was come, and the voice of the turtle was heard in our land." Then, "in the midst of these goodly times," he said, "the Methodists made their appearance and raised no small opposition about doctrines." Upon their arrival, "they took Brother [John] Alderson's track, made his preaching places theirs. Numbers under conviction and in a hopeful way joined them, and although alarmed by the preaching of the Baptists, turned to be their persecutors." By the time the revival was over in the 1780's the Methodists had far out-distanced their rivals.[36]

The other areas of transmontane West Virginia where settle-ment had by 1784 sufficiently progressed to justify Methodist activity were the Monongahela and upper Ohio valleys. In the autumn of 1783 Richard Owings, perhaps at Asbury's request, crossed the Alleghenies and spent about six weeks visit-ing settlements between Laurel Hill and the Ohio River. Owings' reports of a number of Methodists among these settlers led to the creation of the Redstone Circuit the following year. This circuit originally extended up the Monongahela River as far as Morgantown, and in 1785 was pushed westward to the Ohio to include the Northern Panhandle of West Virginia. Rapid expansion of settlements along the Monongahela and upper Ohio resulted in several divisions of the Redstone Circuit. In 1787 its western part became the Ohio Circuit, and, thanks to circuit riders who had extended its bounds, its southern portion became a part of the new Clarksburg Circuit.[37]

In these northern parts of West Virginia, as in the Greenbrier region and elsewhere on the Allegheny frontier, adherents of Methodism included a substantial portion of the political and social leaders, many of whom had gained local renown in winning the land from the Indians and the British or in con-quering the wilderness itself. Prominent Methodists of the upper Ohio Valley, for instance, included Ebenezer Zane, William McMechen, John McCulloch, John Doddridge, and Richard

[36] Semple, *History of . . . the Baptists in Virginia,* pp. 427-28.
[37] Sherwood, "Methodism in West Virginia."

Wells, all border heroes or respected pioneers.[38] This identification with a "natural aristocracy" gave Methodism a prestige which offset any advantage acquired by the Baptists in their devotion to the American cause during the Revolution and their fight for the principles of separation of church and state.

In 1804 ten large circuits—Berkeley, Allegheny, Pendleton, Greenbrier, Ohio, Clarksburg, Randolph, Kanawha, Little Kanawha, and Guyandotte—were required to carry on Methodist work in West Virginia. Two of them, Randolph and Kanawha, seem to have been formed somewhat prematurely in areas where population was either too sparse, even for the Methodists, or where, as in the Kanawha Valley, the Baptists had already become fairly well entrenched. But the first quarter of the nineteenth century brought large accretions to the Methodists, and by 1826 seventeen additional circuits had been established.[39]

The initiative in the formation of Methodist societies among isolated frontier settlements in the Alleghenies was taken in most instances by local preachers or settlers whose Methodist affiliations antedated their migration to their localities. Reece Wolf, whose own acceptance of Methodist doctrines dated at least from the early 1780's when he lived on Maryland's Eastern Shore and who introduced Methodism to the Little Kanawha Valley in April, 1798, was typical of these early Methodists. At the time of his arrival there, Wolf, later a justice of the peace, wrote, "Methodism was unknown in this country. As soon as I came I commenced preaching, and the next fall and winter a revival took place." Wolf soon had a class of twenty-one members and more work than he could manage. He appealed to Bishop Asbury for help. In 1799 Asbury sent Robert Manley to the Little Kanawha, and within a few months a new circuit had

---

[38] Reminiscences of Thomas Scott and Thomas Scott's Journal of the Ohio Circuit, 1793, Thomas Scott MSS, in the possession of the Reverend Lawrence Sherwood, who permitted me to read his transcripts. See also Journal of Robert Ayres, Circuit Rider on the Redstone Circuit from May 16, 1786, to June 16, 1787, Historical Society of Western Pennsylvania. I have used a typescript of Ayres' Journal made by Mr. Sherwood. Other examples of the ability of Methodism to attract leading citizens are in Jacob Young, *Autobiography of a Pioneer; or, the Nativity, Experience, Travels, and Ministerial Labors of Rev. Jacob Young; with Incidents, Observations, and Reflections* (Cincinnati, Ohio [1857?]), pp. 269, 277.

[39] Sherwood, "Methodism in West Virginia."

been organized. The Guyandotte Circuit, organized in 1804 with Asa Shinn as circuit rider, was the result of a petition signed by about a hundred persons and circulated by an old Methodist who had migrated from Pennsylvania.[40]

The yeoman service rendered by local preachers, exhorters, and class leaders both in organizing and sustaining Methodist classes might have been of little avail without the periodic appearance of the circuit riders, whose visits kept the fires of enthusiasm aglow. Although representing the authority and prestige of a centralized hierachy, the traveling preachers "belonged, like the early founders of Christianity, to the toiling classes of the community. They were taken from the plow, the loom, the bench, and the anvil," and, with their intimate understanding of those among whom they labored, they proved singularly effective in setting forth "those soul-saving truths which brought the sinner to dust, and raised the fallen to the blessings of pardon and salvation."[41]

In his very appearance the Methodist circuit rider seemed to attune himself to the solemnity of his mission. Thomas Scott, whose attire was typical of that of scores of his associates, described himself as "dressed in plain, neat, old-fashioned Methodist style: hair parted in front, combed back, hanging down on my shoulders; plain-breasted coat and vest, with flaps and skirts; small clothes, with buttons and buckles at the knees; cotton stockings; stock nicely plaited, and buckled behind; and a low-crown, broad-brimmed hat." To be more presumptuous in dress invited the scorn of uncouth pioneers, as young Henry Bascom, the traveling preacher on the Guyandotte Circuit in 1814, found to his sorrow. Because he was "exceedingly elegant in person and . . . seemed always to dress in the height of fashion," Bascom was scorned as "proud, ambitious, and too aspiring."[42]

[40] James B. Finley, *Sketches of Western Methodism: Biographical, Historical, and Miscellaneous, Illustrative of Pioneer Life*, ed. W. P. Strickland (Cincinnati, Ohio, 1855), p. 455; Wood County Legislative Petitions, December 6, 1804; Sherwood, "Methodism in West Virginia."

[41] Finley, *Sketches of Western Methodism*, p. 250.

[42] Account of Controversy with Doctor Welsh, 1793–1794, Thomas Scott MSS; William Warren Sweet, ed., *Circuit-Rider Days along the Ohio, Being the Journals of the Ohio Conference from Its Organization in 1812 to 1826* (New York, 1923), pp. 38-39.

Even at its best, the life of the circuit rider was fraught with danger and difficulty, but the Allegheny circuits demanded extraordinary qualities of endurance, determination, godliness, and self-denial. The Allegheny circuits of West Virginia which were included in the Ohio Conference were "the largest, most difficult and most dreaded" of any in the conference. Known as "Brush Colleges," they often fell either to young inexperienced ministers or to preachers for whom no other places could be found. Preachers assigned to these circuits faced not only cold, storms, and swollen streams, but also hunger, lack of lodging, danger from wild beasts, and, until 1795, the risk of attack by Indians. John Stewart, who served the Little Kanawha Circuit in 1817–1818, wrote that "some of our rides between appointments were forty miles and more, and much of the way no roads. We would carry the tomahawk with us and blaze our path on the trees through the forest, or follow the blazed tracks that had been made by our predecessors. Notwithstanding the utmost care, we would frequently lose our path." Even the indefatigable Bishop Asbury admitted that in planting Methodism in the mountains of West Virginia he had suffered hardships "known only to God and ourselves."[43]

Material remuneration in the mountainous circuits, moreover, was in inverse proportion to the exactions of the assignments. The stipulated salary for Methodist circuit riders was sixty-four dollars a year, but it is doubtful that many preachers of West Virginia in the early nineteenth century collected that amount. William Burke, a minister on the Guyandotte Circuit, declared that there was "but little prospect of support from the people among whom we labored, and none from any other source." Eighteen-year-old Henry Bascom, appointed to the same circuit in 1814, traveled three thousand miles, preached four hundred sermons, and received $12.10.[44] Yet, in the face of the dangers and privations with which they were confronted, these circuit riders displayed a raw courage and devotion to duty which could

[43] Sweet, *Circuit-Rider Days along the Ohio*, pp. 51-52; Asbury, *Journal*, II, 303; Finley, *Sketches of Western Methodism*, pp. 87, 387, 448-49; Stevens, *History of the Methodist Episcopal Church*, III, 327-28.
[44] Finley, *Sketches of Western Methodism*, p. 87; Sweet, ed., *Circuit-Rider Days along the Ohio*, pp. 38-39.

hardly have failed to win the admiration and respect of pioneers who themselves had undergone similar experiences.

If the Methodist circuit rider found the tangible rewards of his labors small, he must also have found the spiritual and psychological returns immeasurable. He was part of an organization whose confidence and esprit de corps were hardly matched by other denominations. Its small, intimate class meetings with their watch nights, sacraments, and social satisfactions filled a deep need for isolated pioneers. Quarterly Meetings brought together circuit riders, local preachers, exhorters, class leaders, and communicants—often numbering in the hundreds—from the entire circuit. Here the pioneer heard Methodism's most effective preachers, partook of the sacraments and love feasts, sang the rousing Wesleyan hymns, and had his faith renewed. Here, if he had not already heard Francis Asbury on one of the occasions when Asbury had left the beaten path "to seek the outcasts of the people," he perchance beheld the venerable bishop and sensed his own part in a great religious crusade.[45]

As the Methodist Church grew, the Quarterly Conference lost much of its excitement and festiveness, but by then the camp meeting had become a vital part of the Methodist practice. Indeed, the camp meeting was in some respects the outgrowth of the Quarterly Meetings, where because of lack of buildings adequate to accommodate the throngs who attended, services were not infrequently held outdoors. Equally important, perhaps, in the development of the camp meeting was the fervor that accompanied a revival which swept the frontier areas of the state in 1802. The first evidences of the revival appeared in a private prayer meeting, where ministers from Kentucky recognized the "power of spiritual truths over the minds of men, as they had seen it in the West." The date of the first camp meeting in West Virginia is unknown, but it could not have been long after the famous Cane Ridge revival in Bourbon County, Kentucky, in 1801. Yet, to trace West Virginia camp meetings to this

[45] Accounts of Methodist society meetings and Quarterly Meetings abound in *Journal of John Smith . . . on the Greenbrier Circuit,* July 4, 1787, to July 8, 1788; *Thomas Scott's Journal of the Ohio Circuit,* 1793; and the *Journal of Robert Ayres* [Redstone Circuit], May 16, 1786, to June 16, 1787. See also Asbury, *Journal,* I, 427; II, 25, 35, 37, passim.

gathering or to techniques used earlier in Kentucky by James McGready, the Presbyterian minister, might be allotting too much credit to Kentucky precedents and not enough to well-entrenched practices in the Allegheny area.[46]

By any standards, the response to the camp meeting was little short of phenomenal. At a ten-day gathering at Hedges Chapel in Berkeley County in August, 1804, at least sixty-four persons were converted. Daniel Hitt, one of the ministers present, exultantly declared that "it seemed as if I could live and die at such a place and in such exercise." Nor was Hitt alone in his feelings. Jacob Young, a preacher present at the Short Creek camp meeting in 1810, reported that there was "much ministerial help, and our elder exerted himself to the very utmost of his abilities." On the other hand, exuberance must often have exceeded propriety. Bishop Asbury deplored some of the excesses associated with camp meetings, and en route to an assemblage on the Little Kanawha, wrote in his diary: "Lord, prepare me by thy grace for the patient endurance of hunger, heat, labour, the clownishness of ignorant piety, the impudence of the impious, unreasonable preachers, and more unreasonable heretics and heresy!"[47]

Disturbances and misconduct were not uncommon at camp meetings. In an effort to prevent rowdiness at the Hedges Chapel gathering in 1804, guards were maintained both within the congregation and among the tents and wagons during the entire ten days of the meeting, until at its close the congregation "struck tents, blew the trumpets and journeyed." Jacob Young declared that at Short Creek in 1810 "the rowdies annoyed us exceedingly. They pitched their tents on the hillsides round about, and sold whiskey, brandy, and cider. I visited and conversed with them till I found I could accomplish nothing in that way." Thereupon, said the determined Young, "I then took a strong man with me and a hammer, went to their tents,

---

[46] Stevens, *History of the Methodist Episcopal Church*, II, 223; William H. Foote, *Sketches of Virginia, Historical and Biographical*, Second Series, 2d ed., rev. (Philadelphia, 1856), pp. 288-89.
[47] "An Early Camp Meeting in Jefferson County," *Magazine of the Jefferson County Historical Society*, XIV (December, 1948), 15; Young, *Autobiography of a Pioneer*, pp. 269-70; Asbury, *Journal*, III, 346.

knocked in the heads of their casks, and spilled their liquor on the ground." This willingness of leaders to take strong measures was undoubtedly in many instances the only thing which maintained the decorum necessary to such vast gatherings.[48]

Although their spirited meetings and centralized authority promoted cohesiveness, the Methodists were not entirely free of cleavage and dissension. In 1827 latent discontent, reaching as far back as the first General Conference, held in 1792, rose to the surface and shook the foundations of the church structure. The fundamental issues concerned the great power and life tenure of the bishops, the lack of lay representation in the General Conferences, and the arbitrary assignment of ministers and other ecclesiastical officials. The immediate occasion for discord was the suspension of several ministers charged with circulating *Mutual Rights,* a reformist periodical, and criticizing orthodox officials in the church. In some respects, these efforts to democratize the ecclesiastical structure of the church were a religious counterpart of the political liberalism often referred to as Jacksonian democracy. Representatives of the discontented elements met at Baltimore in November, 1827, called themselves Associated Methodist Reformers, and drew up a petition for presentation to the General Conference scheduled to meet at Pittsburgh in May, 1828. They called for reinstatement of the expelled ministers and admission of laymen to the General Conference.

When the Pittsburgh Conference, unmoved by the urgings of persuasive men such as Henry Bascom and the eloquent pleas of Asa Shinn, rejected the petition, the breach between the church leadership and the Reformers seemed irreparable. Several congregations dominated by Reformers severed their connections with the Methodist Episcopal Church, and on November 12, 1828, about a hundred representatives of the liberal groups met at Baltimore and adopted "Articles of Association." Two years later, on November 2, 1830, eighty-three delegates met at Baltimore and formally established the Methodist Protestant Church.

In trans-Allegheny West Virginia, support for the Reformers

48 "An Early Camp Meeting in Jefferson County," p. 15; Young, *Autobiography of a Pioneer,* p. 270.

centered largely in the Monongahela Valley, where influential laymen such as Thomas Barns of Fairmont and John Hacker and David Smith of Hacker's Creek, watched the events of 1827 and 1828 with keen interest. In October, 1829, the Reverend John Mitchell and David Smith organized, under the Articles of Association, a separatist society at Harmony Church on Hacker's Creek and won over virtually the entire congregation. Another society was organized about the same time at Fairmont at the home of Thomas Barns, a brother-in-law of Asa Shinn. When the Methodist Protestant Church was established, trans-Allegheny West Virginia was included first in its Ohio Conference and, after 1833, in the Pittsburgh Conference.

During its first quarter of a century the Methodist Protestant Church experienced substantial growth in West Virginia, particularly in the north-central sections. In 1855 the Western Virginia Conference, consisting of trans-Allegheny West Virginia, was created and Reverend Peter T. Laishley was elected president. The new conference included 50 meeting houses, 19 unstationed ministers, 26 licensed preachers, and 3,036 members. The Morgantown and Pruntytown circuits with 385 and 375 members, respectively, were the largest in the conference, but the Evansville, Jackson, and Braxton circuits, each had more than 300. The Greenbrier Circuit, the largest in southern West Virginia, had only 70 members.[49]

The Methodists and Baptists swept across the Alleghenies in the face of advantages which at the close of the Revolutionary War appeared to rest largely with the Presbyterians. Primarily because of heavy Scotch-Irish immigration, the Presbyterian Church had been the fastest growing religious organization in the colonies during the two generations preceding the war. In New York, New Jersey, and Pennsylvania—the latter two colonies the source of a considerable migration to the Allegheny frontier —the Presbyterians were stronger than all other denominations combined. Indeed, about half of the five hundred Presbyterian communities in the colonies in 1776 were in those areas from which the greatest number of West Virginia settlers were drawn.

[49] I[saac] A. Barnes, *The Methodist Protestant Church in West Virginia* (Baltimore, Md., 1926), pp. 15-19, 68-70, 471-72, passim.

These pioneers naturally looked to their own church for spiritual sustenance. During the 1780's the Presbyterians gave indication that they might meet the challenge.[50]

In the Eastern Panhandle of West Virginia, where it had languished for several years, Presbyterianism took on new vitality. In 1782 and 1783 old congregations were strengthened and new ones were established at several places on the upper Potomac, including Moorefield, Frankfort, Romney, Springfield, and Gerrardstown. The flourishing state of the church in the lower Shenandoah Valley led to the organization in 1784 of the Winchester Presbytery, with five ministers and sixteen churches. About two-thirds of these churches were in West Virginia.[51]

Presbyterian ministers were in the vanguard of those intrepid and dedicated itinerants who crossed the Alleghenies even before the war was over. In the summer of 1775, John McMillan, a recent licentiate of the New Castle Presbytery, made a tour of frontier settlements and spent several days at the end of July preaching to congregations in the Greenbrier and Tygart valleys. John Alderson, the pioneer Baptist minister in the Greenbrier area, declared that during his first seven years in West Virginia he did not see another Baptist minister but that during that time "two or three licensed itinerant Presbyterian preachers passed through the settlement."[52]

Undoubtedly, one of the ministers to whom Alderson referred was John McCue, who was licensed by the Hanover Presbytery in 1782 to serve as missionary to the Greenbrier and Tygart Valley settlements. Directed to establish the "first church on the western waters," McCue organized three congregations in the Greenbrier region in 1783. One of these churches was located near Lewisburg, another at Renick, and the third about

---

[50] William Warren Sweet, *Religion on the American Frontier, 1783–1840; The Presbyterians: A Collection of Source Materials* (New York, 1964), pp. 21-32.

[51] U. S., W. P. A., *Inventory of the Church Archives of West Virginia: The Presbyterian Churches*, pp. 212-20; Maxwell and Swisher, *History of Hampshire County*, pp. 377-78.

[52] Dwight Raymond Guthrie, *John McMillan: The Apostle of Presbyterianism in the West, 1752–1833* (Pittsburgh, Pa., 1952), pp. 21-23, 203-204, 208-209, 212. The latter references are to McMillan's "Journal," which is printed in *ibid.*, pp. 202-72. See also W. H. Cobb, "Presbyterianism in the Tygarts Valley," *Magazine of History-Biography of Randolph County Historical Society*, No. 2, p. 27; Semple, *History of . . . the Baptists in Virginia*, p. 426.

two miles south of Union. McCue's work in the Tygart Valley was strictly that of a missionary. About the same time that McCue was active in these areas, other missionaries appeared in the Kanawha, Monongahela, and upper Ohio valleys.[53]

In spite of its advantageous position in the 1780's and its widespread appeal in western Pennsylvania, Presbyterianism proved, on the whole, ill-adapted to the religious demands of the Allegheny frontier. Of twenty-two Presbyterian churches established in West Virginia between 1773 and 1800, about half were in the socially and economically mature Potomac section. Five were in the Northern Panhandle, which included a number of settlers from the Potomac region, and five were in the Greenbrier Valley, which had a heavy Scotch-Irish population. The remaining church, that at Morgantown, owed its founding in part to the missionary activity of the nearby Redstone Presbytery. On the other hand, as late as 1830, ten large counties of north-central West Virginia, with a population of 60,000, had no settled minister except Asa Brooks, the pastor of the French Creek church.[54] Moreover, Presbyterian missionaries, lacking the organization of the Methodists or the unrestraint of the Baptists, found themselves at an increasing disadvantage.

The disparity between religious opportunity and the quantitative success of the Presbyterians stemmed in part from their insistence upon both an educated ministry and a literate congregation. Men such as John McElhenney at Lewisburg, Henry Foote at Romney, and Henry Ruffner at Charleston did almost as much to advance the educational opportunities of their communities as they did to promote their ·spiritual welfare. These dual demands upon the minister were set forth, for example, by residents of Clarksburg, who in 1830 appealed to

[53] U. S., W. P. A., *Inventory of Church Archives of West Virginia: The Presbyterian Churches*, pp. 108, 110-11; Statement by unidentified person, Draper MSS, 13CC193. Varying accounts of the location of the church near Lewisburg are given in the former, p. 108, which places it on William Feamster's farm, and the latter, which states that it was on Richard Hammond's farm and lists Hammond, William Feamster, and William Hammond as its first elders. For missionary activity in other areas of West Virginia, see U. S., W. P. A., *Inventory of Church Archives of West Virginia: The Presbyterian Churches*, pp. 23, 57, 84, 87, 155.

[54] U. S., W. P. A., *Inventory of the Church Archives of West Virginia: The Presbyterian Churches*, pp. 57-59, 83-87, 107-13, 211-21; [Phineas Chapin] to L. Woods, January 2, 1830, Clarksburg Presbyterian Church Records, 1798–1903.

Andover Seminary for a minister, preferably one who had "received the honors" of that institution. The petitioners made it clear that they wanted no missionary, but a full-time minister for "the education, both spiritual and temporal" of their children. They offered the minister tuition receipts and a pledge by four leading citizens of Clarksburg to supplement these collections, if necessary, in order that he might be assured of $400 per year.[55]

Confronted with the double burden of transplanting two institutions simultaneously, the Presbyterian Church soon found the frontier outracing it. Its effectiveness in West Virginia was limited largely to those areas where population was sufficiently concentrated to support both churches and schools. On the other hand, the Methodists and Baptists, with less cultural baggage, kept pace with advancing settlement and won many converts who had once seemed likely to belong to the Presbyterians.

Even less of a proselyting denomination was the Episcopal Church. In 1840 there were only eleven Episcopal churches in trans-Allegheny West Virginia. Most of them were in the larger towns, such as Charleston, Wellsburg, Wheeling, Moundsville, Follansbee, Morgantown, and Clarksburg. Three of those in the Northern Panhandle were founded by Joseph Doddridge, an Episcopal minister and the author of a classic work on pioneer folkways. Several of the congregations were drawn chiefly from well-to-do immigrants who had held fast to their denominational ties. A typical example was St. John's in the Valley, which owed its existence to the patronage of Judge George W. Summers, who provided it with quarters in an abandoned stillhouse on his farm at Scary on the Kanawha River.[56]

With an emphasis upon ritual and a distaste for the emotional services characteristic of frontier churches, the Episcopalians were even more reluctant than the Presbyterians to resort to an untrained ministry. The Reverend Norman Nash, a man of advanced years, was at first refused permission to preach in

[55] [Phineas Chapin] to L. Woods, January 2, 1830, Clarksburg Presbyterian Church Records, 1798–1903.
[56] U. S., W. P. A., *Inventory of the Church Archives of West Virginia: The Protestant Episcopal Church,* pp. 28-42.

Hampshire County because he had not studied languages. Nash, however, insisted that he was "called of God and moved by the Holy Ghost" to serve the people there. The church authorities finally relented on the ground that in Hampshire County "the ancient languages were but little known and not much required."[57]

Competing denominations on the Allegheny frontier waged their religious battles partly upon doctrinal issues and interpretations of the Scriptures. To be sure, debates and discussions of fine points of theology often produced more heat than light. Ministers often attended religious services conducted by their rivals, sometimes apparently for the express purpose of exposing "unscriptural" tenets. When John Smith, the pioneer Methodist circuit rider in the Greenbrier area, preached at the house of James McClung, he had John McCue, the local Presbyterian minister, in his congregation. At the conclusion of his sermon, McCue raised several questions, one of which was whether Smith believed in the final perseverance of the saints. When Smith replied that he did not, McCue flew into a rage and declared that Smith should "hear from him again." About two weeks later, when Smith was again preaching at McClung's, McCue interrupted his sermon with charges that Smith preached false doctrines and sang hymns which were "rank popery." McCue then reverted to the question of the final perseverance of the saints but found Smith adamant in his beliefs. Then, said Smith, McCue "fell to Abuscing and black-guarding of me And said if his office did not prohibit him to be A Striker that he would lace me well." To this threat, Smith replied that he "believ'd that was not all that hinder'd him." At last McCue departed, and the bloodshed which Smith had expected at any moment was averted.[58]

Fortunately, the interdenominational struggles were not often conducted in such an unchristian spirit. In scores of pioneer settlements rival denominations shared meeting houses, and there were numerous instances in which churches permitted

[57] Meade, *Old Churches, Ministers and Families of Virginia*, II, 309-10.
[58] Journal of John Smith . . . on the Greenbrier Circuit, July 4, 1787, to July 8, 1788, pp. 19, 23-25.

members to attend services of another denomination when ministers of their own faith were unavailable.[59] Even in areas where competition was intense, a spirit of fairness usually prevailed. About 1830, for example, the Disciples of Christ began to make progress within the bounds of the Ohio and West Liberty circuits of the Methodist Church. The Methodists rose to the challenge, and Leonidas L. Hamline, a recently installed pastor of the Wellsburg church, proved so successful that a short time later one Campbellite remarked: "We have no Church; Hamline has preached us out of existence, and yet he has never said any thing about us." Even Alexander Campbell himself could find little to criticize in Hamline's preaching.[60]

Prior to 1840, West Virginia churches, like those of most other sections of the Alleghenies, were but little disrupted by the slavery controversy which had by then begun to stir the country. Of the 430,499 slaves in Virginia, only 18,488 were in West Virginia. Most of the latter were in the Eastern Panhandle, the Greenbrier area, and the Kanawha Valley. Even in these sections there was substantial opposition to the institution. In the Eastern Panhandle, for example, several prominent residents founded the Shepherdstown Colonization Society in 1819 and affiliated it with the American Colonization Society, which sought to encourage free Negroes to settle in Africa.[61]

The lack of serious internal strife over slavery among West Virginia churches was due in part to policies pursued by the Methodists and Baptists, who claimed the vast majority of the

[59] Asbury, *Journal*, II, 37; U. S., W. P. A., *Inventory of the Church Archives of West Virginia: The Presbyterian Churches*, pp. 62-66, 115, 155-56, 215; P[hineas] Chapin to the Quarterly Conference of the Methodist Episcopal Church, December 4, 1830, Clarksburg Presbyterian Church Records, 1798–1903; C. A. Swearingen and Charles Lewis to [Phineas Chapin], December 7, 1830, *ibid;* Record Book for the Zoar Church [1824–1868], May 20, 1826; Records of the Greenbrier Association of Baptists [1825–1868], p. 47. According to tradition, the joint use by Methodists and Presbyterians of a building at Greenbank occasioned some difficulty. When the former used the structure, they had to remove the Presbyterian "anxious seat," and the latter, in turn, had to remove the Methodist "mourner's bench." U. S., W. P. A., *Inventory of the Church Archives of West Virginia: The Presbyterian Churches*, p. 115
[60] Young, *Autobiography of a Pioneer*, pp. 410-13.
[61] Constitution of the Shepherdstown Colonization Society, 1819, Alexander Robinson Boteler Papers, Duke University Library.

state's churchgoers. The Methodist Church, with more than half the congregations in the state, backed away from its strong antislavery position of 1784 and at the Mount Vernon Conference in 1785 partially came to terms with Virginia's "peculiar institution." The Quadrennial Conferences of 1796, 1800, and 1804 removed restrictions upon slaveholding by church members and placed control of the institution in the hands of the Annual Conferences, which were more sensitive to popular attitudes in their respective jurisdictions.[62]

The Annual Conferences embracing territory now in West Virginia concentrated much of their antislavery effort toward discouraging the buying and selling of chattels. In 1812 the Ohio Conference, which included most of trans-Allegheny West Virginia, prescribed terms of service for slaves subsequently purchased by church members. Similar regulations were enforced by the Quarterly Conference of the Berkeley Circuit, which between 1810 and 1818 examined contracts involving the purchase of slaves and specified reasonable terms of service which owners might have from their Negroes prior to freeing them.[63]

The Baptists, even less than the Methodists, were drawn from the slaveholding classes. Moreover, decentralization of authority among the Baptists tended to localize disputes either in the congregation or association. In 1786 the Greenbrier Baptist Church, in response to a query from the New River Baptist Association, went on record as considering "it to be an Evil in keeping them [the slaves] in bondage for life," but begged that "Our Church having but few in their Possesion [sic] we hope our Brethren will not think it hard, if we lie neuter in this matter."

As slavery, a recognized buttress of the social and economic system of the South, came under attack from Abolitionists, attitudes in slaveholding areas of Allegheny West Virginia

[62] Donald G. Mathews, *Slavery and Methodism: A Chapter in American Morality, 1780–1845* (Princeton, N. J., 1965), pp. 3-29; Walter Brownlow Posey, *Frontier Mission: A History of Religion West of the Southern Appalachians to 1861* (Lexington, Ky., 1966), pp. 327-34.

[63] Sweet, *Circuit-Rider Days along the Ohio,* pp. 108-109; Steward's Book for the Berkeley Circuit [of the Methodist Church], 1807–1820, pp. 43, 45, 49, 51, 81, 85, Methodist Historical Society, Lovely Lane Museum.

hardened into the defensive molds prevalent in the South. As early as 1801, the Greenbrier Baptist Church made it clear that "it is thought Expedient that if any of our Negro Brethren or Sisters Should Join this Church by letter or Experience they must Expect to be treated as in the Character of Servants." Nowhere were West Virginia churches prepared to grant Negro members equality with white communicants. Most of the churches constructed in the state during the 1830's and 1840's provided galleries or other sections where Negro members might be segregated from the remainder of the congregation.[64]

Once the churches split nationally, tensions within West Virginia congregations increased. The break in the Methodist Church in 1844 produced cleavages not unlike those which troubled all denominations in West Virginia. Sam Black, a well-known Southern Methodist circuit rider in the mountainous parts of Fayette and Greenbrier counties, had experiences typical of those of many of his associates. In 1847 he found himself "in the hot of battle" with a Northern Methodist on his circuit. It was not long, however, before Black had captured all but two of the appointments on the circuit, and he expected to have one of them within a short time. In one locality he had won over 110 Methodists, leaving "only one northern man and that a woman" to his rival. Five years later the aggressive Black carried his religious battle to the northern part of West Virginia, where his enemies were numerous. Although faced with strong opposition and even imputations against his character, Black persevered and within a short time his rivals were "as silent . . . as frogs in the month of January."[65]

In spite of the zeal of religious leaders and the increasing involvement of churches in political and social questions, thousands of West Virginians in the Allegheny region remained virtually untouched by organized religion as late as the 1840's. The poverty and isolation which retarded educational develop-

[64] The Minutes of the Greenbrier Baptist Church [1781–1835], June 24, 1786, September 27, 1801.
[65] S[am] Black to George W. Smith, June 7, 1847, George W. Smith Papers; Sam Black to George W. Smith, April 9, 1852, *ibid.;* Sam Black to George W. Smith, May 27, 1852, *ibid.*

ment also proved detrimental to the planting of churches. Agents for tract societies reported not only large numbers of illiterate families who did not even possess a Bible but also found nearly grown children who had never seen a minister. Moreover, where churches were established, their existence was often precarious. Bad weather and sickness combined with mountainous terrain to prevent the Zoar Baptist Church in Nicholas County from meeting for four months during the winter of 1826–1827. The Greenbrier Baptist Church, faced with a depletion or apathy of its members, decided on June 24, 1786, that "every member absenting themselves three times without Lawful Excuse, is worthy of Censure." The church was soon forced to modify its unrealistic ordinance, and on July 26, 1788, it instructed its clerk to draw up a list of members and to arrange their names in accordance with the distance which they lived from the church. Those residing near the meeting house must attend once each month, those within a radius of fifteen miles once each quarter, and those who lived more than fifteen miles once each year in order to retain their membership.[66]

The difficulties encountered in isolated, mountainous areas, however, cannot obscure the rapid growth and increasing sophistication of West Virginia churches during the early nineteenth century. By 1840 log meeting houses had largely been supplanted by brick or frame structures. By that time the Methodists had virtually covered the Allegheny areas, and the Presbyterians and Episcopalians had established congregations in most of the major towns and thickly settled sections. Baptist strength, though widely dispersed, was yet concentrated among the poor, the uneducated, and the isolated elements, but more and more men of means and position were now joining them. Significantly, the Greenbrier Baptist Association, in some respects a bellwether of Baptist fortunes in much of West Virginia, served notice in 1846 that it would actively seek such memberships. Believing it necessary to provide every town with a well-qualified minister " 'clothed in the whole armor of God,' "

[66] The Minutes of the Greenbrier Baptist Church [1781–1835], June 24, 1786, July 26, 1788.

and with "good and respectable houses of worship," it declared that it was "high time, that the Baptists should leave the bushes and suburbs, & enter the main streets of every city, town and village of the land."[67] This realization by the Baptists was in itself an indication that the frontier period in the religious history of the Alleghenies was nearing its end.

[67] Records of the Greenbrier Association of Baptists [1825–1868], p. 276.

Chapter Thirteen

The First Flush of Seeming Wealth

Once they had freed their lands of the Indian menace and established their homesteads upon an enduring basis, Allegheny pioneers began to give thought to their need for domestic manufacturing. Cut off by the mountains from eastern and foreign sources of supply, early settlers from the time of their arrival had been forced into simple household manufactures. Fortunately, nature had compensated for their isolation and the ruggedness of the terrain by endowing the land with abundant mineral resources, including salt, coal, and iron ore, covering it with thousands of acres of superb timber, and supplying it with countless streams suited to the development of water power. Only the hand of the industrial entrepreneur appeared needed to transform latent resources into teeming wealth.

The curtailment of foreign imports during the Napoleonic wars and the cessation of trade with Great Britian during the War of 1812 placed the expansion of American manufacturing in the realm of the imperative. In the ultranationalistic western country, including trans-Allegheny West Virginia, Pennsylvania, and Kentucky, establishment of domestic manufactures assumed the character of high patriotic duty, and scores of small industries were set up. From about 1807 to 1815 these nascent enterprises enjoyed remarkable freedom from foreign competition, and during the early postwar years their growth was fostered by protective tariffs, enacted first as essential to national security and subsequently as an obligation of government to a sound and self-sufficient economy.

Among the earliest of West Virginia industries—and one that antedated the arrival of the first white settlers—was the manufacture of salt. The first saltmaking facilities in Allegheny West Virginia were set up at Malden on the Kanawha River at springs which had been frequented by Indians for untold generations.

Joseph Ruffner, the owner, leased the salt property to Elisha Brooks, who in 1797 erected the first salt furnace in the western country. Brooks' furnace consisted of about two dozen kettles set up in two rows, with a flue beneath them, a firebox at one end, and a chimney at the other. Brooks obtained the brine by sinking gums, or large hollow logs eight or ten feet long, into the earth and lifting the salt water by means of a sweep to the end of which was attached a large bucket. In this crude manner, he produced about 150 bushels of salt a day and sold it at the furnace for eight to ten cents per pound. This Kanawha "red salt," so called because of the iron impurities in it, became a favorite in the western country for curing butter and meats.[1]

The first significant advances in salt manufacture along the Kanawha were made by David and Joseph Ruffner, who inherited the salt property upon their father's death in 1802. Seeking a larger and stronger supply of brine than that used by Brooks, the Ruffner brothers sank new gums into the marshy salt lands, but at a depth of sixteen or seventeen feet they struck bedrock. In penetrating the rock strata, the Ruffners revealed uncommon ingenuity and rare gifts for improvisation. By means of a long iron drill with a 2½-inch chisel bit and watertight tubing made of two long semicircular strips of wood neatly fitted together and wrapped from end to end with tarred twine, they drove through forty feet of rock. Their efforts were rewarded in 1808, when they struck a brine which yielded a bushel of salt for each 200 gallons, or 2½ times as strong as that found in the shallower wells. This discovery enabled the Ruffners to produce about 25 bushels, or 1,250 pounds, of salt a day at their furnace and to reduce the price to four cents per pound.

A younger brother of the Ruffners, Tobias, suspected—correct-

---

[1] The original salt lick or "Great Buffalo Lick," which drew attention to the salt resources of the Kanawha Valley, was on the north side of the Kanawha River a few hundred yards above the mouth of Campbell's Creek. It was twelve to fourteen rods in length. In 1755 Mary Ingles, who had been captured by Shawnees near Blacksburg, Virginia, helped her captors make salt there while the party was en route to the Indian towns in Ohio. George W. Atkinson, *History of Kanawha County, from Its Organization in 1789 until the Present Time* (Charleston, W. Va., 1876), pp. 223-27. See also John P. Hale, *Trans-Allegheny Pioneers: Historical Sketches of the First White Settlers West of the Alleghenies*, 2d ed. (Charleston, W. Va., 1931), p. 32.

ly, it proved—that a vast saline reservoir lay beneath the rock strata of the Kanawha Valley. Hoping to find a yet stronger brine, he leased one of his brothers' abandoned wells and began to bore more deeply. Using wrought iron bits and substituting a horse mill for manpower, young Ruffner drilled to a depth of 410 feet, where he tapped a brine so rich that 45 gallons yielded a bushel of salt.

The successes of the Ruffners touched off a veritable frenzy of drilling. Owners of property on both sides of the Kanawha River for a distance of about ten miles above Charleston sank wells and built furnaces. By the end of 1815, 52 furnaces were in operation and producing between 2,500 and 3,000 bushels of salt a day, and still other furnaces were under construction. The Kanawha Salines, as the area was called, became, along with the Onondaga saltworks in western New York and Saltville in southwestern Virginia, one of the most important salt manufacturing centers in the United States.[2]

During the next quarter of a century notable improvements were introduced into saltmaking. Tin, copper, and iron tubing replaced wooden tubing. The "seed bag," a casing made of calfskin or buckskin, enabled drillers to seal joints in the tubing to prevent weak brine from lesser depths from diluting stronger solutions obtained from below. In 1830 William Morris scored a major breakthrough in drilling with the invention of "slips," a device which, used with bits and heavy iron sinkers, accelerated the boring of wells and largely solved the problem of having tools become stuck in the wells. In 1817 David Ruffner experimented with coal as a fuel for his salt furnace with such success that all saltmakers soon discontinued the use of wood. After 1841 many followed the lead of William Tompkins and began to use natural gas for this purpose. Other advances included the introduction in 1827 of the steam engine to pump brine from the wells and in 1835 of the steam furnace, or multiple effect evaporator, an invention of George H. Patrick, who had moved to the Kanawha Valley after failing to impress Onondaga salt

---

2 Atkinson, *History of Kanawha County*, pp. 226-31; Henry Ruffner, "Notes on a Tour from Virginia to Tennessee, in the Months of July and August, 1838," *Southern Literary Messenger*, V (January, 1839), 47.

manufacturers with his apparatus. Because of their success in perfecting tools and techniques used in drilling, Kanawha well-borers were employed by Edwin Drake in sinking the Titusville, Pennsylvania, oil well in 1859.[3]

Salt production at the Kanawha Salines kept pace with technological advances. In 1829 the area boasted 60 salt wells capable of supplying 95 to 100 furnaces. Actually, 72 furnaces had been constructed, and 49 were in operation. These furnaces manufactured 989,700 bushels of salt that year. The capacity of most salt furnaces was between 25,000 and 50,000 bushels of salt per year, but the large furnace of Joseph Friend and Son at the mouth of Campbell's Creek was capable of producing about 100,000 bushels. With a supply of brine "apparently, as inexhaustible as the flow of the Kanawha River itself," salt manufacturers continued to increase production until 1846, when the output reached 3,224,786 bushels.[4]

In taking advantage of the immense salt resources, Kanawha Valley producers very quickly encountered the problems of overproduction and depressed prices. The War of 1812 and the heavy demands by government contractors artificially stimulated the industry almost from the moment of its birth. Seeking a share of the profits, "rapacious adventureres" obtained short-term leases on valuable salt properties and "so roguishly and inattentively" managed their works, leaving impurities and "other offensive matter" in their salt, that they undermined the reputation which Kanawha salt had earned in western markets. The establishment of a salt inspector at the Salines, however, eliminated that problem. More serious was the deflation of the market at the close of the war and the heavy salt imports, chiefly of British origin, which were landed at New Orleans and distributed along the Mississippi and Ohio rivers by steamboat. Because of this competition, Kanawha saltmakers were forced by 1817 to sell their salt at sharply reduced prices, and even then they were left with substantial stocks on hand.[5]

[3] Atkinson, *History of Kanawha County*, pp. 231-39; John P. Hale, *History of the Great Kanawha Valley*, 2 vols. (Madison, Wis., 1891), I, 211-20.

[4] Atkinson, *History of Kanawha County*, pp. 237-38, 249; Kanawha County Legislative Petitions, February 23, 1831.

[5] Kanawha County Legislative Petitions, December 17, 1813.

In order to adjust production to demands in the western country, saltmakers at the Kanawha Salines in 1817 formed the Kanawha Salt Company, agreed to limit the output of salt in 1818 to 450,000 bushels, and assigned quotas to each of the subscribers. The "trust," as it has been called, was given authority to regulate the quality of salt, prescribe proper packaging, establish a joint sales agency, and set prices for salt. In some cases it "dead-rented" salt properties, or paid owners to close their operations, in much the same manner that the federal government in the twentieth century curtailed certain types of agricultural production. The salt combination lasted sixteen years. From time to time thereafter, manufacturers made new agreements, particularly after salt produced at Pomeroy, Ohio, began to cut into western markets.[6]

The stimulus of wartime conditions inspired other efforts to exploit the vast salt resources of Allegheny sections of West Virginia. At Bulltown, on the Little Kanawha, salt was produced by John Haymond and Benjamin Wilson from 1809 until 1823 and intermittently by others until the Civil War. In July, 1814, John G. Jackson opened a well about three miles above Clarksburg on the West Fork of the Monongahela. Although the brine was only 25 or 30 percent as strong as that obtainable on the Kanawha and was pumped by means of "horse power," Jackson was able to supply a substantial part of the local needs and to reduce prices to approximately prewar levels.[7]

Almost as essential to pioneer life was iron, which was used for a variety of agricultural and household purposes. Small, workable veins of iron were found in many parts of the Alleghenies, and numerous small furnaces were erected for smelting the ore and manufacturing bar iron, the raw material of the pioneer blacksmith. The first production of iron in West Virginia, and perhaps the first west of the Blue Ridge, was attempted in 1742 by Thomas Mayberry at Bloomery on the

---

[6] A copy of the "Articles of Agreement" of the salt manufacturers in 1817 is in Elizabeth Cometti and Festus P. Summers, eds., *The Thirty-Fifth State: A Documentary History of West Virginia* (Morgantown, W. Va., 1966), pp. 197-203.

[7] John Davisson Sutton, *History of Braxton County and Central West Virginia* (Sutton, W. Va., 1919), p. 292; Harrison County Legislative Petitions, November 10, 1814.

314 The Allegheny Frontier

lower Shenandoah River. The furnace of Peter Tarr, built on King's Creek near Weirton in 1794, probably produced the first iron manufactured in transmontane West Virginia. Tarr made cooking utensils, iron grates, and household wares. He also supplied some of the cannonballs used by Commodore Oliver Hazard Perry against the British on Lake Erie during the War of 1812.[8]

About the beginning of the nineteenth century important ironworks were established in the Monongahela Valley. The Decker's Creek Iron Works, also known as Rock Forge, was in operation as early as 1798 and after 1800 was managed successively by Samuel Hanway, John Stealey and his sons-in-law, Richard Watts and Jacob Kiger, and Jesse Evans. Stealey is said to have manufactured stoves there prior to 1825. The most extensive ironworks were located on Cheat River. Pleasant Furnace, built on Quarry Run about 1798, produced substantial quantities of bar iron, which its owner, Samuel Jackson, sold for cash, grain, and country products. About 1809 Jackson began to manufacture handmade nails, and in 1822 he installed nail-cutting machinery. Between 1822 and 1848, the Henry Clay, Woodgrove, and Anna furnaces, all within a four-mile radius of Ice's Ferry on Cheat River, were associated with the Pleasant Furnace. As early as 1830 the Jackson Iron Works was pronounced the best in Virginia, if not, indeed, in the entire western country. In 1839 the facilities were purchased by the Ellicott family of Maryland. Under their management a rolling mill, puddling and boiling furnace, nail factory, foundry, various shops, and a large number of dwelling houses were erected. During its peak years in the 1840's the Jackson, or Cheat, Iron Works employed about 1,200 workers.

The availability of iron stimulated other manufacturing industries in the Monongahela Valley. By 1835 Morgantown had a plow factory. Between 1838 and 1841 Joel Nuzum and Henry and Hugh Daugherty established a foundry in the town, and in 1844 Henry Daugherty set up the Durbannah Steam Foundry, which produced stoves, grates, hollowware, and cane mills. At

[8] U. S., Work Projects Administration, Writers' Program, *West Virginia: A Guide to the Mountain State* (New York, 1941), pp. 45, 301-302, 483.

a Whig rally in Morgantown during the Presidential election of 1840, wagonloads of ironworkers threw sample nails into the streets as symbols of prosperity and inadvertently paid tribute to the importance of the iron industry in the economic life of the upper Monongahela Valley.[9]

Iron manufacturing and related industries were important also in the Northern Panhandle and, to a lesser extent, in the Eastern Panhandle. By 1835 rolling mills of the Wheeling Iron Works were producing about 1,000 tons of iron annually. About 300 tons were cut into nails, and most of the remainder was processed into bar, boiler, sheet, and hoop iron. At that time Wheeling also had four foundries and four steam engine establishments, which gave employment to 140 workmen. Perhaps typical of these enterprises was the Wheeling Manufacturing Company, whose foundry and shops were equipped to produce steam engines and other iron products. Centers of the iron industry in the Eastern Panhandle included Martinsburg, with an iron and brass foundry, Glencoe in Hampshire County, which had "an iron forge in great repute," and the Moorefield area, which by 1835 boasted four ironworks, including two forges for making bar iron and two furnaces for manufacturing pig iron and castings.[10]

Coal mining, later to become the economic backbone of the Alleghenies, was but slightly developed during the first half of the nineteenth century and was usually carried on as an adjunct of other industries. In 1840 the estimated coal production of West Virginia, which lagged behind the Pittsburgh area, was 7,600,000 bushels, or about 304,000 tons. About 5,000,000 bushels of this amount were mined in the Kanawha Valley and about 2,250,000 bushels in the upper Ohio Valley, particularly in Brooke County. Owners of rich coal tracts found little demand for their coal as long as abundant supplies of wood remained for use as fuel. Early iron manufacturers long favored charcoal over coal for firing their furnaces, and not until 1817, when David

[9] James Morton Callahan, *History of the Making of Morgantown, West Virginia: A Type Study in Trans-Appalachian Local History* (Morgantown, W. Va., 1926), pp. 132-34; Joseph Martin, *A New and Comprehensive Gazetteer of Virginia, and the District of Columbia* (Charlottesville, Va., 1835), pp. 389-90, 392.

[10] Martin, *Gazetteer of Virginia*, pp. 327, 358, 362, 407; Ohio County Legislative Petitions, December 15, 1827.

Ruffner demonstrated the efficacy of coal as a fuel, did Kanawha Valley saltmakers begin to supplant wood with coal in heating their brine. With about two bushels of coal required to produce one bushel of salt, the demand for coal at the Kanawha Salines rose from about 1,500,000 bushels annually in the early 1820's to about 6,500,000 bushels in 1846. Between 1830 and 1846 the average yearly consumption of coal at the Salines was about 3,500,000 bushels. Because of navigational hazards of the river and the lack of capital for development, Kanawha coal producers made almost no effort prior to the mid-1850's to seek markets outside the Kanawha Valley.

Local industries consumed most of the coal produced elsewhere in the state. A considerable part of the coal mined in the Northern Panhandle fed the industrial machines of Wheeling, where by the 1830's ironworks, foundries, steam engine factories, flour mills, glass factories, distilleries, cotton and woolen factories, papermills, and sawmills required about 1,000,000 bushels of coal annually. Part of the rather negligible amount of coal mined east of the Alleghenies was shipped down the Potomac River by flatboat to the Harper's Ferry arsenal and to foundries and business establishments in Georgetown and Baltimore.[11]

Petroleum and natural gas resources excited but little attention in the western country prior to 1840. Saltmakers who encountered oil in their drilling considered it a nuisance, and Kanawha salt manufacturers diverted so much oil waste into the Kanawha River that the stream was long known to boatmen as "Old Greasy." On the other hand, local residents took advantage of extensive oil seepages along Hughes River by collecting the crude liquid and selling it in Parkersburg, Marietta, and other Ohio River towns, where the oil was used as an illuminant. The existence of natural gas was known to the first white visitors to the Kanawha Valley, who gazed with awe upon the famous Burning Spring about ten miles east of Charleston, but practical

[11] Estimated coal production statistics are taken from Howard N. Eavenson, *The First Century and a Quarter of American Coal Industry* (Pittsburgh, Pa., 1942), pp. 503-10. See also Atkinson, *History of Kanawha County*, p. 249; Otis K. Rice, "Coal Mining in the Kanawha Valley to 1861: A View of Industrialization in the Old South," *Journal of Southern History*, XXXI (November, 1965), 393-416; Thomas Condit Miller and Hu Maxwell, *West Virginia and Its People* 3 vols. (New York, 1913), I, 210; Martin, *Gazetteer of Virginia*, p. 407.

application of this resource was not made until 1841, when William Tompkins successfully used it to fire his salt furnace.[12]

Extensive claybanks and silica resources, and in many instances their proximity to wood and coal, encouraged the development of the pottery and glass industries in the Allegheny sections of West Virginia. Important centers for the making of pottery were Morgantown, Wellsburg, and Wheeling. Potters were at work in Morgantown by 1800. The establishments at Wellsburg, specializing in stoneware, redware, and queensware, were in operation before 1805. By 1814 Wheeling had two potteries. In glassmaking Wellsburg was the principal center in the Northern Panhandle, but, with the impetus given its industries by the completion of the National Road, Wheeling took preeminence. About 1820 or 1821, George Carothers of Brownsville, Pennsylvania, with the aid of Wheeling capital, opened a glass factory with an eight-pot furnace, annealing ovens, and other appurtenances. Failing in his own business venture, Carothers joined the firm of Knox and McKee, which produced large quantities of cylinder glass, green hollowware, and bottles, which it marketed in Boston and in various cities in the South and West. In 1829 John and Craig Ritchie established a flint glass factory in Wheeling and achieved such success that within a few years two other plants were put into operation. By 1835 Wheeling had five glasshouses and two glasscutting establishments, which gave employment to 193 workmen.[13]

[12] Miller and Maxwell, *West Virginia and Its People*, I, 213; Atkinson, *History of Kanawha County*, pp. 234-37.

[13] Martin, *Gazetteer of Virginia*, pp. 322, 392, 407; Callahan, *History of the Making of Morgantown*, p. 130; Thaddeus Mason Harris, *The Journal of a Tour into the Territory Northwest of the Alleghany Mountains; Made in the Spring of the Year 1803* . . . (Boston, 1805), p. 30; F[ortescue] Cuming, *Sketches of a Tour to the Western Country, through the States of Ohio and Kentucky; A Voyage down the Ohio and Mississippi Rivers, and a Trip through the Mississippi Territory, and Part of West Florida, Commenced at Philadelphia in the Winter of 1807, and Concluded in 1809* (Pittsburgh, Pa., 1810), p. 92; Pittsburgh *Mercury*, June 8, 1816, quoted in Eavenson, *First Century and a Quarter of American Coal Industry*, p. 247; Zadok Cramer, *The Navigator; Containing Directions for Navigating the Monongahela, Allegheny, Ohio, and Mississippi Rivers; With an Ample Account of These Much Admired Waters, from the Head of the Former to the Mouth of the Latter; And a Concise Description of Their Towns, Villages, Harbors, Settlements, &c.* . . . (Pittsburgh, Pa., 1814), p. 85; J. H. Newton, G. G. Nichols, and A. G. Sprankle, *History of the Panhandle, Being Historical Recollections of the Counties of Ohio, Brooke, Marshall and Hancock, West Virginia* (Wheeling, W. Va., 1879), p. 238

In sharp contrast with the limited use which they made of the region's vast mineral resources, early residents and pioneer industrialists of the Alleghenies attacked the forests with merciless prodigality. The manufacture of charcoal for iron furnaces required large quantities of wood, and cordwood cutters supplying iron manufacturers stripped hundreds of acres of their timber. Lumber constituted a major export from nearly every section of West Virginia, and virtually every village had one or more sawmills. Lumber from the South Branch, Lost River, and Cacapon valleys was sent by raft or flatboat to markets along the lower Potomac. Much of the lumber from the trans-Allegheny areas of the state found its way to eastern markets by way of the Ohio and Mississippi rivers. By 1820 eastern shipyards engaged in the construction of oceangoing vessels were purchasing white oak from the Monongahela and Kanawha valleys. The slopes of the Alleghenies also provided much of the white pine used in the masts of sailing vessels. By the 1830's sawmills making use of the circular saw and steampower and capable of producing several thousand feet of lumber a day were common in West Virginia. In 1835 Berkeley County alone had fifteen such mills. Shinnston had five sawmills and ten lumber merchants whose business was mostly with the Ohio River towns.[14]

Boatbuilders who provided the craft for inland waterways also made heavy inroads upon the forests. Thousands of settlers bound for Kentucky and other destinations in the Ohio and Mississippi valleys purchased flatboats along the Monongahela, upper Ohio, and Kanawha. Numerous boatyards such as those established at Morgantown, Wheeling, and Point Pleasant and at Cedar Grove on the Kanawha helped to speed this mobile population westward. Agricultural and industrial growth placed new demands upon boatbuilders. In 1829 the saltmakers at the Kanawha Salines required more than 300 flatboats, built at an average cost of $400 each, and their demands continued to increase until 1846. Scores of workmen were employed along the Kanawha between the saltworks and the falls, on Coal River as far as Madison, and on the Elk as far as Sutton in the manu-

14 Miller and Maxwell, *West Virginia and Its People*, I, 211, 216-18; Martin, *Gazetteer of Virginia*, pp. 357, 359, 364, 380, 391, 421, 466, passim.

facture of salt boats. In 1833 Elk River had fifteen sawmills in operation or under construction, all of which supplied the Charleston and Kanawha Salines markets. Single shipments of lumber and boats were valued as high at $10,000 to $12,000. Flatboats sent down the Kanawha, Coal, and Elk to the Kanawha Salines, moreover, were in many cases loaded with gunwales. In 1829 they carried enough barrel staves and hoop poles to keep 200 coopers busy. Flatboat manufacturing cleared many stands of yellow poplar, one of the finest woods in the Alleghenies.[15]

Lacking satisfactory overland facilities and heavily dependent upon water transportation, Allegheny pioneers naturally evinced great interest in steam navigation on inland waterways. A resident of Shepherdstown, James Rumsey, was one of the nation's important pioneers in steam navigation. As early as 1784 Rumsey had designed a mechanical boat, a model of which won the excited admiration of George Washington, who had long been interested in linking eastern and western Virginia by good transportation routes. Rumsey's invention enabled him to obtain from both the Maryland and Virginia legislatures exclusive navigational rights for such craft on the Potomac River. The inventor's crowning achievement came in 1787 when before an enthusiastic crowd of dignitaries and townspeople he demonstrated a boat which moved upstream under steampower and a type of jet propulsion.

Of more immediate significance to the economic development of the Allegheny section of West Virginia was the launching of the *New Orleans* at Pittsburgh in March, 1811. The vessel was built for the Robert Fulton interests under the direction of Nicholas Roosevelt. Her maiden journey from Pittsburgh to her home port of New Orleans was marked by the excitement of passing the falls of the Ohio at Louisville. Although the twelve-foot hull depth of the 371-ton vessel proved too great for the Pittsburgh-Louisville trade, the service of the *New Orleans* on the lower Mississippi indicated that with adaptations of design steamboats could successfully be put into operation on the shallower waters of the upper Ohio.

---

[15] Kanawha County Legislative Petitions, February 23, 1831; Martin, *Gazetteer of Virginia*, pp. 378, 380, 404; Cramer, *Navigator*, pp. 82, 85, 100.

Construction of steamboats for inland water traffic quickly became an important industry along the Ohio. By 1840 steamboats with a total tonnage of 159,511 had been built on western waters. Pittsburgh, Cincinnati, and Louisville, whose craftsmen built more than 90 percent of this tonnage, enjoyed a near monopoly of the business. Pittsburgh alone produced 45 percent of these vessels.

Of the lesser centers of steamboat construction, Wheeling occupied a place of some distinction. Here in 1816 was built the 403-ton *Washington,* designed by Henry M. Shreve and described as the "largest and most pretentious craft that had yet appeared on the western waters." Older accounts represent the *Washington* as having a "flat shallow hull" and floating on the water. More recent research, however, indicates that neither it nor other boats designed by Shreve differed substantially from other steamboats of their day. Whatever the merits or shortcomings of her design, the *Washington's* successful journey from New Orleans to Louisville in twenty-five days clearly established the practicability of steam navigation on the inland rivers and encouraged Shreve and others to challenge any exclusive privileges claimed by the Fulton interests to navigation of the interior waterways.[16]

Aside from contributing to an extensive boatbuilding industry, rushing mountain streams provided countless waterpower sites. About the close of the Revolution, waterpower mills began to supplant the hominy block, grater, handmill, and horse mill with which pioneers had ground their grain. The first water mills were of the tubmill type. The tubmill consisted of a horizontal wheel about four or five feet in diameter attached to the bottom of a shaft, which carried the runner, or upper millstone, and passed through the bedstone. About 1795 the tubmill began to give way to the water gristmill with country stones. By 1820 these improved merchant mills were found at numerous places

[16] Millard Kessler Bushong, *A History of Jefferson County, West Virginia* (Charles Town, W. Va., 1941), pp. 37-50; Archer B. Hulbert, *The Paths of Inland Commerce* (New Haven, Conn., 1922), p. 175; Charles Henry Ambler, *A History of Transportation in the Ohio Valley* (Glendale, Calif., 1932), pp. 114-29; Louis C. Hunter, *Steamboats on the Western Rivers: An Economic and Technological History* (Cambridge, Mass., 1949), pp. 65-77, 105-107.

throughout the state. On his journey down the Ohio in 1807 Fortescue Cuming observed fine mills at Fishing Creek, Middle Island Creek, and other places. Improved mills, including those of Michael Kerns and Samuel Hanway on Decker's Creek, Samuel Jackson on Cheat River, John Coombs at Flickerville, and Abram Guseman at Dellslow, were in operation in the Monongahela Valley by 1810. Ten years later Hampshire County had more than a dozen such mills. The introduction of steam-driven machinery marked a further advance in the milling industry, and by the 1830's a number of important mills were making use of the new source of power.[17]

Improvement in milling and the widespread cultivation of wheat combined to give flour manufacturing an important place in the economy of many areas of West Virginia. The earliest centers of flour milling in the state were in the Eastern Panhandle. At the time of the American Revolution the farms and diversified plantations of Berkeley County alone were producing more than 1,000,000 pounds of flour annually. In 1814 flour made from wheat grown along the Monongahela was "celebrated in foreign markets, for its superiority" and sold for a dollar more on the bushel in New Orleans than that brought in from other places. During the twelve months from May 15, 1819, to May 15, 1820, John Rogers, a Morgantown miller, ground four times as much wheat as corn and manufactured both fine and common grades of flour. Although flour of good quality continued to be made in the Monongahela Valley, the most important flour milling areas of the state in 1830 were in the Eastern and Northern panhandles. The chief centers in the Eastern Panhandle included Gerrardstown, Martinsburg, Wardensville, Moorefield, Glencoe, and Coldstream Mills. In the Northern Panhandle, Holliday's Cove, with four or five mills, produced about 10,000

---

[17] Joseph Doddridge, *Notes, on the Settlement and Indian Wars, of the Western Parts of Virginia & Pennsylvania, from the Year 1763 until the Year 1783 Inclusive, Together with a View, of the State of Society and Manners of the First Settlers of the Western Country* (Wellsburgh, [W.] Va., 1824), pp. 142-43; Hu Maxwell and H. L. Swisher, *History of Hampshire County, West Virginia* (Morgantown, W. Va., 1897), pp. 534-35; James Morton Callahan, *Semi-Centennial History of West Virginia* (n. p., 1913), p. 51; Cuming, *Sketches of a Tour to the Western Country*, pp. 101, 104, 120; Robert L. Scribner, "Mills That Ground Slowly," *Virginia Cavalcade*, IV (Autumn, 1954), 9-12.

barrels of flour a year. Wellsburg exported from 30,000 to 40,000 barrels annually to New Orleans by way of steamboat and flatboat. Other important centers were Wheeling, with three steam flour mills, and West Liberty, which had six mills within a three-mile radius.[18]

One of the most important farm-related industries of the Alleghenies was the manufacture of textiles. The most common cloth made by the pioneer was coarse linsey-woolsey, in which flax provided the "chain" and wool the "filling." The introduction of fulling mills and carding machinery wrought vast improvements in the quality of woolen cloth. In 1807 Robert Marshall put into operation near Wellsburg a carding machine which broke, carded, and wound the wool into rolls. Farmers who brought in wool for processing were required to provide one pound of clean hog's fat or fresh butter with every eight pounds of wool and to remove large chips, burrs, or sticks from the wool. For his services, Marshall charged ten cents a pound, or, if the wool were dyed with colors "handsomely intermixed," twelve cents. Wool thus carded could be spun more quickly, woven more easily, and made into better and more durable yarn, cloth, blankets, linsey-woolsey, and stockings. In 1810 a similar establishment in Monroe County processed about 4,000 pounds of wool, which was formed into "Roles fitt for Spining" and valued at 42 cents per pound. At his factory in Morgantown, John Rogers in 1819 carded 3,732 pounds of wool for 230 customers, some of whom lived 50 miles or more distant. By 1830 woolen factories and carding mills were numerous in mountainous areas. Some of the most important ones in West Virginia were located at Gerrardstown, Martinsburg, Moorefield, Coldstream Mills, Cackley's, Peterstown, Polsley's Mills, Aurora, Buckhannon, Barboursville, Holliday's Cove, Wheeling, and Wellsburg. The last-named town not only had a woolen factory and a carding machine but also boasted a rug factory and a cotton factory, the latter equipped with 1,200 spindles and requiring 60 operatives.[19]

18 Freeman H. Hart, *The Valley of Virginia in the American Revolution, 1763–1789* (Chapel Hill, N. C., 1942), p. 10n; Cramer, *Navigator,* pp. 14-15; John Rogers' Grist Mill Book and Memorandum Book No. 5, 1816–1828, John Rogers Papers; John Rogers' Morgantown Mill Book, Decker's Creek, 1817–1819, *ibid.;* Martin, *Gazetteer of Virginia,* pp. 326-27, 331-33, 357, 359, 361-63, 368, 380, 388, 391, 405, 463.

Among other industries resting upon an agricultural base was the distilling business. Faced with almost insurmountable problems of transportation of their fruits and grains to distant markets and with spoilage if they were kept, many farmers converted their surplus corn and rye into whiskey and their apples and peaches into brandy. One highly successful distiller in the Ohio Valley, who had previously been an equally successful hunter, sold whiskey and the brandy which he made from the fruit of his 3,000 peach trees for prices ranging from 75 cents to a dollar per gallon. In the early nineteenth century it was commonly said that "the best and greatest quantity of rye whiskey" was made on the Monongahela River. Nearly every community had its distillery, but with the growth of religious revivalism and the spread of the temperance movement many farmers were forced to divert their energies into other channels.[20]

The rise of industry wrought significant social and economic changes in the areas of the state in which manufacturing was most extensive. It brought to the industrial centers hundreds of "transient persons" whose outlook upon life and patterns of behavior differed radically from those of agriculturally oriented pioneers who had arrived a generation or two earlier. The Kanawha Salines, for example, drew workers and fortune seekers from all parts of the country. Among them, said Henry Ruffner, there was "horrible profaneness, . . . rioting and drunkenness, . . . quarreling and fighting, . . . gambling and cheating, . . . during the first flush of seeming wealth and prosperity in this region." Anne Royall declared that she had never seen or heard of any people other than those at the saltworks "who gloried in a total disregard of shame, honour and justice, and an open avowal of their superlative skill in petty fraud," but she admitted that they were "hospitable to a fault." She also observed among

[19] Doddridge, *Notes, on the Settlement and Indian Wars, of the Western Parts of Virginia & Pennsylvania,* p. 143; Unpublished United States Census Returns, 1810, Population Schedules, Monroe County, [West] Virginia, Microfilm in West Virginia Department of Archives and History Library; John Rogers' Carding Book, 1819, John Rogers Papers; Morgantown Carding Company Account Book, 1830–1831, *ibid.;* Martin, *Gazetteer of Virginia,* pp. 326-27, 331-33, 357, 361, 384, 391, 393, 407, 418, 421.

[20] Cuming, *Sketches of a Tour to the Western Country,* p. 115; Cramer, *Navigator,* pp. 14-15; Maxwell and Swisher, *History of Hampshire County,* pp. 535-36.

them women who were "modest, discreet, industrious and benevolent, . . . fair and beautiful," in short, " 'diamonds shining in the dark.' " In 1816 a large number of residents, many of them saltmakers, complained to the legislature that existing laws had been drawn up to govern "a thinly Inhabited country composed of a virtuous yeomanry" and were entirely inadequate for dealing with conditions which existed at the Salines. They asked that Charleston be incorporated and that its boundaries be extended eastward for ten miles along both sides of the Kanawha River in such a manner that the salt-producing area might be brought within the province of an effective government.[21]

The salt industry also helped to fasten Negro slavery upon the Kanawha Valley. Prior to the War of 1812 the saltmakers had employed "the hardy sons of . . . [the valley] yeomanry as best adapted to the toils and privations" of their business. At the beginning of the war many of these workers enlisted in the armed services, and the saltmakers were left "almost destitute of hands." With the cutting off of salt imports by way of the Great Lakes and the Mississippi, Kanawha salt manufacturers were in a position to obtain a near-monopoly of the western salt market, and they were not inclined to allow a lack of labor to deprive them of their opportunities. Their response to the problem was to make increasing use of Negro slaves. At the same time, Kanawha salt producers pressed the legislature to deny a request by Kentucky manufacturers, who had obtained leases on Kanawha salt lands, to import Negroes from that state. Although their action undoubtedly sprang partly from fear of competition, the Kanawha saltmakers emphasized a belief that the Kentucky manufacturers had no close connections with the slaveholding sections of the Bluegrass state and that they would bring in the most undesirable and unruly elements of the slave population and thereby create more problems at the saltworks than they would solve.

Even as it laid a slave base to society at the saltworks, the salt industry created a new aristocracy in the Kanawha Valley. The

[21] Address by Henry Ruffner on his Seventieth Birthday; Anne Royall, *Sketches of History, Life, and Manners, in the United States* (New Haven, Conn., 1826), pp. 20-21; Kanawha County Legislative Petitions, December 16, 1816. Charleston was incorporated January 19, 1818.

original aristocracy of the area rested upon land ownership and to some extent upon family background, but the lines between it and the more prosperous yeomanry were blurred. By 1815, Henry Ruffner later noted, the saltmakers had come into "almost unbounded wealth," with the result that "most of them and their families became recklessly expensive in their habits." Among the *nouveaux riches* were members of the Ruffner, Shrewsbury, Lewis, Donnally, Noyes, Brooks, and Tompkins families, who quickly gained prominence in the social and economic life of the valley.[22]

The bustling life of Wheeling revealed other facets of the economic and social impact of industrialization upon an essentially rural area. There, as in many other small industrial towns, diversification of manufactures attracted a variety of artisans, mechanics, and merchants and gave the town a somewhat cosmopolitan character. The rapid growth of industry, in turn, greatly stimulated the building trades, but numerous houses and other structures were built through the use of credit. The failure of their owners, in times of adverse business fluctuations or personal crises, to meet payments imposed serious burdens upon artisans, mechanics, and vendors of building supplies. It led to a strong movement for mechanic's lien laws, which would enable those who provided labor or materials to collect money due them through the sale of the property of defaulting owners and to have priority over any other claims against unpaid-for property. With its large landless laboring class, Wheeling also became the focal point for the first significant labor movement in the state. In 1829 William Cooper Howells, father of the celebrated novelist William Dean Howells, established there a labor organ, *The Eclectic Observer, and Working People's Advocate,* which in its support of "general education" and "equal privileges" was decidedly Jacksonian in spirit.[23]

In spite of auspicious beginnings in a few sections of the state, the industrial development of West Virginia during the early

[22] Kanawha County Legislative Petitions [December, 1811?]; *ibid.,* December 4, 1812; Address of Henry Ruffner on his Seventieth Birthday.

[23] Ohio County Legislative Petitions, December 15, 1829; *ibid.,* December 7, 1830. Otis K. Rice, "West Virginia Printers and Their Work, 1790–1830," *West Virginia History,* XIV (July, 1953), 326; Delf Norona and Charles Shetler, comps., *West Virginia Imprints, 1790–1863: A Checklist of Books, Newspapers, Periodicals, and Broadsides* (Moundsville, W. Va., 1958), pp. 257-58.

nineteenth century hardly matched that of other naturally favored areas of the country. Physiographical features which had earlier retarded the settlement of large parts of the state now stood between manufacturers and outside markets. But physiography alone does not explain the economic retardation of the Allegheny sections of West Virginia. Two other major handicaps to the growth of manufacturing were lack of capital and inadequate transportation facilities, which were in part the result of inaction or inadequate attention on the part of the Virginia legislature.

The shortage of investment capital, lack of credit facilities, and near-absence of an acceptable medium of exchange in West Virginia presented serious problems even before the close of the War of 1812. At the end of the war there was not a single incorporated banking establishment in West Virginia. Indeed, in all of Virginia there were only two banks, and both were in Richmond and of virtually no service to residents of the Allegheny sections of the state.

Lacking banking houses of their own, western Virginians carried on most of their financial transactions with Ohio and Pennsylvania institutions, whose notes constituted the chief circulating media in many counties. Ohio County residents declared in 1815 that they derived no benefits whatever from the banks of Virginia, but obtained most of their paper from establishments outside the state, especially those of Washington and Pittsburgh, Pennsylvania, and Steubenville, New Lisbon, Zanesville, and Marietta, Ohio. In a thinly veiled reproach to the legislature, they noted that although Wheeling did not have a single incorporated bank, there were four banks in Ohio within twenty-two miles of the town and six banks in Pennsylvania within sixty miles of it. In 1816 memorialists from Harrison County complained that no person in their quarter of the state had ever had a note discounted by either of the established banks of Virginia or their branches. Moreover, the directors of the branch of the Bank of Virginia at Winchester, they alleged, had made it clear that they would make no loans to persons "residing so remotely from them."[24]

[24] Ohio County Legislative Petitions, December 6, 1815; *ibid.,* November 15, 1816; Harrison County Legislative Petitions, November 18, 1816.

In their attempts to sustain the "new spring to . . . industry and enterprize" which the war had called forth, businessmen of several towns in West Virginia resorted to the establishment of unincorporated banks. After failing by a single vote in the state senate in December, 1813, to obtain a charter for a bank, a group of Wheeling residents formed a private banking facility known as the Ohio Company, and, with a capital of $60,000 began operation in July, 1814. In the same year the Charleston Manufacturing Company, a joint stock organization with a capital of $200,000, which was to be used "principally for Banking purposes," opened its doors at Charleston. "About the close of the year 1814" industrial-minded residents of Morgantown formed the Monongalia Farmers Company of Virginia and during the ensuing two years conducted a "considerable business." On August 15, 1814, nine Harrison Countians formed a joint stock company which they styled the Farmers Bank of Virginia, but, despite the general approval of delegates from northwestern Virginia, they failed to obtain a charter from the legislature. Persisting in their efforts to promote the improvement of the Monongahela River, the manufacture of salt, iron, wool, cotton, and other products, and the encouragement of agriculture, the group formed a company and, with a capital of $150,000 but still without a charter, by December, 1815, was operating at Clarksburg as the Virginia Saline Bank.[25]

Agitation for banks in the Eastern Panhandle stemmed from agricultural as well as from industrial needs. In 1815 investors, mostly "frugal industrious and substantial farmers far removed from the temtation [sic] and spirit of adventure or speculation," organized the Bank of the South Branch of Potomac at Romney. Their chief purpose was to provide credit for farmers whose "principal and moste profitable agricultural pursuit" was the grazing and stall-feeding of beef cattle for eastern markets. Unable to purchase cattle from western drovers except at heavy advances in prices, many South Branch cattlemen borrowed

[25] Harrison County Legislative Petitions, December 10, 1815; *ibid.*, November 18, 1816; Ohio County Legislative Petitions, November 15, 1816; Kanawha County Legislative Petitions, December 16, 1815; Monongalia County Legislative Petitions, November 22, 1816.

from Maryland and other out-of-state banks, and by 1815 their indebtedness to those banks was estimated at from $50,000 to $100,000. Stockmen residing on the headwaters of the Potomac in Pendleton County also carried on a lively business with the Winchester branch of the Bank of Virginia, which they praised for its "prudent, but liberal, issue of paper and loan of its funds."[26]

Blaming the industrial retardation of their area largely upon the failure of the legislature to provide adequate banking facilities, westerners bombarded the General Assembly with appeals designed to touch both its sense of justice and its feeling of state pride. Ohio County petitioners pointed out that in 1800 Wheeling had been "a place of importance about equal to Pittsburgh," but with the establishment of a branch of the Bank of Pennsylvania at the latter town, Wheeling had rapidly lost ground, remaining stationary while her rival took the lead in every branch of commerce. Promoters of the Virginia Saline Bank at Clarksburg raised the cry of colonialism and declared that the legislatures of Ohio and Pennsylvania "through the instrumentality of their chartered companies governed the medium by which the whole produce of the land and industry of the country was circulated and derived from that source, a revenue of six percentum upon its amount." Although they admitted that this interest was not "intolerable," they branded it as "injurious and humiliating" to Virginia. Like other banking organizations, they charged that out-of-state institutions were hoarding specie, which they declared to be "continually vanishing from circulation [in northwestern Virginia] and burying itself in the Vaults of the numerous banks of Ohio and Pennsylvania." Residents of the South Branch area, who like their trans-Allegheny countrymen derived almost no benefit from the Bank of Virginia and the Farmers Bank of Virginia, significantly took the position that "exclusive privileges [for those institutions] beyond the sphere of the benefits they afford is unrepublican and inconsistent with the Constitution."[27]

[26] Pendleton County Legislative Petitions, December 22, 1815; *ibid.*, November 16, 1816; Hampshire County Legislative Petitions, December 7, 1815; *ibid.*, November 8, 1816.

[27] Ohio County Legislative Petitions, November 15, 1816; Harrison County Legislative Petitions, December 10, 1815; Hampshire County Legislative Petitions, December 7, 1815.

Western discontent over inadequate banking organizations and other problems resulting from legislative indifference came to a head in 1816 and was given forceful expression in the Staunton Convention, which met August 19-23. At that time fifty-nine of the sixty-five delegates representing thirty-five western counties called for a constitutional convention with power to deal with all existing defects in the state's constitution and, by inference, with authority to reapportion representation in the legislature and thereby break the political stranglehold of the East. Although conservatives were able to block the calling of a constitutional convention, they did agree to compromises affecting representation in the state senate and equalization of land values for purposes of taxation.[28]

In a further move toward conciliation, the General Assembly in 1817, after earlier rejecting western demands for the creation of fifteen new state banks, established two important state banking institutions west of the Blue Ridge. The first, the Northwestern Bank of Virginia at Wheeling, with a capital of not less than $400,000, was authorized to set up branches at Wellsburg, Morgantown, and Clarksburg. The second, the Bank of the Valley of Virginia at Winchester, with a capital of $600,000, was empowered to establish a branch in Jefferson, Berkeley, Hardy, or Hampshire counties.[29]

The establishment of the two new western banks temporarily silenced much of the transmontane agitation for banking institutions, but it did not long conceal fundamental differences between East and West on policies relating to banking, credit, and money supply. In the 1830's these matters again became subjects of bitter sectional and political controversy. In general, the East held that the Bank of Virginia at Richmond must assume functions formerly exercised by the United States Bank in maintaining a stable currency and in restraining unwise policies of other banking establishments. During the 1834-1835 session, the Whig-dominated General Assembly increased the stock of the Richmond

---

[28] Charles Henry Ambler, *Sectionalism in Virginia from 1776 to 1861* (Chicago, 1910), pp. 94-96.

[29] *Ibid.*, p. 104; Charles H. Ambler and Festus P. Summers, *West Virginia: The Mountain State*, 2d ed. (Englewood Cliffs, N. J., 1958), pp. 127-28. For some of the difficulties in establishing the Northwestern Bank of Virginia at Wheeling, see Ohio County Legislative Petitions, January 2, 1818.

bank and added new branches in eastern cities. Even after the Democrats gained control of the legislature in 1835, eastern delegates were able to block western efforts to set up additional state banks.

After 1837 Democratic legislatures waged an almost relentless war on the state banks. Western delegates, pressed by the Panic of 1837 and discussions over specie payment and angered by their failure to procure additional banks for their section, struck savagely at the eastern banking power. They subjected the state banks and their branches to searching investigation, refused to increase their capital stock, required them to pay specie on fixed dates or cease operation, and forbade them to declare dividends as long as they refused to pay specie.

With their return to power in 1838, the Whigs proved somewhat more friendly to western interests. New state banks were authorized for the region. State banks were permitted to issue notes in denominations of less than five dollars, and their notes were made legal tender for the payment of taxes and state debts. With this decentralization of banking in the state and with the establishment of the Independent Treasury to supplant the defunct Bank of the United States, western fears of an eastern financial monopoly subsided, and the question of banking ceased to be a major factor in troubled East-West relations in Virginia.[30]

Of no less importance than adequate banking facilities were improved transportation links between eastern and western Virginia. Demands for the construction of highways and canals began almost immediately following the Revolutionary War and grew increasingly vociferous. Expressing sentiments generally held by trans-Allegheny residents, settlers in the Monongahela and Cheat valleys told the legislature in November, 1795, that they had entered the country when it was "an inhospitable wilderness, and thro' peril and all the horrors of Indian Wars . . . [had] maintained their ground." Because of their endeavors, land which "formerly was only the range for an untutored Indian, or the haunt of the Wild Buffalo" was now "covered with flocks graizing," and dotted with "Valleys standing thick with corn."

[30] Ambler, *Sectionalism in Virginia,* pp. 237-39.

Their only outlet for their products was the Mississippi River, but at New Orleans, they lamented, they were "treated with cruelty and Oppressions, and their monies extorted from them at the Will of a despot Governor" and their business "often delaid, amongst a People of a Strange language, and . . . disposition . . . hostile to them." They were less interested, they declared, in future possibilities of the Mississippi River trade than in roads that would connect the trans-Allegheny regions with the Potomac River and Virginia's eastern seaboard.[31]

Few Americans of the post-Revolutionary War era had a keener appreciation of the need for promoting closer commercial relations between East and West than George Washington. With an insight gained partly through several journeys into the transmontane region, Washington wrote to Governor Benjamin Harrison on October 10, 1784, urging that the vast area between the Great Lakes and the Ohio River be brought into Virginia's economic orbit and that the state take immediate steps to prevent its western inhabitants from falling prey to any "lures for trade and alliances" held forth by Spain or Great Britain. Specifically, Washington proposed that the state investigate the feasibility of improving the Potomac and James rivers to their sources and connecting them by means of portages with the Ohio and its tributaries and, through the latter, with streams flowing into the Great Lakes.[32]

Harrison laid Washington's communication before the General Assembly, which on January 14, 1785, acted upon its recommendations by chartering the James River and Potomac companies. These corporations in time became known as the James River and Kanawha Company and the Chesapeake and Ohio Canal Company, respectively. Washington himself served as first president of the Potomac Company and accepted the same position, but in name only, of the James River Company. The latter, actually the more important of the two, completed improvements in the James River for the 220 miles between Richmond

31 Monongalia County Legislative Petitions, November 17, 1795.
32 John C. Fitzpatrick, ed., *The Writings of George Washington from the Original Manuscript Sources, 1745–1799*, 39 vols. (Washington, D. C., 1931-1944), XXVII, 471-80; Ambler, *Sectionalism in Virginia*, pp. 46-49.

and Crow's Ferry and was highly praised by Albert Gallatin in 1808 in his report to the United States Senate on internal improvements in the country. The company's heavy tolls, its evident prosperity, and its failure to comply fully with the terms of its charter, however, evoked serious popular discontent. In 1820 the legislature, after investigation of charges leveled against its directors, stripped the company of its powers and reclaimed them for the state. Criticism of the Potomac Company was also widespread, and in 1823 it, too, lost its charter.[33]

The stimulation to agriculture and industry immediately prior to and during the War of 1812 and the gradual maturation of the western economy, meanwhile, led to increased demands for internal improvements. Although many western cries bore the unmistakeable stamp of local interest, their cumulative effect was to register a massive desire of the Allegheny residents to enter the mainstream of American economic life and to serve notice that consideration of western needs must not be unduly delayed. During the postwar years western residents exerted heavy pressures upon both Richmond and Washington for government aid to improved transportation.

The Virginia General Assembly was by no means oblivious to the needs of the mountainous areas. On February 5, 1816, it created a fund for internal improvements and stipulated that it was to be kept separate from other state monies. The same act created a Board of Public Works with authority to subscribe state funds to desirable projects. The first annual report of the Board, made to the 1816–1817 session of the legislature, recommended that the state invite Ohio, Indiana, and Kentucky to join it in endeavors to link the James with the Ohio and other interior streams by way of the Kanawha.[34]

The General Assembly gave more tangible evidence of its interest in an act of February 17, 1820, which authorized the

[33] Ambler, *Sectionalism in Virginia*, pp. 46-48; Wayland Fuller Dunaway, *History of the James River and Kanawha Company* (New York, 1922), pp. 17-47; Walter S. Sanderlin, *The Great National Project: A History of the Chesapeake and Ohio Canal* (Baltimore, Md., 1946), p. 51; I[saac] F[egley] Boughter, "Internal Improvements in Northwestern Virginia: A Study of State Policy Prior to the Civil War" (Ph.D. dissertation, University of Pittsburgh, 1930), pp. 64-66, 128-34.

[34] Dunaway, *History of the James River and Kanawha Company*, pp. 59-60.

James River Company, by then in reality the agent of the Commonwealth, to construct a road from Dunlap's Creek to the falls of the Kanawha at a cost of $100,000 and to improve the Kanawha River from its falls to the Ohio for the accommodation of boats drawing three feet of water. The turnpike followed the "Old State Road," first authorized in 1785 and completed to the falls of the Kanawha in 1790 and to the Ohio in 1800. The new road was opened to the falls in 1826. Encouraged by assurances from Henry Clay that Kentucky would build a road eastward from Lexington to meet it, the legislature on January 30, 1829, appropriated $50,000 for extending the new turnpike to the mouth of the Big Sandy. For the next twenty years the James River and Kanawha Turnpike was one of the busiest arteries of east-west commerce in the country, but other routes offered competition, and about 1852 its traffic began to decline.[35]

Meanwhile, the company was vigorously at work constructing wing dams and sluices on the Kanawha from Charleston to Point Pleasant. By 1830, largely as a result of agitation by the Kanawha salt manufacturers, it had spent $91,766.72 in improving the stream. Disappointed when the steamboat *Robert Thompson,* which made its way up the Kanawha to Red House in the summer of 1819, was unable to reach Charleston, the saltmakers appealed to the legislature for improvements in river navigation. They declared that the cost of transporting their salt to market equaled 50 percent of its value. These costs, in the words of the producers, "operates upon them like an export duty and is a bounty to their competitors." By 1823 improvements in the Kanawha enabled the *Eliza,* built especially for the salt trade, to go into service. Ten years later half a dozen other steamboats were regularly plying the Kanawha. During the ensuing decade a lively steamboat traffic developed between Kanawha and Ohio river ports.[36]

Despite the flurry of activity during the early 1820's, the James River Company never fulfilled western expectations. The Gen-

[35] *Ibid.,* pp. 66-84; Callahan, *Semi-Centennial History of West Virginia,* pp. 94-97; James Morton Callahan, *History of West Virginia: Old and New,* 3 vols. (Chicago, 1923), I, 174-76.

[36] Dunaway, *History of the James River and Kanawha Company,* pp. 88-89; Kanawha County Legislative Petitions, December 9, 1819; Hale, *Trans-Allegheny Pioneers,* pp. 258-59; Ambler, *History of Transportation in the Ohio Valley,* pp. 151-52.

eral Assembly enacted legislation on March 16, 1832, whereby its properties were transferred to a new joint-stock corporation, the James River and Kanawha Company, to which the state subscribed three-fifths of the stock. The new company fared little better than its predecessors. Sectional interests prevented full state support to the so-called central waterline, advocates of railroad construction attacked an all-water connection between East and West as outdated, and financial problems sapped the company's vitality. Moreover, residents along a substantial part of its route were critical of its efforts. Greenbrier Countians complained that the section of the turnpike from Covington to the falls of the Kanawha was "loosing its orriginal Shape and becoming Lowest in the middle" and failing to drain properly, that timber along its 66-foot right-of-way had grown to a height of 20 feet, and that in places the road was not more than 15 feet wide. Inhabitants of the Kanawha Valley were never satisfied with the improvements made in the river.[37]

When compared with the inadequate facilities linking the James and Kanawha rivers, which prior to 1838 constituted Virginia's most ambitious venture in internal improvements, the success of the National Road, completed from Cumberland, Maryland, to Wheeling in 1818 by the federal government, seemed little short of spectacular. Wheeling, a village of only 120 houses and 11 stores in 1810, was by 1830 the largest town in northwestern Virginia, and, in population, second only to Richmond. In 1822 one mercantile house in Wheeling had consigned to it 1,081 wagonloads of merchandise, averaging about 3,500 pounds each. With five other similar businesses in operation, it was estimated that at least 4,681 wagons were unloaded at Wheeling that year. Costs of transporting the goods from Baltimore to Wheeling were said to be about $390,000. These figures, however, did not take into account the number of wagons which merely passed through Wheeling, probably one-tenth of the total traffic, or of savings in transportation charges, perhaps as much as $300,000, which the road made possible. The beneficial effects of the highway were not confined to towns and

---

[37] Dunaway, *History of the James River and Kanawha Company,* pp. 76, 80-81, 134-55; Greenbrier County Legislative Petitions, January 7, 1830.

villages through which the road passed, but penetrated deep into the hinterland on either side of the route. With its enormous freighting business, heavy stagecoach traffic, and fast mail service, the National Road quickly became for westerners "a visible symbol of the power and fostering care of the national government."[38] Moreover, time provided ample corroboration of the prediction made on March 23, 1816, by John G. Jackson, northwestern Virginia's representative in Congress, that the road would "have an influence over physical impossibilities" and "promote a free intercourse among the citizens of remote places, by which unfounded prejudices and animosities [would be] . . . dissipated, local and sectional feelings . . . destroyed, and a nationality of character . . . inculcated."[39]

The overwhelming approval of the National Road was but one manifestation of interest in federal aid to internal improvements during the postwar years. The report of a 22-member commission headed by John Marshall, which in 1812 viewed the proposed route for linking the James and Kanawha rivers, suggested an appropriation from the federal government for financing the work. The General Assembly of 1814–1815 adopted the commission's recommendation, with the West voting solidly in its favor. At the same session, it passed a resolution directing Virginia's representatives in Congress to request that body "to manifest an interest in internal improvements." Two years later, Ballard Smith, a congressman from Kanawha County, proposed that the federal government be authorized to subscribe two-fifths of the capital stock in any company which Virginia might charter for the purpose of opening communications between the James and Kanawha rivers. During the spring and summer of 1823 residents along the Potomac and in the northwestern counties held mass meetings at which they urged federal support for internal improvements. They exerted such pressures upon the General Assembly that it canceled the charter of the Potomac

[38] Cuming, *Sketches of a Tour to the Western Country*, pp. 94-95; Dan Elbert Clark, *The West in American History* (New York, 1937), pp. 292-93; Philip D. Jordan, *The National Road* (Indianapolis, Ind., 1948), p. 217. See also Thomas B. Searight, *The Old Pike* (Uniontown, Pa., 1894) and Archer B. Hulbert, *The Cumberland Road* (Cleveland, Ohio, 1904).

[39] Jordan, *National Road*, p. 88.

Company, and chartered the Chesapeake and Ohio Canal Company, which proposed to build a canal with both federal and state funds. In the election of 1828 the West gave strong support to John Quincy Adams because he supported federally financed internal improvements.[40]

Hopes of western Virginians that the Chesapeake and Ohio Canal might benefit trans-Allegheny sections of the Old Dominion in the same manner that the Pennsylvania Main Line Canal united Pittsburgh with Philadelphia were not realized. The canal carried a heavy volume of freight, chiefly agricultural, between the Eastern Panhandle and the seaboard, but its advantages were never extended to the transmontane areas. In 1826 opponents of the project held a convention at Charlottesville at which they severely criticized the undertaking and revived a languishing interest in an all-water route from the James to the Kanawha. In 1828 the General Assembly, pressed by eastern opposition to federal involvement in the project, refused to make further appropriations to the Chesapeake and Ohio Canal. Meanwhile, President Andrew Jackson threatened to cut off federal funds unless the company removed its president, Charles F. Mercer, whose popularity and strength were derived from a strong National Republican element along the Potomac. Although the company agreed in 1833 to name ex-Secretary of War John Eaton, a close friend of Jackson, president, Congress itself refused to give further aid to the enterprise.[41]

With the abatement of federal interest in internal improvements, westerners increased their pressures upon the Virginia General Assembly. Wood Countians, in demanding a road from Winchester to Parkersburg, asked how western residents, without "interchange of thought, or of commercial [and] political intercourse" with easterners could have a feeling of brotherhood with them, and then answered their own question by concluding that they could only feel as "outcasts and aliens." The sparse

[40] Sanderlin, *Great National Project*, pp. 51-53; Ambler, *Sectionalism in Virginia*, pp. 98-99, 105-106, 122-23, 134-35.

[41] Ambler, *Sectionalism in Virginia*, pp. 125-26; 184-85; Sanderlin, *Great National Project*, p. 103; Boughter, "Internal Improvements in Northwestern Virginia," pp. 220-24.

population of many of the Allegheny sections through which roads must pass, they declared, made state support essential. In seeking a state-constructed road from Morgantown to the mouth of Fishing Creek on the Ohio, Monongalia Countians declared in 1810 that such a road would traverse thirty miles of unsettled lands, which were in large tracts and belonging to "foreigners" and not likely to be settled for many years.[42]

During the 1830's and 1840's internal improvement projects were buffeted upon the stormy seas of Virginia politics. While in power in the 1830's, the Whigs showed partiality toward the James River and Kanawha Company, whose operation lay in strongly Whig territory. At the session of the legislature of 1834–1835, they granted loans to the company, endeavored to divert all income from the internal improvements fund to its use, and rejected petitions from Democratic strongholds which might have been inimical to the company's interests. Neglected sections of the state bitterly resented Whig policy, and in the elections of 1835 their votes helped to turn the Whigs out of office. Democratic legislatures from 1835 to 1838, on the other hand, gave special consideration to these areas. Their legislation included approval of no less than sixteen charters to companies proposing to construct internal improvements in the western parts of the state.[43]

The most important road built into the Allegheny sections by Virginia during this period was the Northwestern Turnpike, which connected Winchester and Parkersburg. It was constructed partly for the purpose of diverting some of the western trade from the National Road, which, according to Hampshire Countians, was "destroying any thing like a spirit of enterprize and improvement" among the people remote from the highway. Westerners also desired a turnpike which would strike the Ohio at some point where navigation was open throughout the year. While professing a full measure of "that State pride which . . . all . . . Virginians delight in," they declared themselves "offcasts

---

[42] Wood County Legislative Petitions, December 8, 1830; Monongalia County Legislative Petitions, December 11, 1810.

[43] Ambler, *Sectionalism in Virginia*, pp. 239-41.

338 The Allegheny Frontier

and aliens" in the matter of internal improvements. They could no longer, they said, "Shut their eyes against the light, nor . . . quietly Submit to that neglect of their rights and interest under which they . . . [had] so long Suffered."[44]

Although the company was chartered in 1827, construction did not get underway until 1831, when it was reorganized and authorized to borrow $125,000 on the credit of the state. Under the able direction of Charles B. Shaw, who in turn worked under Colonel Claudius Crozet, the road was completed in 1838 at a cost of $400,000. The route chosen passed by way of Capon Bridge, Romney, Rowlesburg, Grafton, Pruntytown, Bridgeport, Clarksburg, Salem, West Union, Pennsboro, and Murphytown. By 1840, the western portion of the road, macadamized from Parkersburg to the Tygart Valley, boasted a daily line of stage-coaches and a regular mail service. Within a few years the area was within relatively easy communication with Winchester and even with Baltimore. The new turnpike contributed significantly to the settlement and development of lands along its route and stimulated the construction of numerous feeder turnpikes.[45]

Also important in the economic development of central West Virginia was the Staunton and Parkersburg Turnpike, authorized in 1824 but not completed until 1847. After considerable con-troversy over a proper route, the turnpike was finally built by way of Monterey, Beverly, Buckhannon, and Weston. Construc-tion of the road proceeded slowly, largely because counties through which it passed did not raise their share of money or failed to meet their commitments on schedule.[46]

Virginia's support for the construction of turnpikes, however, did not compensate for her refusal to permit the Baltimore and Ohio Railroad to build its lines across the central parts of the state. During the 1820's many westerners continued to hope that the state would grant the railroad permission to connect

[44] Hampshire County Legislative Petitions, January 9, 1828; *ibid.*, December 5, 1828; Callahan, *History of West Virginia*, I, 184; Ambler and Summers, *West Virginia*, pp. 151-52.

[45] Callahan, *History of West Virginia*, I, 184-86; Ambler and Summers, *West Virginia*, pp. 152-53.

[46] Callahan, *History of West Virginia*, I, 181-84; Ambler and Summers, *West Virginia*, p. 153.

Baltimore and the Kanawha Valley by way of the Valley of Virginia. In 1844–1845 the General Assembly relented, but only on the condition that the western terminus of the railroad must not be south of Wheeling. Because of Virginia's desire to keep western parts of the state tributary to Richmond and Norfolk, efforts of West Virginians during the 1840's to obtain approval for a route by way of Clarksburg and Parkersburg were in vain. As a result, the completion of the first major railroad in Allegheny sections of West Virginia was delayed until 1853, when the Baltimore and Ohio was opened to Wheeling.[47]

Much of the animosity generated by the construction of turnpikes and roads was sectional in character, but efforts to improve river navigation frequently produced severe local tensions among residents along inland streams. Owners of low-lying properties, businessmen and workers engaged in floating or rafting logs, plank, staves, and scantling, builders of flatboats for western markets, millowners, and fishermen all strongly objected to the construction of locks and dams in rivers essential to their economic welfare. Dozens of petitions to the Virginia legislature sought to prevent incorporation of companies seeking to improve navigation or to restrain others from interfering with existing rights.

Perhaps no internal improvement company in West Virginia faced more determined opposition than the Monongahela Navigation Company. Chartered in 1816, the company was authorized to construct locks and dams in the Monongahela and West Fork rivers sufficient to provide eighteen inches of water at all seasons, to condemn sites for the dams, and to collect tolls on the river traffic. At first, residents along the streams paid little attention to the company's plan, but as its work progressed a large portion of them manifested extreme hostility to the undertaking. They contended that the works contemplated would destroy valuable fording places, require greater freshets to enable flatboats and

---

[47] Wood County Legislative Petitions, December 20, 1827; Greenbrier County Legislative Petitions, December 5, 1827; Monroe County Legislative Petitions, December 6, 1827; Hampshire County Legislative Petitions, December 7, 1827; Mason County Legislative Petitions, December 6, 1827; Ambler, *Sectionalism in Virginia*, pp. 175, 179, 241-42; Dunaway, *History of the James River and Kanawha Company*, pp. 189-90.

rafts to pass over the dams than were needed for navigating the river in its natural state, and flood much of the lowland with stagnant water, which would create a menace to public health.

Opponents of the company also criticized its privileges as "Interfering with land holders private Rights, and Incorporating a body of Men over whome the law has but little controle by which they can create a Menopoly to them selves to the Great Injury of the people." Moreover, the law put "it in the power of a few Large stockholders to procure their own Elections as Directors, . . . thereby creating to themselves an Undue Manopoly." Two years later, objectors to the privileges granted the company declared: "We consider that Incorporated bodys clothed with law in a free Government like ours, savors too much of aristocracy." Still not reconciled to the company's project, residents of the Monongahela Valley were complaining ten years later that they had "borne the deprivation of their rights, the sacrifice of their interests and endangering [of] their health." They charged that the property of many persons who could no longer get their products to market had been "sacrificed under the hammer" and that there had been more cases of bilious fever during the preceding three years than in the previous twenty. The whole purpose of the navigation project, they reiterated, was "private emolument and not public utility."[48]

Whether they based their arguments upon personal injury or abstract principle, opponents of industrial growth and internal improvements waged an unequal battle with the forces of change. For large numbers of West Virginians, as for residents of the Alleghenies elsewhere, the future appeared to be inescapably hinged to industrial and commercial development. That conviction, coupled with the feeling that eastern-dominated governments responded to their needs with either neglect or unconcern, everywhere produced serious tensions between Allegheny residents and their state authorities.

[48] For the works of the Monongahela Navigation Company, see Harrison County Legislative Petitions, October 28, 1815; Virginia, *Fifth Annual Report of the President and Directors of the Board of Public Works, to the General Assembly of Virginia* (Richmond, Va., 1820), pp. 35-45. Objections to the company's project are set forth in Harrison County Legislative Petitions, December 8, 1819; *ibid.,* December 9, 1822; *ibid.,* December 19, 1825; Monongalia County Legislative Petitions, December 26, 1822; *ibid.,* December 19, 1826.

In Virginia, insufficient attention by the state government to economic and political needs of the Allegheny counties, and not clashes over the moral issues relating to slavery, ultimately resulted in disruption of the Old Dominion and the creation of the state of West Virginia.

Chapter Fourteen

Government of and for the People

The motto of West Virginia, *montani semper liberi*, or "mountaineers always free," might well have been applied to most of the American West during the decades following the Revolution. For West Virginians, however, the phrase expressed a hope rather than a reality. As heirs to the ideas and ideals of the Revolutionary era, West Virginians, like other Allegheny residents, subscribed to the philosophy that government should not only protect liberty and property but should be an instrument whereby the people might achieve political and economic fulfillment. Moreover, their preoccupation with providing protection against hostile Indians, clearing homesteads, and establishing economic viability, made them acutely conscious of their need for strong and effective government. The political influence which Allegheny pioneers of West Virginia commanded, however, was far from commensurate with the protection and services which they sought. Indeed, their liberty and opportunity, the very fruits of the Revolution, seemed often in jeopardy. The blame, they reasoned, must rest with either faulty government machinery or self-seeking officials.

Prior to 1830 West Virginians were profoundly influenced by two prevailing tendencies in government. The first was the steadily increasing authority of the federal government and its intervention in the practical and pressing problems of the West. The other was the continued concentration of power in Virginia in the hands of an eastern aristocracy, whose inadequate concern for western needs and aspirations engendered frustration and deep dissatisfaction. If westerners at times found the ever-expanding powers of the federal government disquieting, they were far more concerned over the domination of state affairs by the political and economic interests of the Tidewater and Piedmont. By the early nineteenth century Allegheny West

Virginia had become predominantly liberal and nationalist, but in some areas, notably sections of the Eastern Panhandle, there was a drift toward a states' rights orientation.

During the decade immediately following the American Revolution, the greatest single need of trans-Allegheny West Virginia, and one which perhaps did most to color the attitude of the inhabitants toward government, was defense against hostile Indians. As early as May 22, 1783, George Rogers Clark had informed Governor Benjamin Harrison that he did not expect peace between Great Britain and the United States to foster Indian respect for the United States. At that time Clark proposed to lead an expedition of 2,000 men against the western tribes, but Virginia's depleted finances and the unwillingness of frontiersmen to join in the undertaking forced him to cancel his plan. Scores of Indian forays into West Virginia and Kentucky during the ensuing decade, however, proved the accuracy of Clark's observation. In 1786 Indians raided as far east as the Bluestone settlements, where they left the inhabitants "more Panic struck . . . than they were at anything that happened to them in the course of the last war." Ohio County's thin line of settlements extending for a distance of more than forty miles along the upper Ohio bore the brunt of numerous attacks and constituted "a good barrier to the people of Pennsylvania, who appear[ed] perfectly easy in their situation." Virginia authorities attempted to meet the threat to the frontiers by stationing militia at strategic places, erecting additional military posts, such as Fort Lee at the mouth of Elk River, and keeping scouts on patrol duty along well-known Indian paths.[1]

Adding to the dangers to the West Virginia frontier between 1785 and 1787 were efforts of Sir John Johnson, Joseph Butler, and Joseph Brant, agents of British authorities in Canada, to promote a confederation of tribes northwest of the Ohio River. Like George Clendenin, Kanawha County's delegate in the

---

[1] Clark to Harrison, May 22, 1783, W. P. Palmer, and others, eds., *Calendar of Virginia State Papers and Other Manuscripts*, 11 vols. (Richmond, Va., 1875-1893), III, 488-90; Harrison to the Speaker of the House of Delegates, May 30, 1783, *ibid.*, pp. 495-96; Walter Crockett to Patrick Henry, July 26, 1786, *ibid.*, IV, 159-60; William McMechen and Archibald Woods to Edmund Randolph, December 3, 1787, *ibid.*, p. 363.

Virginia General Assembly, most frontier leaders were convinced that the Indians did not desire peace as long as the British extended them aid and encouragement. By the summer of 1788 British agitation and provocative raids against the Indians by Kentucky frontiersmen had set the stage for a full-scale Indian war. West Virginia's frontier defenses appeared hopelessly inadequate for meeting the threat. Clearly a more vigorous policy, with the backing of far greater military resources, was needed.[2]

Amid these conditions, sixteen West Virginians journeyed to Richmond to attend the convention, which met from June 2 to June 25, 1788, to consider Virginia's ratification of the Constitution. Of the 170 delegates to the convention, 85 had been chosen as Federalists and 66 as anti-Federalists. Three members had not made up their minds, and the attitudes or instructions of 16 others were unknown. Twelve of the latter were from Kentucky and four from trans-Allegheny West Virginia. Several issues discussed during the convention were of major importance to West Virginians, and both supporters and opponents of the Constitution endeavored to capitalize upon them as a means of winning the votes of western delegates.[3]

Opponents of ratification, relying heavily upon the persuasive oratory of Patrick Henry, argued that the Constitution would create a central government with power to bargain away the navigation of the Mississippi, which trans-Allegheny areas regarded as vital to their economic development. With telling effect, they pointed to the unpopular Jay-Gardoqui negotiations of 1785. They also warned inhabitants of the Northern Neck, which included a substantial part of the Eastern Panhandle of West Virginia, that retention of properties which they had

[2] Clendenin to Edmund Randolph, December 18, 1788, *ibid.*, IV, 533-34.

[3] Forrest McDonald, *We the People: The Economic Origins of the Constitution* (Chicago, 1958), pp. 257-58. Delegates from West Virginia included William Darke and Adam Stephen from Berkeley County; George Clendenin and John Stuart, Greenbrier County; Ralph Humphreys and Andrew Woodrow, Hampshire County; Isaac Van Meter and Abel Seymour, Hardy County; George Jackson and John Prunty, Harrison County; John Evans and William McCleery, Monongalia County; Archibald Woods and Ebenezer Zane, Ohio County; and Benjamin Wilson and John Wilson, Randolph County. Hugh Blair Grigsby, *The History of the Virginia Federal Convention of 1788*, 2 vols. (Richmond, Va., 1890), II, 363-66.

obtained from the sequestered lands of Lord Fairfax could be assured only by retaining Virginia's sovereignty over the area and rejecting the Constitution.

More convincing to trans-Allegheny delegates were arguments set forth by proponents of the Constitution, among whom were George Washington, James Madison, Edmund Randolph, Edmund Pendleton, and George Wythe. Only a powerful central government, declared these Federalists, could force the British to withdraw from the Northwest posts, which held the key to their influence over western Indians. Instead of placing the free navigation of the Mississippi in jeopardy, the Constitution offered the surest means of providing a government with power to maintain unobstructed use of the river. The claim that purchasers of tracts from the Fairfax estate risked the loss of their lands should the Constitution be adopted was countered with the argument that Virginia would still possess sufficient authority to protect their rights.[4]

After more than three weeks of debate and political maneuvering, the convention voted on June 25 to ratify the Constitution. The margin of victory was narrow—89 votes to 79. Fourteen West Virginia delegates favored ratification; one Ebenezer Zane, did not vote; and one, John Evans, voted against ratification. The votes of most delegates were determined by local conditions and interests. For the West Virginians, the consideration of transcendent importance was British evacuation of the Northwest posts and removal of the Indian menace. At least eleven West Virginia delegates had been actively engaged in frontier defense, and all had witnessed the ravages of Indian attack. John Stuart of Greenbrier County, who as a soldier and public official had had a "long and intimate acquaintance with the wants and interests of the West," believed that the Indian would continue to be a dangerous foe and that if either England or Spain gained control of all the tribes the result might be "the extermination of the settlers west of the Blue Ridge." Should the Indians come under the domination of either power, "it would require all the resources of the Union to repel the savages and punish them."[5] Unlike the Kentucky delegates, the trans-Allegheny West Virginia delegates considered free navigation of the Mississippi as of secondary importance or believed that it, like frontier defense, could best be secured through a strong central government. Fears that adoption of the Constitution might jeopardize the property of those who had acquired it from the Fairfax estate evidently did not trouble delegates from the Eastern Panhandle, who voted unanimously for ratification.

Economic interests of the West Virginia delegates apparently had little or no influence upon their votes on ratification. All sixteen delegates were farmers or planters, and George Jackson of Harrison County was also a lawyer. At least eleven were slaveholders. Seven held either continental or state securities. No less than eleven had served in some military capacity either during the Revolution or subsequent years.[6] Of far greater significance than economic backgrounds was the fact that, although all were drawn from the local aristocracy of their respective counties, the sixteen delegates were chosen by a relatively broadly based electorate and were representative of the views and interests of their counties.[7]

[5] McDonald, *We the People*, pp. 269-83; Grigsby, *History of the Virginia Federal Convention*, II, 27. West Virginia delegates who had been active in military affairs or frontier defense included William Darke, Adam Stephen, George Clendenin, John Stuart, Andrew Woodrow, George Jackson, John Evans, William McCleery, Archibald Woods, Ebenezer Zane, and Benjamin Wilson.

[6] McDonald, *We the People*, pp. 269-81; Grigsby, *History of the Virginia Federal Convention*, II, 25-30, 55-59, 64-70; Jackson Turner Main, "The Distribution of Property in Post-Revolutionary Virginia," *Mississippi Valley Historical Review*, XLI (September, 1954), 241-58.

[7] A case in point is that of the Greenbrier delegates. John Stuart held only $16 in continental securities, and George Clendenin had no securities at all. Moreover, their county had been threatened in August, 1787, with an insurrection by some 300 men who had reportedly signed a pledge to oppose payment of the certificate tax and any other taxes levied for liquidation of the state's war debt. Yet both Stuart and Clendenin voted for ratification, and the Greenbrier area appeared substantially Federalist in sentiment. J[ames] McClurg to James Madison, August 22, 1787, Worthington C. Ford, ed., "The Federal Convention in Virginia, 1787–1788," Massachusetts Historical Society *Proceedings*, Second Series, XVII (1903), 472-73; J[ames] McClurg to James Madison, September 5, 1787, excerpt quoted in *ibid.*, p. 473; Henry Banks to [Edmund] Randolph, September 1, 1787, Palmer and others, eds., *Calendar of Virginia State Papers*, IV, 336-37; [Edmund] Randolph to Lieutenant Governor of Virginia, September 2, 1787, *ibid.*, p. 338; Henry Banks to [Edmund] Randolph, October 19, 1787, *ibid.*, pp. 349-50. For difficulties in

The new government created by the Constitution soon gave evidence of its concern for frontier defense. In the autumn of 1790 General Josiah Harmar led an army of 1,500 men into the Indian country. The Indians, however, were warned of Harmar's advance. Taking refuge in the forest along the Maumee River, they ambushed the army and killed 183 of his men. Determined that the Indian menace must be ended, the government readied another expedition, which set out in the summer of 1791 under Arthur St. Clair. The 3,000-man expedition moved slowly, building Forts Washington, Jefferson, and St. Clair far beyond the perimeter of settlement. Failing to take the most elementary precautions, they suffered a surprise attack in which 630 men were killed and 283 wounded and left to die on the battlefield.[8]

The disasters that befell the expeditions of Harmar and St. Clair opened the trans-Allegheny West Virginia settlements to new horrors. George Clendenin declared in 1792 that the frontier counties had "never experienced so desparate a summer as this appears to be." Kanawha County, he said, was "one continual scene of depradation" with as many as a hundred Indians roaming about at a time. Indian attacks became so numerous in Ohio County that settlers could not pursue their "necessary occupations," and many "experienced the dreadful effects of the Tomahawk and scalping knife." In the spring of 1793 Hezekiah Davisson informed Governor Henry Lee that Harrison and Randolph counties were "in Geperty, and in more Danger than we have been since the Teadious Indian ware commenced." The Greenbrier frontiers, declared John Stuart in June, 1794, were "much more exposed to danger than I ever knew before."[9]

---

establishing economic motivations for voting on ratification, see McDonald, *We the People*, pp. 261-68, 281-83.

[8] Good brief accounts of these expeditions are in Thomas D. Clark, *Frontier America: The Story of the Westward Movement* (New York, 1959), pp. 156-60; Ray Allen Billington, *Westward Expansion: A History of the American Frontier*, 3d ed. (New York, 1967), pp. 221-24; Dan Elbert Clark, *The West in American History* (New York, 1937), pp. 223-27.

[9] Clendenin to Henry Lee, May 26, 1792, Palmer and others, eds., *Calendar of Virginia State Papers*, V, 561; Clendenin to Lee, September 22, 1792, *ibid.*, VI, 68-69; Ohio County delegates to the General Assembly to [Lee?], November 15, 1792, *ibid.*, pp. 146-47; Davisson to Lee, April 4, 1793, *ibid.*, pp. 325-26; Stuart to Henry Lee, June 9, 1794, *ibid.*, VII, 175.

Failure of the Harmar and St. Clair expeditions and subsequent Indian activity seriously undermined the confidence of West Virginians in the ability of the federal government to deal decisively with the Indian menace. John Pierce Duvall, the lieutenant of Harrison County, believed the St. Clair expedition "an Injury Rather than a protection," and later declared that "the Idea . . . that the Federal troops are a Protection to us, is but a meare shadow without substance." Cornelius Bogard and Abraham Claypool, Randolph County's delegates to the General Assembly, gloomily informed Governor Lee that St. Clair's defeat had been of "sufficient moment" that westerners must, for the protection of their families and constituents, turn to Lee "as the Guardian & protector of our lives, our rights, our liberties." Confidence in measures taken by the federal government was so lacking that William Lowther of Harrison County declared on March 26, 1793, that he could not "conceive that General Wain's army nor the talk of peace Can be any safty to us."[10]

In spite of the doubts that assailed the trans-Allegheny settlers and their leaders, the federal government soon gave convincing evidence of its ability to deal effectively with troublesome Indians. In August, 1794, an expedition under General Anthony Wayne dealt the Indians a decisive blow at the battle of Fallen Timbers. The Indians, some 2,000 strong, who had gathered near Fort Miami, which the British had built on the Maumee River for the protection of Detroit, were deserted by their British allies, who had no intention of engaging in battle against a nation with which Britain was not at war. Left to fight alone, the Indians were demoralized, and early in 1795 their disheartened chiefs gathered at Fort Greenville to sign a treaty dictated by Wayne. By the terms of the agreement the Indians gave up all of Ohio except a small strip along Lake Erie, a tract of land in Indiana, and sixteen sites on strategic waterways for use as trading posts. Except for a few scattered forays in the summer of 1795, Indian attacks upon West Virginia frontiers

---

[10] Duvall to Beverly Randolph, November 27, 1791, *ibid.*, V, 400-401; Duvall to Henry Lee, December 8, 1791, *ibid.*, p. 406; Bogard and Claypool to Lee, December 6, 1791, *ibid.*, pp. 405-406; Lowther to Henry Lee, March 26, 1793, *ibid.*, VI, 317-18.

ceased. So completely did Wayne's victory break the power of the Indians and destroy their faith in their British allies that in December, 1794, George Clendenin and William Morris, Kanawha County's delegates in the General Assembly informed Governor Lee that one militia company was adequate for the defense of Kanawha and Greenbrier counties and that with the "success of our arms in the Westward," little or no winter establishment was necessary.[11]

Meanwhile, the Washington administration had taken steps to induce the British to surrender the Northwest posts and the Spanish to remove barriers to the navigation of the Mississippi. By the terms of Jay's Treaty, signed on November 14, 1794, Great Britain agreed to relinquish the Northwest posts by June 1, 1796, but the United States promised to permit Canadian traders to operate in the area on essentially the same basis as American traders. Jay's Treaty was a natural complement to Wayne's victory at Fallen Timbers. Pinckney's Treaty, concluded with Spain on October 27, 1795, ended more than a decade of turmoil in the Southwest. It opened the Mississippi River to American navigation and provided Americans with a "privilege" of deposit at New Orleans for three years. The opening of the Mississippi, the use of warehouses, and the exemption of American goods from customs duties were essential to the economic development of Allegheny regions cut off from eastern trade centers by mountain barriers.

Although West Virginians were impressed by all of these achievements, they regarded the effort to subdue hostile Indians as of transcendent importance. The priority which they gave to peace with the Indians accounts, more than any other factor, for the failure of transmontane settlers to join the farmers of western Pennsylvania in the Whiskey Rebellion of 1794. Like their Pennsylvania neighbors, West Virginians were mostly small farmers who manufactured their grains into whiskey for easier marketing. They, too, regarded the excise tax imposed upon whiskey in 1791 as discriminatory in nature, excessive in amount, and calculated to drain the western country of its

---

[11] Clendenin and Morris to Lee, December 2, 1794, *ibid.*, VII, 389. Good brief accounts of Wayne's expedition are in Clark, *Frontier America*, pp. 160-65; Billington, *Westward Expansion*, pp. 225-26.

already scarce specie. Yet, they were unwilling to permit even the detested tax to interfere with Wayne's campaign and with the long-sought chastisement of the troublesome western tribes.

On the other hand, the Whiskey Rebellion, which centered in the Monongahela section of Pennsylvania and more particularly in Washington County, elicited strong sympathy from residents of contiguous counties of West Virginia, and they were urged to join in the defiance of federal authority. In Ohio County opponents of the tax attacked Zacheus Biggs, the excise officer, and forced distillers to ignore the law. After warning the collector at Morgantown that his property would be destroyed if he attempted to enforce the law, about thirty men with blackened faces called at his house for the purpose of forcing him to give up his commission, but found upon arrival that the "scaray" officer had already posted his resignation to his door and fled. In Martinsburg opponents of the excise tax attempted to erect a liberty pole but were dispersed by the militia and their pole torn down. Except for these incidents, the northern counties of West Virginia indicated a sullen, but precarious, acceptance of the unpopular measure. Only one West Virginia county—Ohio—complied with the invitation of Pennsylvanians that it send delegations to a meeting at Parkinson's Ferry on August 14 for the purpose of devising methods of bringing the federal authorities to terms and concerting efforts toward that end. William McKinley, William Sutherland, and Robert Stephenson, Ohio County's three representatives, were among those who met with federal commissioners on August 20 to discuss the situation. They and their colleagues agreed, however, to accept the excise tax in return for a guarantee of general amnesty for participants in the disturbances. On August 28, William McKinley told the federal commissioners that "the more I think of the excise the more I hate it, but I have no Intention of opposing it, but in a Constitutional way." His statement undoubtedly reflected the thinking of the majority of the inhabitants of trans-Allegheny West Virginia.[12]

[12] The most convenient accounts of the Whiskey Rebellion in West Virginia are found in letters from David Bradford to John McCally, et al., August 6, 1794, Palmer and others, eds., *Calendar of Virginia State Papers*, VII, 249; H. H. Brackenridge to Tench Coxe, August 8, 1794, *ibid.*, pp. 251-53; Edward Smith to

During the climactic summer of 1794 the serenity of even the frontier churches was broken by the intense feeling engendered by the excise tax. John Corbly, the founder of the Forks of Cheat Baptist Church, was one of the "most violent for Resistance" in Pennsylvania. John McMillan, an influential Presbyterian minister, who had been one of the first of his denomination to visit trans-Allegheny West Virginia, threatened, on the other hand, to excommunicate members of his Pennsylvania congregation who did not sign promises to submit to federal authority. Once the disturbance was over, the Redstone and Ohio presbyteries, which included northern West Virginia churches, followed a suggestion of the Virginia Synod and called for a day of fasting and prayer as atonement for the "late very sinful and unconstitutional opposition . . . to some of the laws of the United States."[13]

The effects of the excise controversy upon religious harmony were temporary, but their generation of sharp political cleavages in the Allegheny sections of Virginia was of enduring significance. For many persons, the excise became the focus for an intense aversion to most of Hamilton's nationalistic financial measures. Once the Indian menace was eliminated, the discontented elements felt free to vent their opposition. Quite naturally, they looked to Thomas Jefferson and James Madison for leadership

Edward Carrington, August 17, 1794, *ibid.*, pp. 267-68; William McCleery to Henry Lee, August 28, 1794, *ibid.*, p. 279; Benjamin Wilson to Henry Lee, September 2, 1794, *ibid.*, pp. 289-90; John Haymond to Henry Lee, September 4, 1794, *ibid.*, p. 294; William Lowther to Henry Lee, September 8, 1794, *ibid.*, pp. 298-99; George Jackson to James Wood, September 9, 1794, *ibid.*, pp. 303-304; George Jackson to Henry Lee, September 9, 1794, *ibid.*, p. 304; Henry Lee to James Wood, September 19, 1794, *ibid.*, p. 318; Edward Carrington to James Wood, September 24, 1794, *ibid.*, pp. 323-24; Thomas Mathews to James Wood, October 6, 1794, *ibid.*, pp. 341-42; and Alexander Wells to Governor [Robert Brooke], November 2, 1795, *ibid.*, VIII, 306-307. See also the proclamation of Governor Henry Lee, August 19, 1794, *ibid.*, VII, 265-66, and Henry Haymond, *History of Harrison County, West Virginia* (Morgantown, W. Va., 1910), pp. 406-408. For the situation in Ohio County, and more particularly for the role of William McKinley, enlightening information is found in William McKinley to [James] Ross, [Jasper] Yeates, and [William] Bradford, August 23, 1794, John G. Jackson Papers, Eli Lilly Library, Indiana University. See also undated Statement by William McKinley and a letter from Daniel Morgan to William McKinley, April 15, 1795, *ibid.*, Leland D. Baldwin, *Whiskey Rebels: The Story of a Frontier Uprising* (Pittsburgh, Pa., 1949), pp. 105, 137, 175, 190, 198, 205-207, 257, passim; John C. Miller, *The Federalist Era, 1789–1801* (New York, 1960), pp. 155-60.
13 Baldwin, *Whiskey Rebels*, pp. 48-49, 198, 205, 218, 257.

and became active supporters of the emerging Republican party. In 1795, George Jackson of Harrison County, a leading opponent of the excise tax, won election to Congress. Jackson had sought reelection to the House of Delegates in 1794 and lost by only five or six votes. During the course of the campaign he had visited Monongalia and Ohio counties, where he found strong opposition to the excise tax. According to one of his political rivals, Jackson then became anti-excise himself in the belief that he would "make a bridge of the Excise Law upon which he would walk into the house of Congress." Others who had been active in opposing the excise tax, including William McKinley and William Sutherland of Ohio County, again held positions of trust in state and local government.[14]

On the other hand, supporters of Hamilton's policies, who believed that the achievements of the federal government far outweighed its deficiencies, stood firm under the Federalist banner. In 1797 the western sections of Virginia elected General Daniel Morgan, who lived in Frederick County but whose district included Berkeley County, and James Machir, who for four years had represented Hardy County in the House of Delegates, to Congress. That both of these men were Federalists is indication of substantial Federalist strength in West Virginia.

The breach between the Republicans and Federalists widened with the passage of the Alien and Sedition Acts of 1798. The Republicans struck back at the Federalist legislation with the Virginia and Kentucky Resolutions, adopted by the legislatures of the two states. The work of Jefferson and Madison, the resolutions set forth a compact theory of government and a vigorous assertion of states' rights. In Virginia, George Keith Taylor, a resident of Prince George County and a brother-in-law of John Marshall, branded the resolutions an incendiary attack upon a perfectly constitutional government. John Taylor of Caroline, on the other hand, upheld the compact theory and the right of the states to prevent usurpation of power by the federal government.[15]

---

[14] Benjamin Wilson to Henry Lee, September 2, 1794, Palmer and others, eds., *Calendar of Virginia State Papers*, VII, 289-90; Alexander Wells to [Robert Brooke], November 2, 1795, *ibid.*, VIII, 306-307.

[15] Ambler, *Sectionalism in Virginia*, pp. 65-71.

Members of the General Assembly representing West Virginia counties voted ten to five against the Virginia Resolutions. In an open letter to their constituents, Magnus Tate and John Dixon, Berkeley County's delegates, defended their votes against the resolutions on the ground that they were couched in terms of invective against the federal government. That government, they contended, was the "result of a compact, not between the States, but between the People of the United States, and as such not under the control of the State Legislatures, but of the people themselves." One of the stoutest defenders of the action of the General Assembly was John George Jackson, son of George Jackson, and brother-in-law of James Madison. In his defense of the resolutions, Jackson, who represented Harrison County in the House of Delegates, had the able support of John Dawson, a congressman from northwestern Virginia and a close political ally of Jefferson and Madison.[16]

One of the most outspoken opponents of the Virginia Resolutions was another congressman, Daniel Morgan, whose constituency included Berkeley County. Declaring that he had never felt "more anxious" for the fate of the country, Morgan in 1799 urged voters to elect "men of sound politics, friends to their country and government" in the coming elections. He vigorously defended the Federalist programs and declared that if the people wanted the protection of government they must be willing to pay for it. He saw no "inconveniency" in the Alien and Sedition Acts and in fact maintained that "no government can exist without them."[17]

Sentiment of the people of West Virginia regarding the Virginia Resolutions was also divided, but generally it coincided with their views concerning other Federalist legislation. The county court of Greenbrier County was so incensed that it destroyed and trampled under foot copies of Madison's *Report* and of the resolutions themselves. In Berkeley County James Ferguson campaigned for the House of Delegates on a platform

---

[16] The statement of Magnus Tate and John Dixon is in the Martinsburg *Potomak Guardian*, January 2, 1799. For Jackson's attitude, see Ambler, *Sectionalism in Virginia*, pp. 71-72.

[17] Morgan's statement is in the Martinsburg *Potomak Guardian*, April 17, 1799. For a similar statement, see Ambler, *Sectionalism in Virginia*, pp. 73-74.

which charged that the Alien and Sedition Acts were "flagrant violations of the Constitution, and absolutely inexpedient and impolitic." He branded a standing army, favored by Federalists, as "destructive of . . . liberties, and the occasion of unnecessary and oppressive taxes." He approved the Constitution, he said, but he reserved the right to his own opinion concerning its administration. Nathaniel Willis' *Potomak Guardian,* West Virginia's only newspaper at the time, excoriated the Federalist legislation, pronouncing the Sedition Act a "dreadful law" which restricted freedom of the press. It questioned the need for a standing army or for a navy as protection to commerce which it charged did not exist.[18]

During the ensuing months the Republicans gathered strength in Virginia. Although the elections of 1799 resulted in Federalist gains in the Tidewater, the transmontane sections of the state leaned toward Republicanism. The General Assembly of 1799–1800 by a vote of 100 to 63 accepted Madison's *Report,* which set forth replies to arguments raised against the Virginia Resolutions. In the expectation that the Presidential race in 1800 would be close, Republicans set up organizations in each county and a five-member central committee in Richmond. Richard Claiborne, a member of the Monongalia County committee, however, informed Governor James Monroe that "from the present temper of the Inhabitants of this county (being federal) not much is to be expected from them towards Republican works—in some owing to the personal influence of a few old Residents, grown into the character of Federalism by habit or premeditation, and perhaps not just reasoning; and in others from a want of literature and a perusal of instructive productions." This situation would continue, he wrote, until "an improved education or some competant [sic] and active Republican can effect a renovation."[19]

With the election of 1800, in which Jefferson carried Virginia

[18] Ambler, *Sectionalism in Virginia,* p. 72; Martinsburg *Potomak Guardian,* January 24, March 27, April 10, 1799.

[19] Ambler, *Sectionalism in Virginia,* pp. 78-79; Richard Claiborne to Governor James Monroe, May 20, 1800, Palmer and others, eds., *Calendar of Virginia State Papers,* IX, 111-12. For a list of the members of the Republican Committees in West Virginia, see *ibid.,* pp. 74-86.

with a majority of 13,363 votes in a total of 20,797, it became clear that Republicanism was in the ascendancy in Virginia. Although the Federalists won the votes of some staunch Presbyterians, Methodists, and Baptists, who were concerned about Jefferson's religious views, the Republicans steadily gained strength, particularly in western sections of the state. The stroke by which the Jeffersonians clinched their hold upon the westerners was the purchase of Louisiana from France in 1803. The collapse of Napoleon's scheme for a new French empire in America in which Louisiana would serve as the granary for valuable West Indian sugar islands provided the United States with an unexpected opportunity to gain control of the vast Mississippi Valley and to calm the fears of westerners who found French possession of the mouth of the great river intolerable. The diplomatic achievements of the Federalists were thus not merely matched but almost dwarfed by the accomplishment of the Republican President.[20]

The acquisition of Louisiana and the uninterrupted navigation of the Mississippi, however, did not solve the economic problems of trans-Allegheny pioneers. Lack of up-to-date information on prices at New Orleans, the long and arduous journey down the Mississippi, competition in a glutted market, and trading amid strange conditions sapped the profits which the pioneer exporter hoped to realize from his agricultural goods. A depression which settled upon the western country in 1808, and which was erroneously attributed to the British blockade of Europe, added to the difficulty. To many residents of West Virginia, Britain, the traditional enemy, was responsible, and they staunchly defended efforts of the federal government, including the Embargo of 1807 and the Non-Intercourse Act of 1809, to bring her to terms.[21]

The War of 1812, not unexpectedly, drew enthusiastic support from trans-Allegheny West Virginia but found less favor in the Eastern Panhandle, where Federalism remained relatively

---

[20] Ambler, *Sectionalism in Virginia*, pp. 79-80; Norman K. Risjord, "The Virginia Federalists," *Journal of Southern History*, XXXIII (November, 1967), 507-508.

[21] For western economic problems, see, for example, Billington, *Westward Expansion*, pp. 268-70.

strong. In a typical display of western nationalism and patriotism, Nimrod Saunders, a captain of cavalry, and James Laidley, captain of a rifle company, wrote to Governor James Barbour from Parkersburg that they wished to use their men "in defense of the violated rights of our beloved country. Though we might feel safe from British outrage—though we may not fear the depredations of the savages—from our peculiar local situation, yet we are members of the great Union, and our lives shall be devoted to the security of the whole." Captains had little difficulty in raising volunteer militia companies; in fact, any need to resort to a draft was considered a mark of a lack of patriotism. Carver Willis of Jefferson County had to report that in raising its quota of men his county had "to their eternal shame and disgrace" been forced to draft 116 recruits, but he took comfort in the fact that the situation had been "confined to the nest of federalists (I will not say Tories) inhabiting this and a few adjoining counties."[22]

During the years immediately following the War of 1812 West Virginians displayed remarkable harmony in their views on national political affairs. The Federalist party was in a state of decline, and the Republicans suffered a minimum of internal bickering and factionalism. Even the deepseated differences between eastern and western Virginia were muffled during this Era of Good Feelings. Although the westerners, generally, condemned the decisions of the Supreme Court in the cases of *Martin* v. *Hunter's Lessee, McCulloch* v. *Maryland,* and *Cohens* v. *Virginia,* they were, whether Republicans or Federalist, decidedly nationalistic in political outlook.

The postwar nationalism of West Virginians, built upon Republican no less than upon Federalist achievements, was buttressed by the needs of a nascent industrial economy, particularly in the trans-Allegheny areas. It manifested itself in the votes of West Virginia congressmen on numerous significant

---

[22] Saunders and Laidley to Barbour, May 23, 1812, Palmer and others, eds., *Calendar of Virginia State Papers,* X, 147; Willis to Governor James Barbour, May 21, 1812, *ibid.,* pp. 146-47. For other expressions of western sentiment, see John Connell to Governor [James] Barbour, September 1, 1812, *ibid.,* p. 162, and September 15, 1812, *ibid.,* pp. 165-66; and James Marshall to Governor [James] Barbour, September 1, 1812, *ibid.,* p. 163.

issues, including the establishment of a second Bank of the United States, the adoption of a protective tariff, and federal expenditures for internal improvements.

At the time of the chartering of the second Bank of the United States, there was not a single incorporated bank in all of West Virginia. Infant industries were hampered by an acute shortage of specie and the necessity of relying upon the paper of numerous shaky banking institutions in surrounding states. A national bank which could emit its own paper and bring some order into the chaotic financial conditions offered encouragement to western industry. Representatives from trans-Allegheny West Virginia voted with the majority of Southern congressmen in favor of the bill to charter the bank.

Sentiment for a protective tariff developed more slowly in West Virginia. The protective features of the tariff of 1816 were supported by the upper Ohio and Monongahela valleys, where the woolen and iron industries had been established, but were opposed by the Eastern Panhandle and the area south of the Kanawha. Even as late as 1820 western Virginia showed little interest in the tariff measure then under consideration by Congress. During the 1820's, however, interest in a protective tariff increased rapidly. Kanawha Valley saltmakers began to experience serious competition from salt imported from the West Indies by way of New Orleans. Iron producers of the Valley of Virginia and the Monongahela and upper Ohio areas began to seek protection for their products, as did wool growers and producers of the northwestern counties. Except for a Kentucky delegation, the two delegates from northwestern Virginia were the only representatives from south of the Potomac at the Harrisburg Convention, which in 1827 drew up a memorial to Congress, calling for the setting of minimum valuations on textiles and additional duties on hemp, flax, hammered bar iron and steel, and other goods. Not surprisingly, West Virginia representatives in Congress voted unanimously for the Tariff of Abominations in 1828.

In their support for federal-financed internal improvements, West Virginia's representatives in Congress were in complete agreement. A bill introduced into the House of Representatives on December 23, 1816, by John C. Calhoun, provided that the profits which the federal government might receive from the Bank of the United States should be set aside for internal improvements. This Bonus Bill received the unanimous support of congressmen representing West Virginia districts, but strong opposition by eastern representatives revealed the clash of fundamental economic interests between eastern and western Virginians. Although it passed the House by the narrow margin of 86 to 84 and the Senate by 20 to 15 votes, the bill was vetoed by President James Madison.[23] Ironically, residents of the Allegheny sections of Virginia were now forced to place much of their hope for internal improvements upon the General Assembly, which was dominated by the very elements which opposed federal aid to such projects.

With regard to the Missouri controversy of 1820, which stirred the dormant slavery question, West Virginians were in substantial agreement with eastern Virginians. The "fire bell in the night," so distinctly heard by Jefferson, failed to arouse any antislavery impulses in even those areas of West Virginia where the peculiar institution scarcely existed. Congressman James Pindall, like other Southerners, maintained that the slavery provision of the Northwest Ordinance of 1787 applied only to the territorial stages of the Northwest Territory and was not a precedent for later legislation. Power over the institution rested with the states and had not been granted to the federal government by the Constitution, which, declared Pindall, was "a national, or rather international compact" between the states themselves and the states and the federal government. Pindall agreed with Ballard Smith, his colleague from the Kanawha area, that extension of slavery did not increase, but merely diffused it. The Clarksburg *Republican Compiler,* while opposed to the extension of slavery and favoring a constitutional amendment giving Congress authority to abolish it, contended that Congress did not possess "any constitutional power to prohibit slavery in any state." Only five of Virginia's twenty-three con-

23 Ambler, *Sectionalism in Virginia,* pp. 97-107, 110-24; Risjord, "The Virginia Federalists," pp. 511-14; Thomas P. Abernethy, *The South in the New Nation, 1789-1819* ([Baton Rouge, La.], 1961), pp. 426-33.

gressional votes were cast in favor of the Missouri Compromise. None of those favoring the measure represented West Virginia constituencies.[24]

Although West Virginians generally opposed what they considered an unwarranted and unconstitutional assumption of authority by Congress in the Missouri controversy, their essentially nationalistic orientation was patently demonstrated in the elections of 1824 and 1828. Counties in which there was a strong interest in internal improvements voted in 1824 for John Quincy Adams or Andrew Jackson, both of whom were considered friendly to such federal projects. Henry Clay, the advocate of the American System, carried Ohio County, where the National Road was contributing to the development of Wheeling into an industrial center. William H. Crawford showed some strength in undeveloped areas along the Ohio and Cheat rivers, but his major support lay in eastern Virginia.

Far more exciting was the election of 1828, in which the popular vote was nearly two and one-half times that of 1824. In western Virginia the crucial issue was again that of internal improvements. Jackson carried most of the Monongahela Valley, the northern half of the Northern Panhandle, and an area south of the Kanawha River. Adams, a known friend of federal appropriations for internal improvements, won the votes of the Ohio County area, a belt of counties lying between Winchester and Parkersburg, and the Greenbrier-Kanawha region.[25] An analysis of the vote is difficult, since both candidates drew support from industrialized as well as from essentially rural areas.

The approval which West Virginians generally gave to policies of the federal government contrasted sharply with their growing discontent with their own state government in Richmond. When the Virginia constitution was adopted in 1776, the West Virginia counties were basically agricultural, and landholding was relatively broadly distributed among small farmers. At that time

---

[24] Glover Moore, *The Missouri Controversy, 1819–1821* (Lexington, Ky., 1953), pp. 120, 121, 232; Ambler, *Sectionalism in Virginia*, p. 107; Clarksburg *Republican Compiler*, February 4, 1820; Charles S. Sydnor, *The Development of Southern Sectionalism, 1819–1848* ([Baton Rouge, La.], 1948), p. 129.

[25] Ambler, *Sectionalism in Virginia*, pp. 127–36.

neither suffrage requirements nor the basis for representation in the General Assembly placed the Valley and Allegheny regions at any serious political disadvantage vis-à-vis the Tidewater and Piedmont. Between 1790 and 1830, however, the population and economic life of West Virginia, particularly the Allegheny areas, underwent drastic change. The white population increased from 50,593 in 1790 to 157,084 in 1830. The white population of the remainder of Virginia during the same period rose from 335,551 to 360,282, but a substantial part of the increase was in the Valley and southwestern sections. Thousands of West Virginians in 1830, particularly in the industrial areas, were artisans, un-skilled laborers, and merchants, who lacked the fifty acres, later reduced to twenty-five, or the town house and lot, required for voting in Virginia.[26]

Restrictions upon suffrage, which disfranchised an estimated 31,000 out of 76,000 men of legal voting age in Virginia in 1829, drew strong condemnation from the Allegheny residents. Al-though West Virginia's share of the disqualified, by the very nature of her population increases, was growing, objections to the qualifications derived also from political principle. As early as 1799, James Ferguson of Berkeley County, an unsuccessful candidate for the General Assembly, declared that the right to vote should be extended to "all persons who contribute to the support and defense of government, by paying taxes, performing militia duty, &c. with the restriction, perhaps, of a short term of residence." More vitriolic tones were employed by the Clarks-burg *Republican Compiler,* which noted that "when the taxes are levied, when the roads want working, when jurors are wanted at court, when war is declared and soldiers are wanted, then no freehold is necessary; no distinction is made—and if there is any distinction, it is universally in favor of the rich. But when the election day is here, and we approach the polls to enjoy the greatest blessings of heaven, 'tis then we hear the ridiculous and impudent question, '*Are you a freeholder?*'" It was an astound-ing fact, the editor declared, that "a free negro in the state of Pennsylvania has ten thousand times more liberty than nearly

[26] *Ibid.,* pp. 137-38; Ohio County Legislative Petitions, December 15, 1812.

two thirds of the white free born sons of Virginia."[27]

In the interest of fairness, it is worth noting that property requirements for voting probably affected eastern Virginians as adversely as residents of the Valley and Allegheny regions. For many residents of the Tidewater, land was dear and almost unobtainable, whereas cheap wildlands were abundant in transmontane sections. Many persons in mountainous areas acquired necessary acreages at minimal cost for the express purpose of qualifying as voters. Hugh Phelps and John G. Henderson, who failed in 1800 to win election as delegates to the General Assembly from Wood County, accused the victors, Abner Lord and Joseph Spencer, of gaining their seats by conveying to 37 persons tracts totaling 1,900 acres of allegedly nonexistent land as a means of capturing their votes.[28]

A frequent complaint, and one in which satisfaction involved no threat to the existing power structure in Virginia, was that many eligible voters were effectively disfranchised because of the great distances which they had to travel in order to cast their ballots. Most Allegheny counties had few polling places, and to reach them voters had to contend with poor roads, flooded streams, cold weather, and other inconveniences. Partly because of large election districts, only 275 to 325 of Greenbrier County's 700 freeholders ordinarily voted in the 1820's. Residents of mountainous areas presented dozens of memorials to the legislature requesting that voting precincts be broken up into more convenient units.[29]

The enfranchisement of all adult white males would not have solved the more serious problem of underrepresentation of many western counties in the General Assembly. Under a constitutional provision which allotted each county, irrespective of its population, two seats in the House of Delegates, rapidly growing western counties had no greater voice in legislative affairs than

[27] Ambler, *Sectionalism in Virginia,* p. 138; Martinsburg *Potomak Guardian,* March 27, 1799; Clarksburg *Republican Compiler,* quoted in Wheeling *Virginia North-Western Gazette,* August 29, 1818.

[28] Wood County Legislative Petitions, December 4, 1800; Ambler, *Sectionalism in Virginia,* p. 138.

[29] Greenbrier County Legislative Petitions, December 12, 1827. For similar requests, see Kanawha County Legislative Petitions, December 5, 1828; Hampshire County Legislative Petitions, December 4, 1823; *ibid.,* December 9, 1824; Greenbrier County Legislative Petitions, December 9, 1811.

small eastern counties where population was either static or declining. Indeed, the very number of eastern counties assured the Tidewater and Piedmont of control of the House of Delegates. The creation of 18 new counties in West Virginia after 1783, bringing the total number to 23 in 1830, in no way disturbed the political supremacy of eastern Virginia. The disparity in population of the constituencies of the delegates placed Allegheny residents at a disadvantage in legislation concerning taxes, education, internal improvements, and other vital matters.[30]

Time after time West Virginians branded the inequities in representation as inconsistent with democratic political principles. "No doctrine," declared a Wood County memorial, "has received a more universal assent than that in a republican government the will of the majority should be the law of the land. And yet in a state, boasting of the pure republican character of its institutions, this first and fundamental principle of republicanism does not exist." The government of Virginia, it contended, was in the hands of a minority, and "still more pernicious to the general interests, in the hands of a minority, inhabiting a particular section of the state." The petitioners noted that 49 counties in the eastern and southern parts of the state, together with 3 boroughs within their borders, had a majority in the House of Delegates, even though in 1810 their 204,766 white inhabitants were 72,138 less than one-half the white population of Virginia. According to the Wood Countians, the Tidewater should also have 7 rather than 13 state senators, while areas west of the Blue Ridge should be granted 9 instead of 4.[31]

As part of the western effort to break the power of the Tidewater and the Piedmont, petitions were circulated in most West Virginia counties in 1822 calling for removal of the capital from Richmond to some place in the Valley of Virginia. Advocates of changing the seat of government cited statistics provided by the 1820 census, which revealed that the majority of white Virginians lived west of the Blue Ridge. They feigned great

[30] Typical complaints of West Virginians about the system of representation are set forth in Pendleton County Legislative Petitions, December 14, 1824.
[31] Wood County Legislative Petitions, November 20, 1816.

concern for the vulnerability of Richmond in case of an attack by a foreign power. Noting that most of the state was agricultural and that Richmond had a mercantile orientation, they questioned whether the "enlightened population of highly polished manners" of that city could contribute more to the "Wisdom or despatch of public measures or . . . to the perpetuity of a Republic, than [the] frugality, economy, and simplicity of manners," which by inference characterized western and rural areas.[32]

Westerners found no more satisfaction in their county governments, which in many respects had even greater immediate effects upon their lives than did the state administration. Like all pioneers, residents of the Alleghenies wanted local governments brought close to the people. Prime targets of popular attack were the county courts. These bodies, consisting of the justices of the peace, were appointed by the governor upon recommendation of the sheriffs, who themselves were ordinarily drawn from the court membership. Clothed with executive, legislative, and judicial power, the court appointed civil officials of the county and all military officers below the rank of brigadier general, laid the county levies, and filled numerous honorary and remunerative positions. The most lucrative county office, that of sheriff, was ordinarily passed around among members of the county court, but actual duties of the office were usually assigned to deputies.[33]

Common complaints against the county courts centered around the undemocratic method by which members were chosen, the prevalence of nepotism, their inefficient administration, neglect of isolated areas of the counties, and lack of responsibility to the public which they were to serve. Residents of Ohio County, where twelve of the twenty-seven justices had served more than ten years, declared in 1822 that they "religiously" believed that most of their troubles had "their origin in the present local situa-

[32] Monongalia County Legislative Petitions, December 20, 1821. See also Kanawha County Legislative Petitions, December 5, 1822; Pendleton County Legislative Petitions, December 5, 1822; Mason County Legislative Petitions, December 4, 1822; Monongalia County Legislative Petitions, December 4, 1822; Greenbrier County Legislative Petitions, December 5, 1822; Wheeling *Virginia North-Western Gazette*, February 8, 1823.

[33] Ambler, *Sectionalism in Virginia*, pp. 139-40.

tion of the courts." Members of the court, they told the General Assembly, were "imbued with the prerogative of perpetuating their own existence without the intervention of the people, [and were] . . . wholly irresponsible to them for the all important power of taxation and appropriation." They pointedly reminded the legislature that it was the "declared right of taxing America, without representation, which produced the severance of these U[nited] States from their parent country." Hampshire Countians, branding the method of filling the offices as one of the most "palpable & Glaring" defects in county government, accused their county court of either providing or withholding sufficient magistrates to various sections of the county "according as the political sentiments of such Sections & persons as they appoint, or Omit, may square with or differ from their own." Other appointments by the court were allegedly based upon family connections rather than merit. Extensions of the franchise, the petitioners maintained, could have little benefit as long as citizens were "deprived of the Blessings of the Liberty of being governed in their Counties, by men of their own Choice." The people, they declared, should have the right to vote not only for justices of the peace, but also for sheriffs, coroners, constables, overseers of the poor, school commissioners, and militia officers.[34]

Other criticisms were leveled at the court system. "Our present County Court Jurisprudence," charged Monongalia County memorialists, "is nothing more than Mock Justice." They proposed that the law be amended to provide justices of the peace with jurisdiction in suits not exceeding $50, with the right of appeal to superior courts. Petitions were circulated in numerous counties urging that individual justices be empowered to deal with cases involving no more than $20. One plea, with the usual catalog of hardships incident to traveling long distances to court and collecting witnesses, cited a case in which a plaintiff was awarded a judgment of $11.44 but won little more than a moral victory inasmuch as his "ruinous bill" of costs amounted to $11.28. In an effort to bring justice within the reach of all, western

[34] Wheeling *Virginia North-Western Gazette,* April 5, 1823; Ohio County Legislative Petitions, December 6, 1822; Hampshire County Legislative Petitions, December 8, 1825; Harrison County Legislative Petitions, December 10, 1806.

counties sent to the legislature dozens of appeals calling for the creation of new district and chancery courts.[35]

Few legislative acts relating to legal procedures occasioned more criticism in the Allegheny and Valley areas than Virginia's law process tax, which imposed additional costs upon plaintiffs in court cases. Harrison Countians declared that it was "a tax imposed upon the POOR for the benefit of the RICH" and the "most unjust and unequal" of all the taxes in the Commonwealth. The process tax, said a group of Hampshire County residents, was another confirmation that the "rich land and slave holder is enjoying the advantages of government, . . . [and] the poor man is taxed . . . because he is poor." For impecunious West Virginians, the costs of obtaining justice exacerbated other grievances and even evoked charges of class legislation.[36]

Demands for reforms, both political and economic, led to the Staunton Convention, which met from August 19 to 23, 1816. Sixty-five delegates from thirty-five western counties aired their grievances and called for suffrage for all taxpayers and militiamen and a fair apportionment of seats in the General Assembly. Impressive weight was added to western demands by Thomas Jefferson, whose famous letter to Samuel Kercheval urged free white manhood suffrage, representation based upon white population, and popular election of the governor, judges, and county officials. The Staunton gathering ended its discussions by calling for a constitutional convention to rid the state government of its defects and to effect needed reforms.[37]

Although it was unwilling to make provision for a constitutional convention, the conservative-dominated legislature did attempt to appease western feelings. It agreed to a reapportionment of

[35] Monongalia County Legislative Petitions, December 9, 1818. Typical of memorials requesting authority for justices of the peace in cases of less than twenty dollars are Monongalia County Legislative Petitions, December 4, 1806; Harrison County Legislative Petitions, December 8, 1801; *ibid.,* December 9, 1802. For appeals for extension of chancery and district courts, see Wood County Legislative Petitions, December 5, 1811; Greenbrier County Legislative Petitions, December 21, 1802; Kanawha County Legislative Petitions, December 11, 1800; Harrison County Legislative Petitions, December 6, 1810.

[36] Harrison County Legislative Petitions, December 5, 1834; Hampshire County Legislative Petitions, December 10, 1823.

[37] Ambler, *Sectionalism in Virginia,* pp. 94-96. See also Wood County Legislative Petitions, November 20, 1816.

the Senate on the basis of white population, endeavored to insure more equitable assessments on land, created a Board of Public Works with authority to plan roads and canals, appropriated additional funds for internal improvements, and established banks at Wheeling and Winchester. The mollifying effects of these concessions were of but brief duration, and in 1824 and 1825 numerous mass meetings and conventions were held in various sections of the state to reharness the forces of reform.

Among the most important of the conventions was that held at Staunton in July, 1825. In an emotional atmosphere, its members, numbering more than a hundred, lashed out at the federal basis for representation by which slave property would increase the strength of eastern counties in the General Assembly and called for representation in accordance with white population. The suffrage, it insisted, must be conferred upon all white males over twenty-one years old. These reforms could be achieved only by amending the state's constitution. The ground swell of sentiment for reform by this time had enlisted the support—albeit it with varying degrees of enthusiasm—of both the Richmond *Whig* and the Richmond *Enquirer*, two of Virginia's most influential newspapers.[38]

The call of the Staunton delegates for a constitutional convention was echoed throughout West Virginia. The Clarksburg *Intelligencer* declared that "if every *freeholder* of Virginia was . . . 'by nature equally free,'" then changes in the constitution were essential in order to remove inequalities in representation. On the other hand, there were genuine fears even in western counties that a convention with unlimited powers might devise an instrument of government as unsatisfactory as the existing constitution. To prevent the convention from destroying parts of the constitution which were acceptable and from engaging in prolonged and expensive debate, Hampshire Countians proposed that it be empowered to amend only sections of the constitution authorized by the people.[39]

[38] Ambler, *Sectionalism in Virginia*, pp. 137-43; Claude H. Hall, *Abel Parker Upshur: Conservative Virginian, 1790-1844* (Madison, Wis., 1963), pp. 36-40.

[39] Clarksburg *Intelligencer*, August 13, 1825; Hampshire County Legislative Petitions, December 8, 1825; Monongalia County Legislative Petitions, December 12, 1825; Pendleton County Legislative Petitions, December 8, 1825.

In spite of the growing clamor for democratization of Virginia's government, eastern conservatives, in undisguised uses of power, beat down moves in the General Assembly to provide for a constitutional convention. In 1826 the reformers mustered even fewer votes than in 1825. Finally, in 1828 the legislature yielded. In the ensuing referendum supporters of the convention cast 21,896 votes; opponents numbered 16,646. As expected, about seven-eighths of the Tidewater and about half of the Piedmont votes were negative, but the Valley voted almost unanimously for a convention. Approximately three-fourths of the trans-Allegheny votes were in favor of a convention.

Despite the substantial majority by which the public voted for constitutional change, the General Assembly was slow to act. After weeks of debate, in which western delegates endeavored to secure authorization for a census and representation in the constitutional convention based upon the new population statistics, the legislature directed that each of the state's twenty-four senatorial districts select four delegates. Senatorial districts were then based upon the census of 1810. Only qualified voters were permitted to participate in the election of delegates. The western counties were at the outset placed at a distinct disadvantage in the convention.[40]

The convention, which assembled in Richmond on October 5, 1829, sparkled with men of distinction and talent. Among its members were two former Presidents of the United States, James Madison and James Monroe; Chief Justice John Marshall; two United States Senators, John Tyler, himself a future President, and Littleton W. Tazewell; and eleven congressmen, among whom were John Randolph, Charles F. Mercer, Philip P. Barbour, and Philip Doddridge; prominent judges, including John W. Green and Abel P. Upshur; and well-known lawyers such as Benjamin W. Leigh, Chapman Johnson, and Lewis Summers. With its distinguished personnel and significant agenda, the convention attracted national attention and drew numerous spectators, both native and foreign.[41]

---

40 Ambler, *Sectionalism in Virginia,* pp. 144-45; Hall, *Abel Parker Upshur,* p. 47.
41 West Virginians chosen as representatives from their senatorial districts were William McCoy, Pendleton County; Andrew Beirne, Monroe County; William Smith, Greenbrier; John Baxter, Pocahontas; Hierome L. Opie and

After unanimously electing James Monroe as its president, the convention began its work by setting up four committees—the Bill of Rights, the Legislative, the Executive, and the Judiciary, chaired by Samuel Taylor, James Madison, William B. Giles, and John Marshall, respectively. Each committee, with one member from each of the twenty-four districts, was responsible for a segment of the constitution, which it reported to the Committee of the Whole. The committees carried on their work in closed sessions and kept no official minutes. The conservatives dominated all of the committees except the Legislative.

With the exception of that of the Legislative section, the committees were able to make their recommendations, all favoring the conservatives, without undue delay. The Legislative Committee included twelve reformers and eleven conservatives, with Madison seeking to exert a moderating influence. The most serious clashes in the committee involved representation and the suffrage. The reformers, under the leadership of Doddridge, a delegate from Brooke County, insisted that membership in both houses of the legislature be based upon white population and that there be an extension of the suffrage. The conservatives, whose chief spokesman was Leigh, held out for a mixed basis, or a formula utilizing both white population and direct taxes. Madison favored a white population for the lower house but not for the Senate. Under these circumstances, Doddridge's strategy was to offer separate resolutions covering the Senate and the House of Delegates. Both called for representation based upon white population. Madison voted with the reformers to recommend the white population as the basis of representation in the House but joined the conservatives to prevent its use for the Senate. The report which the committee adopted recommended the incorporation into the constitution of the white population basis for representation in the House but omitted a similar recommendation for the Senate. It also approved an extension of the suffrage.[42]

Thomas Griggs, Jr., Jefferson; William Naylor and William Donaldson, Hampshire; Elisha Boyd and Philip C. Pendleton, Berkeley; Edwin S. Duncan, Harrison; John Laidley, Cabell; Lewis Summers, Kanawha; Adam See, Randolph; Philip Doddridge and Alexander Campbell, Brooke; Charles S. Morgan and Eugenius Wilson, Monongalia. *Proceedings and Debates of the Virginia State Convention, of 1829–30* (Richmond, Va., 1830), pp. 3-5.

On October 27 the convention began its debates on substantive constitutional issues by considering the resolution of the Legislative Committee that representation in the House should be based upon "white population exclusively." Judge Green moved an amendment to substitute the words "and taxation combined" for "exclusively." In their defense of the white basis, the reformers, dominated by westerners, drew their arguments from the Declaration of Independence. They laid heavy stress upon the concepts that men were born free, that they had inalienable rights, that government existed for the common good of the people and drew its powers from them, and that when government failed to serve popular interests the people had a right to alter or abolish it. Older conservatives, such as Madison, Monroe, Randolph, Tazewell, and William B. Giles, who feared the rising power of the western sections of the state, subscribed to the same philosophy but favored a strict construction of the Declaration. Other conservatives, such as Leigh and Upshur, argued that all men were not born free and equal, rejected the contention that a majority had the right to amend or abolish a government, and insisted that the acquisition and possession of property was an inalienable right. Despite their differences in philosophy, the conservatives generally presented a united front in voting.[43]

One of the most forceful speeches setting forth the conservative views was made by Abel P. Upshur, who countered the demands of the reformers with the argument that there was a "majority *in interest* as well as a majority in numbers." This principle, said Upshur, meant that "those who have the greatest stake in the Government shall have the greatest share . . . in the administration of it." Upshur contended that history had shown that the safety of man depended upon the rights of property and cited the example of the French Revolution as an instance in which universal male suffrage had brought disaster to a nation. He set forth the belief, already voiced by easterners, that rejection of representation for the slave population in Virginia would make

---

[42] *Proceedings and Debates of the Virginia State Convention, of 1829–30*, pp. 45-46; Ambler, *Sectionalism in Virginia*, pp. 147-48; Hall, *Abel Parker Upshur*, pp. 50-51.
[43] *Proceedings and Debates of the Virginia State Convention, of 1829–30*, p. 46; Ambler, *Sectionalism in Virginia*, pp. 149-52.

it virtually impossible for Virginia to oppose efforts to abolish the three-fifths ratio for representation in the United States House of Representatives. He refused to accept any western guarantees of restraints upon the powers of taxation and appropriation and called for continuation of the existing system on the ground that experience was the "best guide in Government."[44]

Replies to Upshur's address were set forth by Chapman Johnson and Alexander Campbell of Augusta and Brooke counties, respectively. Voicing the views of the western counties, Johnson rejected Upshur's contention that there were no first principles of government and that expediency governed the affairs of mankind. Such arguments, he contended, cast aside the views and accomplishments of the Founding Fathers and denied the very birthright of Virginia. Campbell, one of the most eloquent spokesmen for the mountainous areas, attacked Upshur's idea of a majority in interest and declared that representation for property rights must of necessity be accompanied by representation for intellect, physical strength, scientific accomplishment, or literary art, which were as important to many men as material possessions. After nearly three weeks of debating the matter of representation, the convention rejected the Green amendment by a vote of 49 to 47. During that time the reins of power slipped out of the hands of the moderate conservatives, such as Madison, Monroe, and Giles, who had hoped for some compromise and into those of more extreme conservatives. At this time the balance of power rested with a small group of uncommitted members from the Piedmont, which had for some years held "the equipoise between the West and the East" in the legislature. Fearing that adoption of the white basis would undermine their advantage, the Piedmont delegates threw their support to Upshur and the conservatives. Their move proved decisive, and on November 14 the convention, by a margin of one vote, rejected representation on the basis of white population.[45]

---

[44] *Proceedings and Debates of the Virginia State Convention, of 1829–30*, pp. 65-79; Hall, *Abel Parker Upshur*, pp. 51-55; Ambler, *Sectionalism in Virginia*, pp. 152-53.

[45] *Proceedings and Debates of the Virginia State Convention, of 1829–30*, pp. 116-24; Ambler, *Sectionalism in Virginia*, pp. 154-60; Hall, *Abel Parker Upshur*, pp. 55-57.

Compromise offered the only way out of the impasse. To this end five major plans were offered. That of John R. Cooke of Frederick County proposed the use of a combination of federal numbers and white population for representation in the Senate and white population alone for the House of Delegates. Marshall advocated a combination of white population and federal numbers for both houses, while Leigh proposed an average of the white population and mixed bases. Reformers were mildly attracted to Marshall's plan but rejected Leigh's. Upshur presented a more complicated plan by which each of the four major sections of the state would be allocated seats in both houses on the basis of a formula which took into account white population, federal numbers, and the mixed basis, with periodic reapportionments.

The fifth proposal, that of William F. Gordon of Albermarle County, became the basis of compromise. Recognizing no particular principle and lacking a provision for future reapportionment, it nevertheless provided at least temporarily a fair distribution of seats in both houses. After some modification, membership in the Senate was set at 32, with 19 senators from the East and 13 from the West. Of the 134 members provided for the House of Delegates, 36 were allotted to the Tidewater, 42 to the Piedmont, 25 to the Valley, and 31 to the trans-Allegheny region. In 1841 there might be a reapportionment, provided that two-thirds of each house of the legislature agreed, but the number of senators was not to exceed 36 and the number of delegates 150. Partly because it avoided commitment to any principle, westerners opposed the plan and voted almost unanimously against it, but conservatives and moderates united behind it, and it passed by a vote of 55 to 41.

Once it had disposed of the matter of representation, the convention turned to the question of suffrage. Reformers defended free white suffrage as a natural right, but the conservatives argued that it was a conventional right and should be restricted to those most capable of exercising it judiciously. Those in favor of an extension of the suffrage pointed out that twenty-two of the twenty-four states had abandoned property qualifications and that New York and North Carolina even permitted free Negroes to vote. Military service, long residence, and payment of taxes, they declared, indicated as great an interest in government as did the ownership of land. Charles S. Morgan of Monongalia County maintained that universal manhood suffrage would unite the citizens of the state in common interests and increase the security of slave property. Many conservatives, however, feared that enfranchisement of propertyless classes would undermine responsible government, perhaps lead to revolution, and without question, shift the balance of political power in the state westward. Debates on the question of suffrage were acrimonious, but the conservatives triumphed, and the right to vote was further extended only to small groups of leaseholders and housekeepers.

Other grievances of the western counties were left virtually untouched by the convention. A proposal by Doddridge that the governor be elected by popular vote was endorsed by Upshur and other conservatives, but it was defeated by one vote, and the office continued to be filled by the legislature. Moreover, the court system survived. John Marshall spoke against election of judges, even at the lowest levels, arguing that their election by joint ballot of the General Assembly or appointment was necessary to prevent their becoming political figures. Long tenure for judges, he declared, was both traditional and essential to true justice.

Although the final document was not entirely satisfactory to any single faction, it was approved by a vote of 55 to 40. Cooke was the only delegate from west of the Blue Ridge to vote for the constitution. Of the 40 negative votes, 39 were cast by delegates from west of the Blue Ridge. These delegates seethed with bitterness and frustration, and Alexander Campbell contemplated calling them together for the purpose of holding a separate convention with the prospect of secession from Virginia.[46]

The people of the western counties were equally outraged. As early as December 11, 1829, Wheeling residents, in a mass meeting, lashed out at the existing constitution, which enabled "an ambitious minority . . . to lord it over a majority of the people." They condemned the composition of the constitutional convention because "a decisive majority of the members" represented

[46] Ambler, *Sectionalism in Virginia*, pp. 161-66, 168-70; Hall, *Abel Parker Upshur*, pp. 57-62.

a minority of the people. As soon as it became clear, they said, that the convention was "definitely determined . . . to disregard the basis of white population in organizing the popular branch of the Legislature," their representatives, in whom they had complete confidence, and other friends of reform should withdraw and take no further part in the proceedings. Free laborers of the west, they declared, were not on a par with eastern slaves or European peasants.[47]

When the convention adopted the constitution, the Wheeling *Compiler* presented the completed document to its readers with "unfeigned sorrow." It held forth no "hopes of a rejection of this MONSTER, more odious than the 'serpent' that has so long reigned over us." The constitution, it declared, had been "GIVEN to the West" in much the same manner as a European monarch might present one to his subjects. Citizens of Ohio County shared these views, and in a mass meeting declared that the document was "unfit for the government of a free people."[48] A writer in the Wheeling *Gazette* called for a division of the state "peaceably if we can, forcibly if we must."

Western hopes that somehow the constitution might fail of ratification were quickly doomed. Every county east of the Blue Ridge, except Warwick and Lancaster, voted overwhelmingly in favor of ratification. The heaviest vote for the document was recorded in the northern and western Piedmont and the Shenandoah Valley. Only two trans-Allegheny counties, Washington and Lee, in southwestern Virginia, gave their approval to the constitution. All trans-Allegheny counties of West Virginia voted overwhelmingly against it. In Ohio County only 3 votes out of 646 were cast in favor of ratification. Brooke County, the home of Campbell and Doddridge, did not record a single favorable vote, and Harrison County counted only 8 out of 1,128. Despite the heavy opposition in the western counties, the constitution was ratified by a vote of 26,055 to 15,566.[49]

Once again there arose serious talk of dismemberment of the Old Dominion. On October 1, 1830, a mass meeting at Wheeling

47 Wheeling *Compiler*, December 23, 1829.
48 *Ibid.*, January 27, 1830; Ambler, *Sectionalism in Virginia*, pp. 170-71.
49 Ambler, *Sectionalism in Virginia*, pp. 170-72.

considered the possibility of withdrawing from Virginia and adding to Maryland that part of West Virginia lying north of a line drawn from the southwestern corner of Maryland to Parkersburg. A series of articles signed "Senex," and appearing in several newspapers, urged separation as a means of self-preservation for the trans-Allegheny region. The disaffection of the western counties appeared so great that a considerable sentiment developed in the Valley, as well as in eastern Virginia, to let them depart in peace. Gradually more moderate views prevailed, and westerners became somewhat reconciled to remaining with Virginia.[50]

The great debate in the constitutional convention over fundamental differences between eastern and western Virginia had far-reaching consequences. Until 1830 residents of Allegheny sections of West Virginia retained substantial hopes for redress of grievances. With an extension of the suffrage to free white males, a redistribution of seats in the General Assembly on the basis of white population, and election of county officials, government might yet be responsive to the needs of the people. With political influence commensurate with its increasing population, the western sections might belatedly obtain economic reforms and internal improvements. The crushing of western hopes with the adoption and ratification of the new constitution bred only greater dissatisfaction and frustration. After 1831 the slavery question further divided eastern and western Virginia. It is difficult to determine to what extent western attacks upon the institution were inspired by Abolitionist sentiment and to what extent they were the result of a conviction that slave property in eastern Virginia was inimical to the interests of the west. The discontent in the West Virginia counties, kindled during the earlier decades of the nineteenth century and fanned into flames in 1829–1830, smoldered menacingly for the ensuing twenty years. In 1850–1851 a new constitutional convention quenched some of the fires of western discontent, but by the end of the decade they were burning once more. By 1863 they had become part

---

[50] *Ibid.*, 172-74. For sentiment against separation from Virginia, see, for example, Lewisburg *Palladium of Virginia and the Pacific Monitor,* February 27, 1830.

of an even greater conflagration, which engulfed the whole nation and accentuated the cleavages between residents throughout the Alleghenies and the southern Appalachians generally, on the one hand, and their political masters, on the other. In the heat of that holocaust, the Old Dominion was rent asunder, and West Virginia emerged as a separate state.

Chapter Fifteen

An Enduring Past

Although his descendants looked back upon the frontier era with nostalgia as a time of romance and accomplishment, the truth is that the settler who cut his way into the Alleghenies wanted to get the pioneer period behind him as quickly as possible and to establish the political, social, and economic institutions which seemed essential to the fulfillment of the promise of American life. The conquest of the Alleghenies proved no easy undertaking, and in the attempt the pioneer himself seemed likely to be subdued. Indeed, his efforts to cast off the restrictive influences of a frontier environment and at the same time to preserve those values which became ingrained during the process constitute the very warp and woof of the first century of Allegheny history.

The texture of the historical fabric of the Alleghenies has been determined in large part by the geographical strands. Abundant natural resources enabled the pioneer to survive in a rugged and isolated area, but mineral wealth and timber pointed toward an industrial orientation for much of the region. In West Virginia, for example, the iron-producing sections of the Northern Panhandle in the early nineteenth century developed into an impressive steel center in the twentieth; the saline reservoir of the Ohio and Kanawha valleys, which sustained a flourishing salt industry then now supports a thriving chemical industry; the heavy stands of timber on the Allegheny slopes, tapped by the pioneer for cabins, houses, flatboats, and lumber, now feed numerous factories in the eastern United States; and coal, first tied to the salt and iron industries, became a hundred years later the lifeblood, not only of West Virginia but of most of the Allegheny region. In the nineteenth, as in the twentieth, century, industries were primarily extractive and presented unusual opportunity for exploitation and profit.

The very abundance of natural resources in the Alleghenies bred a reckless prodigality. The pioneer launched a merciless attack upon the forests and their wildlife and gave little thought to conservation. The prolonged frontier experience of the mountain pioneer undoubtedly accentuated this destructiveness. Absentee owners—in control of much of the region's land and resources by 1830—were even then intent upon wringing profits from their possessions and little concerned about political, social, and economic betterment. Heavy scars of this destructiveness and exploitation, both by its own people and by nonresidents, are everywhere apparent, and, despite sections of great progress and prosperity, the region is a conspicuous part of that depressed area known in the mid-twentieth century as Appalachia.

Geography has also presented other major problems. Rugged terrain made transportation and communication difficult, and, during the years when the great tide of population was moving westward, deprived substantial portions of the Alleghenies, including much of West Virginia, of many sturdy and optimistic yeomen. Settlers who entered the mountain fastnesses of West Virginia were for generations cut off from easy contacts with other parts of the Old Dominion and of the country. Railroad construction of the late nineteenth century was determined less by their needs than by those of industrial entrepreneurs. Not even the coming of the automobile entirely relieved the isolation of many of the state's residents. Even yet, West Virginia is in great need of better north-south communications. Unable to solve their transportation problems, West Virginians in the early nineteenth century looked in vain, first to the federal government and then to Virginia. Their difficulties did not differ in kind from those of their twentieth-century descendants, whose hopes for improved communication, like those of other Allegheny residents, rest heavily upon a combined federal-state assault upon the geographical and financial problems which have retarded communications.

The transportation difficulties and isolation of the formative years of Allegheny history inevitably gave rise to strong particularistic feelings and preserved customs, manners, and folkways which the pioneers carried into the region or developed during their initial frontier experiences. Long exposure to primitive conditions strengthened these ways of life and gave them a vitality which endured well into the twentieth century. Local and sectional feelings that developed during those formative years have survived in many cases to the present day.

Of major importance among the cultural patterns established during the pioneer period were religious affiliations. The fluidity that had characterized the religious life of the Alleghenies in the eighteenth century gave way by 1830 to strong identification with evangelical Protestant churches, particularly the Methodists, Baptists, and Presbyterians. The influx of thousands of eastern and southern Europeans into industrial centers in the mountains in the post–Civil War years in no way disturbed the basic religious structure established during the late eighteenth and early nineteenth centuries. In West Virginia, the cooperation found among pioneer churches and the later admixture of non-Protestant with predominant Protestant groups prevented widespread intolerance. Traditions of religious freedom and toleration combined with existing circumstances in 1960, for example, to give the vote of the state's Democratic presidential primary, despite some predictions to the contrary, to John F. Kennedy, a Roman Catholic.

Few problems of the Alleghenies in the twentieth century appear more staggering than those related to education. Significantly, however, nearly every major difficulty had its counterpart in the early nineteenth century. The problems of recruiting teachers, procuring finances, and overcoming popular apathy toward learning, which retarded educational development a century and a half ago, have by no means disappeared. In spite of major efforts to overcome some of its handicaps, the area still ranks low in educational achievements. Just as local efforts in the early nineteenth century failed to solve the underlying problems, so have they proved inadequate in the twentieth century, and many residents look increasingly to the federal government for help with major tasks.

The experience of the Alleghenies with federal benevolence is not new. The earliest pioneers of the mountainous regions sought and obtained federal assistance in pacifying hostile Indians, removing the menace of British occupation of the Northwest posts, opening the Mississippi to their commerce, and providing a highway linking them with eastern commercial centers. As frustration piled upon frustration in their efforts to induce the Virginia government to render necessary services, many West Virginians became increasingly nationalistic in their outlook. Similar attitudes were developed by other Allegheny residents who also clashed with the seats of power in their respective states. Their seeking of federal aid, however, has usually been balanced by a strong support of federal government. It is perhaps natural that Allegheny residents, early benefactors of federal help, should look to Washington for assistance in solving some of the great social and economic problems of the twentieth century, particularly those arising out of past neglect and exploitation.

Lest the dependence of the people of the Alleghenies upon government benevolence be viewed in an entirely negative light, let it be remembered that few people in the United States have waged a more one-sided battle with their environment or with forces of greed and exploitation. In believing that government, whether federal or state, exists for the people and their service, they have exhibited traditional concepts of democracy. For their part, West Virginians have time after time rallied to the support of American ideals and government. In this respect they are even today little different from their pioneer forefathers.

Bibliography

Manuscripts

[Alexander, James?]. Greenbrier County Ledger, 1800 [1799]-1814. West Virginia Department of Archives and History Library.

Ayres, Robert. Journal [Redstone Circuit], May 16, 1786, to June 16, 1787. Historical Society of Western Pennsylvania.

Boardman, Daniel. Papers, 1803-1826. West Virginia University Library.

Boteler, Alexander Robinson. Papers, 1776-1898. Duke University Library.

Brooke County Court Records, Land Tax Books, 1779. Microfilm, West Virginia University Library.

[Cabell and Trimble?]. Account Book, 1823-1824. West Virginia Department of Archives and History Library.

Clarksburg Presbyterian Church. Records, 1798-1903. West Virginia University Library.

Clarksburg Presbyterian Church. Records, 1832-1894. West Virginia University Library.

Cunningham, George W. Papers, 1784-1903. In possession of George W. Cunningham. (Microfilm, West Virginia University Library.)

Deakins Family. Papers, 1778-1925. West Virginia University Library.

Draper Manuscripts. State Historical Society of Wisconsin. (Microfilm, West Virginia Department of Archives and History Library.)

Ewin Family. Papers, 1784-1877. West Virginia University Library.

Ewin, James. Pendleton County Assessment Book, 1797. West Virginia University Library.

Forks of Cheat Baptist Church. Records, 1775-1830. Typescript, West Virginia University Library.

Fox Family. Papers, 1762-1859. West Virginia University Library.

Griggs, Dr. Lee. Account Book, 1821-1831. West Virginia Department of Archives and History Library.

Haymond Family. Papers, 1783-1867. West Virginia University Library.

Haymond, Luther. Diary, 1809-1830. West Virginia University Library.

Jackson, John G. Papers, 1781-1825. Eli Lilly Library, Indiana University.

Kanawha Falls Account Book, 1829-1831. West Virginia Department of Archives and History Library.

Laishley, Peter T. Papers, 1809-1915. West Virginia University Library.

Legislative Petitions, 1754-1863. Virginia State Library. (Petitions examined included those for Greenbrier, Hampshire, Hardy, Harrison, Kanawha, Madison, Monongalia, Ohio, Pendleton, and Wood counties.)

McCoy Family. Papers, 1761-1903. West Virginia University Library.

The Minutes of the Greenbrier Baptist Church, [1781-1835]. Baptist Historical Collection, West Virginia Department of Archives and History Library.

Miscellaneous Manuscripts. Box CII, 1737-1786. West Virginia Department of Archives and History Library.

Monongalia County Court Records, Delinquent Tax List, 1814. Microfilm, West Virginia University Library.

Monroe County Court Records, Minute Books, 1804-1821. Microfilm, West Virginia University Library.

Muse, Battaile. Papers. Duke University Library.

Ohio County Court Records, Land Tax Books, 1814; Survey Books, 1779-1859; Order Book, 1778-1786; Minute Books, 1815; Land Tax and Licensing Books, 1814. Microfilm, West Virginia University Library

Plats of Surveys [for Henry Banks]. In possession of Joseph M. Holt, Lewisburg, West Virginia. (Photostats, Office of the Auditor of the State of West Virginia.)

Record Book for the Zoar Church, [1824-1868]. Baptist Historical Collection, West Virginia Department of Archives and History Library.

Records of Presbyterian Church, Clarksburg, [1798-1803]. West Virginia University Library.

Records of Presbyterian Church, Clarksburg, [1832-1894]. West Virginia University Library.

Records of the Greenbrier Association of Baptists, [1825-1868]. Baptist Historical Collection, West Virginia Department of Archives and History Library.

Rigsby Family. Papers, 1755-1898. In possession of Leon Louisa Rigsby, Catlettsburg, Kentucky. (Microfilm, University of Kentucky Library.)

Rogers, John. Papers, 1777-1857. West Virginia University Library.

Ruffner, Henry. Papers. Historical Foundation of the Presbyterian and Reformed Churches, Montreat, North Carolina.

Scott, Thomas. Manuscripts. In possession of the Reverend Lawrence Sherwood, Oakland, Maryland.

Smith, George W. Papers, 1818-1885. West Virginia University Library.

Smith, John. Journal . . . on the Greenbrier Circuit, July 4, 1787, to July 8, 1788. Garrett Biblical Institute. (Typescript owned by the Reverend Lawrence Sherwood, Oakland, Maryland.)

South Branch Valley Manuscripts, 1762-1940. West Virginia Department of Archives and History Library.

Stevens, Alexander, and Company Account Book, 1817-1818. Monroe County Court Records. (Microfilm, West Virginia University Library.)

Steward's Book for the Berkeley Circuit [of the Methodist Church], 1807-1820. Methodist Historical Society, Lovely Lane Museum, Baltimore, Maryland.

Subject Indexes to Monongalia, Ohio, and Brooke County Court Records. West Virginia University Library.

Survey of Patterson's Creek Manor of Lord Fairfax by Joseph Neavill, November 20, 1762. Typescript, West Virginia Department of Archives and History Library.

Tavenner-Withers Papers. Duke University Library.

U. S., Bureau of the Census. Census Returns, 1810: Population Schedules. Microfilm, West Virginia Department of Archives and History Library.

Ward, Henry Dans. Journal, [1843-1862]. In possession of Charles

Carpenter. (Microfilm, West Virginia University Library.)
West Virginia Land Grants. Virginia State Library. (Transcripts, Office of
the Auditor of the State of West Virginia.) Examination was made of
grants lying in Bath, Botetourt, Fincastle, Greenbrier, Hampshire, Hardy,
Harrison, Kanawha, Monongalia, Montgomery, Ohio, Pendleton, Ran-
dolph, Russell, and Wythe counties.
Wilson and Stribling Families. Papers, ca. 1781-1934. West Virginia
University Library.
Wood County School Commissioners. Reports, 1820-1841. West Virginia
University Library.

Public Documents

Commonwealth of Virginia. *Fifth Annual Report of the President and
Directors of the Board of Public Works, to the General Assembly of
Virginia.* Richmond, Va., 1820.
*Governor's Letter, Transmitting a Statement of the Accounts of the Literary
Fund, for the Year Ending 30th September, 1825.* Richmond, Va., 1825.
Hening, William Waller, comp. *The Statutes-at-Large: Being a Collection
of All the Laws of Virginia from the First Session of the Legislature in the
Year 1619.* 13 vols. Richmond, Va., 1809-1823.
Kennedy, John Pendleton, and McIlwaine, H. R., eds. *Journals of the
House of Burgesses of Virginia, 1619-1776.* 13 vols. Richmond, Va.,
1905-1915.
McIlwaine, H. R., Hall, Wilmer, and Hillman, Benjamin J., eds. *Executive
Journals of the Council of Colonial Virginia.* 6 vols. Richmond, Va.,
1925-1966.
*Minutes of the Provincial Council of Pennsylvania from the Organization
to the Termination of the Proprietary Government, 1683-1775.* 10 vols.
in *Colonial Records of Pennsylvania.* 16 vols. Philadelphia, 1851-1853.
Palmer, W. P. and others, eds. *Calendar of Virginia State Papers and Other
Manuscripts.* 11 vols. Richmond, Va., 1875-1893.
Proceedings and Debates of the Virginia State Convention, of 1829-1830.
Richmond, Va., 1830.
*The Proceedings of the Convention of Delegates held at the Capitol in the
City of Williamsburg in the Colony of Virginia, . . . May, 1776.* Richmond,
Va., 1816.
*Second Auditor's Report on the State of the Literary Fund, and Proceedings
of the School Commissioners, in the Different Counties, for the Year End-
ing September 30, 1831.* Richmond, Va., 1831.
*Second Auditor's Report on the State of the Literary Fund, and Proceedings
of the School Commissioners, in the Different Counties, for the Year
Ending September 30, 1832.* Richmond, Va., 1832.
*Second Auditor's Report on the State of the Literary Fund, for the Year
1834, and Preceedings of the School Commissioners, in the Different
Counties, for the Year Ending September 30, 1833.* Richmond, Va. 1834.
*Second Auditor's Report on the State of the Literary Fund, for the Year
1836, and Proceedings of the School Commissioners, in the Different*

Counties, for the Year Ending September 30, 1835. Richmond, Va. 1836.
Second Auditor's Report on the State of the Literary Fund, for the Year 1837, and Proceedings of the School Commissioners in the Different Counties, for the Year Ending September 30, 1836. Richmond, Va., 1837.
Second Auditor's Report on the State of the Literary Fund, for the Year 1838, and Proceedings of the School Commissioners in the Different Counties, for the Year Ending September 30, 1837. Richmond, Va., 1838.
Second Auditor's Report on the State of the Literary Fund, for the Year 1839, and Proceedings of the School Commissioners in the Different Counties, for the Year Ending September 30, 1838. Richmond, Va., 1839.
Second Auditor's Report on the State of the Literary Fund, for the Year 1840, and Proceedings of the School Commissioners in the Different Counties, for the Year Ending September 30, 1839. Richmond, Va., 1840.
Second Auditor's Report on the State of the Literary Fund, for the Year 1841, and Proceedings of the School Commissioners in the Different Counties, for the Year Ending September 30, 1840. Richmond, Va., 1841.
Sims, Edgar B. *Making a State.* Charleston, W. Va., 1956.
————. *Sims' Index to Land Grants in West Virginia.* n. p., 1956.
U. S., Bureau of the Census. *Agriculture of the United States in 1860; Compiled from the Original Returns of the Eighth Census.* Washington, D. C., 1864.
————. *Compendium of the Enumeration of the Inhabitants and Statistics of the United States, as Obtained at the Department of State, from the Returns of the Sixth Census.* Washington, D. C., 1841.
————. *The Seventh Census of the United States: 1850, Embracing a Statistical View of the States and Territories, Arranged by Counties, Towns, Etc.* Washington, D. C., 1853.

Newspapers and Periodicals

Charleston *Kanawha Banner.*
Charleston *Kanawha Republican.*
Charleston *Western Courier.*
Charleston *West Virginia and Kanawha Gazette.*
Charlestown *Gazette.*
Charles Town *Farmer's Repository.*
Christian Baptist.
Clarksburg *Enquirer.*
Clarksburg *Republican Compiler.*
Clarksburg *Scion of Democracy.*
Frankfort (Ky.) *Franklin Farmer.*
Martinsburg *Potomak Guardian.*
Morgantown *Monongalia Herald.*
Millenial Harbinger.
Shepherdstown *Impartial Observer: or Shepherd's-Town, Charles Town, & County Advertiser.*
Shepherdstown *Potowmac Guardian, and Berkeley Advertiser.*
Wheeling *Repository.*

Wheeling *Eclectic Observer, and Working People's Advocate.*
Wheeling *Times and Advertiser.*

Contemporary Sources

Agricultural Almanac for the Year of Our Lord, 1830. Charleston, W. Va., 1830.

Alderson, Emma Frances, ed. "The Minutes of the Greenbrier Baptist Church, 1781–1782," *West Virginia History,* VII (October, 1945), 40-53.

Ambler, C. H., ed. "The Clarksburg Educational Convention of September 8-9, 1841," *West Virginia History,* V (October, 1943), 5-54.

Ambler, Charles H., Atwood, Frances Haney, and Mathews, William B., eds. *Debates and Proceedings of the First Constitutional Convention of West Virginia, 1861–1863.* 3 vols. Huntington, W. Va., n. d.

[Asbury, Francis]. *Journal of Rev. Francis Asbury, Bishop of the Methodist Episcopal Church.* 3 vols. New York, n. d.

Brock, R. A., ed. *The Official Records of Robert Dinwiddie, Lieutenant-Governor of the Colony of Virginia, 1751–1758.* 2 vols. Richmond, Va., 1883-1884.

Bowers, Claude G., ed. *The Diary of Elbridge Gerry, Jr.* New York, 1927.

Burnaby, Andrew. *Travels through the Middle Settlements in North America, in the Years 1759 and 1760 with Observations upon the State of the Colonies.* London, 1755.

Chalkley, Lyman. *Chronicles of the Scotch-Irish Settlement in Virginia, Extracted from the Original Records of Augusta County, 1745–1800.* 3 vols. Rosslyn, Va., 1912.

Cometti, Elizabeth, ed. "Concerning the First Survey of the Northern Neck," *West Virginia History,* II, (October, 1940), 52-64.

————, and Summers, Festus P., eds. *The Thirty-Fifth State: A Documentary History of West Virginia.* Morgantown, W. Va., 1966.

Cox, Jacob D. *Military Reminiscences of the Civil War.* 2 vols. New York, 1900.

Cramer, Zadok. *The Navigator; Containing Directions for Navigating the Monongahela, Allegheny, Ohio, and Mississippi Rivers; with an Ample Account of These Much Admired Waters, from the Head of the Former to the Mouth of the Latter; and a Concise Description of Their Towns, Villages, Harbors, Settlements, &c. . . . .* Pittsburgh, Pa., 1814.

[Cross, John]. *Five Years in the Alleghanies.* New York, 1863.

Cuming, F[ortescue]. *Sketches of a Tour to the Western Country, through the States of Ohio and Kentucky; A Voyage down the Ohio and Mississippi Rivers, and a Trip through the Mississippi Territory, and Part of West Florida, Commenced at Philadelphia in the Winter of 1807, and Concluded in 1809.* Pittsburgh, Pa., 1810.

Doddridge, Joseph. *Notes, on the Settlement and Indian Wars, of the Western Parts of Virginia & Pennsylvania, from the Year 1763 until the Year 1783 Inclusive, together with a View, of the State of Society and Manners of the First Settlers of the Western Country.* Wellsburgh, [W.] Va., 1824.

"An Early Camp Meeting in Jefferson County," *Magazine of the Jefferson County Historical Society,* XIV (December, 1948), 15.

Finley, James B. *Sketches of Western Methodism: Biographical, Historical, and Miscellaneous, Illustrative of Pioneer Life.* Edited by W. P. Strickland. Cincinnati, Ohio, 1855.

Fithian, Philip Vickers. *Journal, 1775–1776, Written on the Virginia-Pennsylvania Frontier and in the Army around New York.* Edited by Robert Greenhalgh Albion and Leonidas Dodson. Princeton, N. J., 1934.

Fitzpatrick, John C., ed. *The Diaries of George Washington, 1748–1799.* 4 vols. Boston, 1925.

———. *The Writings of George Washington from the Original Manuscript Sources, 1745–1799.* 39 vols. Washington, D. C., 1931-1944.

Foote, William H. *Sketches of Virginia, Historical and Biographical.* Second Series. 2d ed., rev. Philadelphia, 1856.

Ford, Worthington C., ed. "The Federal Convention in Virginia, 1787–1788," *Massachusetts Historical Society Proceedings,* Second Series, XVII (1903), 449-510.

Gaddis, Maxwell Pierson, Sr. *Foot-Prints of an Itinerant.* Cincinnati, Ohio, 1855.

Hamilton, Stanislaus Murray, ed. *Letters to Washington and Accompanying Papers.* 5 vols. Boston, 1898-1902.

Harris, Thaddeus Mason. *The Journal of a Tour into the Territory Northwest of the Alleghany Mountains; Made in the Spring of the Year 1803. . . .* Boston, 1805.

Hinke, William J., trans. and ed. "Letters regarding the Second Journey of Michel to America, February 14, 1703, to January 16, 1704, and His Stay in America till 1708," *Virginia Magazine of History and Biography,* XXIV (July, 1916), 289-303.

———, and Kemper, Charles, eds. "Moravian Diaries of Travels through Virginia," *Virginia Magazine of History and Biography,* XI (October, 1903), 113-31; XII (January, 1904), 225-42; XII (April, 1904), 370-93; XII (July, 1904), 55-82; XII (October, 1904), 134-53; XIII (January, 1905), 271-84.

Jefferson, Thomas. *Notes on the State of Virginia.* Edited by William Peden. Chapel Hill, N. C., 1955.

Kellogg, Louise Phelps, ed. *Frontier Advance on the Upper Ohio, 1778–1779.* Madison, Wis., 1916.

———. *Frontier Retreat on the Upper Ohio, 1779–1781.* Madison, Wis., 1917.

Kemper, Charles E., ed. "Documents relating to Early Projected Swiss Colonies in the Valley of Virginia, 1706–1709," *Virginia Magazine of History and Biography,* XXIX (January, 1921), 1-17; XXIX (April, 1921), 180-81.

———. "Some Valley Notes," *Virginia Magazine of History and Biography,* XIX (October, 1921), 413-22.

Kercheval, Samuel. *A History of the Valley of Virginia.* Edited by Oren F. Morton. 4th ed. Strasburg, Va., 1925.

Kinnaird, Lawrence, ed. *Spain in the Mississippi Valley, 1765–1794.* American Historical Association *Annual Report, 1945.* 4 vols. Washington, D. C., 1949.

[Lewis, Thomas]. *The Fairfax Line: Thomas Lewis's Journal of 1746.* Edited by John W. Wayland. New Market, Va., 1925.

Martin, Joseph. *A New and Comprehensive Gazetteer of Virginia, and the District of Columbia.* Charlottesville, Va., 1835.

Michaux, F. A. *Travels to the Westward of the Allegany Mountains, in the States of Ohio, Kentucky, and Tennessee, and Return to Charlestown, through the Upper Carolinas; . . . Undertaken in the Year X, 1802. . . .* London, 1804.

"Morton's Diary," *Virginia Historical Register, and Literary Note-Book,* IV (July, 1851), 143-47.

Mulkearn, Lois, ed. *George Mercer Papers relating to the Ohio Company of Virginia.* Pittsburgh, Pa., 1954.

Pittsburgh Magazine Almanac for 1824. Pittsburgh, Pa., n. d.

Prolix, Peregrine. *Letters Descriptive of the Virginia Springs: The Roads Leading Thereto and the Doings Thereat.* 2d ed. Philadelphia, 1837.

Reed, Isaac. *The Christian Traveller, in Five Parts, including Nine Years and Eighteen Thousand Miles.* New York, 1828.

Rights, Douglas L., and Cumming, William P. eds. *The Discoveries of John Lederer, with Unpublished Letters by and about Lederer to Governor John Winthrop, Jr.* Charlottesville, Va., 1958.

[Rogers, Henry]. *Directions for a Family Medicine Chest, Put up and Sold by Henry Rogers, Chemist and Druggist, Charleston, Kanawha County, West Virginia.* Charleston, W. Va., [1830?].

Royall, Anne. *Sketches of History, Life, and Manners, in the United States.* New Haven, Conn., 1826.

Ruffner, Henry. "Notes on a Tour from Virginia to Tennessee, in the Months of July and August, 1838," *Southern Literary Messenger,* V (January, 1839), 44-48.

Stewart, John. *Highways and Hedges; or, Fifty Years of Western Methodism.* Cincinnati, Ohio, 1872.

Stuart, John. "Memoir of Indian Wars, and Other Occurrences," *Virginia Historical and Philosophical Society Collections.* Volume I. Richmond, Va., 1833.

Sweet, William Warren, ed. *Circuit-Rider Days along the Ohio, Being the Journals of the Ohio Conference from Its Organization in 1812 to 1826.* New York, 1923.

————. *Religion on the American Frontier; The Baptists, 1783–1830: A Collection of Source Materials.* New York, 1931.

————. *Religion on the American Frontier, 1783–1840: The Methodists; A Collection of Source Materials.* New York, 1964.

————. *Religion on the American Frontier, 1783–1840: The Presbyterians; A Collection of Source Materials.* New York, 1964.

Thwaites, Reuben Gold, and Kellogg, Louise Phelps, eds. *Documentary History of Dunmore's War, 1774.* Madison, Wis. 1905.

————. *Frontier Defense on the Upper Ohio, 1777–1778.* Madison, Wis. 1912.

————. *The Revolution on the Upper Ohio, 1775–1777.* Madison, Wis. 1908.

Transactions of the Medical Society of the State of West Virginia, Instituted April 10, 1867. Wheeling, W. Va. 1870.

U. S., Work Projects Administration, Historical Records Survey, *Inventory of the Church Archives of West Virginia: The Presbyterian Churches.* Charleston, W. Va., 1941.

U. S., Work Projects Administration, Historical Records Survey, *Inventory of the Church Archives of West Virginia: The Protestant Episcopal Church.* Wheeling, W. Va., 1939.

Walker, Thomas. *Journal of an Expedition in the Spring of the Year 1750.* Edited by William Cabell Rives. Boston, 1888.

Withers, Alexander Scott. *Chronicles of Border Warfare.* Edited by Reuben Gold Thwaites. New ed. Cincinnati, Ohio, 1903.

Young, Jacob. *Autobiography of a Pioneer; or, the Nativity, Experience, Travels, and Ministerial Labors of Rev. Jacob Young; with Incidents, Observations, and Reflections.* Cincinnati, Ohio [1857?].

Unpublished Manuscripts

"Baptist Church History," Typescript, West Virginia Historical Records Survey, Box 208, West Virginia University Library.

Boughter, I[saac] F[egley], "Internal Improvements in Northwestern Virginia: A Study of State Policy Prior to the Civil War" (Ph.D. dissertation, University of Pittsburgh, 1930).

Holmes, Marjorie Moran. "The Life and Diary of John Jeremiah Jacob" (M.A. thesis, Duke University Library, 1941).

McNeel, Isaac. "History of the Baptist Churches." Typescript, Baptist Church Records, West Virginia Historical Records Survey, Box 208, West Virginia University Library.

Malone, Miles Sturdivant. "The Distribution of Population on the Virginia Frontier in 1775" (Ph.D. dissertation, Princeton University, 1935).

Secondary Works—Books

Abernethy, Thomas P. *The South in the New Nation, 1789–1819.* Baton Rouge, La., 1961.

———. *Three Virginia Frontiers.* University, La., 1940

———. *Western Lands and the American Revolution.* New York, 1937.

Alden, John Richard. *The American Revolution, 1775–1783.* New York, 1954.

Aler, Vernon. *History of Martinsburg and Berkeley County, West Virginia.* Hagerstown, Md., n. d.

Alvord, Clarence Walworth. *The Mississippi Valley in British Politics: A Study of Trade, Land Speculation, and Experiments in Imperialism Culminating in the American Revolution.* 2 vols. Cleveland, Ohio, 1917.

———, and Bidgood, Lee. *The First Explorations of the Trans-Allegheny Region by Virginians, 1650–1674.* Cleveland, Ohio, 1912.

Ambler, Charles H. *George Washington and the West.* Chapel Hill, N. C., 1936.

———. *A History of Education in West Virginia from Early Colonial Times to 1949.* Huntington, W. Va., 1951.

————. *A History of Transportation in the Ohio Valley.* Glendale, Calif., 1932.

————. *Sectionalism in Virginia from 1776 to 1861.* Chicago, 1910.

————, and Summers, Festus P. *West Virginia: The Mountain State.* 2d ed. Englewood Cliffs, N. J., 1958.

Atkinson, George W. *History of Kanawha County, from Its Organization in 1789 until the Present time.* Charleston, W. Va., 1876.

Bailey, Kenneth P. *The Ohio Company of Virginia and the Westward Movement, 1748–1792: A Chapter in the History of the Colonial Frontier.* Glendale, Calif., 1939.

————. *Thomas Cresap: Maryland Frontiersman.* Boston, 1944.

Baker-Crothers, Hayes. *Virginia and the French and Indian War.* Chicago, 1928.

Baldwin, Leland D. *Whiskey Rebels: The Story of a Frontier Uprising.* Pittsburgh, Pa., 1949.

Barclay, Wade Crawford. *Early American Methodism, 1769–1844.* 2 vols. New York, 1949.

Barnes, I[saac] A. *The Methodist Protestant Church in West Virginia.* Baltimore, Md., 1926.

Bell, Sadie. *The Church, the State, and Education in Virginia.* Philadelphia, 1930.

Billington, Ray Allen. *Westward Expansion: A History of the American Frontier.* 3d ed. New York, 1967.

Bittinger, Foster Melvin. *A History of the Church of the Brethren in the First District of West Virginia.* Elgin, Ill., 1945.

Brown, William Griffee. *History of Nicholas County, West Virginia.* Richmond, Va., 1954.

Buck, Solon J., and Buck, Elizabeth Hawthorn. *The Planting of Civilization in Western Pennsylvania.* Pittsburgh, Pa., 1939.

Buley, R. Carlyle. *The Old Northwest: Pioneer Period, 1815–1840.* 2 vols. Bloomington, Ind., 1951.

Bushong, Millard Kessler. *A History of Jefferson County, West Virginia.* Charles Town, W. Va., 1941.

Callahan, James Morton. *History of the Making of Morgantown, West Virginia: A Type Study in Trans-Appalachian Local History.* Morgantown, W. Va., 1926.

————. *History of West Virginia: Old and New.* 3 vols. Chicago, 1923.

————. *Semi-Centennial History of West Virginia.* n. p., 1913.

Caruso, John A. *The Appalachian Frontier: America's First Surge Westward.* Indianapolis, Ind., 1959.

Clark, Dan Elbert. *The West in American History.* New York, 1937.

Clark, Thomas D. *A History of Kentucky.* Lexington, Ky., 1954.

————. *Frontier America: The Story of the Westward Movement.* New York, 1959.

Cook, Roy Bird. *The Annals of Fort Lee.* Charleston, W. Va., 1935.

————. *The Annals of Pharmacy in West Virginia.* Charleston, W. Va., 1946.

————. *Washington's Western Lands.* Strasburg, Va., 1930.

Dayton, Ruth Woods. *Greenbrier Pioneers and Their Homes.* Charleston, W. Va., 1942.

————. *Pioneers and Their Homes on the Upper Kanawha.* Charleston, W. Va., 1947.

Dick, Everett. *The Dixie Frontier: A Social History of the Southern Frontier from the First Transmontane Beginnings to the Civil War.* New York, 1948.

Dodson, Leonidas. *Alexander Spotswood: Governor of Colonial Virginia, 1710–1722.* Philadelphia, 1932.

Downes, Randolph C. *Council Fires on the Upper Ohio: A Narrative of Indian Affairs in the Upper Ohio Valley until 1795.* Pittsburgh, Pa., 1940.

Dunaway, Wayland Fuller. *History of the James River and Kanawha Company.* New York, 1922.

————. *The Scotch-Irish of Colonial Pennsylvania.* Chapel Hill, N. C., 1944.

Eavenson, Howard N. *The First Century and a Quarter of American Coal Industry.* Pittsburgh, Pa., 1942.

Evans, Willis F. *History of Berkeley County, West Virginia.* n. p., 1928.

Faust, Albert Bernhardt. *The German Element in the United States.* 2 vols. Boston, 1909.

Fenneman, Nevin M. *Physiography of the Eastern United States.* New York, 1938.

Freeman, Douglas Southall. *George Washington: A Biography.* 7 vols. New York, 1948-1957.

Gardiner, Mabel Henshaw, and Gardiner, Ann Henshaw. *Chronicles of Old Berkeley: A Narrative History of a Virginia County from Its Beginnings to 1926.* Durham, N. C., 1938.

Gewehr, Wesley M. *The Great Awakening in Virginia, 1740–1790.* Durham, N. C., 1930.

Gipson, Lawrence Henry. *The British Empire before the American Revolution.* 12 vols. to date. New York, 1936-

Grigsby, Hugh Blair. *The History of the Virginia Federal Convention of 1788.* 2 vols. Richmond, Va., 1890.

Guthrie, Dwight Raymond. *John McMillan: The Apostle of Presbyterianism in the West, 1752–1833.* Pittsburgh, Pa., 1952.

Hale, John P. *History of the Great Kanawha Valley.* 2 vols. Madison, Wis. 1891.

————. *Trans-Allegheny Pioneers: Historical Sketches of the First White Settlers West of the Alleghenies.* 2d ed. Charleston, W. Va., 1931.

Hart, Freeman H. *The Valley of Virginia in the American Revolution, 1763–1789.* Chapel Hill, N. C., 1942.

Haymond, Henry. *History of Harrison County, West Virginia.* Morgantown, W. Va., 1910.

Henderson, Archibald. *Dr. Thomas Walker and the Loyal Company of Virginia.* Reprint from *Proceedings* of American Antiquarian Society. Worcester, Mass., 1931.

Henlein, Paul C. *Cattle Kingdom in the Ohio Valley, 1783–1860.* Lexington, Ky., 1959.

Higginbotham, Don. *Daniel Morgan: Revolutionary Rifleman.* Chapel Hill, N. C., 1961.

Hildreth, E. A. *A Contribution to the History of Medicine, with a Biography of Deceased Physicians in the City of Wheeling, for the Last Hundred Years.* Wheeling, W. Va., 1876.

Hulbert, Archer B. *The Cumberland Road.* Cleveland, Ohio, 1904.

————. *The Paths of Inland Commerce.* New Haven, Conn., 1922.

Hunter, Louis C. *Steamboats on the Western Rivers: An Economic and Technological History.* Cambridge, Mass., 1949.

James Alfred P. *The Ohio Company: Its Inner History.* Pittsburgh, Pa., 1959.

Jennings, Walter Wilson. *Transylvania: Pioneer University of the West.* New York, 1955.

Johnson, Allen, and Malone, Dumas, eds. *Dictionary of American Biography.* 20 vols. and 2 supps. New York, 1928-1958.

Johnston, David E. *A History of the Middle New River Settlements and Contiguous Territory.* Huntington, W. Va., 1906.

Jordan, Philip. *The National Road.* Indianapolis, Ind., 1948.

Kibler, J. L. *A Historical Sketch of Rehobeth M. E. Church, South, Monroe County, W. Va., Delivered at the Centennial Celebration, July 20, 1884.* "Methodist Shrine Edition." Glenville, W. Va., 1960.

Koontz, Louis Knott. *Robert Dinwiddie: His Career in American Colonial Government and Westward Expansion.* Glendale, Calif., 1941.

————. *The Virginia Frontier, 1754–1763.* Baltimore, Md., 1925.

Lewis, George E. *The Indiana Company, 1763–1798: A Study in Eighteenth Century Frontier Land Speculation and Business Venture.* Glendale, Calif., 1941.

Lewis, Virgil A. *First Biennial Report of the Department of Archives and History of the State of West Virginia.* Charleston, W. Va., 1906.

————. *Second Biennial Report of the Department of Archives and History of the State of West Virginia.* N. p., n. d.

Malone, Dumas. *Jefferson, the Virginian.* Boston, 1948.

Mathews, Donald G. *Slavery and Methodism: A Chapter in American Morality, 1780–1845.* Princeton, N. J., 1965.

Maxwell, Hu. *The History of Randolph County, West Virginia, from Its Earliest Settlement to the Present.* Morgantown, W. Va., 1898.

————, and Swisher, H. L. *History of Hampshire County, West Virginia.* Morgantown, W. Va., 1897.

McDonald, Forrest. *We the People: The Economic Origins of the Constitution.* Chicago, 1958.

McMurtrie, Douglas C. *The Beginnings of Printing in West Virginia, with Notes on the Pioneer Newspaper and Early Book and Pamphlet Imprints.* Charleston, W. Va., 1935.

Meade, William. *Old Churches, Ministers and Families of Virginia.* 2 vols. Philadelphia, n. d.

Miller, John C. *The Federalist Era, 1789–1801.* New York, 1960.

Miller, Thomas Condit, and Maxwell, Hu. *West Virginia and Its People.* 3 vols. New York, 1913.

Moore, Glover. *The Missouri Controversy, 1819–1821.* Lexington, Ky., 1953.

Morton, Oren F. *A History of Pendleton County, West Virginia.* Franklin, W. Va., 1910.

————. *A History of Preston County, West Virginia.* 2 vols. Kingwood, W. Va., 1914.

Newton, J. H., Nichols, G. G., and Sprankle, A. G. *History of the Panhandle: Being Historical Recollections of the Counties of Ohio, Brooke, Marshall, and Hancock, West Virginia.* Wheeling, W. Va., 1879.

Norona, Delf, and Shetler, Charles, comps. *West Virginia Imprints, 1790–1863: A Checklist of Books, Newspapers, Periodicals, and Broadsides.* Moundsville, W. Va., 1958.

Parkman, Francis. *History of the Conspiracy of Pontiac.* Boston, 1851.

Peckham, Howard H. *Pontiac and the Indian Uprising.* Princeton, N. J., 1947.

Posey, Walter Brownlow. *The Baptist Church in the Lower Mississippi Valley, 1776–1845.* Lexington, Ky., 1957

————. *Frontier Mission: A History of Religion West of the Southern Appalachians to 1861.* Lexington, Ky., 1966.

Sanderlin, Walter S. *The Great National Project: A History of the Chesapeake and Ohio Canal.* Baltimore, Md., 1946.

Savelle, Max. *George Morgan: Colony Builder.* New York, 1932.

Scharf, J. Thomas. *The Chronicles of Baltimore; Being a Complete History of "Baltimore Town" and Baltimore City from the Earliest Period to the Present Time.* Baltimore, Md., 1874.

Searight, Thomas B. *The Old Pike.* Uniontown, Pa., 1894.

Semple, Ellen Churchill, and Jones, Clarence Fielden. *American History and Its Geographic Conditions.* Rev. ed. Boston, 1933.

Sosin, Jack M. *The Revolutionary Frontier, 1763–1783.* New York, 1967.

————. *Whitehall and the Wilderness: The Middle West in British Colonial Policy, 1760–1775.* Lincoln, Nebr., 1961.

Stevens, Abel. *History of the Methodist Episcopal Church in the United States of America.* 3 vols. New York, 1864.

Sutton, John Davisson. *History of Braxton County and Central West Virginia.* Sutton, W. Va., 1919.

Sydnor, Charles S. *The Development of Southern Sectionalism, 1819–1848.* Baton Rouge, La., 1948.

Talbert, Charles Gano. *Benjamin Logan: Kentucky Frontiersman.* Lexington, Ky., 1962.

Turner, Frederick Jackson. *The Frontier in American History.* New York, 1920.

U. S., Department of Agriculture. *Soils and Men: Yearbook of Agriculture, 1938.* Washington, D. C., 1938.

U. S., Work Projects Administration, Writers' Program. *West Virginia: A Guide to the Mountain State.* New York, 1941.

U. S., Works Progress Administration, Writers' Program. *Historic Romney, 1762–1937.* N. p., 1937.

Volwiler, Albert T. *George Croghan and the Westward Movement, 1741–1782.* Cleveland, Ohio, 1926.

Wainwright, Nicholas B. *George Croghan: Wilderness Diplomat.* Chapel Hill, N. C., 1959.

Wayland, John W. *The German Element of the Shenandoah Valley of Virginia.* Charlottesville, Va., 1907.

Wish, Harvey. *Society and Thought in Early America: A Social History of the American People through 1865.* New York, 1950.

Secondary Works—Articles

Ambler, Charles H. "Poor Relief (Kanawha County, Virginia, 1818–1847)," *West Virginia History,* III (July, 1942), 285-304.

Bates, Robert L. "Middleway, A Study in Social History," *West Virginia History,* XI (October, 1949-January, 1950), 5-43.

Brooks, Maurice. "A Community Records Its History," *West Virginia History,* XVII (April, 1956), 252-61.

Carrier, Lyman. "The Veracity of John Lederer," *William and Mary Quarterly,* Second Series, IX (October, 1939), 435-45.

Cobb, W. H. "Presbyterianism in the Tygarts Valley," *Magazine of History-Biography of Randolph County Historical Society,* No. 2, pp. 26-36.

Downes, Randolph C. "Dunmore's War: An Interpretation," *Mississippi Valley Historical Review,* XXI (December, 1934), 311-19.

Draper, Lyman C. "The Expedition against the Shawanoe Indians in 1756," *Virginia Historical Register,* V (April, 1852), 61-76.

England, J. Merton. "Some Early Historians of Western Virginia," *West Virginia History,* XIV (January, 1953), 91-107.

Fortney, Harold Bruce. "Maryland–West Virginia, Western Boundary," *West Virginia History,* XIX (October, 1957), 5-37; XIX (January, 1958), 101-27.

Harrison, Fairfax. "Western Explorations in Virginia between Lederer and Spotswood," *Virginia Magazine of History and Biography,* XXX (October, 1922), 323-40.

Kenamond, A. D. "Early Shepherdstown and Its Churches," *Magazine of the Jefferson County Historical Society,* XI (December, 1945), 34-41.

"A List of Early Land Patents and Grants," *Virginia Magazine of History and Biography,* V (October, 1897), 173-80.

Main, Jackson Turner. "The Distribution of Property in Post-Revolutionary Virginia," *Mississippi Valley Historical Review,* XLI (September, 1954), 241-58.

Martin, Raymond V., Jr. "Eminent Virginian—A Study of John Beckley," *West Virginia History,* XI (October 1949-January, 1950), 44-61.

McAllister, J. T. "Incidents in the Pioneer, Colonial and Revolutionary History of the West Virginia Area." In Henry S. Green, *Biennial Report of the Department of Archives and History of the State of West Virginia, 1911–1912, 1913–1914* (Charleston, W. Va., 1914).

Poling, Dorothy. "Jesse Bennet, Pioneer Physician and Surgeon," *West Virginia History,* XII (January, 1951), 87-128.

Rice, Otis K. "Coal Mining in the Kanawha Valley to 1861: A View of Industrialization in the Old South," *Journal of Southern History,* XXXI (November, 1965), 393-416.

―――. "Importations of Cattle into Kentucky, 1785–1860," *Register of the Kentucky Historical Society,* XLIX (January, 1951), 35-47.

————. "The Sandy Creek Expedition of 1756," *West Virginia History,* XIII (October, 1951), 5-19.

————. "West Virginia Printers and Their Work, 1790–1830," *West Virginia History,* XIV (July, 1953), 297-338.

Risjord, Norman K. "The Virginia Federalists," *Journal of Southern History,* XXXIII (November, 1967), 486-517.

Scribner, Robert L. "Mills That Ground Slowly," *Virginia Cavalcade,* IV (Autumn, 1954), 8-12.

White, Edward T. "Andrew and Oliver Beirne of Monroe County," *West Virginia History,* XX (October, 1958), 16-23.

Williams, Elizabeth Whitten. "Mercer Academy: A Brief History Thereof, 1819–1862," *West Virginia History,* XIII (October, 1951), 41-55.

Index

Abercromby, James, 52, 328

abolitionism, 374

absentee ownership of land, vii-viii, 149

academies: motives for founding, 236, 237; financial support of, 251-52; enrollments of, 253-54; and literary societies, 259; mentioned, 235. *See also* names of academies

Adams, John Quincy: western support of, 336, 359

Adams, Thomas, 130

"Address to Our Fellow Citizens," 227

Agricultural Almanac: lists home remedies, 193, 196, 199-200

agriculture: north of Ohio River, 5; landholdings, 154; unscientific practices in, 163

—crops: barley, 3, 156; beans, 3; corn, 3, 155-56; flax, 3, 156-57, 357; oats, 3, 156; rye, 3, 156; hemp, 156-57, 357; buckwheat, 156; wheat, 156, 163; apples, 163; peaches, 163

—livestock: cattle, 7, 41, 96, 102, 156, 158-60, 165, 327-28; horses, 41, 96, 158, 162; hogs, 156, 158, 161-62; sheep, 158, 160-61

ailments: chill fever, 190; malarial, 191-92; rheumatism, 192; coughs and colds, 193; pleurisy, 193; pulmonary, 193; asthma, 194; consumption, 194; croup, 194, 205; children's diseases, 194-95; dysentery, 195, 198; smallpox, 195; skin, 196, 205; itch, 196, 205; corns, 196; felons, 196; eye, 197-98, 205; diarrhea, 198; typhoid, 198; snakebite, 199; burns and scalds, 199-200; wounds, 200; "cold plague," 200; Asiatic cholera, 200-201, 205

Alburtis, John: founds *Berkeley Intelligencer*, 263; founds *Lay-Man's Magazine*, 265

Alden family, 146

Aldermanic Law, 214-15

Alderson, John: founds Greenbrier Baptist Church, 278; extends Baptist faith, 278-79, 280; remuneration of, 283; views Arminianism, 287; mentioned, 131n, 278, 281, 282, 287, 292, 300

Alderson: Baptist church at, 278; mentioned, 237

Alexander, Archibald, 44

Alexander, James, 131n

Alexandria, Virginia: cattle market of, 158; mentioned, 5, 92

Alien and Sedition Acts, 352, 353

Allegheny Circuit (Methodist), 293

Allegheny College, 255

Allegheny Front: barrier to settlement, 4; mentioned, viii, 1

Allegheny Highlands: described, 1, 6-8; effects of, on pioneer life, 1-2, 8, 150; and westward migration, 1, 6-7; wildlife of, 7; climate of, 8; foster particularism, 9, 377-78; Indian occupants of, 11-12; natural resources of, 12; persistent geographical influences of, 376-78; mentioned, 4, 14-15, 29, 34, 36, 54, 64, 65, 73, 79

Allegheny River, 5, 15

Allegheny Valley: fur trade of, 15

Ambler, Charles H.: notes failure of district free school plans, 233; comments on Mercer Academy, 250

American and Foreign Bible Society of Philadelphia, 286

American Bible Society, 226

American Colonization Society, 304

American System (Clay's), 359

American Tract Society, 210

Amherst, Jeffrey: captures Louisbourg, 52; advocates smallpox infection for Indians, 56, 56n; in Pontiac's War, 57

Anderson, John: attitude of, toward land commissioners, 130-31

Andover Seminary, 302

Anglican Church: interested in education, 242; in Potomac Valley, 267, 268; effects of the Great Awakening in, 272; and origins of Methodism, 287; mentioned, 276, 288

Anna Iron Furnace, 314

Monongalia County (*continued*):
67; maturing economy of, 167; illegal distilling in, 181; theft in, 183; court sentences slave to death, 184; shortage of ministers for performing marriages in, 188; physicians in, 202; attitude toward Literary Fund in, 216; poverty limits school attendance in, 217; represented at Clarksburg Educational Convention, 226; residents demand internal improvements, 337; opposition to excise tax in, 352; Republican party in, 354; criticisms of county court system in, 364; mentioned, 99, 138, 139, 238, 241, 344n, 368n, 372

Monongalia Farmers Company of Virginia, 327

Monroe, James: at Virginia Constitutional Convention of 1829-1830, 367, 368, 370; and Declaration of Independence, 369; mentioned, 354

Monroe County: horses in, 162; merchants in, 164-65; economic maturation of, 167; illegal distilling in, 181-82; gambling in, 185; early school in, 211; teacher shortage in, 219; sets up free public schools, 223; abandons free public school system, 223; in Greenbrier Circuit, 291; carding machinery in, 322; mentioned, 184, 188, 204, 367n

Montague, Edward, 71

Montcalm, Marquis de, 53

Monterey, 338

Montgomery, John, 44

Montgomery County: Henry Banks' lands in, 137; mentioned, 131, 140

Montour, Andrew: and Treaty of Logstown, 36-37

Montreal, 53, 92

Moore, Andrew: proposed as land commissioner, 130

Moore, Jeremiah: and religious liberty, 276

Moorefield: settlements at, 25; Presbyterian church at, 300; iron industry at, 315; flour milling at, 321; textile industry at, 322; mentioned, 11

Moravian Church: missionaries visit South Branch, 27-28; missionaries warn of attacks by Indians, 95, 114; missionaries describe life on South

Moravian Church (*continued*):
Branch, 152; and Eastern Panhandle, 272-74; mentioned, 150

Morgan, Charles S.: views suffrage question, 372; mentioned, 368n

Morgan, Daniel: vows aid to Bostonians, 88; joins Washington's army, 89; disperses Loyalists, 113; defends John Claypool, 113-14; elected to Congress, 352; opposes Virginia Resolutions, 353; defends Alien and Sedition Acts, 353; mentioned, 141n

Morgan, George: fears Indian war, 94; in charge of Indiana Company land office, 119; and Westsylvania, 119; appears before Virginia commissioners, 121; seeks Congressional confirmation of Indiana grant, 123, 125; offers to arbitrate Indiana claim, 124-25; mentioned, 118, 120

Morgan, John, 65

Morgan, Morgan: settles at Bunker Hill, 18-19; founds Christ Church (Anglican), 268

Morgan, William, 66

Morgan, Zackwell: settles at Morgantown, 66; suppresses Loyalists, 92

Morgan County: Fairfax lands in, 24; incompetent teachers in, 221

Morgan's Chapel. *See* Christ Church (Anglican)

Morgantown: settlement of, 66; tobacco inspector at, 157; hogs at large in, 161; early physicians of, 201; Presbyterians at, 201; academy at, 237; interest in academies at, 240-41; proposed location for college, 241-42; newspaper at, 262; Episcopal Church at, 302; iron manufacturing at, 314-15; pottery industry at, 317; boatbuilding at, 318; milling at, 321; carding machines at, 322; banking at, 327, 329; Whiskey Rebellion at, 350; mentioned, 10, 56, 99, 138, 180, 182, 202, 204, 246, 259, 292, 337

Morgantown Circuit (Methodist Protestant): membership of, 299

Morgantown Circulating Library: activities of, 259

Morgantown Female Seminary, 242

Morgantown *Monongalia Gazette*: publishes Clemmons murder story, 184

Morris, Benjamin, 70

New Orleans (*continued*):
goods at, 349; market conditions at, 355; mentioned, 108, 319, 320, 321, 322

New Orleans: and inland river navigation, 319

New River: and settlement of West Virginia, 4-5; gorge of, 7; discovery of, 14; visited by Thomas Walker, 29; settlements on, 31, 35, 44n; rumors of French forts on, 39; mentioned, 2, 44, 44n, 55, 59n, 61, 73, 139

New River Baptist Association: includes Greenbrier churches, 281; and slavery question, 305

New River Valley, 9, 35

newspapers: establishment of, 262-64; difficulties of, 264; mentioned, 235. *See also* names of newspapers

Newton, Enos W.: at Clarksburg Educational Convention, 226; notes significance of Clarksburg Educational Convention, 228

New York: Indian attacks in, 104-105; Presbyterians in, 299; mentioned, 94, 233, 311, 371

New York City, 146

Nicholas, George, 239

Nicholas, Wilson Cary: landholdings of, 136, 139-40

Nicholas County: residents attack Virginia land system, 145, 148; poverty limits schools in, 217; sparse population limits schools in, 217; moral qualities of teachers in, 220; Baptists in, 279; church attendance in, 307; mentioned, 262, 284

Nichols, Austin, 142

Nichols family, 65

Nolichucky River: settlements on, 64

Nonhelema: warns of Indian alliance with British, 95; at Fort Randolph, 102

Non-Intercourse Act: supported by West, 355

Norfolk, 339

Northampton, Massachusetts: revival at, 271

North Branch of the Potomac: settlements on, 4-5; mentioned, 24, 73

North Carolina: offers lands to Graffenried, 17-18; mentioned, 10, 64, 73, 272, 275, 288, 371

Northern Neck of Virginia: disputed ownership of, 17, 23; surveyed, 23-24

Northern Panhandle: Indian depredations in, 94; sheep-raising in, 161; horses in, 162; academies in, 237; Presbyterians in, 301; Episcopal Church in, 302; iron manufacturing in, 315; coal mining in, 316; glass and pottery industries in, 317; flour milling in, 321-22; in election of 1828, 359; mentioned, 11, 63, 69, 73, 197, 246, 257, 292, 376

North Fork of the South Branch, 10

North Mountain, 21

Northwestern Bank of Virginia: and Wheeling University, 255-56; founded, 329

Northwestern Turnpike: constructed, 337-38

Northwestern Virginia Academy: founded, 240

Northwest Ordinance of 1787; views of James Pindall on, 358

Northwest posts: British retention of, 345, 349

Northwest Territory, 188, 358

Notes, on the Settlement and Indian Wars, . . . : describes pioneer life, 266

Noyes family, 325

Nutter, Levi: defective land titles of, 145

Nutter family, 66

Nuzum, Joel: foundry of, 314

Oakland, Maryland, 10

Ogle, Joseph: and defense of Fort Henry, 95-96; and Foreman's Massacre, 98

Ohio: banks serve West Virginia, 326, 328; mentioned, 11, 241, 257, 258, 310n, 332

Ohio Circuit (Methodist): formed, 292; mentioned, 293, 304

Ohio Company (banking facility), 327

Ohio Company of Virginia: land grant to, 34, 35; opposition to, 35-36; membership of, 36; and Treaty of Logstown, 36-37; disputes with Corbin group, 37; settlements of, 37; storehouse of, 37-38; opposes Treaty of Easton, 54; absorbed by Walpole Company, 72; demise of, 127; grant